Business Continuity Management

Since the publication of the first edition in 2001, interest in crisis management has been fuelled by a number of events, including 9/11. The first edition was praised for its rigorous yet logical approach and this is continued in the second edition, which provides a well-researched, theoretically robust approach to the topic combined with empirical research in continuity management. New chapters are included on digital resilience and principles of risk management for business continuity. All chapters are revised and updated with particular attention being paid to the impact on smaller companies. New examples include: South Africa Bank, Lego, Morgan Stanley Dean Witter; small companies impacted by 9/11; and the New York City power outage of August 2003.

Dominic Elliott is Paul Roy Professor of Business Continuity and Strategy at the University of Liverpool Management School, UK. He has published widely in the fields of crisis and strategic management, and has worked with organisations including IBM, Philips and BNP-Paribas. He is the co-editor of *Risk Management: An International Journal*.

Ethné Swartz is Associate Professor of Entrepreneurship, and Chair of the Marketing and Entrepreneurship Department at the Silberman College of Business, Fairleigh Dickinson University, US. She publishes and teaches in the fields of entrepreneurship, strategic management, and crisis and continuity management.

Brahim Herbane is Principal Lecturer in Strategy and Continuity Management at Leicester Business School, De Montfort University, UK. He researches in strategic management, crisis and business continuity management.

Business Continuity Management

A Crisis Management Approach

Second Edition

Dominic Elliott, Ethné Swartz
and Brahim Herbane

Routledge
Taylor & Francis Group

NEW YORK AND LONDON

First published 2001
by Routledge
270 Madison Avenue, New York, NY 10016

Second edition published 2010
by Routledge
270 Madison Avenue, New York, NY 10016

Simultaneously published in the UK
by Routledge
2 Park Square, Milton Park, Abingdon, Oxon OX14 4RN

Routledge is an imprint of the Taylor & Francis Group, an informa business

Typeset in GaramondThree by
RefineCatch Limited, Bungay, Suffolk
Printed and bound in the United States of America on acid-free paper by
Sheridan Books, Inc.

Library of Congress Cataloging in Publication Data
Elliot, Dominic, 1963–
   Business continuity management: a crisis management approach /
   Dominic Elliott, Ethné Swartz, and Brahim Herbane. – 2nd ed.
     p. cm.
   1. Crisis management.   2. Emergency management.   3. Business
   planning.   I. Swartz, Ethné, 1961–   II. Herbane, Brahim, 1969–
   III. Title.
   HD49.E44 2010
   658.4'056 – dc22   2009024938

ISBN10: 0–415–37108–2 (hbk)
ISBN10: 0–415–37109–0 (pbk)
ISBN10: 0–203–86633–9 (ebk)

ISBN13: 978–0–415–37108–7 (hbk)
ISBN13: 978–0–415–37109–4 (pbk)
ISBN13: 978–0–203–86633–7 (ebk)

Contents

Preface

Since the first edition of this book was prepared and subsequently published, the world seems to have changed. The first decade of the twenty-first century has witnessed constant reminders of the power of natural forces of the planet we inhabit. The South East Asian Tsunami of 2004, earthquakes in China, Italy and Pakistan, hurricanes striking the islands of the Caribbean and the US coastline, famine in Africa, flooding in the UK and along the Danube, forest and bush fires in Australia, Greece and Indonesia may all have been triggered by human activity but caused tremendous problems for people, communities, businesses of all kinds, governments and even politicians. Human activity in the forms of terrorism struck Britain, India, Pakistan, Russia, Spain and of course the attacks of 9/11 in New York and Washington. Our global society has become ever more connected, be it through trade, communication, the Web, ease of travel of people, viruses and pollution, global warming and our dependence upon one another and certain key but finite resources. This mutual dependence has been reinforced by the so-called credit crunch, which, at the time of writing in April 2009, appears to be triggering an economic downturn in many parts of the world. These are the macro, media grabbing events, but business continuity is concerned, often, with the minutiae of organisations, with micro as well as macro triggers and as dependencies have increased so has the vulnerability of all organisations.

Against this backdrop, the need for business continuity in its broadest sense has never been greater. The need for inter-organisational business continuity, from a strategic to an operational level, has never been more urgent. The need for creative approaches to continuity, grounded in rich insight but manifest in adaptive and flexible capability, in place of rigid, "safe" but ineffective solutions is also clear. This edition has been prepared in the spirit of desiring to make a contribution to the practice of business continuity. We wish to thank friends, associates and sponsors from the business continuity community, particularly the anonymous contributors to our research, and colleagues from Taylor & Francis for ongoing support and patience. We would like to thank our colleagues from De Montfort University, Silberman College of Business and University of Liverpool.

This book has benefited from many interactions, but ultimate responsibility for the book in its final form rests with its authors.

Finally, for their forbearance and support, we wish to thank our families and to dedicate this book to our children David, Hannah, Jasmine, Jessica, Lucy, Megan, Philip and Thomas.

The Plan of the Book

This book is structured around the key concept of business continuity management (BCM) and the underlying assumptions that accompany theoretical and practical approaches to this process. It is logical that the book should be structured in line with the strategic management process, starting with the main environmental issues first and then focusing on the internal, organisational influences and process. Figure 1.1 illustrates the BCM process and factors that influence the activities necessary to put continuity management in place within an organisation.

In Chapter 1, we consider why organisations should adopt BCM through a consideration of the strategic importance of being able to deal with crises and interruptions effectively. Furthermore, we examine the historical legacies and antecedents of BCM and predict that organisations should be focused on developing a business continuity capability in order to be both better prepared to deal with crises or interruptions and competitively differentiated.

Chapter 2 considers the regulatory and legislative environment within which continuity planning and management must operate. The ethical and legal responsibilities of organisations must work in parallel with continuity management, particularly as organisations' liability in the event of a crisis may have consequences for its survival. Although there is little specific legislation for business continuity, a wider range of rules and regulations can influence the responsibilities of an organisation before and after an interruption.

Having considered the strategic and regulatory or legislative need for continuity management, Chapter 3 considers the influence on life in a digital age and its implications for BCM. The chapter considers the drivers to further exploit digital technologies within organisations, the increased dependence on digital technologies, digital threats facing organisations, and the implications of failing to achieve digital resilience.

Chapters 4–7 introduce and detail the four stages of the business continuity process, from initiation to implementation as depicted in Figure 1.1. Chapter 4 examines how organisations initiate BCM and put into place structural, managerial and resource requirements in order to proceed with planning for business continuity (Chapter 5). Chapter 6 examines how organisations can and should implement BCM by exploring change management. From this, organisations are in a position to proceed to the operational management of business continuity (Chapter 7) in which they continuously maintain and test their plans. In addition, Chapter 7 examines how organisations manage recovery operations in the event of a crisis.

Chapter 8 concludes with an examination of the new challenges and developments that are shaping the current and future business environment. In so doing, we identify the prospect of such developments having an influence on BCM in the future.

1 Continuity Management in Historical Context

Introduction

The objective of this chapter is to review the development of business continuity management (BCM) into its current form from its origins in disaster recovery planning. The focus is on the evolution of the practice, from its origins in disaster recovery to contingency planning and finally to a more strategically focused management concern. The roots of BCM lie in information systems but then extended beyond this as organisations became more dependent upon technologies that drove core business processes. Hence, pushed by changing stakeholder and organisational needs, BCM has, over the last twenty years, moved from a technical focus to a compliance focus and has now moved towards a strategic focus, within some businesses. The chapter concludes by envisioning how BCM might move into the future through the development in some organisations of a business continuity (BC) capability.

The Ubiquity of Technology

> [A] frog if put in cold water will not bestir itself if that water is heated up slowly and gradually and will in the end let itself be boiled alive, too comfortable with continuity to realize that continuous change at some point may become intolerable and demand a change in behavior.
> (Handy, 1990: 9)

The boiled frog syndrome has entered the management literature as a warning to those who fail to detect environmental change and take action (Handy, 1990; Frost, 1994). Examining the reintroduction to the social world of those isolated from normal life for long periods of time enables us to detect the stark changes in them that the rest of us barely notice. Nelson Mandela's autobiography describes how, on his release from prison in 1990 after serving a twenty-six-year sentence, a television crew "thrust a long, dark and furry object at me. I recoiled slightly, wondering if it were a new fangled weapon developed while I was in prison. Winnie informed me that it was a microphone" (Mandela, 1994: 673). After undergoing voluntary exile from the "real world" during his ten-year premiership, former prime minister Tony Blair acquired his first mobile telephone (*Sky News*, 2006) and had to master new competences such as learning how to use it. Such technology had become ubiquitous during his term in office and any nine-year-old might have been a knowledgeable tutor for the former premier.

Since the first edition of this book was written, terrorist attacks in North America (9/11), London (7/7), Istanbul, Madrid, Beslan, Mumbai and the Maldives, to name but a few, have had a tremendous impact, both physically and emotionally. Very human disasters have been triggered by natural events, including the South East Asian Tsunami of 2004, Cyclone Nargis of 2008 which devastated Myanmar, and the pounding of New Orleans by Hurricane Katrina in 2005. New records for high summer temperatures, with unseasonal flooding elsewhere, have seen forest fires rage across the Peloponnese in Greece while English towns were struck by flooding not experienced within human memory.

Such events grab the headlines and undoubtedly trigger business inter-ruptions for small and large organisations alike. Given that lives are often put at risk in many crises, we have learned that such events will have a disproportionate impact upon management considerations compared to the more mundane, but more probable, interruptions likely to befall man-agers and their organisations. Whether the trigger is viewed as a major event or a more trivial systems failure, BCM a process intended to support organisations in building resilience and, where necessary, to recover key activities as quickly as possible in order to minimise organisational impacts and protect key stakeholders.

Tension has arisen because the focus upon great events is detrimental to the exploration of the minutiae of everyday life. This tension is also evident in the fields of BC and crisis management. Historians fall into one of at least two camps: those who are primarily concerned with the great figures of history, kings and presidents, and those who seek to better understand the experiences and practices of those everyday people who often remain nameless yet are the ancestors of the majority of us. Similarly, within this book, although reference is made to well-known incidents and recoveries, this indicates the relative ease of access to such cases whose data are available in the public domain. Conversely, the sparse reference to small businesses and mundane examples hides the fact that the value of BC is in building day-to-day resilience and the associated recovery capability.

The routines of organisational and personal life depend today more than ever upon digital tools. The developed world has seen a rapid growth in online shopping, ever more sophisticated data-mining opportunities and supply chain management. Retailers have learned how to exploit the data available from loyalty cards, enabling detailed consumer profiles to be drawn. Google provides about three-quarters of the "external referrals for most websites" reports Google Watch (2007), worrying that such dominance undermines the principles of the World Wide Web. Finkelstein (2007) suggests a threat to privacy since a wide range of internet service providers may maintain detailed records of customers' activities and thus their interests. He also reports the allegation that Yahoo! assisted the Chinese authorities to imprison dissidents. The digital age provides an opportunity for the kind of Big Brother surveillance of which not even Orwell could conceive.

In banking, the personal touch was superseded by the telephone interface, itself increasingly replaced by internet services, and, as we turn full circle, personal banking is now being reintroduced as a "value added service". With a plethora of goods from which to choose, customers have become more demanding and less tolerant of sloppy service or delays. As such change occurs incrementally we hardly notice it, but for those such as Nelson Mandela and Tony Blair who have been temporarily isolated, the changes associated with stepping back into the real world were immense. They were not concerned only with great events but with the humdrum minutiae of living everyday life, from shopping to speaking to friends, and using social networking technologies.

Change, fuelled by new information and communication technology (ICT), may be seen as a constant — it is estimated by award-winning scientist and futurist Ray Kurzweil that such communications technologies double their capacity and power each year, while the hardware is becoming smaller by a factor of 100 every decade (Kurzweil, 2007). Linked to this, in business the reliance on technology and on fellow members of the organisational supply chain has increased both dependencies and the potential for interruptions. The need to ensure BC is in place has never been greater.

BCM is a maturing discipline. Although its origins lie in Information Systems (IS) protection, it is evolving into a full business-wide process. Kurzweiler (2007) posits that the greater affordability and miniaturisation of technology has democratised access to technology so that no single individual remains untouched by technological change. However, this text is less concerned with the technology itself than with the concomitant changes to the organisational processes, systems and operations which new developments have made possible. Organisations are socio-technical systems, and to manage them effectively for continuity, all elements must be considered. The roots of the experiences of the three authors of this book lie in a variety of sub-disciplines, including strategy, industrial crisis and Information Systems. Inevitably, these have shaped this book and the theoretical approach to BCM. Throughout this text we use the Business Continuity Institute's (BCI, 2007a) definition, which closely fitted our earlier definition (see Elliott et al., 2001), and has provided the basis for the definition of British Standard 25999:

> Business Continuity Management is a holistic management process that identifies potential impacts that threaten an organisation and

provides a framework for building resilience and the capability for an effective response that safeguards the interests of its key stakeholders, reputation, brand and value creating activities.

(BSI, 2006)

This definition of BCM is firmly rooted in a crisis management approach (see Shrivastava, 1987a; Smith, 1990; Pauchant and Mitroff, 1992) and is broader in scope than more traditional approaches, which emphasise hard systems (see, for example, Doswell, 2000). The next section outlines what is meant by a crisis management approach. Then, Chapter 1 considers the strategic importance of being able to deal with crises and interruptions effectively; how "service continuity" might be a more appropriate term than "business continuity". Finally, we examine the historical development of BCM.

A Crisis Management Approach to Business Continuity

A key part of this book's contribution to the development of BCM lies in its crisis management approach, which underpins all aspects of this text. Such an approach may be defined as one that:

- recognises the social and technical characteristics of business interruptions;
- emphasises the contribution that managers may make to the resolution of interruptions;
- assumes that managers may build resilience to business interruptions through processes and changes to operating norms and practices;
- assumes that organisations themselves may play a major role in "incubating the potential for failure";
- recognises that, if managed properly, interruptions do not inevitably result in crises;
- acknowledges the impact, potential or realised, of interruptions upon a wide range of stakeholders;
- clearly recognises that a crisis unfolds through a series of salient phases, often providing managers with several points at which an intervention can be made to limit the impact of the threat faced by the organisation.

Figure 1.1 illustrates how a crisis management view of BC acknowledges first that the organisation is part of an environment characterised by uncertainty and change, leading to new challenges. Inside this environment, regulation, legislation and stakeholders help to shape the BC process within individual organisations. That process will be shaped by the historical legacy of the continuity process and the accumulated knowledge within an organisation. In addition, a key driver is the strategic

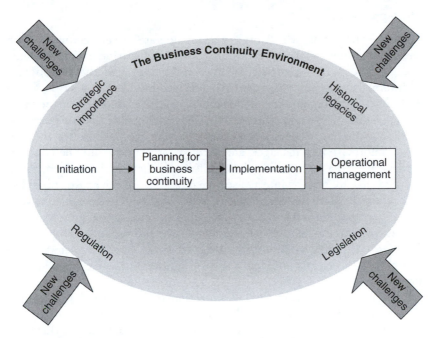

Figure 1.1 The continuity management process in context.

importance that business continuity management is regarded as having, both inside and outside the organisation.

Earlier BC publications (see, for example, Ginn, 1989; Andersen, 1992; Strohl Systems, 1995) have restricted their attentions to IS management and protection. More recent practical guides and case studies have a broader range of interests extending to all facilities (see, for example, Hiles and Barnes, 1999; Vancoppenolle, 1999) and, in some cases, to reputation management (Elliott et al., 1999a).

This broadening of BC reflects the underlying assumption that crisis incidents or business interruptions are systemic in nature, comprising both social and technical elements. Such a view has been well developed within the field of crisis management (Turner, 1976; Turner and Pidgeon, 1997; Shrivastava, 1987a; Smith, 1990; Pauchant and Douville, 1993; Perrow, 1997; Castillo, 2004). For example, the Challenger disaster (1986) arose from the convergence of technical failure (faulty seals) and the NASA culture. This created assumptions about the ability of staff to always succeed and the organisation became "deaf" to concerns about safety. Thus when specific safety issues were raised, the culture conspired to push ahead with the launch, resulting in tragedy (see Schwartz, 1987; Starbuck and Milliken, 1988; Pauchant and Mitroff, 1992; Vaughan, 1997). Within such a framework, the focus of disaster recovery upon the hardware is inherently flawed in that little or no consideration is given to human, organisational or social aspects of the system, nor to the interaction between components (Lewis, 2005).

Strategic Importance

The environment in which organisations operate is very complex, with change and innovation driven by increased competition and technology change. The judicious management of technology and the exploitation of Information Systems in particular are recognised as key skills which will determine organisational advantage in the "Information Society" (Bangemann, 1994, quoted in Crowe, 1996). Pilger (1998) disputes the label "information society", arguing that "media age" is more apt and that much information is managed and filtered for good or ill. The concerns expressed by the Google Watch organisation seem pertinent here, given the data that are held by internet service providers, search engine providers and retailers about the detail of our wants and preferences. Such a view recognises that the technology which makes information processing so easy is programmed and controlled by people and organisations: that is, there are social as well as technical dimensions. This is depicted in the case of fear uncertainty and doubt (FUD) and Sun Microsystems, shown in Box 1.1.

The prominence given to the protection of IS has been highlighted earlier and forms a key consideration within this text but does not encompass the full scope of BCM. An underlying assumption of this book is that BC permeates all areas of activity. Box 1.1 highlights two high-profile "interruptions" with far-reaching consequences for the organisations involved.

Box 1.1 FUD – Fear, Uncertainty and Doubt

Emerging from the early days of the personal computer industry, "fear, uncertainty and doubt" (FUD) is a term used to describe the actions of rivals that seek to propagate misinformation about a product or technology. In so doing, the FUD factors will lead consumers to disregard the product or technology, thereby protecting the position of incumbent suppliers of the technology.

The FUD technique is said to have originated at IBM during the 1970s, when one of its most senior managers, Gene Amdahl, left the company to set up a rival concern. He became a victim of FUD as the salespeople of his former employer undermined Amdahl products, giving rise to the term "fear, uncertainty and doubt".

By the 1980s, FUD had become a widespread marketing and sales technique within the computer industry. When the small British company Amstrad launched a range of affordable home computers, it found that rivals (whose products were often twice the price) quickly pointed out that the computer did not have a cooling fan and that this could lead to the overheating of internal components and subsequent loss of data. However, the Amstrad computer had been designed to operate without cooling fans because the power supply unit was not housed within the main case. Nonetheless, rivals' FUD tactics seemed to have generated reluctance and doubt in consumers' minds. Consequently, Amstrad was forced (unnecessarily) to install a cooling fan into its computers, at great expense and market damage to itself (given the unnecessary recognition of the unwarranted criticism).

FUD shows no signs of going away. Indeed, tensions between Microsoft and Sun Microsystems have given rise to the official and ongoing monitoring of statements relating to their products. Sun Microsystems, for instance, has a website dedicated to FUD statements, alongside official comment and rebuttal.

In a response to critics of Microsoft's new Vista product, Stefanik (2007), a seemingly well-informed advocate of Microsoft attacked the "FUD . . . being repeated (over and over) about Windows Vista by the press and bloggers . . . just a few hours before the official launch . . . that started a whole round of misinformation, speculation and paranoid conspiracy theories". Stefanik (2007) continues:

> The thing that really annoys me the most, however, is that you have these techno-pundits who have never actually used Vista simply regurgitating things that they've read on someone else's blog or some article in the trades. It's like a book reviewer who glances at the cover, reads a paragraph or two of the foreword and then writes a scathing review denouncing it as rubbish because they've read a previous book by the same author that they didn't like. Not only is it disingenuous, it's patently unfair to both the author and the potential readers. The same principle applies here. If you haven't actually used the operating system (and I mean really use it, not just install it), then you have no business writing about its vices or its virtues.

Stefanik's seemingly independent rebuttal is arguably more believable than an official Microsoft statement. What this example clearly illustrates is that in either consumer or corporate markets, wherever there is the threat of FUD activities emanating from a rival, there is also the propensity for a crisis to arise.

Sources: Sun Microsystems (2001, 2007); Irwin (2001);
Stefanik (2007)

Mercedes A-Class

More than a billion deutschmarks had been invested in the development and manufacture of the "Baby Benz", formally known as the

Mercedes-Benz A-Class. Scheduled for launch in late 1997, this radical new vehicle marked a major shift for the company into smaller sized vehicle segments, thereby capturing mass-market sales revenues. However, such visions soon became a nightmare for the company when on 21 October five Swedish motoring journalists managed to topple the vehicle at a mere 60 kph during an object-avoidance manoeuvre, known as the "elk" test.

Alone, this widely reported handling shortcoming represented a major crisis for the company fabled for its quality and safety. But, the lack of an immediate response to an incident perceived by the company to be inconsequential (given that the car had been tested for over eight million kilometres) merely served to compound the media interest in the story. When, a few days later, the company made its first public comments about the Baby-Benz, it sought to deflect attention away from Mercedes' contribution to the failed elk test, suggesting instead that the blame resided with Goodyear's tyres, which it suggested were insufficiently stiff for the vehicle's requirements.

Eight days after the initial failure of the vehicle in Sweden, Mercedes began to accept some responsibility for events and the behaviour of the vehicle by offering an expensive electronic modification to the car and making tyre changes. In the aftermath of the crisis, the company spent an estimated £100 million on retrofitted components and delayed re-launch for twelve months. Furthermore, the crisis had wider effects. Daimler-Benz, the parent company and one of Germany's largest industrial conglomerates, found its stock price diminished at its worst point by nearly 32 per cent.

Opinion is divided over whether Mercedes-Benz (at the time part of the Daimler-Chrysler group) will have suffered in the long term over the A-Class crisis. Production and order books have now reached target levels (180,000 vehicles per year), and the company's hi-tech Rastatt factory, along with the innovative vehicle, has become widely admired within the motor industry. Mercedes' response to the crisis was, however, less so.

Sources: Olins and Lynn (1997); Prowse (1998)

Firestone – Precedented Crisis, Unprecedented Changes

Product recalls in the motor industry are far from unusual. In the early 1970s, Ford faced public outrage following its unwillingness to respond to fatal design flaws in its Ford Pinto vehicle. Later in the decade, tyre manufacturer Firestone was forced to recall 14.5 million tyres, said to risk explosion under normal driving conditions. The magnitude of these crises suggested that neither of these companies would be found wanting again.

Never in the history of the car industry had production plants been closed in order to generate surplus stocks of new components for customers until the onset of one of the largest tyre recalls in history. Ford's plant closures released 70,000 new tyres, but Firestone (part of Japan's Bridgestone) recalled some 6.5 million in August 2000. A fault that led to tyre tread separation has been linked to 271 deaths and 800 injuries in hundreds of accidents in the US, Venezuela and the Middle East, with repercussions for tyres fitted to Ford's Explorer and Ranger 4 × 4 models across the world.

Sharing in both the causes and the effects of the crisis, Bridgestone and Ford faced several hundred lawsuits arising from individual and collective litigants. In spite of their shared exposure to significant out of court settlements or court-imposed damages, the companies continue to wrangle over the blame and response to the crisis. Ford had been criticised for not acting quickly and openly with the public media and authorities, for having ignored early warning signs and for having failed to recognise the role of the vehicle as a contributory factor. Equally, Firestone was criticised for its perceived role in the crisis, and was further criticised by Ford for its lack of openness and communications during the crisis.

The closure of the three plants to release the 70,000 tyres is estimated to have cost Ford $100 million, and the redeployment of Ford employees to assist in the replacement of tyres at motor dealerships proved to be one of the largest logistical operations of its type for the Ford Motor Company. Furthermore, in 2001, Ford announced that the company would offer, for the first time, its own warranties for tyres to supersede those offered by the tyre manufacturer, presenting a first step on a long road to corporate image recovery. In October 2005, Bridgestone settled the dispute with Ford, paying the car manufacturer $240 million to bring the long-running dispute to an end, by which time the tyre replacement programme is estimated to have cost in the region of $3 billion.

Sources: Bowe (2001); Tait (2001); Taylor (2000); BBC (2005)

Mercedes (Daimler-Chrysler) and Ford achieved ongoing success for much of the twentieth century and looked well positioned for the twenty-first. Both cases demonstrate how interruptions can be self-induced, in even the most successful of companies. Few commentators would deny that the crisis responses of Mercedes, Ford and Firestone were perceived to be inappropriately slow. Although continuity management is closely associated with ensuring that organisations can recover quickly from the loss of key facilities, we argue that the same principles can be applied to interruptions of a strategic nature. Breaks in operational continuity represent an interruption in the provision of products or services to customers. Facilities are restored in order that an organisation can continue to meet the needs of its customers and other stakeholders; recovery is a means to an end rather than an end in itself. Key lessons emerging from these two cases include:

- the potential threat to continuity from moves into new markets;
- technical failures arising from the complex interaction of factors including scientific knowledge, management interpretation and the demands of achieving business objectives, quickly – the old adage "act in haste, repent in leisure" seems apt as the costs to Ford and Mercedes approach an estimated £80 million and £100 million respectively;
- the potential transfer of damage from one product market to threaten an organisation's reputation in all areas;
- a slow and ineffective response may exacerbate the impact of an interruption;
- the dangers of ignoring early warning signals;
- the relevance of continuity management to new product development.

Although finance, marketing and operations have been subsumed within general management, they have retained their professional distinction. It is our view that continuity management will follow and be one of those areas for which all managers have some responsibility. Of course there will always be the need for discipline experts but success requires that a continuity mindset be absorbed by managers of all types and at all levels.

From Hardware Continuity to Service Continuity

Box 1.2 describes how Royal Sun Alliance recovered quickly in restoring "business as usual" when its offices in Manchester (UK) were destroyed in an explosion. Theirs is a typical scenario and highlights the dependence of organisations upon their facilities, obvious as it may seem. Organisations increasingly depend upon each other and upon key services and technologies; this has been a major development of the late twentieth century. A negative aspect of this is that the growing dependence upon IS requires that they will always be available for use. Inevitably, this is not always the case, and when problems arise, "drastic" solutions may be sought. For example, the failure of privatised electricity companies in California led that state to embark on transferring the utilities back to public ownership.

Box 1.2 Manchester – Royal Sun Alliance 1996

Manchester's business and retail quarter was devastated, although early warnings enabled police to evacuate shoppers and workers. The Royal Sun Alliance's offices were severely damaged, with the loss of hardware, data, paperwork and communication systems. Also thirty-four people had been working in the building that day, all of whom were mentally or physically injured in the blast. There seemed little chance of business as usual for Monday after the blast. Royal's recovery plan swung into action within twenty-four hours and by Monday alternative office space had been found, although access to the blasted building was not possible for some days. By chance, the Royal's headquarters in Liverpool had some space. Other Royal departments were split across offices in Manchester and a Comdisco recovery site at Warrington. A warehouse was set up to deal with recovering data from damaged hardware and documents taken from the ruins.

Source: Royal Sun Alliance (1996)

We often make assumptions about the dependability of technology-based systems. Technological breakthroughs quickly become absorbed into daily routines because of the ubiquitous nature of technology and ICT systems. Such systems eventually become used by all and questioned by none. The case of Electronic Point of Sale (EPOS) Systems is instructive here – most people only notice their dependence upon such systems when they are unable to pay for their goods in a store because of a breakdown in computer systems. The extent of an organisation's "hidden technology" such as its IS may only be highlighted when matters go wrong. Pauchant et al. (1992) describe how a fire in a Chicago telephone switching centre caused disruption to one and a half million business and domestic customers. The immediate effects lasted for some three weeks, at an estimated cost of $200–300 million. The pre-incident attitude of many were summed up by the comment of one manager: "I always thought the dialtone came from God!"

If it is accepted that ICT will help determine organisational advantage (by Earl, 1996; Awazu et al., 2009), the protection of such systems has become vitally important. It is essential that managers approach the protection of such systems from a strategic perspective so that opportunities presented by new technologies might be better exploited. There is a danger, however, that protection of the system becomes the objective rather than an attempt to ensure that the desired outcomes are achieved, as Thames Water's case in Box 1.3 indicates.

Box 1.3 Continuity as a Means to an End

Thames Water in London, UK refers to BC as "service continuity". When a water main burst, interrupting supplies, the company originally defined this as a technical problem to be solved by repairing the burst pipe. However, when reconsidering this, Thames Water realised that customers were less concerned with repairing the water pipe than with ensuring that clean water was delivered to their properties, by tanker if necessary. A story was told of how a burst water main had flooded a garden due to host a wedding two days later. Service continuity included not simply fixing the pipe but also restoring the garden for that weekend in order that the wedding could go ahead.

When Sunderland City Council, in the North East of the UK, prepared for possible disruptions triggered by the millennium bug, it identified alternative power generation as a key vulnerability. Key sites, initially, were held to be security lighting on council premises and building developments. Slowly, there was the recognition that if power supplies were interrupted, council residential homes for the elderly and disabled would be without electricity and protection of human life was a higher priority than the protection of property. The Council had simply not considered the possibility of a major power failure in its residential care homes.

Box 1.3 shows that organisational continuity should be extended beyond merely IS. Its two examples clearly indicate that BC is incomplete when it is internally and hardware focused. The management of organisational facilities and IS offer a means to an end but are not ends in themselves. Service continuity, as a concept, emphasises that organisational assets, soft and hard, are a means to the end of satisfying customers and maintaining the explicit and implicit service-level agreement between supplier and client.

This chapter now turns to examine the development of BC as a discipline. It is not the intention to introduce the reader to a prescriptive approach, as we do not subscribe to the view that there is "one right way" of doing continuity planning. All organisations differ and it therefore would be foolhardy to presume such an approach to be feasible. Indeed, in an ongoing study Elliott and Johnson (2008b) report evidence of effective BCM emanating from organisations in which root cause analysis provided the underlying methodology for developing continuity plans and processes. Rather, we present a perspective that we hope will stimulate debate and offer new ways of understanding the issue. Our approach regards people as being at the heart of the issue of ensuring organisational preparedness. Without a body of committed employees who engage in the planning process, who challenge organisational assumptions and who enact whatever continuity plans the organisation has constructed, organisational preparedness will remain a chimera. Second, an organisation forms part of a wider system and emphasising this interdependence is crucial. BCM should therefore be based upon the recognition of these issues and the planning process should reflect these realities.

Historical Legacies, Evolution and Stages of Development

It is well recognised that products and services often follow common life-cycle patterns (see, for example, Levitt, 1965; Gibson and Nolan, 1974; Shipley, 1998). Even the diffusion of management ideas appears to follow common patterns of development and demise (see, for example, Egan, 1995a). With regard to IS, such an evolution (from a technical to a broader organisational focus) has been observed (see, for example, Nolan, 1979; Earl, 1989; Galliers and Sutherland, 1991). An organisation's underlying assumptions about the nature of information systems and strategy will be revealed by the approach taken. For example, technocratic approaches emphasise ICT hardware and the importance of control by ICT professionals. Technocratic approaches are no longer sufficient, however, in the era of open innovation (Chesbrough, 2003). Online communications permeate our organisational lives, crossing organisational boundaries and, as we demonstrate in Chapter 3, it is not feasible today for any organisation to deny the fact (and accompanying opportunity) that technology enables contributions to be made by a variety of internal and external stakeholders. Hence, those organisations that have an understanding of Web 2.0 technologies and how to integrate them into a company's strategy will be able to focus on how best to manage the new forms of ICT as they interact with the social part of the organisation.

Despite their limitations, life-cycle models have been extremely influential because they emphasise a well-recognised pattern – in the IT field they document the switch from a focus upon technology to one on resource management and, latterly, to value creation as development moves beyond the initiation stage. Put simply, concern switches to seeking ways of exploiting IT for competitive advantage (Awazu et al., 2009). The speed of change may be determined by the nature of the technology (Earl, 1989) or by the degree to which the management team understands the importance of systems to the success of their business (Hirschheim et al., 1988).

Within the IS management literature, the use by Sutherland and Galliers (1994) of Waterman et al.'s (1980) Seven S framework may be seen as both reaction to and development from earlier evolutionary models (see also Pascale and Athos, 1982). Developed by McKinsey and Company during the 1970s, the Seven S framework emphasised the systemic

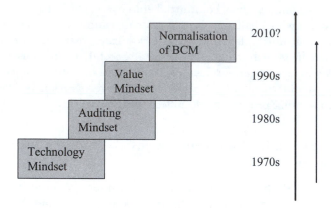

Figure 1.2 Evolution of BCM concept and drivers.

Source: Elliot et al. (2002)

properties of organisations. Sutherland and Gallier's (1994) resulting stages of growth model mapped out the organisational characteristics associated with the six stages of development.

In an attempt to apply the stages of growth model to BCM, Swartz et al. (2003) identified at least three stages from a study based on data collected from six organisations, shown in Table 1.1. During the 1990s, two mindsets dominated the BCM literature and organisational practice, which Swartz et al. (2003) label the "technology" and "auditing" mindsets. A third, arising from their analysis, is described as a "value-based" mindset, which at that time appeared to gain influence over practice. The authors posited a potential evolutionary path for BCM since the 1980s from the initial focus upon technological activities and concerns predominantly with hardware towards a growing interest in the value of BCM. There is no suggestion, argue Swartz et al., that these mindsets are restricted to specific decades; rather, they suggest that each represented the dominant paradigm for a particular period. In reality, these mindsets may live alongside one another within the population of organisations in an industry sector and even in any one organisation.

Implicit in Table 1.1 is a potential evolutionary path for BCM, extending from a technology-focused to a capability-based activity found within some organisations today. These mindsets are historically contingent and, to be properly understood, should be considered against the context of the dominant technologies and organisational forms of the different periods. In presenting Table 1.1, it is not suggested that these perspectives are restricted to specific decades; it is argued that the first two mindsets represented the dominant paradigm for a particular period. The latter two, value and capability based, represent ideal types to which, it might be claimed, better practice organisations aspire. Accordingly, mindsets

Table 1.1 Exploring Assumptions about BCM Provision

Emerged during this decade	Mindset	Scope	Triggers	Process
1970	Technology	Limited to technology Focus upon on large corporate systems, e.g. mainframes	External physical triggers, flood, fire, bomb	Contingency measures focused on hard systems
1980	Auditing	All facilities All systems – both corporate and departmental office	As above and legal or regulatory pressures	Contingency measures outsourced; compliance driven
1990	Value-based	Maintain competitive advantage Includes customers and suppliers Entire organisation, including human, social issues	Organisational stake-holders in value system	BCM developed as business process focused on business managers
2000	Capability-based	Integrates CSR, risk management and digital resilience	The desire to further embed well developed BCM practices	BCM is an ongoing and continuous organisation-wide responsibility

coexist within the population of organisations and even within any one organisation. When the first edition of this text was published, in late 2001, it seemed that the events of 9/11 would see greater recognition of BCM as a central and strategic issue with the potential to add value. However, as we shall indicate, there is evidence to suggest that the auditing mindset is strengthening. Key characteristics of each mindset are summarised in Table 1.1.

In Table 1.1, *scope* refers to whether BCM is regarded as functional or organisation-wide in its focus. *Triggers* indicate the nature of the event that led to initiation of the BCM process within an organisation. *Process* refers to whether BCM is regarded as a technocratic or business activity, to the degree of involvement of key staff and the underlying assumptions made about how BCM should be embedded within the organisation. We discuss the different stages and mindsets below.

Technology Mindset

The technology mindset has as its exclusive concern the protection of computer systems and facilities. During the 1970s, a common assumption was that business disruptions were triggered by technology failure. There are numerous examples of the practical guides to BCM emanating from practitioners which fit within the technology mindset. These may be judged on their merits either within the terms of reference they set themselves or within a broader critical review of the BCM literature. For example, Wieczorek et al.'s (2002) study of business continuity is subtitled *IT Risk Management for International Corporations*, allowing no ambiguity about the subject matter. Toigo (2003), responding to the events of 9/11, produced a third edition of his text *Disaster Recovery Planning* solely concerned, not surprisingly, with facilities management. Doswell's (2000) work perhaps typifies the technology mindset and its primary concern with the protection of computer systems and facilities. The introduction to this text makes clear the author's view of the close ties between BCM and disaster recovery and makes significant reference to the importance of BS 7799, the British Standard for Information Security. Such a view is reinforced by the examples provided and the focus upon interruption to IS. Implicit is the view that interruptions affect the organisation, with little consideration of the involvement of other stakeholders other than as groups to be communicated to in the event of a crisis (Doswell, 2000: 43). Underpinning Doswell's work is the widely shared assumption that business disruptions are triggered by technology failures; thus the emphasis placed upon the protection of hard systems such as corporate mainframe systems (Pritchard, 1976; Broadbent, 1979; Kuong and Isaacson, 1986). This hardware focus is identified by Kuong and Isaacson (1986) as an instigator for business continuity planning (BCP), which they suggest was first seen in Electronic Data Processing (EDP) departments as organisations from many sectors recognised their reliance upon their computer systems. Ginn (1989) asserted that IT disaster recovery (recovery of systems after disruption has taken place) can be traced back to the US banking industry's desire to protect their corporate data centres in the early 1970s. This was when the vice president for IS of a major US bank sought a solution to being disturbed at night by telephone calls from the data processing centre about potential disasters threatening IT security. Out of this arose the idea to systematically plan back-up or recovery sites and many of the concepts and practices which are still in use today in disaster recovery. The dominance of corporate mainframe systems allowed for a centrally driven, technology driven approach.

The emergence of personal computers during the 1980s and the diffusion of control of IS among organisations (Panko, 1988) provided a basis for developing an auditing mindset in which a task for central IS departments was to regulate and police. It should be noted that while the recognition of growing reliance upon IS was a key driver, elsewhere other drivers were also present. For example, within the UK the perceived threat of terrorism, largely focused upon the financial institutions of the City of London during the early 1990s, were viewed as significant drivers of BCM. More recently, threats associated with animal rights activists and poor laboratory practices have raised the profile of BC within veterinary and medical research respectively.

Auditing Mindset

The auditing perspective regards BC as a "cost" required by regulations, corporate governance initiatives or customer requirement. For example, specific federal legislation has acted as a driver in the US. Within the UK, the BC British Standard (BS 25999, 2006) is expected to encourage and facilitate the spread of BCM from large corporate customers to smaller suppliers. The Financial Services Authority's (FSA) "Benchmarking Resilience" exercise has sought to raise standards across the finance sector.

The auditing mindset assumes a broader scope for BCM than its predecessor. It is regarded as vital insurance. This functional perspective, however, places little emphasis upon BC within the process of value creation. Consequently, the BC process is still concentrated upon contingency measures for hard systems protection, perhaps outsourcing certain tasks to disaster recovery consultants. The major focus of the auditing perspective is still on the technology, the plan itself, and on how continuity can be established through protecting essential business activities. This became increasingly important as end-user computing spread through organisations during the 1980s. For Ginn (1989), this type of continuity planning has two distinct phases:

- planning to lessen the risk of disaster;
- concentrating upon the development of a survival plan to ensure survival and recovery from a disaster.

While phase 1 might concentrate upon IT systems and the corporate data centre, phase 2 is concerned with how to prevent or survive disruption caused by the loss of people, buildings or other resources required to conduct business. Swartz et al. (2003) argued that the auditing mindset retained the technology focus of the preceding phase, but sought to achieve outcomes through different means. New drivers such as federal legislation within the US, especially within the finance sector, saw BCM compliance emerge as a key issue; for example, the US Foreign Corrupt Practices Act required that publicly owned organisations have internal control provisions to safeguard assets (Kuong and Isaacson, 1986). In the UK, Turnbull's (1999) guidance on internal controls and the IS Security Standard (BS 7799) triggered consideration of an organisation's information systems and security. More recently, the BS 25999, published in late 2006, deals directly with BC. Wieczorek et al. (2002) cite the influence of the Basel Committee on Banking Supervision (1999) in considering risk through identifying a range of "risk areas", including external, processes, systems and people. This is further explored in Chapter 2 of this text. Such initiatives appear to have played an important role in developing further the scope of BCM. Nevertheless, a weakness of such approaches is that they are dependent upon the interests of the regulators and scope may be limited to what is set down in writing. For example, Wieczorek et al.'s own examples are concerned with the tangible risks associated with hardware or facilities failures rather than with less tangible issues such as reputation risk.

While the auditing perspective does consider people as part of the BCM process, the focus is principally upon how to "engineer" compliance. There is no elaboration of the impact of the human contribution to disruption (neither as cause nor prevention) or to its influence upon implementation of the BC process. In contrast, in the value-based mindset it is proposed that these factors are central to the process (Herbane et al., 1997).

Value-based Mindset

The value-based perspective is concerned less with compliance, regulations or technology failure than with the needs of the business itself. Crucially, in this mindset BCM is regarded as having the potential to add value to the organisation, not just consume revenues. The value-based perspective departs from the technology and auditing perspectives in the assumptions that are made about the scope and purpose of BCM. The scope is perceived as constituting the entire organisation including employees, who are regarded as presenting the biggest challenge in terms of implementation and management of the BC process. Organisational stakeholders are regarded as being the most important driver for change and hence for BCM. In essence, BC is regarded as the integration of social and technical systems that together enable effective organisational protection (Swartz et al., 1995). In organisations which adopt this approach, BCM expertise is often brought into the new product development process, and actively exploited in marketing strategy. Therefore, BCM not only protects but also contributes to the value-adding process through more efficient systems, or provides value-adding benefits to customers through superior responsiveness, reliability and security.

Within the value-based approach, Herbane et al. (1997) argued that the human contribution to disruption (either as cause or prevention) is seen as central to BCM. The other mindsets consider BCM as a cost; for example, the CCTA (1995a, 1995) state that, like insurance, BCM is a cost which may show little evidence of tangible reward.

The value-based approach draws upon a more strategic view of BC than previous mindsets. Influential tools such as value chain analysis, developed by Porter (1985), emphasised the linkages and interdependencies that created value and formed the basis for competitive advantage (Ramsay, 1999, suggests that the value chain can be used as a tool for crisis and emergency planning). Simply protecting and replicating facilities and hardware might not be sufficient to protect the value-adding capabilities that underpinned organisational success. At one level, practitioner authors such as McManus and Carr (2001) recognise that a flu epidemic, labour dispute or shortage may create a more significant disruption than an IS failure. Thus, BCM should not simply be concerned with tangible assets but with all its resources. At a second level, the value-based approach emphasises the importance of understanding how an organisation adds value. The resource-based view of the firm (Barney, 2001, 2007) and the notions of core competences and strategic capabilities, put simply, suggest that value may be added through linking disparate activities better than do competitors. For example, it might be argued that Sony has consistently linked R&D, marketing, production and distribution better than their competitors. The basis for Sony's competitive advantage may depend upon the organisation's ability to develop capabilities through shared tacit knowledge, organisational resources and assets within its various activities.

The protection of corporate knowledge provided the basis for an investigation by Beazley et al. (2002) which identified the threat of knowledge loss within the so-called knowledge economy. Although other texts similarly make some reference to less tangible resources, Beazley et al. (2002) are exclusively concerned with intellectual and human capital. They argued that these differ from other assets and describe them as a stream rather than a physical entity. Knowledge, they argued, resides in the minds of employees rather than in space controlled by an organisation. The priority Beazley et al. ascribe to a non-physical asset may provide a pointer to the future of BCM. Considering this contribution, Elliott et al. (2002) argued that, if this is the case, BCM must be a strategic activity and must be properly grounded in an understanding of how competitive advantage is achieved. Ferre (2000), in a guide published by the UK's Institute of Directors clearly positioned to raise consideration of BCM to a strategic level, argued for a proactive, broad-scope approach (see Figure 1.3).

Business Continuity Capabilities – Reflecting a New Mindset for the Twenty-First Century

There is evidence to support the emergence of BC *capabilities* as the most recent manifestation of BC practice (Figure 1.2). These capabilities build upon, but are distinct from, the resources necessary for BCM per se. An organisational capability has been conceptualised as "the capacity for a team of resources to perform some task or activity. While resources are the

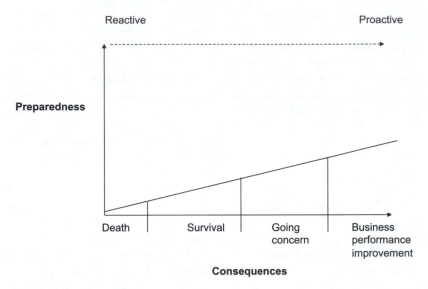

Figure 1.3 Business continuity continuum.

Source: Ferre (2000)

source of a firm's capabilities, capabilities are the main sources of its competitive advantage" (Grant, 1991: 119). Crucial to the effectiveness of such a BCM capability is the cooperation and coordination of resources that may reside in diverse locations within the organisation.

The notion of BC *capabilities* which create a recovery advantage (relative either to the absence of BCM or to the capabilities of those of organisations facing the same interruption) are distinct to BC *management*. BCM is an activity characterised by discernible skills, approaches and styles. Management is a process, whereas a capability is an organisational possession that is the combination of several organisational resources. The task or activity that a BC capability is designed to accomplish is to provide effective prevention and recovery for the organisation while maintaining competitive advantage and value system integrity. An organisation may achieve an advantage by being able to actively avoid the disadvantages faced by other organisations in the same environment (Powell, 2001). From a conceptual standpoint, a BC capability is characterised by its embeddedness and resource bundling, and is knowledge rich, path dependent and context dependent (vizualised in Figure 1.4). As such, these central motifs characterise a BC capability and influence its uniqueness.

The configuration of resources is principally dependent upon the embeddedness and bundling of resources. As an *embedded* resource, BC is no longer a purely functional activity carried out by "someone else". This elevates and democratises BCM into a strategic and organisation-wide undertaking (Herbane et al., 2004; Foster, 2005). The tasks of BCP are

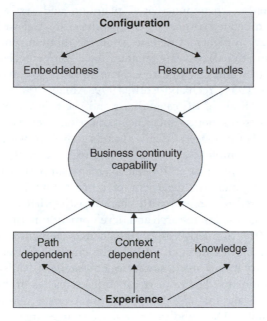

Figure 1.4 Building business continuity capability.

shared and BC processes and plans are owned by those for whom the plan is designed. Furthermore, a broader responsibility for thinking about BC is engendered within the organisation. In addition to operational and strategic considerations, managers and employees need to think continuously about BC issues within their organisations and have a mechanism to capture ideas and feedback in a continuous improvement manner. Real-time feedback and signal detection mechanisms are essential in high-reliability organisations (La Porte and Consolini, 1991) in which the consequences of a system failure are grave. The ongoing requirement for a rapid response to new and emerging threats calls into question the practice of using BC planning as a one-off project (Elliott et al., 1999a) or leaving plans in place untested and unmodified for long periods. Pitt and Goyal's study of BC practices (2004) found that 15 per cent of respondent organisations had never tested their plans and only 20 per cent of organisations audited their plans more than once per year. Auditing and testing, which form the critical link between planning and implementation, are considered in further detail in Chapter 7. Despite the wider dissemination and awareness of BCM of late, many firms still appear to regard it as a highly seasonal process. Whether the timing of a large interruption matches the availability of the most contemporary versions of the organisation's plans (that should include provisions for scenarios that consider new threats) is a matter more of chance than design. In a digital world, the pace, vector and implications of threats that reside within it (Chapter 3) further necessitate continuous rather than punctuated planning and testing cycles, thus making the embedded nature of BC capabilities more desirable.

The *bundling* together of diverse resources (human, financial, technological, organisational) to create organisational competencies has long been documented in studies seeking to explain sustainable competitive advantages (Barney, 1989; Yeoh and Roth, 1999; Afuah, 2002). Such bundling also lies at the heart of BC capabilities and their development. Resource bundling represents not simply the connections between resources but their *synthesis*. For instance, specialised skills combined with organisational structures allow employees to join ad hoc teams quickly. Also in-house technologies and genuine senior management support will enable rapid response development in the event of a crisis that has not previously been encountered or foreseen with characteristics that are similar to the "Cheetah teams" used in research and development functions (Engwall and Svensson, 2001). Similarly, supply chain management resources can be coupled with BC resources to address the challenge of ensuring supply chain continuity in low-stock, stock free or "fragile" (Zsidisin et al., 2005) supply environments. The value of capabilities resides in their integration of both tangible and intangible resources to provide a more appropriate set of BC provisions. The bundling of such resources may emerge without intention, but a careful understanding and management of resources at one's disposal is a starting point in formulating effective combinations of capabilities.

The knowledge richness, and path and context dependency of BC capabilities are components of the experience that the organisation has in responding to crises and interruptions. Indeed, successful responses to crises may become cultural artefacts in the forms of stories (Levitt and March, 1988; Schein, 1992). BC capabilities are *knowledge rich* because of the integration of tacit and explicit knowledge. Organisations will accumulate a large amount of information (know-*what*) from both planning and testing activities that can be readily codified and transferred to others within the organisation. In addition, individuals will have know-*how* that is derived from operational experience, mistakes, observations and social interactions. This complex and specific information further informs organisations about how they should or might respond during a crisis. Tacit knowledge about group interaction may also allow teams to form and begin functioning more quickly and prevent the delays that arise from team maladaptation.

BC capabilities do not emerge overnight or during the course of a short period. Their development is *path dependent*. As Barney (1995: 53) notes, "as firms evolve, they pick up skills, abilities, and resources that are unique to them, reflecting their path through history. These resources and capabilities reflect the unique personalities, experiences, and relationships that exist in only a single firm." In a BC context, a firm that has a long presence in a particular location, as did several tenants of the World Trade Centre in

2001 and who had had experience of the terrorist attack in 1993 (Herbane et al., 2004), will demonstrate not only a can-do attitude but will also have developed their responses through the organisational learning that followed the restoration of interrupted processes.

To add to the already distinct nature of BC capabilities, they are also *context dependent*. Organisations face idiosyncratic situations (Ahuja and Katila, 2004) in which problems and opportunities are weighed up as managers consider a course of action. A firm that is one of the first to confront and respond to a particular type of threat (as did Johnson & Johnson faced with the malicious product tampering of its Tylenol product in 1982, or BMW faced with the recall of the Mini shortly after its launch in September 2001) will need to make a decision that may exhibit high levels of uncertainty and while having little or no background knowledge to inform (or distort) subsequent decisions. The same applies to organisations encountering for the first time a specific crisis with unique characteristics — a product recall (Chapter 2), or cybercrime (Chapter 3), etc. Idiosyncratic situations are important in the BC context because by their very nature they cannot be precisely replicated by another organisation. Consequently, the benefits and learning gained from the response to the situation are causally ambiguous. Knowledge exchanges, such as The Business Continuance Group in the UK (http://www.tbcg.org.uk), can help to overcome the experiential limitations of novice firms but are not a substitute for ongoing exposure to BC activities over a long period of time.

BC capabilities represent the future development of BC resources and build upon the legacy and sustenance of BCP and management. Without these, as Figure 1.2 shows, BC capabilities cannot exist.

Which Mindset?

Despite Herbane et al.'s (1997) assertion concerning the development of a value-based approach, it may be seen that the auditing mindset is still in existence at the time of writing. Reiman's (2002) consideration of the role of internal audit with regard to BCM provides strong evidence of this. Gerlach (2002) provides a review identifying the growth in controls broadly concerned with BCM, primarily but not exclusively concerned with the finance sector. Gerlach (2002) cites the importance of the events of 9/11 as a driving force for many of these initiatives. What seems more likely is that those tragic events encouraged greater dissemination and acceptance of the regulations reviewed. Furthermore, these events demonstrated the coupled and complex nature of economic, financial, technological and infrastructure systems and the need for laggard organisations (whether public or private) to catch up with and comply with the higher-quality BC provisions in place at other reliant organisations. Although Gerlach (2002) is concerned with European and US regulations, the establishment of standards in Australia, Japan, Mexico, Singapore and the UK indicates the global awareness of BCM and its measurement (see Chapter 2).

Within the UK, the Financial Services Authority (FSA) benchmarks the preparedness of key financial organisations. The key instrument includes hundreds of items or questions to which respondents must reply. Robinson (2006), one of the authors and designers of the instrument, advocates the use of a well-devised mechanical control with clearly identified tolerances to ensure that BCM is efficiently managed within a dynamic context. Robinson cites the example of the refrigerator that keeps food chilled but not frozen and will be set up such that a deviation of one degree from its setting will lead to a self-correcting response. Robinson's (2006) background in metrics and control systems was manifest in his key role as author of the diagnostic tool employed by the UK's FSA Resilience Benchmarking Project (2005). This project brought together the Tripartite Authorities (FSA, HM Treasury and the Bank of England) to consider the resilience of the UK finance sector in the face of a major disruption, its ability to recover and to examine how further resilience might be built. The report's conclusions were based upon responses from sixty firms from the finance sector and its supporting infrastructure, answering around 1,000 questions each. Robinson's (2006) paper is especially relevant as it provides some insight into the assumptions of the Tripartite Authorities which underpinned the benchmarking project. This approach would indicate support for a view that detailed standards, well-developed metrics and high rates of sampling are the primary means of control.

Henry (2006), reviewing Robinson's work, argued that standardised measurement within a system of controls could only add to the credibility of BCM. Green (2006), in a review of his organisation's approach to benchmarking BCM, identified disaster recovery, staff welfare and respect, facilities and logistics as pillars of the process. Green (2006) identified the Business Continuity Institute's (BCI) ten standards as the starting point from which a series of questions were developed as a means of generating values linked to the BCI's competencies. These questions originate from a post-9/11 review and reflect subjective assessments by members of the Bank of England. The method used in Green's research included a pre-determined weighting given to each item (higher weightings were given to items that could be evidenced) as well as the value provided by respondents. In Green's (2006) description of the process, it is clear that the questionnaire instrument forms only a part of an interactive discursive process, which appears markedly different to the seemingly more mechanistic approach advocated by Robinson (2006) and used by the Tripartite Authorities.

Another view, that would not reject out of hand the value of such metrics and efforts to benchmark, would point to a body of knowledge which reports that regulation often leads to a low common standard of behaviour in which fulfilling the letter of the law becomes more important than abiding by the spirit of regulation (see, for example, Elliott and Smith, 2006). Elliott and Smith (2006) also argue that regulation, if enforced in a punitive manner, tends to stifle learning and lead to sub-optimal outcomes. The basis of BC capabilities, as has been argued, relies upon rich knowledge which results from the integration of tacit and explicit knowledge. While explicit knowledge may be evaluated through metrics to some extent, the nature of tacit knowledge makes it less access-ible to quantitative, positivistic methodologies.

Although this book presents an ideal-type, in the Weberian sense, and a systematic model of BCP, and considers key issues around the management process, we argue that effective BC capabilities require both explicit and tacit knowledge. This has implications for managing the process and for evaluation. For example, while we would not reject the usefulness of metrics, we would argue that a more qualitative approach such as in "pro-cess benchmarking", as identified by Trosa and Williams (1996), might generate greater learning opportunities.

Robinson's (2006) metaphor of the refrigerator and the role of metrics to maintain temperature provide a clear example of single-loop learning (Argyris, 1994) in which learning takes the form of single, negative, feed-back loops during which organisations review and learn from actions that they or others have taken. Such learning takes place within a given paradigm and is based upon asking a one-dimensional question to elicit a one-dimensional answer. Alternatively, double-loop learning takes an additional step or, more often than not, several additional steps. It turns the question back on the questioner. Argyris says "in the case of the thermostat, double loop learning would wonder whether the current set-ting was the most effective temperature at which to keep the refrigerator, and, if so, would question whether the present heat or cooling source was the most effective means of achieving it. A double loop process might also ask why the current setting was chosen in the first place" (Argyris, 1994: 78–79). Thus, well-developed metrics and high rates of sampling may provide a useful means of control, but the assumptions on which the metrics are based must be made clear and open to challenge.

In an earlier study by the authors of this text (Herbane et al., 1997), a BCM continuum was developed which subsequently evolved into the original version of the mindsets identified above. It is argued that what we now term a value-based mindset constituted "better practice" compared to the "standard practice" of the technology mindset.

The continuum, depicted in Figure 1.5, identified a number of dimen-sions against which "practice" might be assessed. The first two dimensions refer to the types of staff employed on continuity projects and to the scope of their work. Standard practice is concerned with IT systems and employs only IT staff while better practice organisations employstaff from a diver-sity of backgrounds on a project which is business wide in scope. A range

'Standard practice'	'Better practice'
Old	New
Disaster Recovery	**BCM**
IT focus	Value chain focus
IT staff	Multi-disciplinary team
Existing structure	New structures
Protect core operations	Protect entire organisation
Sustain current position	Create sustainable advantage
Parochial view	Open system view
Recovery emphasis	Prevention emphasis

Figure 1.5 Old and new BCM approaches compared.

Source: adapted from Herbane et al. (1997)

of forces, including board-level champions and support, manager appraisal and a persuasive communications strategy, drove effective continuity. Better practice organisations combined these and other measures to successfully drive the BC process; standard practice firms had little use for such initiatives because they were seen as a task for IT alone. In such organisations, there was little need for new structures because IT could deal with continuity. In better practice cases, new structures of coordinators were identified with responsibility for the continuity process being delegated to each business unit and the dedicated continuity team providing a supporting role. The final differences between the two extremes concern strategy. Better practice saw continuity as a strategic issue both in terms of protecting its place in the supply chain and in marketing activities. The continuum provides a snapshot of continuity practice.

This focus upon practice has led us to reconsider how the evolution of BCM identified in Figure 1.2 might be redrawn, with less emphasis upon the drivers and a greater consideration of BCM in practice. Figure 1.6 depicts an emergence from disaster recovery as a post-event response, through BCP, the more integrated BCM to an embedded BC capability.

The remainder of this book aims to provide an academically grounded, practically useful guide to the BC professional on a journey towards embedding a BC capability within their organisation. The notion of capability, identified as the fourth stage, suggests a number of key issues for the BCM professional. First, capability suggests managing cooperation and the coordination of organisational resources and competences and is

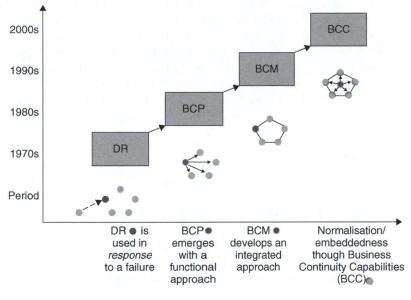

Figure 1.6 The evolution of BCM concept and practice.

thus a key task for the BCM professional. Second, where traditional approaches to BCM emphasise internal resources, we acknowledge the complementary importance of external formal and informal networks and relationships as a key resource. The notion of harnessing social capital is one that has been almost absent from consideration of BCM. Third, embedding BCM requires promoting effective organisational learning and knowledge management. Within the literature dealing with capabilities, it is acknowledged that long-term competitive advantage may emerge when the tacit knowledge base is nurtured and protected. Fourth, such knowledge and the maintenance of links may provide a solid platform for organisational resilience. Note that resilience is considered as a socio-technical phenomenon which, while implicit in many approaches, is often treated as a solely technical exercise. Fifth, the notion of a capability rising from the functions suggests a strategic role for BCM.

Summary

This chapter has introduced the concept of BC and has identified a range of approaches to it. We have argued that effective continuity management needs to be focused upon business processes and assets as means to an end. The growing reliance of organisations upon one another and upon technology and infrastructure has also been cited as supporting the view that BCM matters more today than at any other point in history. The arguments in this book are founded upon what has been termed as a crisis management approach; this assumes that soft and hard system elements must be considered together and that organisations themselves may incubate the potential for interruptions. Managerial intervention plays a vital role in causing crises or in mitigating their effects. While no methodology can guarantee that interruptions will be avoided, it is argued that adopting the broad methodology developed in this book will assist organisations to be better prepared.

Study Questions

1   What are the advantages of applying a BC approach to strategic decisions?
2   Examine the newspapers for a fourteen-day period and identify examples of service continuity.
3   How does service continuity differ from BC?
4   What are the characteristics of good BC practice?
     How would you expect to see this implemented in:

     a   a large retailer?
     b   an internet service provider?
     c   a football club?

Further Reading

Billings, R., Milburn, T. and Schaalman, M. (1980) "A model of crisis perception", *Administrative Science Quarterly*, 25: 300–316.
Drennan, Lynn T. and McConnell, A. (2007) *Risk and Crisis Management in the Public Sector*, London: Routledge.
Herman, C.F. (1963) "Some consequences of crisis which limit the viability of organisations", *Administrative Science Quarterly*, 12: 61–82.
Mitroff, I.I. and Alpaslan, M.C. (2003) "Preparing for evil", *Harvard Business Review*, 81 (4): 109–115.
Turner, B. and Pidgeon, N. (1997) *Man-made Disasters*, 2nd edn, London: Butterworth-Heinemann.

2 Legal Drivers and Business Continuity Management Standards

Introduction[1]

In chapter 1 we examined the development of business continuity (BC) into its current form – business continuity management (BCM) – from its origins in disaster recovery planning. The transition stages of this approach have moved from a technical focus to one driven by the needs of compliance and finally to one based on the needs of the strategic management of the organisation. In the twenty-first century, not only is BC a strategic concern, but it is once again heavily influenced by the heartbeat of technology (Chapter 3) and the pressure from external bodies to comply with standards and regulations. The latter is the focus of this chapter.

Despite the uncertainty which managers may face in determining the precise timing and types of crises that an organisation may face, regulations, legislation and good practice standards affecting an organisation in a crisis or business interruption are well established. In this chapter, we navigate through some of the important areas of legislation of which managers should be aware. It is important, prior to any attempt to plan for crises, that managers are acquainted with those legal and regulatory issues that will influence or affect the plans they seek to develop. We begin by considering legal drivers and BCM standards as control systems within BC through an integrated framework, which identifies their source, type, purpose and appropriateness, and proceed to evaluate the influence that stakeholders have upon external controls such as legislation and regulation. From this we examine self-regulation as alternatives to legislative provisions. While having many benefits compared to legal provisions, this chapter highlights the nature of regulatory approaches and examines how the role of regulators has evolved. Next we set out to identify some of the important domestic, international and sectoral regulation – regulations and standards that require or influence the adoption of BCM. Finally, we examine some of the legislation that relates to product liability, product recalls and mass torts. Readers should note that this chapter is not designed to be exhaustive but to demonstrate that an exercise in the analysis of compliance and good practice is an important prerequisite in both the initiation of BCM (Chapter 4) and the maintaining and enhancement of BCM provisions (Chapter 7).

Legal Drivers and Business Continuity Management Standards as Control Systems

Alongside the commercial and technological stimuli for organisations to adopt and develop BC practices, legal and regulatory provisions have presented a parallel series of developments that have made BC provisions more of a necessity than a luxury in a modern operational context. These come to form a macro-environment of control systems which can influence, shape or enforce desired behaviours to prevent, pre-empt, respond to and recover from an organisational interruption (Figure 2.1) It has been argued that "Just as good strategic planners will pay attention to changes in their competitive environments – and in some cases attempt to shape it – there is scope for business continuity managers to move beyond the legal or regulatory pull factors of national, industry or technology obligation. However, since these pull factors provide the analytical baseline for planners, they merit identification" (Herbane et al., 2004: 441). These pull factors act as external control mechanisms upon organisational planning and behaviour.

Unlike legislation, which is embodied in acts of parliaments or statutes, a regulation may be defined as a set of principles and rules created (in some cases to supplement legislation) by statutory or regulatory bodies to control the behaviour and ensure compliance with established norms of behaviour of organisations within their jurisdiction. Both, however, have similarities in compulsion and control.

Contingent upon their origin, controls influence or determine an organisation's actions. Control systems are processes that enable an evaluation of

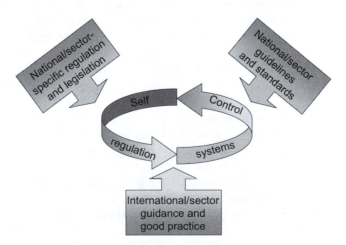

Figure 2.1 Internal and external behavioural drivers and influences.

whether objectives and goals are being met in four major ways: coping with complexity; coping with and adapting to environmental complexity; enhancing efficiency by minimising costs; and maintaining standards (Herbane and Rouse, 2000). Controls are important in guiding and determining the behaviour of organisations and their employees. The types of control examined and evaluated in this chapter (such as regulation and legislation) determine the degree to which behaviour is *compelled* and BCM good practice guidelines *influence* behaviour. The need for control systems in the implementation and integration of BCM within an organisation is subject to the same exigencies as the actions needed to incorporate improved quality programmes or new administrative processes.

The provenance of controls can be both external and internal. With differing degrees of influence and appropriateness, an organisation is faced with many reasons why its processes and actions must adhere and conform to prescribed standards. Figure 2.2 presents a hierarchy of controls that organisations are subject to. Legislation, regulation and internal controls are the three control *types* which have been identified. We can observe from Figure 2.2 that the *source* of control types ranges from externally derived sources, such as regulation and legislation, to those developed internally, such as administrative systems, procedures, mentoring, appraisal systems, budgets and rewards. Such internal controls are highly tangible yet will vary between organisations. Control types also vary in their *appropriateness* and their *purpose. Appropriateness* is considered in terms of the congruence of control types within an organisation, given the unique nature of its resources, operations and history. This varies from generic legislation,

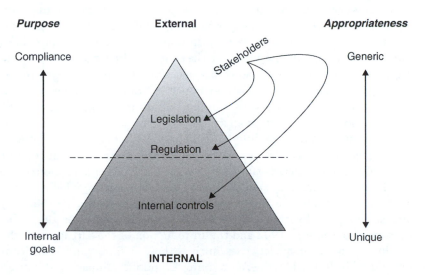

Figure 2.2 Hierarchy of controls.

to which all organisations within the boundaries of a jurisdiction must conform, to regulations which may deal with specific industries, activities and processes, and finally to the unique control systems which individual organisations have in place and which are determined by factors such as age, history, environment and leadership. *Purpose* refers to the rationale behind the control type, such as whether organisations are meeting the expectations determined externally about their behaviour, such as compliance, or whether activities are achieving internally established goals, reflecting performance aspirations.

Stakeholders and Control

In the previous chapter, we introduced and examined the relationship between stakeholders and organisations, with the attendant requirement for organisations to be aware of their ability to ensure both the continuity of commercial trading and production and the continuity of stakeholder relationships. Stakeholder groups are not only unique between organisations, but their relationship with an individual organisation can also be characterised by dynamism, particularly during crises. Crisis events serve to challenge day-to-day operations, and may also change the relationship between stakeholders as the effects on differing stakeholder groups may vary. In the process of an organisation invoking continuity plans, the necessity arises for the organisation to implement a series of planned activities designed to achieve the resumption of operations (often referred to as a "timeline of recovery"). This may shift stakeholder relations from the existing dynamic complex of relations with a large group of stakeholders to a more limited set of groups which has been designated as those on whom the organisation must rely, or who are in turn reliant upon the organisation during the recovery phase. The shifting dynamics of stakeholders during a crisis not only play an important role in the subsequent turnaround period but also influence the controls which prevail within the organisation. For instance, a car component manufacturer facing a product recall will prioritise the media and franchised dealership network more highly that the university with which it has an ongoing, but unrelated, research and development programme since this latter group, albeit an important stakeholder in a different context, does not constitute a priority in the activities designed to resolve the aftermath of a major product recall. The role of stakeholders is significant for each type of organisational control. New legislation may arise due to the influence of stakeholders, such as in the introduction of a Treasury-funded re-insurance scheme following intense lobbying by the UK insurance industry soon after the Baltic Exchange bombing in 1992 and the introduction of the Sarbannes–Oxley Act in response to financial crises, such as those at Enron and Worldcom. Introduced in July 2002, the Act requires US public companies to indicate the effectiveness of their controls for financial activities and has been interpreted as a driver in the quest for greater enterprise-wide resilience (Giles, 2005).

Regulations (from governments and industry groups) may reflect changing public tastes and social change, such as the introduction of voluntary schemes for improved animal husbandry (such as the Freedom Food initiative starting in 1995), the ban placed upon the testing of cosmetics products on animals imposed by the British government in November 1998, and The Council of The European Union's Council Regulation No 834/2007 (June 2007) on organic production and labelling of organic products.

The stakeholder influence on internal controls is equally discernible. Stakeholder expectations in competitive industries with publicly quoted companies create a form of market control whereby the expectations and actions of shareholders drives the need for organisations to have in place controls that ensure that expectations (such as investment returns, but increasingly in terms of socially responsible conduct) are met.

Regulation and Business Continuity Management

Regulation and Control

Regulation is a further set of controls upon organisations and their behaviour. Often developed and supervised by extra-organisational authorities, they are designed to direct the decisions and actions of individual organisations operating within specified economic sectors of activity. They are still external, generic and compliance-based controls, but to a lesser degree than legislation, although, regulations may supplement a more generic set of legislative instruments within specific contexts (industries and activities) as seen later in this chapter. Equally, regulations may have elements of wider law associated with them in order to ensure compliance. In having their origins beyond the boundaries of an organisation, such controls coexist in the context of the controls developed within organisations during their growth and development. The source of such controls determines the way they are assimilated into an organisation's everyday process.

By their very nature, controls originating from outside an organisation are *imposed* since the regulatory authority in question will normally have statutory powers to enforce compliance with their regulations. In contrast, internal controls may develop in a *voluntary* manner, reflecting a more organic process of bargaining, consensus and human resource practices which differ between organisations. In making a clear distinction between imposed controls and voluntary controls, we can acknowledge fundamental differences between them and identify how their integration into processes and activities vary. Both voluntary and imposed controls coexist in the organisational environment in which BCM prevails. The composition of controls (whether external or internal) will clearly differ according to the organisation's operating context. However, the imperative facing BC managers is the need to understand the balance between controls. This will not only determine the content of BC provisions in place, but may also affect the necessity to have specific provisions in place.

Regulatory Approaches

Regulation can exist in two forms: statutory regulation, underpinned by statute, or self-regulation, underpinned by voluntary agreements between organisations. A two-tiered regulatory regime can be observed where both types of regulation are used to govern the activities of organisations. A further distinction is provided by Hemphill (1996: 27) between "industry regulation", which focuses upon an individual industry, and "social regulation", which is "issue-related and non-economic in nature, crosses industries in its impact, and affects the manufacturing processes and physical characteristics of products". Smith and Tombs (1995: 620) define self-regulation as where organisations "ensure that they comply with current legislative requirements, without the direct policing of, and subsequent interference by, the various regulatory bodies". The existence of regulators, in their view, is testament to the inability of employers to regulate themselves without compromising safety or responsible behaviour.

Reflecting the view that safety through compulsion is unlikely to be achieved without an organisational desire to change, a number of studies have advocated varying degrees of self-regulation (Mintzberg, 1983a; Braithwaite and Fisse, 1987; Kharbanda and Stallworthy, 1991):

> In industry, management inevitably know more than anyone else about the type of risk involved in the operations within their plants, and the implications for the community at large. . . . It is in their own interest for management to self regulate . . . their own affairs and to do their best to ensure that such disasters never occur.
>
> (Kharbanda and Stallworthy, 1991: 88)

For Mintzberg (1983a) trust alone is insufficient. He argued that managers should be relentlessly pressured and constrained by a framework of regulation. In addition, efforts should be made to integrate a range of stakeholders into decision-making processes. Braithwaite and Fisse (1987) argue that self-regulation must be made to work, that the basis for an effective system requires that compliance personnel be given informal authority and top management support, that line managers be given clearly defined responsibility for compliance and careful monitoring of performance, and that effective communication of problems is made to those capable of acting. What is evident from these studies is the range of opinion regarding the most effective means of controlling organisational behaviour.

The relevance of regulation in a continuity management context is salient. The improper, imprudent, careless or negligent behaviour of organisations and their agents can promulgate or cause crises for which BC plans must be invoked. In order to prevent or reduce the propensity towards the occurrence of crises, regulatory systems of both an internal and an external nature must be thoughtfully considered.

Doyle (1994) suggests that the need for regulation of either type should be determined by whether detailed and formal legal contracts are required to undertake an economic transaction. In many cases of economic exchanges, formal contracts are incomplete or missing altogether. The structure of an industry's competition will provide a partial solution to inappropriate behaviour should a vendor not fulfil their obligations to the purchaser. If an organisation behaves in such a way that it fails to protect its consumers, a highly competitive market would provide an incentive (yet not a guarantee) to improve and sustain better working practices, since to do otherwise would lead to inferior financial performance. In effect, this invisible hand serves, partly, as a tacit regulator. In a less competitive market, there is a lower competitive incentive for organisations to ensure that their business practices meet public expectations. The appropriateness of regulatory approaches can be determined by competition, structure, activities, innovation and information. See Figure 2.3 where we highlight the context and position of self-regulation.

The problems of regulation are exacerbated where industries and organisations operate both within and beyond national boundaries, and have to manage the (often major) differences between accounting, legal and supervisory systems. Moreover, in a sector such as financial services, different product types may fall within the remit of different regulatory bodies whose level of supervision and authority may vary. Two subsidiaries of the same organisation operating in the same product but separate geographic markets will have similar operations yet face a different statutory environment, which is then determined by different legislatures, which are in part influenced by individual stakeholder groups. The challenge for BC planners is to develop internally consistent continuity systems operating within divergent industrial, geographical, operations and legal domains. As we discuss in Chapter 6, clear structural linkages must exist between the BCM team and functional representatives to ensure contextual relevance in BC activities.

Self-Regulation

The introduction of standards for product testing, ethics, certification and accreditation are increasingly used by industry associations as criteria for membership. Such actions by industry and trade associations represent a process of self-regulation that is becoming ever more popular. However, as Jacobs and Portman (1998) found, self-regulation may serve the public interest but equally expose associations to legal liability in areas such as anti-trust laws, negligence, discrimination and defamation. Associations

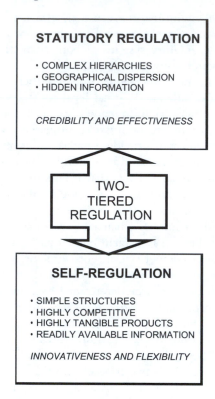

Figure 2.3 Regulatory approaches.

will be liable if their self-regulation guidelines lead to anti-competitive activity, particularly where membership of the association (contingent on meeting standards) leads to distinct groupings of competitors (members and non-members). Associations will also be liable should procedures for ethics, standards and membership be shown to be unfair. Due process in common law should be seen not only in the criteria upon which organisations are evaluated but also in the clarity of the decision-making process undertaken by the association in determining conformity with standards or membership entitlement. Where self-regulation is undertaken by an industry association, it may also be liable to third parties affected by the actions of a member that has been certified as compliant with the association's standards. The element of associations' liability forms an extension to the legal liability that may transpire in a product recall, as discussed later in this chapter in the US pedicle bone screw case.

It is in the context of liability and the embryonic nature of BC that there is an absence of regulation directly associated with BC. In its place, a piecemeal consideration of legislative provisions and their impact upon continuity issues has occurred. For instance, the *IT Law Today* publication produced a guide to legal liability and the Y2K problem, highlighting issues such as contracts and express warranties, liability, mounting claims, implied contract terms and guidance on who is liable in disputes between two or more parties (*IT 2000*, 1997).

Box 2.1 Self-Regulation in UK Financial Services

The UK financial services sector provides a salient example of the problems facing both regulatory and commercial organisations. The system of self-regulation was introduced in 1986 alongside the Financial Services Act (1986) and the Conservative government's credo of increasing self-regulation throughout the British economy. The Securities and Investments Board became the main regulatory organisation in the finance sector, with responsibility for another five self-regulatory organisations (SROs), nine professional bodies and a small number of specialised regulators. In 1994, four of the SROs merged. In the first, the Life and Unit Trust Regulatory Association and the Financial Intermediaries, Managers and Brokers Regulatory Association became the Personal Investment Authority. In the second, the Association of Futures Brokers and Dealers and the Securities Association became the Securities and Futures Authority.

Under this two-tiered system, each SRO would register an institution in a contractual arrangement that could only be rescinded in court. As an interim measure, organisations could be given formal reprimands, but no statutory provision was in place for levying fines on organisations found to have broken the SRO's rules. In contrast, the US financial services sector has in place a statutory regulation regime under the remit of the Securities and Exchange Commission (SEC). Founded in 1934 and still active today, US federal law made malfeasances such as insider dealing both a civil and a criminal offence, and substantial fines – up to three times the profits made by the insider trader – can be imposed. In the UK, insider dealing only became a criminal offence in 1980. Moreover, US federal law requires conviction on the balance of probability rather than beyond all reasonable doubt as in the UK (Doyle, 1994).

However, in the wake of several financial scandals, by the early to mid-1990s several financial institution executives openly began to question the effectiveness of the self-regulation approach. A further exacerbation of the situation occurred with increasing public dissatisfaction due to the lack of punitive measures available to regulators. The lack of a coercive regulatory environment has led to one in which regulatory bodies became an administrative adjunct to the industry's structure without being the catalyst for changes towards good working practices, improved industry performance and the protection of the public interest, as had been originally intended.

The shortcomings of the two-tiered system operating to govern the UK financial services industry can be seen in the aftermath of the Barings scandal of 1995, where the Securities and Futures Association (SFA) and the Bank of England were criticised for their lack of vigilance. Furthermore, the inability of the SFA to impose punishments on Barings' executives exacerbated the problem. In contrast, the employee at the centre of the crisis, Nick Leeson, received a rapid conviction in a Singaporean court. The nature of the industry and the system of self-regulation arguably contributed to an environment in which crises such as the BCCI and Barings collapses, and the Maxwell pension scandal, could occur:

> The complex hierarchical structure of a modern merchant bank operating on exchanges across the world also presented difficulties for internal governance, let alone external governance. . . . The reliance upon a cumbersome system of considerable self regulation in UK financial services would seem to have enabled more rather than less unacceptable practices. . . . The preponderance of SROs certainly exacerbated the problem of inconsistency, expense and duplication.
>
> (Doyle, 1994: 41)

When Gordon Brown (then chancellor of the exchequer), introduced plans for reform of the system of self-regulation on 20 May 1997, he indicated to parliament that the two-tier system was "inefficient, confusing for investors and lack[ed] accountability and a clear allocation of responsibilities" (Imerson, 1997). The Financial Services Authority (FSA) replaced the separate SROs for the UK financial services industry and re-emphasised consumer protection. The Authority also played an important role in the development of guidelines in relation to BCM (discussed later in this chapter). Unlike its predecessors, the FSA had a statutory obligation to measure the cost effectiveness of its regulations, in order to prevent the augmentation of bureaucratic costs which had previously encumbered the self-regulation of the industry. The UK financial services sector highlights the complex and dynamic environment in which SROs attempt to create minimum standards of behaviour without having sufficient authority to impose heavy sanctions upon organisations which fail to conform. The crises that have precipitated reform of the regulatory environment were high-profile cases in the public and media eye and yet were difficult to observe and control by outside parties. These conditions, in conjunction, provided a formula for a failure in the supervisory regime in this sector and the subsequent lack of credibility which ensued. The loose regulatory framework introduced by the FSA has now been criticised for its role as one of the tripartite supervisors (along with the Bank of England and HM Treasury) in an operating environment in which the UK financial services sector became exposed (and contributed) to the global financial crisis that began in 2008 (Hughes et al., 2009).

Stakeholders and Self-Regulation

The US approach to deregulation in the mid-1990s began with the "reinventing government" program aimed at simplifying and reducing state-directed regulation. Changes in the areas of environmental protection and health and safety were introduced in parallel with simpler documentation for businesses, a lower use of punitive fines and greater flexibility in interpretation of federal rules (Hemphill, 1996).

Stakeholders play an important role in developing self-regulation following crisis incidents. The Coalition for Environmentally Responsible Economies (CERES), established in 1989, developed a voluntary code comprising ten principles designed to improve the environmental protection practices of organisations. Named after the oil spill in the same year, the "Valdez Principles" have been adopted by over eighty companies, including Mobil, General Motors and Polaroid. CERES is a coalition of thirty-two environmental and pressure groups, including investment and pension funds. Similarly, the Aerospace Industries Association of America, the Chemical Manufacturers Association and the American Petroleum Institute have incorporated environmental, health and safety codes of conduct into their by-laws for membership (Hemphill, 1996).

The existence of regulation within an economic sector of activity may indeed be one of the main influences on the formal establishment of a BCM team. It is also evident, from a study of better practice organisations, that organisations (in this case a US bank) regarded regulation as constituting a starting point for internalising control systems:

> About six years ago it was first of all, "the regulations say we have to have it", then it became, "well, there is some impact on us financially if we don't operate in a certain period of time" and then, "well, I suppose our customers would be a bit upset" . . . Last year that had completely turned around, now it is customer expectation first, the financial impact second and federal requirements third . . . the reason for that is that federal requirements should not be driving your business, your business should be driving your business.
>
> (Herbane et al., 1997: 24)

In other sectors (such as university education, automobile manufacturer and retailing), the will to implement BCM as a formal business function may arise from factors such as learning from crisis incidents, the influence of best-practice rivals and the requirements of buyers and/or suppliers.

Problems with Regulators and Regulations

The conflict between regulation, self-regulation and stakeholders can be seen in the move by the British government to make UK-based chemical companies more responsible for the risk assessment of chemicals. At the European Union level, an absence of funds has led to only ten of some 10,000 "recognised" chemicals being assessed since 1993. Moreover, the total number of man-made chemicals is known to number around 100,000. The government favoured an approach in which policy would be developed in consultation with stakeholders comprising chemical companies and the Chemical Industries Association, researchers and the general public. In contrast, the move towards a two-tiered approach was seen by the environmental group Friends of the Earth as a concession to businesses that would compromise the nation's health and the environment (*Chemical and Industry*, 1998).

The actions of regulators have contributed to crises. A drastic fall in saccharin use followed the US Food and Drug Administration's announcement in 1977 that the artificial sweetener was linked to cancer in laboratory rats. Typical of the regulatory logic that has been called "Condemn now, nail down the science later" (Huber, 1997: 114), the announcement from a regulator precipitated a crisis for saccharin producers. This case was not accompanied by vast numbers of litigants in the intervening period, before saccharin was found to be non-carcinogenic, but more recently, as we have seen earlier, the legal liability of regulators is growing. Huber argues that the blame for the actions of regulators is attributable to lack of accountability that regulators have for their claims. The absence of any requirement for regulators to evaluate both *ex ante* and *ex post* the scientific evidence supporting an announcement is clearly different from a situation in which "regulators who take things out of the food supply should be held to the same standards as private companies that put them in" (1997: 114).

Goodhart (1998) argues that when regulation fails, it is not due to the regulators themselves, but rather to the inherent conflict between, and separation of, the external regulatory activity and the internal management controls within organisations. Regulations which compare financial measures between players in the same industry are susceptible to the differences in accounting practices, business operations and the reliability of information provided to regulators. In order to ensure comparability of data between organisations, the role of the regulator would have to become increasingly costly and officious. The impositions on, and disturbance for, organisations would also generate a greater resistance towards cooperation with regulators. Furthermore, the dynamism of change within many industries also renders the controls and regulations used by regulators redundant at worst, or minimal at best. Goodhart argues that many of the highly publicised crises have arisen from poor internal controls rather than regulation, but the latter tends to attract blame since its fundamental role is one of supervision in the public interest. This problem is exacerbated due to the asymmetry of information between regulators and the regulated, leading to a problem of causal ambiguity (Reed and DeFillippi, 1990). Under such conditions, the cause-and-effect relation cannot be fully understood unless all the factors in the relationship are known.

A distinction should be made between an organisation's control systems and the behaviour it successfully or unsuccessfully elicits. The systems of control through procedures, meetings and measures can be in place, but in circumstances where improper or careless behaviour is not identified, the system and its agents are negligent. Conversely, where, in spite of controls, such behaviour is condoned, the control system can be deemed to be irrelevant in shaping employees' behaviour and, indeed, could be construed both as clouding the actions of employees and as a veil beneath which improper practices are obscured. As Goodhart points out, "internal risk [or other] control mechanisms, however technically advanced, cannot be more reliable than those humans who manipulate them" (1998: 23). Even where regulators develop complex techniques for supervision and control, the lack of compliance (deliberate or otherwise) needs to be addressed predominantly as an internal matter. Were a regulator to pursue a change in the culture of behaviour and practices within an industry, the intangibility and subjectivity of culture and decisions derived on the basis of it would expose regulators to charges of lacking due process and bias and could in return leave regulators facing litigation (Goodhart, 1998). Moreover, the causal ambiguity over how an organisation's culture contributed to improper behaviour would, inter alia, be great and could lead to speculative decisions regarding conduct and performance: "everybody may have 'known' that BCCI had a shady reputation, but the Bank of England needed objective proof before it could act" (Goodhart, 1998: 23). The process of both internal and external supervision could be improved by increasing the amount and extent of supervision. This, however, is hampered by further problems of resistance. Both internal and external auditing may not be considered value-creating activities, and those responsible for them may be relegated to a lower status than those who are the subject of supervision and who are better remunerated and regarded. This lower relative status makes this profession unattractive, demoralised and, in some cases, underqualified. Regulators, however proficient, are in a perpetually unenvious position. In their role as a supervisor of the penultimate resort (the judiciary represents the final resort), their inability to identify improper behaviour will be met with criticism. Equally, the improper behaviour of an organisation deemed to be proficient and compliant by a regulator will meet with a similar response towards the regulator concerned.

With changes in economic, financial and trading circumstances, organisations may alter their priorities vis-à-vis issues which could influence the propensity for a crisis to occur. A further problem of self-regulation at an organisational level is the assumption that existing customs and practices are acceptable and, in being so, create an endorsement which regulators may find difficult to challenge given the "limitations" of their knowledge of specialised businesses. Smith and Tombs (1995) and Reason (2008) offer the example of the *Herald of Free Enterprise* ferry disaster in 1987, caused by the long-standing and accepted practice of departing from ports with bow doors still open.

National Legislation and Regulation Relating to Business Continuity Management

The legislative and regulatory ambit of BCM could best be described as a patchwork of provisions that lack a single integrating "Business Continuity Act". This does not signify an absence of compulsion for firms in certain sectors to adopt provisions to respond to operational interruptions. Indeed, the continual development of both highlight the changing requirements for operational continuity as summarised in Table 2.1.

Some of the earliest legal provisions to influence disaster recover and BC ideas can be traced back to the US financial services sector. The 1977 Foreign Corrupt Practices Act is often cited as an important develop in firms' reorientation of the perceived threats and impacts. Designed primarily as a legal mechanism to combat bribery and the destruction of

Table 2.1 National or Sector-Specific Regulation and Legislation

National/sector-specific regulation and legislation

Title	Geographical influence	Type	Sector	Date of origin/ amendment
Foreign Corrupt Practices Act	USA	Reg	FS	1977 (1998)
Office of Comptroller of Currency (OCC) Directive 177	USA	Reg	Finance	1987
The Expedited Funds Availability Act	USA	Reg	Finance	1989
Health Insurance Portability and Accountability Act (HIPAA)	USA	Leg	Health	1996
Gesetz zur Kontrolle und Transparenz im Unternehmensbereich (Law for the Control and Transparency in the area of organizations)	Germany	Leg	All listed	1998

Data Protection Act	United Kingdom	Leg	All	1998
Presidential Decision Directive 63 (PDD-NSC-63)	USA	Other	Public	1998
Presidential Decision Directive 67 (PDD-NSC-67)	USA	Other	Public	1998
The US Financial Services Modernization Act (Gramm-Leach-Bliley Act GLBA)	USA	Leg	Multi	1999
FRB-OCC-SEC Guidelines for Strengthening the Resilience of U S Financial System Federal Reserve System [Docket No. R-1128] Department of the Treasury Office of the Comptroller of the Currency [Docket No. 03–05] Securities and Exchange Commission [Release No. 34-47638; File No. S7-32-02]	USA	Reg	All	2002
Sarbannes–Oxley Act (2002)	USA	Leg	Multi	2002
NASD Rules 3510/3520 NYSE Rule 446	USA	Reg	Finance	2002–2003
Financial Institution Supervision: Risk Assessment and Information and Technology System (Bank of Thailand, 2003)	Thailand	Reg	Finance	2003
NFA Compliance Rule 2–38	USA	Reg	NFA members	2003
Civil Contingencies Act 2004	United Kingdom	Leg	Public	2004
The Australian Prudential Regulation Authority (APRA) Standard on Business Continuity Management (BCM) Prudential Standard APS & GPS 222 Business Continuity Management	Australia	Reg	Finance	2005
Reserve Bank of India DBS.CO.IS Audit.No. 19/ 31.02.03/2004–05 Operational Risk Management – Business Continuity Planning	India	Reg	Finance	2005

documents that would cover up bribery, corporate managers would be held personally liable for protecting assets with sanctions of imprisonment. Its relevance in a continuity management content is largely in its amplification of a recognition that both hard *and* soft systems can be the cause of human error, intervention, and interaction that can promulgate the destruction of records which could hamper criminal investigations. Such records could be paper or computer based and the necessary protection of these records would follow in the form of secure back-ups and off-site storage and vaulting. The act formally set down a requirement for the "reasonable protection of information systems" (section 13b). The elevation of responsibility to the boardroom further signalled the need for a systematic approach (possibly through a BC plan) to the planning process for devising and maintaining a system of adequate internal accounting controls.

By the 1980s, customer-facing and back-office technologies had become well established within the financial services. Illustrative of the priority placed on information systems recovery was the 1987 OCC (Office of Comptroller of Currency) 177 directive which stipulated that all US Banks (whether located in the USA or not) were to have recovery times of longer than 72 hours. With the Expedited Funds Availability Act of 1989 (also developed by the US Comptroller of Currency), US financial institutions were obliged to possess and BC plan to ensure that customer deposits were available the next business day (Gartner, 2001). In another sector-specific act of legislation, the US Health Insurance Portability and Accountability Act of 1996 required that healthcare providers must have disaster recovery procedures in place to prevent the loss or misuse of patient data.

Two pieces of European legislation heightened company liability for information security. The UK Data Protection Act (DPA) of 1998 established eight data protection principles to safeguard the handling of electronic and paper (manually structured) personal data. As part of the principles date storage security, protection and transfer are paramount and there is clear potential for an organisation's DPA and BCM policies to dovetail together to provide further digital resilience (Chapter 3). Also brought into law in the same year was Germany's corporate control and transparency law (*Gesetz zur Kontrolle und Transparenz im Unternehmensbereich*). The act was designed to apply to listed and large German companies and required the board of directors to introduce risk identification measures and to report the risk profile of the company in a formal manner (echoing the UK Turnbull report published in 1999).

In a public sector context, May 1998 saw the introduction of Presidential Decision Directive PDD-NSC-63 "Protecting America's Critical Infrastructures". Presidential Decision Directive 63 focuses on the resilience of critical and interconnected infrastructures, such as essential government services, telecommunications, banking and finance, energy, and transportation. The directive also identifies the importance and interdependence of public and private sector organisations. In October 1998, PDD-NSC-67

"Enduring Constitutional Government and Continuity of Government Operations" required US federal agencies to put in place provisions for the "continuity of operations" (a public sector synonym for BC) with particular focus on US critical infrastructure. In the UK, The Civil Contingencies Act (2004) sets out a coordinating framework for public and private/ multi-agency responses to large-scale emergencies. Among these arrangements, so-called "Category 1" organisations, such as the emergency services, health authorities and local government agencies, are now required to have BCM provisions in place, have predetermined stakeholder communication plans and cooperate with other agencies to improve the coordination of recovery efforts (HMSO, 2004; UKresilience, 2006).

A number of associated regulations and non-statutory arrangements amplify the roles and responsibilities of Category 1 and 2 responders set out in the Civil Contingencies Act (2004). For instance, local authorities and emergency services must:

- Assess the risk of emergencies occurring and use this to inform contingency planning;
- Put in place emergency plans;
- Put in place BCM arrangements;[2]
- Put in place arrangements to make information available to the public about civil protection matters and maintain arrangements to warn, inform and advise the public in the event of an emergency;
- Share information with other local responders to enhance coordination;
- Co-operate with other local responders to enhance coordination and efficiency; and
- Provide advice and assistance to businesses and voluntary organisations about business continuity management (Local Authorities only).

(Cabinet Office, 2005: 2)

The Contingency Planning regulations refer to the duty of local authorities in the UK to provide advice and assistance to business and voluntary organisations: "The duty on local authorities to give advice and assistance to business and voluntary organisations in relation to business continuity management (BCM) is an integral part of the Act's wider contribution to building the UK's resilience to disruptive challenges" (Cabinet Office, 2005: 110). Furthermore, public authorities are required to provide advice to businesses and voluntary organisations which may recommend "business continuity consultants" or to provide assistance with obtaining advice from such sources.

The US financial services industry, both prior to and in the aftermath of 9/11, has faced a continuous stream of regulations and legal requirements to impose greater and more stringent BC and risk management provisions. Under sections 501 and 505 of the US Gramm–Leach–Bliley Act of 1999 (also known as the Financial Services Modernization Act) financial institutions are compelled to provide safeguards for the security and confidentiality of customer information and records. While the act does not refer specifically to BC, it specifies that safeguards need to be administrate, physical and technical in nature and that the purpose of the act is designed to counter the increasing risk of external threats to digital resilience (Chapter 3), which is one of the dependencies on BCM. The Federal Reserve System, Office of the Comptroller of the Currency, Securities and Exchange Commission Interagency paper *Sound Practices to Strengthen the Resilience of the U.S. Financial System* (SEC, 2002a) highlighted three new BC objectives that emerged in the post-9/11 environment for all US and US-based financial firms:

- Rapid recovery and timely resumption of critical operations following a wide-scale disruption.
- Rapid recovery and timely resumption of critical operations following the loss or inaccessibility of staff in at least one major operating location.
- A high level of confidence, through ongoing use or robust testing, that critical internal and external continuity arrangements are effective and compatible.

Based on the experiences of the US financial system on 9/11, the interagency paper also explicated four aspects of good practice in BCM. These were to:

- identify clearing and settlement activities in support of critical financial markets;
- determine appropriate recovery and resumption objectives for clearing and settlement activities in support of critical markets;
- maintain sufficient geographically dispersed resources to meet recovery and resumption objectives;
- routinely use or test recovery and resumption arrangements.

Further enhancement of the regulatory framework for US financial services organisations came in the form of the US Securities and Exchange Commission (SEC) approved the National Association of Securities Dealers Rules 3510/3520 and NYSE Rule 446 in April 2004. These rules oblige (and will lead to compliance monitoring of) members of the National Association of Securities Dealers and the New York Stock Exchange to have BC plans in place. Members' plans must consider mission critical systems, assessments of finances and operations, data-back-up and recovery, alternative communication systems for clients and employees, alternative operational locations, impact analyses for critical stakeholders, regulatory reporting and communication with regularity bodies, and continuity of customer access securities and funds (SEC, 2002b, 2003). Furthermore, under Compliance Rule 2–38 of 2003, the US National Futures Association requires that each

> Member must establish and maintain a written BC and disaster recovery plan that outlines procedures to be followed in the event of an emergency or significant business disruption. The plan shall be reasonably designed to enable the Member to continue operating, to re-establish operations, or to transfer its business to another Member with minimal disruption to its customers, other Members, and the commodity futures markets.
>
> (NFA, 2003)

The Sarbanes–Oxley Act of 2002 (known as SOX) represents one of the most marked changes to US federal regulation of public corporate governance since the Securities Exchange Act of 1934 (upon which it builds and extends). In the aftermath of high-profile accounting and fraud scandals such as WorldCom and Enron, the act has been designed to raise confidence in and instil greater reliability in financial reporting and also applies to non-US companies that are listed in the US. In particular, two sections of the act are relevant to BCM: first, under section 302 (4c) companies are required to "have evaluated the effectiveness of [their] internal controls"; second, in section 404 companies must assess and attest to the adequacy and effectiveness of internal controls (Sarbanes–Oxley, 2002). (SOX does not refer explicitly to BCM, but it may be argued that the requirements of the act can be enacted through both risk management and BCM).

The introduction of BCM-specific regulations in the financial services sector is clearly not confined to the US and UK. For instance, the Australian Prudential Regulation Authority (APRA) Standard on BCM APS 222 (for deposit taking institutions) and GPS 222 (for general insurers) published in April 2005 (ARPA, 2005a, 2005b) requires Australian financial institutions to implement a whole of business approach to BCM. Its BCM process consists of the following stages:

a   risk assessment;
b   business impact analysis;
c   consideration of recovery strategies;
d   business continuity planning (BCP);
e   establishing BC or crisis management teams;
f   review and testing.

Elsewhere, the Reserve Bank of India (RBI) found that some Indian banks did not yet have fully developed BC plans. Document DBS.CO.IS

Audit.No. 19/31.02.03/2004–05 sets out a requirement for Indian banks to fully implement BCP, presents a planning methodology, and further specifies a template for plan content. Banks are required to submit recovery time objectives for critical systems to RBI's Department of Banking Supervision at the end of each financial year and to report major failures and response activities or prevention measures on a quarterly basis (Parthasarathi, 2005).

Legislation and its subordinate in the form of regulation have increasingly come to require firms in a number of strategically and economically important sectors to formally develop BC plans. These forms of control mechanism have emerged to compel many firms to have BC plans and management systems in place but generally tend to require other sources to supplement knowledge of detailed BCM processes. These supplementary sources may include national and international guidelines and standards for BCM.

National and International Guidelines and Standards

National Guidelines and Standards

Unlike a law or regulation which mandates compliance, guidelines and standards are voluntary in legal terms, although they may be a de facto requirement of doing business. Some of the seminal national guidelines and standards developed since the year 2000 are presented in Table 2.2.

Before examining the development of standards that have driven BC practice, our attention should be drawn to the ideas of *mimetic adoption* and *order qualifying criteria*. These posit the reasons why requirements in one industry or zone of jurisdiction may find their way into another. Mimetic adoption connotes the emulation of observable best practice processes in organisation both within and beyond the industry sector or scope of activity undertaken by the adopter (Greve, 1998). Once firms recognise that there is both a relevance and a benefit arising from the practices that are known to exist within another organisation, the level of incentive to develop, emulate, match or exceed the observed practices increases. Similarly, the idea of order qualifying criteria suggests that firms must exceed minimum acceptable standards in both the service/provision being traded and the wider skills and resources that are necessary to carry out their activities. As part of new or renewed trading relationships and contracts with other firms in a supply chain, contracted parties may change the *force majeure* provisions that deal with unexpected situations and may require suppliers to have minimum standards of preparedness for business interruptions.

Intended for use within the UK's Ministry of Defence and Armed Forces, Joint Service Publication 503 (MOD, 2006) sets out a BCM approach that addresses both technical dimensions of BCP and organisational culture

Table 2.2 National/Sector-Specific Guidelines and Standards

National/sector guidelines and standards

Title	Geographical influence	Type	Sector	Date of origin (revision)
JSP 503 – Business Continuity Management	United Kingdom	Guidance	Military	2000 (3rd edition 2005)
National Institute of Standards and Technology (NIST) Special Publications (SP) 800 Series	USA	Guidance	Public	2002
North American Electric Reliability Council (NERC) Security Guidelines for the Electricity Sector	USA	Guidelines	Electricity	2002
King II	SA	Guidance	All	2002
HKMA Supervisory Policy Manual TM-G-2: Business Continuity Planning	Hong Kong	Non-statutory guideline	Finance	2002
PAS 56	United Kingdom	Standard	Multiple	2003
FFIEC BCP Handbook	USA	Guidance	Finance	2003
State Bank of Pakistan: Risk Management Guidelines for Commercial Banks & DFIs	Pakistan	Guideline	Finance	2003
Monetary Authority of Singapore (MAS)	Singapore	Guidance	Finance	2003
SS507	Singapore	Standard	BC/DR Service providers	2004
Technical Reference (TR19: 2005) on BCM	Singapore	Standard	Multi	2005
Tripartite Authorities (FSA, Bank of England and HM Treasury) – Business Continuity Management Practice Guide	United Kingdom	Guidance	Multi	2006

factors which determine training needs and implementation challenges. Joint Service Publication 503 that defines BCM as "The systematic identification of risks to the normal continuation of an organisation's activity and the effective management of those risks to ensure a basic level of output/service following a disruptive event" (MOD, 2006: 4). The methodology is based around the Business Continuity Institute's BCM approach but presents a novel approach to implementation using a balanced scorecard (Annex E2) as part of this methodology.

In the US, the National Institute of Standards and Technology Special Publication 800–34, Contingency Planning Guide for Information Technology (IT) Systems provides guidance for government IT contingency planning. While clearly having a focus on information systems, its seven-stage planning methodology bears a close resemblance to a BCM planning approach, which includes the development of the contingency planning policy statement, business impact analysis, identification of preventive controls, development of recovery strategies and an IT contingency plan, plan testing, training and exercises. The process continues with planned maintenance (NIST, 2002). In terms of sector specific guidelines and arising from PDD-63, the North American Electric Reliability Council (NERC) Security Guidelines for the Electricity Sector guidelines include BCP ("Continuity of Business Processes") as one of four components of its security guidelines for electricity sector organisations (NERC, 2002). The Federal Financial Institutions Examination Council (FFIEC) guidance on BCP highlights the relationship between BCM in the availability of critical financial services (FFIEC, 2003). The guidance rescinds and replaces the Corporate Contingency Planning matter of the 1996 FFIEC's Information Systems Examination Handbook. Founded in 1979, the FFIEC establishes standards for the supervision of federal examination of financial institutions. The BCP guidance has been developed to determine the effectiveness and quality of an organisation's BCP processes. The guidance highlights that BCM should be an organisation-wide undertaking, founded around business impact analysis and risk assessment, based on the recovery of physical and human resources, regularly tested and frequently updated.

The US Office of the Comptroller of the Currency (OCC) (which charters, regulates and supervises all US national banks) uses the FFIEC BCP Handbook as its standard reference matter for BC. Many other OCC handbooks refer to BCM (see, for instance, OCC, 2006).

The Hong Kong Monetary Authority's (HKMA) Supervisory Policy Manual TM-G-2 Business Continuity Planning (HKMA, 2002) sets out good practices that the HKMA expects financial institutions to observe. The HKMA BCP approach explicates the following:

- Board and senior management oversight.
- Business impact analysis and recovery strategy.

- Development of BC plan (including business resumption, technology recovery, BC models, vital record management, public relations and communication strategy, and other risk mitigating measures).
- Alternate sites for business and technology recovery institutions.
- Implementation of BC plan (including testing and periodic maintenance).

Similarly, the Monetary Authority of Singapore (MAS) BCP guidelines issued in 2003 are based around seven principles which conceive of BCM as an "over-arching framework" of "policy, standards and procedures" (MAS, 2003: 5):

- Board and management should take responsibility for the BCP preparedness of their institution.
- Institutions should embed BCP into their business-as-usual operations, incorporating sound BCP practices.
- Institutions should test their BCP regularly, completely and meaningfully.
- Institutions should develop recovery strategies and set recovery time objectives for critical business functions.
- Institutions should understand and appropriately mitigate inter-dependency risks of critical business functions.
- Institutions should plan for wide area (zonal) disruptions.
- Institutions should practise separation policy to mitigate concentration risk.

Singapore is also the source of two BCM standards. Developed by the Infocomm Development Authority of Singapore and the IT Standards Committee, the SS507 Standard has been developed to provide guidance in the choice of BC/disaster recovery service providers, thereby assuring end users of capability levels that are certified against high-level benchmarks (ISA, 2004). Launched in September 2005 and developed by SPRING (Standards, Productivity and Innovation Board Singapore), the Technical Reference (TR19: 2005) framework on BCM is based around risk analysis and review, business impact analysis, strategy, business continuity plans, testing and programme management. TR19 is intended to become a national standard of international recognition and is supported by "SPRING", the Economic Development Board and the Singapore Business Federation (SPRING, 2005).

Both the MAS and HKMA guidelines offer reasonable detailed guidelines. Elsewhere guidance is less prescriptive and suggests the desired presence of BC. For instance, within its guidelines for operational risk, the State Bank of Pakistan's guidelines merely state that "Banks should have in place contingency and BC plans to ensure their ability to operate as going concerns and minimise losses in the event of severe business disruption" (State Bank of Pakistan, 2003: 39) without recourse to a pre-defined series of parameters, key performance indicators or methodology.

Two important developments in standards and guidelines for BCM in the UK can be found in PAS 56 and the Tripartite BCM Practice guide. The Publicly Available Specification 56 Business Continuity Management was published in 2003 by the British Standards Institution in association with the Business Continuity Institute and Insight Consulting. The guide represents the first stage towards the development of a British standard and is based on known good practice. In this context, PAS 56 is a precursor to British Standard BS 25999 Code of Practice for BCM (discussed below). The Tripartite Authorities (which consist of the Financial Services Authority, the Bank of England and HM Treasury) issued its Business Continuity Management Practice Guide as an outcome of its 2005 Resilience Benchmarking Project (FSA, 2006). The BCM Practice Guide has been published to inform and disseminate good practice from a study of sixty companies. It is designed to complement rather than replace Financial Services Authority guidance. The guide divides the resources of BCM into five modules of good practice in respect of corporate continuity, crisis management, systems, facilities and people.

Within a broader corporate governance agenda, BC has emerged as an increasingly import theme in South Africa. Building on the 1994 King I report (which followed the CSR development of the UK Cadbury and US Treadway reports), the King II report published in 2002 sets out best practice principles in a number of areas of corporate governance, including risk management. The report proposes that there should be "a documented and tested process in place which will allow the company to continue its critical business processes in the event of a disastrous incident impacting its activities. This is commonly known as a business continuity plan, and should cater for a worst case scenario (Section 5.2.5.)". While broadly voluntary in nature, it is considered a de facto standard for listed companies in South Africa (Nielsen, 2006).

International Standards and Guidelines

Three clusters of internal standards and guidelines have emerged in recent years that are of direct interest to BC managers: those which deal with technology resilience; standards relating to risk management; and holistic BCM standards (Table 2.3). As with other international standards that pertain to, for example, quality management systems and environmental management systems, technology resilience, risk management and BC standards could become a form of competitive differentiation as buyers look to identify and contract with suppliers who are less likely to jeopardise supply chain BC (which we consider in greater detail in Chapter 5)

A number of international technology resilience (security and service delivery) standards embrace or require BCM processes to be in place

Table 2.3 International/Sector-Specific Guidelines and Standards

International/sector guidance and good practice

Title	Geographical influence	Type	Sector	Date of origin (revision)
Technology Resilience Standards				
Control Objectives for Information and related Technology (COBIT) 4.0	Global	Guidance	All	1992 (2005)
ITIL BS 15000 (IT Service Management Standard)	International	Standard	All	2000
ISO/IEC 17799	International	Standard	Multi	2000 (2005)
The ISFs Standard of Good Practice – The Standard for Information Security (Version 4.1)	International	Standard	All	2005
ISO (2008) ISO 24762 Security techniques – Guidelines for information and communications technology disaster recovery services	International	Standard	Multi	2008
Risk Management Standards				
AS/NZS 4360 Risk Management Standard	Australia/New Zealand	Standard	Multi	1995 (2004)
Basel II Capital Accord	International	Reg	Finance	2007
Business Continuity Standards				
NFPA1600	USA	Standard	Multi	1995 (2004&2007)
BCI Good Practice Guidelines	Global	Standard	All	2002 (2005)
The Business Continuity Management Standard HB 221: 2003/4	Australia/NZ	Standard	All	2003
BCI 10 Standards of professional competence (Shared with DRII's professional practices for BC professionals)	Global	Standard	All	2003
BS25999-1 Code of Practice for Business Continuity Management	United Kingdom	Standard	Multi	June 2006

(Continued Overleaf)

Table 2.3 Continued

International/sector guidance and good practice				
Title	Geographical influence	Type	Sector	Date of origin (revision)
BS25999-2 Specification for Business Continuity Management				
ISO (2008) ISO/DIS 22399 Societal security – Guidelines for incident preparedness and operational continuity management	International	Standard	Multi	2008

for certification to succeed. For instance, COBIT is an international best practice framework developed by the Information Systems Audit and Control Association and the IT Governance Institute in 1992. In its most recent guise Control Objectives for Information and related Technology (COBIT) 4.0 covers four domains: plan and organise; acquire and implement; deliver and support, and monitor and evaluate. Part of the high-level control objectives for deliver and support is "DS4", which refers to a need to "Ensure Continuous Service", within which BCM is a recognised solution. Echoing many of these dimensions is the Information Security Forum (ISF) Standard, which identifies strategic aims and objectives for information security coupled with a statement of good practice for digital resilience (ISF, 2005). Originally derived from the British Standards Institute's Code of Practice for IT Service Management – DISC PD 0005: 1998 – and developed by the UK government, ITIL (the IT Infrastructure Library) has become widely adopted in Europe as an IT service standard and is based on best practice in public and private sectors nationally and internationally. The IT Infrastructure Library forms the basis of the BS 15000 (IT Service Management Standard) standard. BCM is one of the five service delivery disciplines within ITIL and contingency planning (or BCM) is required within BS 15000 (BSI, 2005).

From its roots in the British Standard BS 7799 of 1995 the ISO 17799 Security Standard (2000) has been revised in the form of ISO/IEC 17799 (2005). The standard identifies ten areas of best practice in the domain of information security. The ten areas include BCM alongside security policy; organisation of information security; asset management; human resources security; physical and environmental security; communications and operations management; access control; information systems acquisition, development and maintenance; information security incident management; and compliance (International Organization for Standardization, 2005). The standard explicates processes for BCM process, business impact analysis, planning and plan authorships and testing, echoing the approach taken in this book.

Beyond the broad risk management advice found in corporate governance reports such as the Turnbull report (Turnbull, 1999) the AS/NZS 4360 Risk Management Standard and Basel II Capital Accord represent two totemic exemplars of how the field of risk management is no longer separable from BCM – whether this be in terms of the similarity of analytical technique, shared objectives, or shared activities. Since its launch in 1995, the Australian and New Zealand AS/NZ 4360 Risk Management Standard is in its third incarnation published in 2004. The standard, which has become popular in the Asia-Pacific region, dovetails with standards and guidelines relating to BCM, outsourcing and information security and sets out a process with which to identify, analyse, evaluate and treat risks (risk management is considered further in Chapter 5). Furthermore, the Australian/New Zealand Business Continuity Management Standard has been designed to actively merge with the AS/NZS 4360 Risk Management Standard.

Commonly known as Basel II (but formally as "International Convergence of Capital Measurement and Capital Standards: A Revised Framework") this Bank for International Settlements (BIS) standard was developed from a preceding capital accord which focuses on the level of capital allocations that needed to be put aside from high-risk loans. The revised framework continues with the development of international banking risk management standards but it also refers to operational risk whereby "operational risk is defined as the risk of loss resulting from inadequate or failed internal processes, people and systems or from external events" (BIS, 2006: 144). To an extent, Basel II challenges the zeitgeist of risk management and since the BIS's Basel Committee on Banking Supervision has a membership comprising central backs from over fifty countries, the increased coupling of financial and operational risk management signposts future business reliance concerns and priorities. While not referring explicitly to BCM, it can be strongly argued that it forms part of improved operational risk management (Herbane, 2004).

Table 2.3 suggests that the development of BC standards has been an incremental process in which national standards are internationalised through alliances between national standards agencies or de facto industry associations. In the case of national standards agencies, the National Fire Protection Association (NFPA) 1600 Standard on Disaster/Emergency Management and Business Continuity Programs builds on its role as an organisation which develops codes, procedures, standards and training practices for both US and international organisations. The NFPA 1600 standard is designed for public and private disaster management and addresses disaster mitigation, preparation, response and recovery (National Fire Protection Association, 2004, 2007). NFPA 1600 began as a recommended practice in 1995 but became a standard in 2000 bringing together both emergency management and BCM through collaboration with the US Disaster Recovery Institute International and the UK Business Continuity Institute. The standard covers all ten of the BCI and DRII Professional Practices subject areas (see below). In another case of collaboration, the Business Continuity Management Standard HB 221: 2003/4 was developed jointly by Standards Australia and Standards New Zealand. HB 221 (2004) has been revised from its 2003 version to align with the of AS/NZS 4360 Risk Management Standard. Influenced by the BCI and DRII, the handbook sets out a wide socio-technical view of BCM and a framework designed for general application of firms of all sizes and sectors (Standards Australia, 2004).

First published in 2002 (and influenced by the empirical work of Elliott et al., 1999a and Elliott et al., 1999b), the BCI's good practice guidelines (BCI, 2002) represent one of the most extensive bodies of knowledge in the field of BCM and has led to PAS 56 (discussed earlier in this chapter), the internationally recognised BCI and DRII professional standard and the forthcoming BS 25999 Business Continuity Management Standard. The BCI and DRII's standards of professional competence have become a de facto standard for BC management professionals and have influenced the development of standards elsewhere internationally. The ten areas of the standard include:

1 Initiation and management.
2 Business impact analysis.
3 Risk evaluation and control.
4 Developing BCM strategies.
5 Emergency response and operations.
6 Developing and implementing business continuity and crisis management plans.
7 Awareness and training programmes.
8 Maintaining and exercising business continuity and crisis management plans.
9 Crisis communications.
10 Coordination with external agencies (BCI, 2003).

Published in draft form in June 2006, BS 25999 Code of Practice for Business Continuity Management and BS 25999–2 Specification for Business Continuity Management (published in late 2006) are intended to form the two pillars of a British (and subsequently International) standard in BCM. The standard was developed by the British Standards Institute (BSI) along with the BCI and Insight Consulting (the organisations responsible for the development of PAS 56). BS 25999 is structured around the following ten elements dimensions:

•   Determining cope and applicability

- Terms and definitions
- What is BCM?
- Overview of BCM
- The business continuity management system
- Programme management
- Understanding the organisation
- Determining BCM options
- Developing and implementing a BCM response
- Exercising, maintenance, auditing and self-assessment of BCM arrangements (BSI, 2006).

Two further international standards that specify or relate to BCM activities are ISO (2008a) ISO/DIS 22399 *Societal security – Guidelines for incident preparedness and operational continuity management* and ISO (2008b) ISO 24762 *Security techniques – Guidelines for information and communications technology disaster recovery services*.

The Public Available Specification for ISO/DIS 22399 integrates the Plan-Do-Check-Act approach from continuous improvement techniques synthesised with best practice knowledge and "Incident Preparedness and Operational Continuity Management" so that the public and private sector organisations can plan and prepare for disruptive incidents (Tangen and Seigel, 2008). ISO 24762 *Security techniques – Guidelines for information and communications technology disaster recovery services* (ISO, 2008b) sets out guidelines for disaster recovery services (whether in-house or third party), such as emergency computing centres (hot, warm or cold sites). Specific dimensions of the guidelines refer to facility and service requirements, suppliers capabilities, recovery site selection and continuous improvement monitoring of service suppliers.

In the course of approximately ten years, the landscape of BCM has transformed from one in which esoteric organisation-centric approaches represented known best practice (Elliott et al., 1999a; Herbane et al., 1997) to a topography in which a consensus is emerging from national and inter-national standards (for both public and business sectors) along with the exigencies of regulation and legislation about the generic dimensions that constitute BCM (Herbane et al., 2004). These generic dimensions coupled with an analysis of an organisation's specific legal, geographical and polit-ical context, tangible and intangible resources, cultural dimensions and risk analysis provide the bedrock of BCM for the twenty-first century.

Product Liability

One of the major crises which an organisation can face is the discovery of a product defect leading to measures to ensure the return of a potentially dangerous product back to the manufacturer, retailer or distributor. These measures are generally known by the term "product recall". Product recalls are of particular note in BCM since a defective product is a type of potential crisis for which there are specific acts of legislation and statutes, and procedural requirements in many jurisdictions. Furthermore, the presence of product recall plans in an organisation may exist alongside existing BCM provisions or entirely separate to them. Product recall crises should be a central consideration in the continuity plans of all manufacturers, particularly since the liability of organisations for their products is well-established in legal systems worldwide. Table 2.4 provides a small sample of product recalls which provide a flavour of the problems that organisations can face – whether this be contamination, packaging failure, poor design, or supplier problems. The table also shows that some of these problems (such as broken glass and fuel tank location) are defects which manifest themselves repeatedly.

The legal liability of organisations selling products which cause injury is known under the umbrella term "product liability". More specifically product liability has be defined as "the liability of any or all parties along the chain of manufacture of any product for damage caused by that product" (Cornell, 2006) with US legal provisions of product liability stemming from the precedent laid down in *Greenman* vs. *Yuba Power Products Inc.* (1962). Within the US Uniform Commercial Code, the implied and express warranties of merchantability and fitness for particular purpose in the sales of goods that are enshrined within §§2–314 and 2–315 and is elucidated though common and Torts law. Both the European Union (through the 1985 Directive on Liability for Legally Defective Products onwards) and Japan (Product Liability Law No. 85 1994 in which a defect is deemed to be a "lack of safety that the product ordinarily should provide") have come to broadly reflect the US legal framework for product liability (McCubbins and Mosier, 1998). Each system is underpinned by the concept of *res ipsa loquitur*, whereby a plaintiff must show that they were injured by a product in such a way that would not have occurred had the manufacturer not been negligent.

From the Ford Pinto to Perrier mineral water, all products sold carry an implied warranty that they are safe and fit for use. In the food industry, ranging from production to catering, the requirement for inspection, hygiene and training cannot provide a reasonable defence against a litigant. Sirignano (1997) argues that commercial product liability litigation in the US is problematic, giving rise to frivolous and opportunistic lawsuits, whereupon the defendant has the burden of proof to show that their duty of care to the buyer has been maintained. For example, R.J.R. Nabisco successfully defended a case in which a child had eaten a snack which contained a pin by showing that the incorporation of the pin into the product could not have taken place at any stage in the production process:

> The raw ingredients were filtered and carefully inspected for foreign materials, the finished products were passed through metal detectors,

Table 2.4 Product Recalls

Year	Product	Reason/defect	Company
2009	Aquafresh Milk Teeth Toothpaste	Formulation cause allergic reaction	GlaxoSmithKline
2008	Infant Formula Milk	Contaminated with toxic melamine	Sanlu Group (China)
2006	Cadbury's chocolate	Salmonella contamination	Cadbury
2006	Contact lens solution	Associated with Fusarium infection	Bausch & Lomb
2005	Chili powder	Toxic dye Sudan I added to chili powder	Many different food producers
2004	Vioxx	Risk of heart attacks and strokes	Merck
2004	Dasani Water	Bromate levels exceeded UK legal standards	Coca-Cola
2003	French Set Yoghurts	Metal particles found	Asda
2002	Zanussi tumble dryer	Fire hazard on model TD4212W	Zanussi
2001	Carte Noir Coffee	Glass particles found	Kenco
1998	Ladybird Rattle	Caused suffocation	Lego
1998	A-Class	Unstable vehicle	Mercedes-Benz
1998	Aluminium cans	Tin lining unstable	Various food companies
1990	Mineral water	Benzine contamination	Perrier
1986	Lawn mower	Battery close to fuel tank	John Deere
1985	Breast implants	Causes auto-immune disease	Dow Corning
1984	Pharmaceuticals	Limited warnings on label	Ortho Pharmaceuticals
1978	Pinto motor car	Fuel tank design fault	Ford
1974	Dalkon shield	Birth control device caused pelvic disease	A.H. Robins
1967	Cola	Exploding bottles	Coca-Cola Company
1963	Fireworks	Powerful firework found in domestic firework set	T.W. Hand Fireworks Co
1944	Cola	Mouse found in bottle	Coca-Cola Company
1941	Bread	Contained fragments of glass	Canada Bread Company
1937	Elixir of Sulfanilamide	Contained diethylene glycol and killed 107	S.E. Massengill Co

Source: McCubbins and Mosier (1998), Nocera (1995), Authors

the wrapped bars were placed in sealed cartons, the type of pin was not used in the manufacturing facility, and all employees were prohibited from wearing jewellery.

(Sirignano, 1997: 7)

In the US, government agencies with regulatory authority for product safety and recalls include the Food and Drug Administration, the Consumer Product Safety Commission (for most non-food recalls), the Environmental Protection Agency (pesticides), and the National Highway Traffic Safety Administration (Motor Vehicles). The application of product liability law in the USA has undergone several changes with a re-examination of the interpretation of why a plaintiff may have wilfully destroyed a defective product, thereby destroying the central evidence in a product liability suit. Where this is found to be the case, the jury can be directed to favour the defence's case and/or the exclusion of the plaintiff's expert witnesses (Goetsch, 1996). A second change has occurred in the liability facing companies which fail to provide adequate warnings about the use of a product or its hazards. No longer is it a requirement for juries to consider whether warnings could have been better (strict liability), but rather if such warnings were unreasonable (negligence). Siegfried (1998) argues that closer involvement of legal experts in the development of labelling and instructions for buyers will not only prove to be precautionary but also enable a strong defence, helping a company to better defend against litigation. This should reduce expensive settlement payments and discourage others from litigation. This requires extensive data to be collected, under the supervision of legal experts, of information associated with the product (substances, materials and packaging) and potential hazards. Once these are known, comprehensive, clear and accessible information on usage should accompany the product. In practical terms, we can see this in many household items. Take, for instance, a food item which is labelled that it "may contain nuts", safety caps and dosage instructions of pharmaceutical products, and Braille text on cleaning products. However, Steves (2006) claims that "mislabelling" was the most frequent cause for a product recall in 2005, whereby the instructions for use (dosage etc.) rather than an inherent problem with the product itself exposed the consumer to an unacceptable risk of harm, injury or death.

In the UK, part 1 of the Consumer Protection Act 1987 implements the European Community directive Product Liability Directive (85/374/EEC) on product liability and imposes strict liability on the producers of goods for any harm, injury or death to consumers caused by the product. Through the process of a civil action, compensation claims are not based on the presence of neglect but rather on the presence of a defect and its connection with an injury. The UK statute of limitation for claims is three years from the time of the injury or death. In addition, and resulting from Directive 2001/95/EC of the European Parliament and of the Council of 3 December

2001 on general product safety, the General Product Safety Regulations (2005) places a general safety requirement for producers and suppliers to not produce, supply or place on the market a product unless the product is safe. Since 2004, the European Commission has provided guidance on corrective action and product recalls within Europe (Intertek, 2004) and which is endorsed by bodies such as the Product Safety Enforcement Forum of Europe, the Union of Industrial and Employers Confederations of Europe, the Retail, Wholesale and International Trade Representation to the EU and the European Consumers' Organisation. The guidance includes an appendix which uses probabilistic risk management techniques reflecting a *de minimis* risk approach (Chapter 5) to assist organisations in deciding whether or not to proceed to a product recall based on the severity of injury, the probability of injury and whether the product is intended to be used by "vulnerable" people such as young children, the elderly or people with disabilities. From an international perspective, the product liability laws of Australia, Taiwan, Japan, China and Hong Kong are broadly convergent with US and UK provisions, and the international ISO 9004 quality management standard requires that companies need to identify "safety aspects of products or processes with the aim of enhancing safety (Section 19)" (Bowman and Brooke LLP, 1999).

The implications of a product recall crisis and product liability litigation cannot be ignored. Not only may an organisation face the costs of legal action but also the revenue losses from direct sales, the cost of public relations activities and the costs of redesign (where design is at fault) raise the cost of such crises. Moreover, the reputation of an organisation and its brand may have further repercussions beyond the ambit of a single recalled product. In being intangible, the effect of a crisis upon a reputation is immense. A corporate and product reputation takes many years of investment and effort to build, yet little time to destroy and the reputation of a company can be affected not only by the fault itself but also by the manner and nature of the actions taken by the company after a recall. Indeed, reputation may be central to an organisation's competitive advantage (Hall, 1992). Even where an organisation has managed to recall products without injury to customers, the organisation may find itself in an inferior competitive position than prior to the recall. A closer link between lawyers specialising in product liability and research and development (R&D) teams has been suggested by Goodden (1996) as a way in which organisations can not only pre-empt the likelihood of a product failure leading to injury to users but also provide documented evidence which can provide a "state-of-the-art defence". This refers to where an organisation can claim that it was reasonable in ensuring the safety of the product given the best prevailing knowledge it had at the time it designed and produced the product. Furthermore, as Siegfried (1998) indicated earlier, accrued benefits could also include a deterrent and cost-saving effect. The approach suggested mirrors the Failure Mode and Effects

Analysis process used in R&D and seeks to factor out any actions which could be seen as negligent should a product subsequently injure a consumer. Furthermore, documentation supporting this process can be used as evidence that a company has taken reasonable steps to prevent foreseeable product liability and should be known to BC managers whose role may involve managing the media during a crisis. The types of questions to be considered include:

- What are the reasonable and foreseeable uses of the product?
- What might end-users do with the product that the manufacturer has not anticipated?
- What are the various ways that the products could injure users or cause property damage?
- Are such dangers obvious?
- To what unusual and climatic or environmental conditions might the product be exposed?
- What kinds of warning labels or instructions should be included in the product?
- What legal implications can reasonably be predicted following the launch of the new product?
- What types of testing should be done to ensure that products or their materials will be reliable? (Goodden 1995, 1996)

Malicious Product Tampering

In contrast to accidental product failure, damage or contamination, malicious product tampering refers to the deliberate act (or claim of) sabotage of equipment and products by an employee or third party with the intent to cause harm to the consumer of the product and to the manufacturer through the need to recall the product, reputational impact and extortion. Some of the most publicised cases of include:

- 1982 The lacing of Tylenol with cyanide kills seven people (USA).
- 1981–1992 Cooking oil laced with industrial lubricant kills 1,000 people (Spain).
- 1984 Claims that Mars chocolate bars had been laced with rat poison (UK).
- 1986 Cyanide found in Benson and Hedges cigarettes (UK).
- 1989 Heinz – glass in baby food (only 10 out of 170 million were contaminated) (UK).
- 2006 Microsoft PowerPoint vulnerability allows installation of key-logging software (Global).

In addition to the provisions that an organisation might have for a product recall, additional resources (and in perhaps a slightly different recall plan and response) may be needed to provide access to specialist laboratories at short notice, to liaise with the police and the extortionist, to deal with the media (for whom information may not be as freely available) and to trigger product or process redesign (for example, packaging).

Industry Associations and Liability

The link between professional and industry associations, their members and product liability has recently been highlighted with the pedicle bone screw litigation in the US (Jacobs and Portman, 1998). Around 2,000 patients found that the screw (used in spinal fusion surgery) had broken, leading to further painful and protracted surgery for the removal of the device. This case is of particular importance because not only does the manufacturer of the pedicle bone screw face litigation, but medical societies (the equivalent of an industry association) have also found themselves facing prosecution since it has been alleged that the screw was not approved by the Food and Drug Administration for spinal fusion surgery and that they were responsible for the promotion of the screw on behalf of the manufacturer. Specifically, it was claimed that the manufacturer and medical societies had worked together to organise seminars, attended by doctors and spinal surgeons, to promote and sell the product. In addition, the societies received financial incentives for recommending the device to fellow medical practitioners. Despite several unsuccessful attempts to have proceedings dismissed, the medical societies now face prosecution for recklessly selling a product that was not approved for the use suggested by the societies' promotional activities, and liability for injury, pain and lengthy convalescence of spinal fusion surgery patients. The implications of this case reach far beyond the medical industry and its representatives. It marks the extension of liability from companies whose goods are defective to industry associations which have provided assistance in the promotion of members' products:

> The best precaution that associations can take to reduce the risk of such liability is to ensure that full disclosure is made to seminar participants about financial relationships with corporate sponsors and the regulatory status of products, discussed, displayed or exhibited at such events. Although these precautions cannot prevent a law suit from being filed, having a documented record of disclosures of financial interests and regulatory status of featured products can discourage product liability plaintiffs from including associations in such litigation.
>
> (Jacobs and Portman, 1998: 82)

Another development concerns mass torts in which plaintiffs group together and enact legal proceedings against an organisation, as highlighted in the box below. The mass tort approach, with many hundreds, if not thousands, of plaintiffs represented simultaneously, offers several advantages to prosecution lawyers by creating legal economies of scale that would counteract the corporate legal resources of large organisations who are better equipped to defend against a single litigant and lawyer.

Box 2.2 Mass Torts as Crises

Litigation against the manufacturers of silicone breast implants illustrates the major impact of large-scale product liability (mass torts) and how the reaction of an organisation prior to, during and following a crisis can influence the outcome of judicial proceedings. A salient issue in the breast implant case from a product liability perspective is that conclusive and comprehensive medical research to support the link between silicone breast implants and anti-immune disease has yet to be produced. Yet, mass torts and their subsequent settlements have been responsible for the bankruptcy of Dow Corning and the major settlements paid by Bristol-Myers Squibb, 3M and Baxter healthcare. The product has been available in the US since 1964, a time in which it was deemed to be a medical device rather than a pharmaceutical product, and thus not subject to the same stringent testing, licensing and approval procedures by the Food and Drug Administration.

Within Dow Corning, the largest manufacturer of implants, several memoranda (subsequently used in evidence) had questioned the long-term safety of the product, but these had not been informed by formal medical study. These speculative documents (known later as the "Dow Documents"), while inadmissible as proof of medical risk, were used as evidence to convince a jury that Dow Corning had been negligent. In July 1985, plaintiff Maria Stern was awarded $1.7 million damages. As Nocera (1995: 64) notes, "for any complicated law suit to sprout into a mass tort, something more is needed than a victory or two against a company. There has to be a climate of fear . . . and a group of angry users." The outcome of this case was significant, as the medical risk of the product had still not been established. In fact, in November 1991, the Food and Drug Administration publicly (but largely ignored) announced that silicon breast implants should not be withdrawn from sale. In January 1992, the FDA became privy to the "Dow Documents" and imposed a temporary restriction on silicon breast implants for cosmetic uses, thereby augmenting the number of litigants.

The effect of a product recall quite clearly threatens the continuity of an organisation's operations and may have more widespread economic and reputational effects than merely a single product or organisation. The causes of such recalls may arise from supplier defects, malicious acts, errors in research and development, and poor manufacturing and quality control. During a recall crisis, several functions of an organisation undertake higher levels of involvement: legal affairs, in dealing with the threat or actuality of litigation; marketing, in its attempt to restore the image and reputation of the organisation and its products; and the manufacturing function, in resolving physical causes of defects. The BC team/plan can play a major role in coordinating the activities of these different functions in the course of a crisis turnaround. Prior to this, the continuity plan (Chapter 4) should include a consideration of, and a contribution from, these important functions. As we have seen, a parochial approach is counterproductive to prevention and recovery of business operations in the wake of a product recall and could indicate, inter alia, negligence, unreasonableness and a failure to act with due care.

Summary

The beginning of the twenty-first century has marked a period of continuously developing legislation, regulation and best practice guidance both nationally and internationally. Such developments have embraced both the public and the private sectors of the economy and reflect a recognition of the importance of BCM for organisations and an emerging consensus about the constituent elements of BCM. This chapter has examined the conceptual nature of legislation and regulation as a control mechanism alongside an overview of the most import developments that BC managers should consider as a new or continuing rationale for resilience planning activities. The chapter also considered product recalls (including malicious product tampering) since they constitute one form of crisis for which there is both specific legislation and (often) the need for highly specialised plans. In this and the previous chapter we have seen that, in a BCM context, organisations are exposed to competitive, strategic, regulatory, legislative and stakeholder pressures, which increase the need for the adoption of BC. In the next chapter, we examine, in the light of such pressures, how the BC process is initiated prior to the processes of planning, implementation and management.

Study Questions

1   Here are some figures:

- We have sold 12.5 million units of product XYZ but there is a fire hazard fault in the product.
- The cost to remedy the defect will be $11 per unit.
- The total cost of the *recall* and defect repairs will be $137.5 million.

However, we have forecast the following deaths, injuries and damaged products:

	Deaths	Injuries	Damaged
	180	180	2,100
Costs	$200,000	$67,000	$700
Total	$36,000,000	$12,060,000	$1,470,000
Total cost of compensation: $49.5 million			

Would you recall the product and why?

2   Identify a recent product recall that has occurred during the past 12 months. How was the crisis communicated to the general public and to what extent were regulatory bodies or safety agencies involved?

Further Reading

Fairgrieve, D. (ed.) (2005) *Product Liability in Comparative Perspective*, Cambridge: Cambridge University Press.

Freeman, R.E. (1994) "The politics of stakeholder theory: some future directions", *Business Ethics Quarterly*, 4: 409–421.

Gibson, D. (2002) "The cyber-revolution in product recall public relations", *Public Relations Quarterly*, 45 (2): 24–26.

Haider, M.W. (2006) "Product liability: retention and risk management solutions", *Information Management Journal*, Jan/Feb, 40 (1): 56–62.

Larsson, G. and Enander, A. (1997) "Preparing for disaster: public attitudes and actions", *Disaster Prevention and Management*, 6 (1): 11–21.

Nerht, C. (1998) "Maintainability of first mover advantages when environmental regulations differ between countries", *Academy of Management Review*, 23 (1): 77–89.

Schneider, R. (2000) "Knowledge and ethical responsibility in industrial disasters", *Disaster Prevention and Management*, 9 (2): 98–104.

Siomkos, G.J. and Kurzbard, G. (1994) "The hidden crisis in product-harm crisis management", *European Journal of Marketing*, 28 (2): 30–41.

Yelkur, R., Morrison, J., Steiner, E.H. and Schmehl, I. (2001) "Product liability: its impact of the auto industry, consumers, and global competitiveness", *Business Horizons*, March/April, 44 (3): 61–66.

3 Digital Resilience and Business Continuity Management

Introduction

In Chapter 1 we introduced the term "digital resilience" to indicate the capability that arises from the conflation of an organisation's risk posture, its defensive resources, behavioural and cultural dimensions, and the strategic development of its information and communications technologies (ICT). In Chapter 2, we considered how an increasing umbrella of regulation and legislation alongside the legacy of disaster recovery planning reflects the broader use of, and threat towards, ICT. In this chapter, we introduce a discussion of digital resilience – its importance, form and diagnosis. Central to this consideration is the distinction between electronic security and digital resilience. The latter echoes, corresponds and aligns with the prevention and recovery management precepts of BCM that we set out in Chapter 1 and developed in the following chapter. As will be argued here, the concept of "digital" has many consequences, including an interrelationship with factors such as commercial, technological, behavioural and cultural ones. From a BCM manager's perspective, not least of these is the how, where, when and why things are done in an organisation. Since, in the simplest sense, BCM is about restoring the way things are completed in an organisation, an understanding of these wide consequences is required. This chapter deconstructs and reconstructs the concept of "digital". In doing so, we reveal and develop the importance of coupling human, group and organisational behaviour (the "do-ware") with hardware and software in the context of a changing environment.

Understanding Digital Resilience

Digital resilience represents a spearhead in the active prevention of business interruptions that distinguishes modern *crisis-prepared* organisations. Digital resilience is the capability that an organisation develops to either withstand or recover from digital threats, and deal in an effective manner with the consequences of interruptions, failures or deliberate violation of digital systems.

The rate of introduction of new technologies is rapidly escalating. As this happens, the gap increases between our ability to manage and the potential for something to go awry. "Digitality" (Negroponte, 1996) describes the lifestyle that digital technology makes possible: assumptions about the 24/7 contact with others through cellular technology, near instantaneous information through the World Wide Web, communicating through email and other electronic forms only now being spawned. Nicholas Negroponte's book *Being Digital* could not envisage the potentially negative consequences that would accompany digital information – some deliberate, others unintended, including viruses, loss of anonymity, spam, remote access to data, cyber crime and the potential for increased vulnerability through the very ubiquity and portability that has become possible today.

The need to inculcate digital resilience into the framework of continuity management arises from the continued development of new technologies and the implications of this for the way organisations are managed. Resilience cannot be delivered through technology alone, but must be based upon developing organisational routines that *build* organisational resilience. Organisational resilience arises from an understanding of behavioural dimensions and drivers both within and beyond the organisation. It is this recognition of behavioural dimensions that elevates the integration of digital resilience within BCM to a strategic management, rather than technical, consideration. Organisational resilience, together with a maximising of technical security measures, will create the ability to recover from failures or attacks. Given that the door or walls of organisations are porous, they can no longer be protected in old ways (Rothschild, 2006). Effective BCM in the twenty-first century will require a combination of organisational resilience and digital resilience. Figure 3.1 represents the influences upon the organisation, and the environment within which such a capacity has to be fostered, and visualises digital resilience as a protective mantle around the organisation; it is one element of the wider organisational resilience to other (non-digital) threats. An organisation's digital resilience comprises of physical, broad BCM and e-continuity measures (to deal with, inter alia, facilities, utilities and staff) along with greater connectedness between systems and web-based communications tools (to allow staff to work remotely), off-site back-up and restoration at hot-sites or business recovery centres. All these are enhanced with a greater understanding of the behavioural dimensions of resilience.

The need for (greater) digital resilience is raised by digital threats, drivers, dependencies and consequences that constitute the digital resilience environment. *Digital threats* such as digital vandalism, data leaks and theft, distributed denial of service[3] (DDoS) attacks and cyber-fraud such as web-spoofing and phishing represent well-known forms of malicious behaviour against digital systems. DDos attacks are especially problematic for websites whose sales patterns are highly cyclical and expose the owner

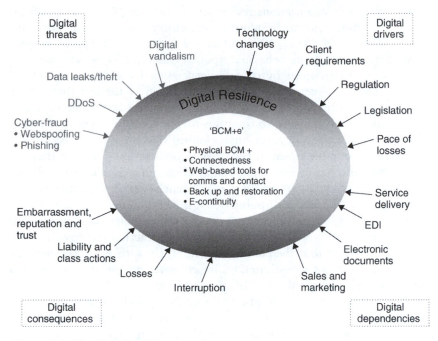

Figure 3.1 The digital resilience environment.

to a period where a large volume of transactions could be lost, such as gambling websites (Dietrich et al., 2004). Such behaviour may emanate from within the organisation as well as from outside it, although there is evidence to show that managers underestimate the degree of threat arising from misconduct or inadequate training (Ernst and Young, 2004). The same study showed that among the top ten causes of unscheduled outages that had occurred, five had generally originated from within the organisation (hardware failure, software failure, system capacity, operational errors and employee misconduct). Williams (2007) reports that politically motivated attacks are growing in number including targets such as air traffic control, financial markets and government networks. There were suspicions, unproven, of a state sponsored attack on Estonian information systems around the time of a dispute with Russia.

Digital drivers include: a number of forms such as competitive pressures to adopt emerging and established technologies (which include mobile computing, wireless networks and virtual servers, removable storage media and internet telephony); the higher pace of losses as a greater number of commercial or financial transactions take place in a digital environment; and silent failures in the form of lost connectivity for system users. With the tapestry of regulatory and legal drivers (such as those discussed in Chapter 2), organisations must often practise and demonstrate high levels of compliance in terms of information systems security. In a survey of 1,300 organisations researchers found that 60 per cent of firms attributed improvements in information security practices to regular compliance (Ernst and Young, 2005). Once again, from a behavioural perspective, organisation-level behaviour (policies and practices) are partially influenced and enforced by outside agencies and regulatory or judicial bodies. This, however, needs to be balanced against the fact that a large proportion of firms do not necessarily perceive compliance to be a primary driver. Even with the need to comply with the terms of Section 501(b) of the Gramm–Leach–Bliley Act,[4] it is claimed that some US banks are less concerned about the financial penalties of non-compliance than they are about the risk rating and reputational effects of a publicised violation (Smith and Frisby, 2004). In the case of financial services, the increases in identity theft cases and well-publicised losses of (or unauthorised access to) confidential data are not uncommon – occurrences which have been shown to lead to a significant negative stock market reaction (Campbell et al., 2003). Clearly there is the potential for interplay within and between the four dimensions of the digital resilience environment that warrants a strategic analysis by senior and BCM managers.

Digital dependencies highlight the increasing technology reliance on organisations to carry out many of the production or service provision activities, whether this is in the form of delivering a service, electronic/ online sales and marketing, or the creation and transfer of electronic documents and electronic data interchange. Such exchange may take the form of inter-organisational linkages in value chains such as CAD/CAM in R&D and security links such as payment verification. These new digital dependencies lead to changing behaviour to increase use of technology and therefore new or greater training needs.

Digital consequences further the pressure for organisations to enhance their digital resilience. Perceptions may be reinforced by the behaviour of individuals or organisations in response to a digital threat or crisis. A failure to respond adequately – to deter, prevent and recover – may not only lead to public embarrassment and a deterioration in reputation and trust, but the aftermath of a digital intrusion or interruption may also include litigation in the form of individual or class actions. For example, the actions filed by plaintiffs Eric Parke and Royal Sleep Clearance Center, Inc. following the CardSystems Solutions security violation (in which potentially 40 million cards were exposed to fraudulent usage, Kelleher, 2005). Bloor (2004) notes that in the case of *Maine Public Utilities Commission (PUC)* v. *Verizon* (2003), Maine PUC successfully argued that Verizon had been negligent in their countermeasures to deal with the slammer worm that had led to an infrastructure failure. The American Civil Liberties Union settled out of court with the State of New York after the loss of confidential data allegedly caused by a third party security provider.

Several large-scale studies highlight the effects of cyber-crime in a corporate environment. The UK's National Hi-Tech Crime Unit (2004) estimated that, in 2003 alone, a conservative estimate of the cost of dealing with attacks in the UK was £195 million. The study found that 83 per cent of UK firms had been victims of hi-tech crime at the time of the study and that the rate of cyber-crime incidents was three per organisation per month. In another study of cyber-crime from the Federal Bureau of Investigation (cited in Evers, 2006), the cost of such crime for US businesses was estimated to be in the order of $67 billion per year with an average cost per incident of $24,000. Although neither study indicates the extent to which the survey sample sites had digital resilience capabilities in place, they do highlight the cost and frequency of such threats.

Our concept of digital resilience is comparable, though different in emphasis, to the CERT[5] definition of "Survivable Network Systems" (Ellison et al., 1999a). Survivability is defined as "the capability of a system to fulfil its mission in a timely manner in the presence of attacks, failures or accidents" (Ellison et al., 1999b: 2). For a system to survive, it should have the capacity to continue functioning after an attack in a manner that preserves data integrity, data confidentiality and system performance, allowing completion of its mission. The difference in emphasis between survivability and resilience is that the CERT survivability concept focuses on technical and systems design aspects. Resilience assumes that the human element of the system requires to be developed along similar lines such that recovery can take place.

Bellovin (2001) argues that security problems stem from the nature of internet architecture and buggy software. The work of CERT supports this view (Ellison et al., 1999a, 1999b). Bellovin (2001) contends that most software code is full of bugs; combine this with users who do not fully understand the technology they are using, the highly decentralised and distributed nature of the internet, and the stage is set for security violations and breaches. Some of these breaches clearly will have roots in user ignorance and cannot truly be categorised as "crime", while others originate out of a deliberate attempt to exploit any space created by such circumstances. Hence, we should distinguish between cyber or digital crime and interruptions caused by human–computer interactions. CERT distinguishes between "failures" that are internally generated and the result of such human–computer interactions, and "accidents" which are the result of external triggers or attacks on the system.

Figure 3.2 provides a means of categorising these incidents. As illustrated, an employee launching (through human error) a virus that spreads through organisational computing systems is very different in nature from a denial of service attack. The former is the consequence of human error that combines with a systems failure, resulting in negative outcomes for the organisation. In contrast, the denial of service attack (cyber crime) has a human trigger (deliberate intent, with malice intended) that finds a system weakness, resulting in negative consequences.

Breaches or interruptions can therefore be categorised based on whether

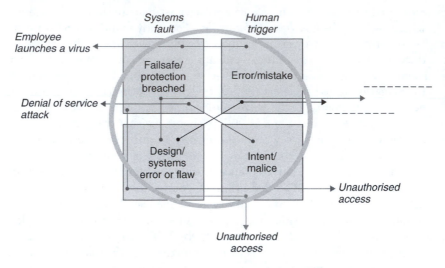

Figure 3.2 Categorising security breaches or interruptions.

the human trigger was an error, or intentional, together with a systems fault, which could be due to either failsafe protection being breached, or a design system flaw being exploited. Taking into account the fundamental architectural problems of software and the internet (Bellovin, 2001), we therefore wish to suggest that our search for more robust systems should focus upon the human element within the organisation – it is here that a search for resilience could produce an accentuating effect to the technology-based security precautions that organisations employ. For example, the human–computer interaction may be seen at the root of a number of recent losses of personal data. In one case, a package of two disks containing the personal and bank account details of twenty-five million people was lost by the UK's Revenue and Custom's service (Croft and Eaglesham, 2007). The data had been posted instead of being digitally transferred. In another case in early 2008, a laptop containing the details of 600,000 military recruits was lost, raising fears for their safety during a time of heightened security concerns (Norton-Taylor, 2008).

Development of a Metasystem

The "second-generation" internet (Camp and Tsang, 2001) where users are continually online means that systems are now more tightly coupled and enmeshed in one huge "metasystem" in which system control and the isolation of that system (once it becomes necessary) can become problematic. Of course, it is inconceivable to think of the world without such 24/7 connectivity. As an example, consider Amazon without the second-generation internet – the quality of service in the early days of the internet made for poor comparison with the technology and ease of use of today. But, such positive benefits are traded against the loss of other system features. For instance, Grimshaw and Wulf (1997) argue that computer systems today do not adequately address the problem of site autonomy. Site autonomy denotes that users are still able to control technological resources locally, while being part of a global computer network or infrastructure. Hence, users may employ a physical means of ensuring security (unplugging computers or dislocating from a network) from threats to a digital system. However, it is clear that with the second-generation internet such control becomes more problematic. Consider, for example, the emerging technologies that offer (often free) services that link users into web-based communities or offer "do-it-yourself" applications. *Business Week* (2006) has credited Tim O'Reilly of O'Reilly Media with popularising the term Web 2.0 and enabling a shorthand reference to the more complex "participatory" internet applications of today.

This participatory or community aspect of the internet implies that the human component of the systems require to evolve also, in line with the more sophisticated technology. In order to tackle this issue, let us consider some lessons imparted via a simple children's story. Madeleine L'Engle (1995), in her classic children's novel *A Wrinkle in Time*, provides a wonderful example of a "metasystem", in the existence of IT – a giant, disembodied brain that controls several planets in the universe, and all inhabitants. As they succumb to IT, all objects and places become alike as they march to the rhythm that IT uses to hypnotise them. Two children, Charles Wallace and his sister, Meg, investigate the disappearance of their physicist father, who had been researching the fifth dimension of time and space travel, and through his scientific work had discovered IT, and the terrible fate that befalls planets and their inhabitants once they fall prey to its rhythmic pulsations. Mr Wallace is captured and kept prisoner. The children, with assistance from some celestial creatures called Mrs What, Mrs Who and Mrs Whatsit, locate their father, while Meg is able to resist the powers of IT because of her capacity to love and be loved by others. She is able to do so because of an internal psychological strength rather than the use of cerebral functioning only. Thus, *A Wrinkle in Time* provides a metaphor for systems evolution into more complex systems, eventually attaining the status of a metasystem. Resistance and control of independent thought and rational action results from having in place sound values and norms that guide behaviour.

In computing, a metasystem refers to a complex system in which subsystems are linked together, and there is an additional mechanism which controls the behaviour and production of the subsystems (Turchin and Joslyn, 1999). A hierarchy of control emerges, which, in the case of computer technology, can become very complex depending on the nature of the languages used to create and compile software (Grimshaw and Wulf, 1997). A computing metasystem implies an expansion of computing power, increases in bandwith, shrinking of distance between computer users and the irrelevance of the location of users and their computing resources, as well as ubiquity of the network once it is digital. Digital further implies that we no longer have islands of technology or hardware – an interconnectedness achieved without the use of cables, etc. Levels of control over the whole and parts of the system also become more complex, heightened by the fact that systems are now digital and continuous, via the second-generation internet (Camp and Tsang, 2001) – the first-generation internet in contrast was available to most users only through a traditional telephone connection that had to be consciously activated by a user.

Similarly, CERT envisions a metasystem as a "large-scale system of systems" (Ellison, 1999a: 1). CERT distinguishes between earlier networks that were spatially and electronically bounded. In contrast, today new networks are unbounded and key features of such unbounded networks are that:

- traditional organisational boundaries have been obliterated;
- local operations are transformed into components of comprehensive, network-resident business processes;
- administrative control becomes distributed rather than centrally controlled;
- there is a lack of information about the entire network;
- organisational dependence on networks are heightened;
- risks and consequences of network failure are increased.

The lack of control that comes with greater integration of systems is reflected in research conducted by the Pew Research Trust (Fallows, 2003) into email communications in the US. In a survey of email users in 2003, 75 per cent of users were concerned at not being able to control spam, and that this lack of control caused them sufficient concern to tail off their email usage. Hence, user response was to effect local control in a physical manner by not logging on to email, judiciously choosing which emails to open, or deleting what they considered to be spam. This lack of control over what travels into inboxes occurs despite the attempts by internet service providers to filter what is allowed through to email. Firewalls and spam killer software can enhance our ability to control, but does not provide complete protection. In fact, by linking into the second-generation internet, we accept that such intrusions are inevitable. Corporations have, however, become more sophisticated in their approach to security, accepting that it should not only be externally focused, but also internal in that threats may arise from employee use of systems, or may simply lurk inside software, to be unleashed at some point in the future (Rothschild, 2006).

As organisations have developed information systems over many years, building layer upon layer of data, connectivity and functionality, the recognition of metasystems as distinct entities requiring formal analysis is necessary to ensure both a strategic and an operational view of digital resilience. As new technologies and platforms are rolled out, opportunities arise to enhance resilience, or increase vulnerability by failing to put into place dynamic security measures that anticipate and circumvent problems in real-time. The idea that layers of technologies can increase or decrease risk is similar to the idea of Reason's "Swiss cheese" model (Reason, 1997) in which an organisation's vulnerabilities are commensurate with the alignment of the holes in a series of slices of Swiss cheese. The alignment of the holes allows the threat to pass through. In contrast, a number of countermeasures can partially or wholly prevent the entry and impact of a threat. Figure 3.3 combines this idea of layers of vulnerability (or, conversely, protection) with the idea of metasystems development. The figure shows four types of system characterised by their size and vulnerability. Each metasystem comprises of a number of subsystems coupled by a resilient or vulnerable linkage. The arrows between the four metasystems denote the path that an organisation can take in its technology roadmap and development by either disregarding or embracing digital resilience within its broader BCM approach.

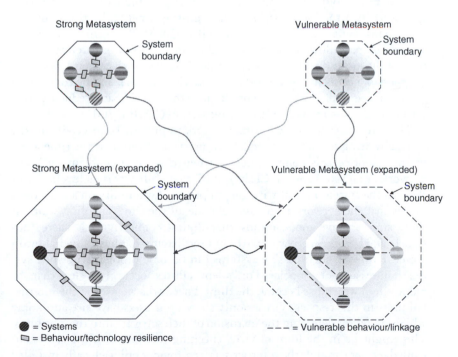

Figure 3.3 Metasystems resilience.

Why is "Digitality" Important for Business Continuity Management Managers?

The concept of digitality has wide consequences – commercial, techno-logical, behavioural and cultural – not least for the BCM manager because of the how, where, when and why things are done in an organisation. Since, in the simplest sense, BCM is about restoring the way things are done in an organisation, an understanding of these wide consequences is required. Table 3.1 summarises the different connotations of digital, and presents the risks and benefits associated with digital networks.

Speed and Availability

Speed of communication and transaction, as well as availability of the system, comprise the most salient features of digital technology. A bene-ficial outcome of this is that credit card companies can today, through the use of neural networks, know within 2 seconds after a credit card is swiped, whether the card is being used fraudulently or not (Marlin, 2005). This assumes of course that the relevant person or authority has notified the company of loss, theft or identity theft. Digital networks have delivered decreased transaction costs as networks become more efficient. This is due to both technology improvements and more interconnectedness afforded by that technology. For a retailer, it is now possible to have transaction approvals in 2 to 3 seconds, using a high-speed network, as opposed to 30 seconds using a dial-up system (Marlin, 2005). Real-time monitoring of systems has allowed the main credit card issuers a greater ability to control the losses due to credit card fraud. Visa claims that their losses have dropped to 5 cents in every $100 in transaction volume, and by continuing to use more sophisticated technologies, they anticipate reducing this further to 2 cents in every $100 in transaction (Marlin, 2005).

The internet enables the digital network to provide connectivity all the time, obviating the need to specifically intervene. Ironically, the time when we most notice this connectivity is when there is a problem with the network or an interruption. Clearly, 24/7 availability creates less buffer or slack in the system to deal with interruptions. Availability on a 24/7 basis means that the network is in passive mode all the time, enabling seamless processing. Passive mode means that digital connectivity is there con-stantly and becomes activated without users having to physically dial into a server. However, such passive systems can become problematic when sys-tem failures are not enunciated or "silent failures" occur. It is clear that the metasystem which has become the digital networks we use via the internet fail users in this respect. Viruses only show up if users have site autonomy which allows for detecting the intrusion of such software into their systems. This might be in the form of virus checking software or if a locally con-trolled (either through the internet service provider or by a locally installed

Table 3.1 Connotations of "Digital"

Connotation of digital	Risks for the organisation	Benefits for the organisation
Speed	The pace of potential loss is heightened due to the speeds of single transactions and data transfer.	Real-time monitoring can provide signal detection to provide early intervention.
Availability – 24/7	Less time, buffer, slack, redundancy, etc., to deal with interruptions.	The commercial benefits in terms of service levels are evident, and the organisation is able to spread its transactions over a wider period (thereby reducing the loss per hour that would have arisen from a non-24/7 operation).
Accessibility – "off-site"	With systems and data access available "off-site" – the points of access (and points of vulnerability) are widened.	Reduces the potential impact of a loss involving a single facility.
Portability	Portable devices provide an additional way in which organisations can lose assets and information.	Portable devices allow employees to carry out a variety of tasks without the necessity to access premises.
Modernity	The assumption that new is better may not be valid. Technologies may not be more productive and efficient but less resilient in their infancy.	As technology standards are replaced, they may no longer benefit from the same levels of security support as their newer counterparts.
Ease of use	Ease of use means that less experienced users of a technology may inadvertently expose a system and data to a vulnerability.	With training, digital resilience can be partly developed to users, creating a shared sense of responsibility for the integrity of an organisation's ICT.
Transferability	Information can be transferred from one location/system/standard to another and exploited in a malicious manner.	Developments such as data ghosting or mirroring benefit from the instantaneous. streaming of back-up data that has arisen from file transfer technology.
Interconnectedness	Threats can spread from one point of impact to another.	Resilience measures can be applied across a system.
Levels/hierarchy of control	Complex levels of control (users, administrators etc.) create multiple access rights and responsibilities.	Responsibility for resilience measures can be top-down with responsibility partly devolved to users.

program on a user computer) firewall alerts the user to the fact that a virus has found its way into a computer system. If users lack this degree of protection, the first intimation of infection will usually be when files are destroyed or the system plays up in some other way. With regard to spam or adware, a different trajectory to discovering a problem exists. Research shows that users are often unaware that this type of software has become embedded in their systems – the "threat from within" (Rothschild, 2006). Pew Internet Life research (Fox, 2005) shows that users have altered their online behaviour because of an awareness of the threat of intrusions, but many others may be completely unaware exactly when an intrusion *has* occurred. In effect, enunciation often does not occur because the software comes bundled with other, legitimate software that the user might have installed by choice. For instance, the screensaver "ScreenScenes" automatically installs GAIN Adserver and allows a network of advertisers to monitor the interests of those who use the computer (Fox, 2005).

Box 3.1   AT&T, Inc. and High Availability Networks

AT&T, Inc. is the result of a merger in November 2005 between SBC Communications and AT&T Corp. The company today is the largest telecommunications provider in the US and one of the largest in the world. Its networks carry 5.4 petabytes of traffic and the company claims 99.99 per cent availability. In 2005 the company achieved $42,862,000 in revenues, with 187,100 employees. AT&T, Inc. serves customers around the world, through provision of services such as traditional and IP-based voice, broadband internet, data transport, entertainment, wireless and video services in eighty countries. They also offer security and support services. The company ranks second in the telecommunications industry by revenue and profit.

AT&T, Inc.'s approach to BCM encompasses the entire system, including software, hardware and people. Information security plays a crucial role in this because, logically, the loss of information would have the same impact as the loss of a building or a system. The telecommunications network is at once an enabler of enhanced security and a heightener of risk. The network is most likely to be the source of an attack. From a physical perspective, the network provides availability, but it also enables a distribution of access and provides the means to replicate and build in redundancies. BCM today dictates that the network be exploited for geographical distribution of access, making use of multi-locational sites and storage grids.

The idea of ultra-available systems rests upon the principle of eliminating a single point of failure. Hence, systems today make use of dual points of entry and dual paths to the network, as well as making use of technological diversity in building availability.

Hence, from a security perspective, provision is made to exploit network-based solutions to security. For instance, instead of using a path that provides 99 per cent malware and 1 per cent good content, using a network-based security solution provides the space to screen "contacts" being made with the system, so that anomalies in transactions can be investigated and vulnerabilities be identified. Security becomes proactive and defensive – once an anomaly is detected, users or customers globally can be alerted that a particular accident or failure had occurred. This allows defensive routines to come into play and systems to be protected.

Governance is vital and forms part of a deliberate process; AT&T has developed a process to identify gaps and new risks. For instance, in the US, terrorism was never as serious a risk as it is today, or the threat of a bird flu epidemic and its consequences for continuity management. The company is cognisant of the strain on systems if, for instance, people have to work from home. There are huge implications for broadband access, data security and work scheduling for categories of employees such as call centre employees who would need calls to be routed to their homes.

AT&T anticipate new customer needs through the use of three criteria that drive availability:

- components
- architecture
- process for detection, break/fix routines and return to service.

Successful strategies around process depend upon how well people are trained to respond once system monitoring detects the need to protect availability. Analyses are done on how failure in one system component might lead to failure elsewhere, and simulations enable additional learnings to be done.

Basic IT architecture consists of an access network that penetrates the system through things such as load balancers and a firewall (see Figure 3.4). Following this is an application that sits on middleware, which sits on a server; this then sits on some type of back-end storage area network, which talks to some storage. In a "smoking-hole" disaster, the entire system can be lost.

But, if you have a failure or fault of some component, you may have lost your server, but storage is intact, and the system can be recovered. So the general approach to develop a disaster recovery architecture is to say, "Because everything can fail locally, I want to have this to be resilient within the site. So, I take my server and may have a cluster. I may take my storage and I may insert local RAID (Redundant Array of Independent Disks) in which I may locally mirror the data or use mechanisms such as parity striping, so that no

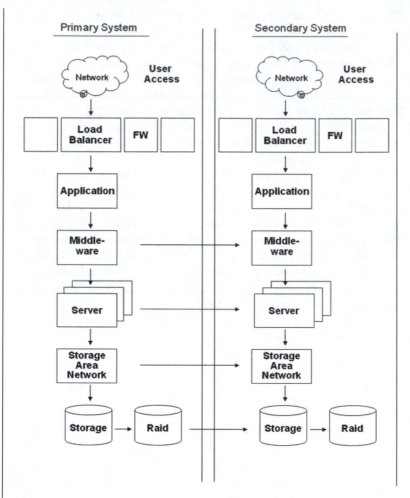

Figure 3.4 AT&T high availability network example.

single loss (for example, loss of a hard drive) will cause data to be lost." Other data loss can also be protected against, for example, middleware: "I may have a database that spits out a log of transactions so that I can recover from the outage or crisis by going back to the log and recover updates. I can do things such as high availability architecture for things such as load balancers and firewalls, or have a switch-over to another firewall so that in the event of firewall failure, the system can continue processing with a firewall intact." I can distribute the applications across the server cluster so that the load balancers interact. Load balancers distribute processing and communications activity evenly across a network to prevent single devices being overloaded and failing. There are products available that provide dual connections between servers, and a storage device. Storage Area Network (SAN) fabrics can be built to be highly resilient so that there is no single point of failure and there is dual interconnections between the SAN and the disk itself. That is the way in which most IT architectures are built today – certainly anything that is mission critical. This kind of architecture is resilient from a physical perspective, except that it does not protect against a bomb going off and taking out the entire system, or from a virus infecting the system. So, the basic real high-availability architecture, that is a business continuity architecture, says that I take the entire system and its redundancies, and duplicate in a secondary site. Just having the site does not help. For example, three weeks of transactions, does not help. An organisation needs to replicate the capacity to process transactions at the second site, *and* make sure that you have data stored at the secondary site. There are four major architectural ways to achieve this. The first is to say that any data written to this storage device, the storage device will talk to its corresponding counterpart at the other location. This is known as disk mirroring, replication, and many other terms. So, there is little or no loss. Second, the SAN can be used to copy data. Any data written to the storage device is intercepted by the SAN and sending it to the second device. This is becoming more prevalent with intelligent storage area networks that can do virtualisation within the SAN, even if the storage device is very dumb. EMC was the best performing stock on the NYSE from 1990 to 2000 based on their ability to manufacture a device that can provide Synchronous Remote Data Security (SRDS). The third thing is to have servers talk to each other. This means the file system in the server captures the transaction being written down through the SAN to the storage device, and sends a copy to the server (secondary) to do the same kind of write. The last is transaction mirroring. As the transaction comes in, the transaction itself is mirrored. An appropriate choice will be made from these in line with the characteristics of the organisation. There are advantages and disadvantages to each of these methods. Those are the basic architectures today.

Sources

Online: http://att.sbc.com/gen/investor-relations?pid=5711
  (accessed 12 July 2006).
Plunketts Research, Ltd, 2006.
Interview with AT&T Source, June 12 and 16, 2006.
Online: http://www.webopedia.com/TERM/R/RAID.html (accessed
  12 July 2006).

Accessibility and Portability

With systems and data access available "off-site", points of access and (potentially) points of vulnerability are widened, given the proliferation of flexible working practices. The Institute of Employment Studies survey of European companies showed that nearly half the companies participating in their survey were engaged in some form of remote working, or e-work (Huws and O'Regan, 2001). Of these companies, 12 per cent had employees who were involved in some form of e-work on behalf of the company. New technologies also appear to be a popular choice to make multi-locational telework possible (Huws and O'Regan, 2001). Among these firms, around 43 per cent reported using new communications technologies for outsourcing purposes, often to other countries. The locations where work is being done are becoming more distributed. This dislocation of work is mirrored by data moving outside the physical boundaries of the organisation, both over networks facilitated by the internet and by portable data storage devices such as computers, PDAs and flash memory cards. Points of access to this data have multiplied and the control and ownership of this data is becoming more complex. *The Wall Street Journal* reports a number of leaks of customer or employee data over the last few months (The Wall Street Journal Report Online, 2005):

- Bank of America announced on 25 February 2005 that computer owners back-up tapes were lost, containing customer data, including social security numbers. The consumers affected in this case were 1.2 million federal government charge cards.
- Lexis-Nexis announced on 9 March 2005 that social security numbers and driver's licence numbers were compromised due to unauthorised use of customer logins and passwords.
- MCI admitted on 23 May 2005 that the social security numbers of 16,500 current and former employees of the company had been compromised when a laptop was stolen from a car at the home of an MCI financial analyst.

The Mastercard vignette below details the case of CardSystems Solutions and the failure of the company to comply with security practices of the major credit card companies, including Mastercard. On 22 May 2005, under pressure it would appear from Mastercard, CardSystems Solutions alerted 40 million customers of all the major credit card companies that a hacker had broken into their computer network and stolen card codes and account numbers. CardSystems Solutions operates as an intermediary between vendors (they target small and medium-sized companies) and credit card companies to facilitate payment processing. It would appear that though the company had been certified as compliant with the data security measures that the major credit card companies such as Visa and

Mastercard use to combat credit card fraud, it was not. The company admitted to incorrectly storing consumer credit card data in breach of security practice. Neither had they taken precautions to encrypt account data (Marlin, 2005). Analysis after the event showed that the company had been in violation of compliance standards with regards to storing data and encryption since April 2004, at least a year before the security breach was made public. None of the credit card issuers had done anything about this until May 2005 (Marlin, 2005).

**Box 3.2 MasterCard Vignette: Card Data Exposure –
When Security and Human Behaviour Don't Mix**

One of the largest security breaches in financial information systems developed in the spring and summer of 2005. While the scale of the incident was headline grabbing, the case was another of many involving the unauthorised access of (seemingly) secure consumer information. When the global payments company MasterCard, the security firm Ubizen and a client bank investigated the pattern and characteristics of unauthorised payments in April 2005, the trail led to CardSystems, a third party subcontractor used by MasterCard. On the 22 May 2005, CardSystems became aware of an attempt to access their systems by an unauthorised individual and, by the following day, it had contacted the Federal Bureau of Investigation. Alerted by real-time fraud monitoring software, an initial analysis indicated that a total of 40 million credit card accounts could have been exposed and compromised through the theft of card data, including 13.9 cards using the MasterCard payment system. MasterCard initiated its established notification and security procedures to alert clients, limit the impact of the data theft, and to monitor Card-Systems' remedial security measures to ensure compliance with its own standards. The attack was seemingly caused by a hacker installing a piece of software designed to appropriate cardholder information. This included the three- or four-digit security code that is one of the more recent security countermeasures introduced by card issuers. Furthermore, the stolen data had not been encrypted. Both MasterCard and CardSystems, in separate press statements released on 17 June 2005, claimed to have identified the security breach. CardSystems began the process of remedying the security flaw and improving the resilience of its information systems and data from unauthorised access with the assistance of a third party technology security company.

As one of several companies that process transactions on behalf of MasterCard, banks, retailers and other merchants, the CardSystems case highlights the potential vulnerability of firms to the actions of organisations elsewhere in the supply chain, not simply in terms of commercial and reputational losses but also compliance with regulatory within their industry. In this case, MasterCard publicly lamented the fact that the provisions of the US Gramm–Leach–Bliley Act (Financial Services Modernisation) of 1999 which impose strict requirements to protect the confidential nature of customer records against threats and misuse would only apply to MasterCard and not to CardSystems, since that latter did not have direct contact with consumers. To compound the challenges and demands of the original systems security attack, MasterCard also had to deal with an intensification of an ongoing form of cyber-crime – phishing (a form of email and internet fraud designed to trick users into divulging their account access information). This provided a far from benign environment in which MasterCard and CardSystems had to manage the hacking attack.

Within days, MasterCard was able to establish the full extent of the hacking attack at CardSystems. Of the 13.9 million cards within its remit, some 68,000 MasterCard branded cards (or 0.48 per cent of cards) were considered to be at high risk of fraudulent manipulation. Less reassuring was the disclosure that CardSystems should not have stored and retained the data that had been stolen in the first place – in contravention to MasterCard and Visa's rules that cardholder account information should not be retained once a transaction is completed. CardSystems claimed that the company had retained the information for "research purposes" and was to be used to improve its fraud detection systems.

This case usefully highlights a number of dimensions that are prevalent within the domain of digital resilience. Real-time detection and monitoring systems provided limited signal detection against known threats in cases where users compromise countermeasures – tight coupling of inter-organisational information systems, card processing companies (MasterCard, Visa), card processing subcontractors/merchant processors (CardSystems etc.) and card issuers (MBNA, Citigroup, etc.). Many of these parties develop and are bound to agreed standards and processes.

The use of third parties to support security audits in the event of a breach have a dual effect: to verify the integrity of changed systems, and to provide public reassurances that systems have returned to a resilient state. Both companies claimed that they had discovered the breach first. The race to notice first is as important (in reputation terms) as the ability to respond to the threat itself. A behavioural dimension (retaining the data) led to a vulnerability having a greater impact than would have been the case without such a deviation in procedure. Basic errors (such as the failure to encrypt) data can emasculate the defensive measures that an organisation has in place. The combination of continuous threats and periodic sudden attacks along with a propensity for human error to impede the technological countermeasures strengthen the case for organisations to develop a general capability of digital resilience.

Sources

BBCi (2005) "Up to 40m credit cards 'hacked' ", BBC News, online: http://news.bbc.co.uk/1/hi/world/americas/4107236.stm (accessed 22 June 2005).

CardSystems (2005) *Statement from CardSystems Solutions, Inc.*, 17 June, online: http://www.cardsystems.com/news.html (accessed 22 June 2005).

Dash, D. (2005) "Lost credit data improperly kept, company admits", *New York Times*, 20 June, online: http:// www.nytimes.com/2005/06/20/technology/20credit.html (accessed 22 June 2005).

Leyden, J. (2005) "MasterCard hack spawns phishing attack", *The Register*, 20 June, online: http://www.theregister.co.uk/2005/06/ 20/mastercard_phishing/ (accessed 22 June 2005).

Leyden, J. (2005) "Unauthorised research opened door to MasterCard breach", *The Register*, 21 June, online: http:// www.theregister.co.uk/2005/06/21/mastercard_follow-up/ (accessed 22 June 2005).

MasterCard (2005) "News Release: MasterCard International identifies security breach at CardSystems Solutions, a third party processor of payment card data", 17 June, online: http:// www.mastercardinternational.com/cgi-bin/newsroom.cgi? id=1038 (accessed 22 June 2005).

Vance, A. (2005) "MasterCard fingers partner in 40m card security breach", *The Register*, 18 June, online: http:// www.theregister.co.uk/2005/06/18/mastercard_breach/ (accessed 22 June 2005).

What is very revealing about cases such as CardSystems/Mastercard is that consumers are learning about breaches of this kind due to political pressure from a number of different states, led by California, which requires commercial organisations to publicly notify consumers when data has been compromised. This security breach notice law took effect in California on 1 July 2003 and compels organisations to give notice to customers should electronically held customer data have been compromised (Searcey, 2005). Companies are clearly keen to limit the amount of damage to their reputation by complying with the regulation and not to compound the problem once discovered. Some are able to recover well and even benefit from the event because of their very responsible handling of it, while others appear to struggle to recover. CardSystems Solutions appear to fall into the latter category as Visa and American Express, two of their largest clients, have indicated that they would be ending their relationship with the organisation (Cardline, 2005). Pay By Touch took over the troubled CardSystems Solutions in December 2005 and, in February 2006, settled Federal Trade Commission charges resulting from the case (FTC, 2006).

Ironically, accessibility at an off-site location brings with it the advantage of reducing the impact of a loss involving a single facility. The experience of Morgan Stanley Dean Witter during the morning of 9/11 illustrates this perhaps best. The company was the largest tenant in the World Trade Center and had also been through the events of the 1993 bombing of the building. This experience had led to well practised disaster contingency plans that enabled the company, in 2001, to escape with the loss of only six lives out of the total 3,700 employee complement. According to Robert Scott, then president and chief operating officer for the company, by 9:30 am that morning, employees had walked twenty blocks to the company's back-up site and activated back-up computers there (Walsh, 2001).

Modernity and Ease of Use

"Digital" may connote modernity and ease of use for end users and technology strategists alike. The inference is that as technology (whether in hardware or software form) develops, the succession of new forms are more robust and resilient to threats and interruptions compared to antecedents. The switching costs of moving from one technology to another should also take into account mal-adaptation costs – that is, the costs associated with operators making errors as they become accustomed and familiar with the new technology. With the backwards compatibility of many information systems, in terms of data and operation, this ease of use means that less experienced users of a technology may inadvertently expose a system's data to systems vulnerability, raising issues about information technology and security skills auditing and training. A study by Dhamija and colleagues (2006) found that 23 per cent of the participants in a study of internet users ignored browser-based security information that indicated whether a site was a genuine and secure bank/payment website, while other users misinterpreted security information. The study also found that a simulation of a spoof/phishing website was able to fool 90 per cent of the sample comprising university staff and students. Since there is evidence to suggest that spam (which often foments a visit to a spoof website) is on the increase relative to computer viruses, the study highlights that the development of secure technologies and countermeasures may be ineffectual if users do not understand current forms of internet fraud or do not fully understand the nature and purpose of new and existing security measures. Another study (Wagner, 2006) found that IT security incidents arising from human error had risen from 47 per cent of cases to 60 per cent between 2005 and 2006, yet only 29 per cent of companies surveyed made an attempt to understand their employees information and technology security training needs. Within organisations, the ubiquity of modern storage technologies such as universal serial bus (USB) drives may not be perceived as a security threat. In an experiment in which twenty USB drives (containing password and ID harvesting programs) were left lying around in a financial services company's building, fifteen of the drives were picked up and used by members of staff in the company's computers (Lemos, 2006).

The likelihood of flaws that generate interest and exploitation from those with malicious intent increases as new software and operating systems are introduced. The assumption that new is better may not be valid. Technologies may be more productive and efficient, but less resilient in their infancy. As technology standards are replaced, they may no longer benefit from the same levels of security support as their newer counterparts. So, assumptions about the modernity of digital systems may drive the adoption of the newest rather than most suitable technology in BCM terms – that is, those which present the lowest known risks to the organisation. The modernity and ease of use of new technologies may create or reinforce assumptions and behaviours which raise the vulnerability of the organisation to digital threats (see Table 3.1), thereby elevating the need for training to create and reinforce a shared sense of responsibility for the integrity of an organisation's ICT.

Transferability and Interconnectedness

The USB drive case above demonstrates that the ability to transfer data, either electronically or through removable media, presents a double-edged sword. The emergence of metasystems has, in many instances, given rise to the transferability and interconnectedness that characterise modern information systems. In terms of transferability, high transfer rates and bandwidth, along with possibilities for end-user intervention, allow information to be transferred from one location, system or standard to another and be exploited in a malicious manner. Conversely, developments such as data ghosting or mirroring benefit from the instantaneous streaming of back-up data that has arisen from file transfer technology. Comparex's response to the Windsor Tower fire (see Chapter 5) is a case in point. The interconnectedness of systems – whether they be through email of intra-, inter- or extra-net connectivity provide the potential scope for viruses, worms, malware and spambots to wreak havoc on information systems. When a metasystem is weak, threats can spread from one point of impact to another, while resilient metasystems represent the implementation of resilience measures (human, technical and behavioural) applied across and between systems. The increased use of "endpoint security" which controls the entry and exit of data from USB drives, PDAs and portable AV devices such as MP3 players is designed to countervail the negative effects of transferability. Similarly, the introduction of stricter policies for laptop security such as two-factor authentication, data extract logging and encryption have been introduced by the US government following a number of well-publicised government laptop thefts or losses (Martin, 2006).

Levels and Hierarchy of Controls

Traditional systems will typically have a hierarchy of controls to ensure integrity, with a systems administrator who can monitor, control and impose sanctions in the event of a security breach. In a metasystem, controls become more complex because no one system component can assert overall control or authority (Ellison, 1999a). Site autonomy can be effected and enable local mechanisms to be deployed for protective action. However, as the AT&T example shows, networked software security today relies on a multitude of layers of security to safeguard parts of the system. Much redundancy is also built in. As systems develop into metasystems, complex levels of control (users, administrators, etc.) create multiple access rights and responsibilities. In part, this system security evolution is based on the assumption that organisations have to deal with externally generated threats. Hardened system boundaries in the form of firewalls do not recognise the reality that organisation boundaries today are porous (Chesbrough, 2003) due to employee entrance and egress, as well as through information spillover.

Some system threats penetrate organisations through "legitimate" routes such as email that subsequently become vectors for an attack or interruption (Keeney et al., 2005). Keeney and colleagues studied the vulnerabilities suffered by organisations from employees (or ex-employees) with system access. They undertook research to develop an aggregated case analysis of insider incidents in the US critical infrastructure sector over the period 1996 to 2002. Public and private sector organisations were included. The results indicated that many threats were "incubated" inside the organisation and, in 51 per cent, insiders were exploiting vulnerabilities with which they were familiar. Simple methods of attack predominated, in the form of insiders using legitimate user commands and physical attacks, based on their deep knowledge as users or developers of the system.

Employee recruitment can itself serve as one means of ensuring that the system will be accessed by individuals who can be trusted to understand the importance of complying with certain protocols.

My employees do not have to be told to do regular back-ups of critical systems. They take the initiative. We actively recruit individuals who demonstrate this type of mindset.

(Interview with the owner of a small company in New Jersey)

This approach is echoed by the findings of the insider threat study done by CERT (Keeney et al., 2005); background and security checks should be done on those who will have access to computer systems, especially those involved in administration of the system. The CERT study quotes a systems developer who admits to installing unauthorised code to allow them to make system access more efficient. However, no amount of employee background checking can prevent malicious behaviour due to disgruntlement (Cappelli, 2005). In the CERT survey, the motives of insiders who had sabotaged systems or committed fraud were primarily revenge (84 per cent) or a response to a negative employment event (92 per cent) and fewer than 1 per cent were motivated by financial gain. Incidents were identified and harm done to systems or the organisation catalogued before being traced back to when the idea of committing the security breach first occurred to the individual. In the majority of cases, it would appear that other employees were often aware of the intentions of the insider, and that the main reason the breaches occurred was due to systematic vulnerabilities in technology, policies or procedures. In the main these were sloppy controls, non-existent or poor monitoring, or physical access controls lacking in rigor. Reason's (1997) Swiss cheese model of human error suggests that when an alignment of the holes occurs, its creates a vulnerability to trigger events such as a negative employment incident. Most of these incidents were internally incubated and preventable. Table 3.2 summarises the main methods of attack and the access controls that may help prevent these.

Perhaps the most important finding and recommendation from the CERT study is the need for organisations to have formal grievance

Table 3.2 Insider Threat Study Findings on Method of System Attack and Potential Controls

Method of attack	Access level	Access control
Technically sophisticated (40% of cases in study)	Scripts, programs and autonomous agents	Separation of duties, with two-person rule for system admin functions. Release of malware usually requires some collaboration
Simple attacks (60% of cases)	Legitimate user commands Physical attacks Information exchanges	Fine-grained controls required Two-person control of critical system and data modification

Source: Based on CERT survey by Keeney et al., 2005

procedures, as well as whistleblower procedures for employees to use to resolve employment concerns, concern about security and other job-related matters. Such procedures should also be consistently enforced and employee concerns in the case of whistleblowers should be taken seriously and investigated.

Balancing the Digital Resilience Agenda – Implications for BCM

In Chapter 1 we examined the evolution of BCM from its roots in the technology-passive disaster recovery approaches to IT systems. Since then, the proliferation of information and communication technologies in commercial, consumer, domestic and cultural terms has once again refocused attention to the reliance and vulnerability of organisations on information technologies that necessitate planning for digital resilience – a new form of disaster recovery. While digital resilience is important, it is necessary to ensure that it does not monopolise planning for BC. Other-wise, disaster recovery will have come full circle in focusing on one part of an organisation's vulnerable resources to the detriment of a focus on facil-ities, production and service provisions, supply chains and human resources. Digital resilience demonstrates the importance of information and communications technologies as a metasystem and as a socio-technical system. In each of these, individual and group behaviour is intimately involved in determining whether digitality helps or hinders general busi-ness resilience.

Our deconstruction of digitality and digital resilience raises a number of issues that are encapsulated in the approaches to BCP and management in the following chapters:

- Digital resilience is one of several pillars of general organisational resilience.
- Human/organisational behaviour and interactions with systems and metasystems must be understood to effect prevention and recovery from digital threats.
- An explicit analysis of the business resilience environment is necessary.
- Understanding digitality is central to understanding the risks and opportunities that organisations face in rolling out new technologies, processes and practices.

Beyond the legal and regulatory drivers to improve their information security and digital resilience, companies may use this imperative to introduce BCM in a green-field context (as many did in the advent of millennium bug projects). In the next chapter we turn to the requirements and challenges facing organisations setting out to introduce BCM programmes.

Summary

The age of digitality has catapulted organisations and individuals into a new age of connectedness that requires much greater vigilance to safeguard digital assets. What is required is the development of digital resilience – a term that denotes the need to be aware that threats to digital assets can arise internally as well as externally. Digital resilience is similar to the CERT notion of a system capable of surviving an attack and completing its mission, except that the resilience refers to the human component of the socio-technical system. Intentional or accidental disruption of systems can result from the human component of an information and communication system or technology and organisations should establish clear policies that guide behaviour in the event of disruption. More importantly, this chapter sought to draw attention to the fact that organisational culture, the type of employees recruited to work in an organisation, routines and training all collectively contribute to whether an organisation is digitally resilient or not. These fundamentals of organisational behaviour will ultimately determine whether the organisation can recover and how well it recovers from an attack on its infrastructure or systems. This chapter considered the manner in which large, complex infrastructure companies structure technology to ensure that the "holes" in the Swiss cheese do not line up and allow intrusion. Similarly, we considered the layered nature of protective measures that ensure that physically and digitally the organisation protects itself. However, the chapter further explored how many interruptions can be internally incubated and that sound personnel practices should be in place to ensure that employees have a means of airing grievances or concerns. In the next chapter we examine how best to initiate and plan for BCM to inculcate this awareness of digital resilience such that it becomes part of an organisation's culture.

Study Questions

1   Conduct an audit of an organisation you know well based on the digital resilience framework set out in Figure 3.1. Your analysis should concentrate on the four quadrants in the framework, including digital drivers, threats, dependencies and consequences. Consider how the organisation might improve its resilience through implementing best practices in BCM.
2   Visit the CERT page at Carnegie Mellon University's Software Engineering Institute (http://www.cert.org) and conduct research on the prevalence of insider threats in organisations. What will be the

impact of social media on such threats as the influence of Web 2.0 becomes more pervasive?

3   Research a recent incident where a company experienced a digital security breach. How did the company manage the incident and what was the impact of this breach on the company long term? Develop recommendations for improving the digital security and resilience.

4 Initiating, Redefining and Planning for Business Continuity Management

The Scope of Business Continuity Management

Introduction

The purpose of this chapter is to investigate the preliminary steps in the BCM process. Our aim is to demonstrate that while the generic process is applicable to most organisations, the starting point in that process will differ between organisations. The point at which an organisation commences the continuity process will depend on a range of factors including industry context (for example, some industries have a more obvious dependence upon information systems or upon tightly coupled supply chain linkages), organisational experience of business interruption (utility breakdown, supplier failure or exposure to the consequences of extreme weather conditions), and the professional background of the manager tasked to lead and manage the BC process. The drivers of change have a tendency to change. For example, Swartz and colleagues (1995) and Honour (2002) reported the influence of terrorism in the City of London and New York as key drivers for BC within the finance sector, respectively. In a more recent survey (Woodman, 2006: 4) highlighted the growing influence of corporate governance and legislation (Chapter 2) as drivers, in addition to raised awareness among a wide variety of stakeholders including insurers, auditors, potential and existing customers and government. Although corporate governance has recently overtaken existing customers as the most reported driver of engaging in BCM, it is clear that the decision to initiate and redefine the process is motivated by many influences.

Several strategies may be adopted by organisations in their efforts to establish continuity management within their organisations. Each of these – reactive, proactive and interactive – is introduced as a precursor to the sequence of activities that have been found to provide the most suitable foundation for the initiation of planning for BC (Chapter 5).

This chapter then examines the sequence of activities regarded as important to the initiation of continuity management within organisations. Following this, it concludes with a consideration of why we need a shift in the mindset which influences the way crises are examined so that planning focuses on both recovery and prevention, while continuously learning from an organisation's experiences, and those of others.

The Continuity Management Process

Figure 4.1 portrays the BCM process as comprising four distinct phases: initiation and redefinition, planning, implementation and operational management. BS 25999 refers to the first of these stages as "understanding the organisation", which emphasises an important aspect of initiation; namely, that the entire process must be firmly rooted within the context of existing organisational processes to prevent BCM appearing to be an alien, incongruous and ill-fitting addition. This is a similar approach to the planning approaches used for business or strategic planning, where managers establish corporate goals and then undertake a strategic analysis of the organisation and its environment in order to choose the most appropriate strategy. This is followed by the implementation of the chosen strategy. Typically, this process of analysis, choice and implementation is known as "strategy formulation" (Mintzberg, 1994). This formulated approach to planning (that is, analysis + choice = the successful implementation of strategy) is not without its pitfalls (Huy and Mintzberg, 2003). Changes beyond the control of the organisation may render the choice of strategy a failure. Equally, unexpected opportunities may lead to a change in the organisation's intended strategy.

The BCM process portrayed in Figure 4.1 differs in two importance respects from the wider activity of strategic or business planning. In many cases, organisations have long established departments, activities and experiences of strategic planning. Since the first edition of this book, BCM has, in some organisations, matured as a business process and in such cases rather than initiation of BCM from a position of absence, this stage involves a periodic redefinition of the goals and scope of BCM to reflect the changing posture of threats which an organisation might face. For example, threats such as a flu pandemic might be more aptly considered to fall under the remit of a BC team today than it did even four years ago. Cooper (2006) cites data from the experience of an outbreak of SARS (Severe Acute Respiratory Syndrome) in Toronto, Canada. Tourism in the province of Ontario lost an estimated C$2 billion due to visitor cancellations, with the hotel industry bearing a loss of C$125 million. Four major conventions were cancelled in Toronto, resulting in 50,000 room reservations being cancelled. Across Ontario 15,000 people were quarantined.

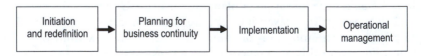

Figure 4.1 The continuity management process.

Increasingly, it may be argued that, in addition to business and service continuity, the unit of analysis should be the supply chain. The recall of millions of Dell and Apple laptop batteries shone the light of publicity on these two companies although the battery manufacturer was Sony (Fowler, 2006). Retailers in particular have long recognised the importance of supply chain issues as evidenced by the speed with which they seize the initiative in cases such as Perrier Water and Cadbury's chocolate contaminations. However, for many organisations, initiation appears the most apt term given that BCM is still not on the management agenda. This view is supported by an extensive survey of UK managers from which Woodman (2006) reported that 49 per cent of respondent businesses engaged in BC, a fall of 2 per cent on the previous year. Hurley-Hanson (2006) surveyed US companies in New York City and the west coast, and found that firms that had been directly affected by the World Trade Centre disaster were less likely than counterparts on the west coast to have improved their crisis preparedness planning. These results echoed similar findings in surveys conducted by the Society for Human Resource Management (SHRM) in the US (SHRM, 2001, 2002).

In contrast to strategic management, BCM seeks to put into place resources, activities and processes that, it is hoped, will never be used. The challenge of initiation and redefinition is to establish need, interest, support (financial and leadership) and a clear remit for ongoing continuity planning activities (Chapter 5). A further difference is the inclusion of operational management in addition to implementation (see Figure 4.1). Implementation (Chapter 6) considers how organisations can manage the process of change to incorporate and integrate continuity management where previously it did not exist. The operational management of continuity management (Chapter 6) refers to the instigation of recovery activities in the event of a crisis.

The continuity management process should be regularly reviewed and updated to ensure that the resulting plans remain appropriate. Redefinition emphasises the importance of revisiting the scope of such activities as expertise and understanding evolves (which, then, is influenced by the testing and auditing of BC plans as we discuss in Chapter 7 along with continuous scanning of the BC environment). However, before we begin our examination of initiation and redefinition, it is appropriate to examine some general principles of planning which apply equally to this chapter and the next, in which the planning processes specifically concerned with BC are considered in greater detail.

Planning to Plan

Planning without discovery is a time-consuming and expensive self-fulfilling prophecy. If, *ex ante*, we understand the issues that will give rise to the plan itself, why should the manager undertake any analytical activities? Planning, therefore, and planners themselves should be immersed in the discovery of what is *not* known, often found in places where it is *not* expected. For instance, a BC manager in a car manufacturing company might assume that there is no risk of virus attack to the long-established electronic purchasing system used with its suppliers of components, only to find that the company has decided to introduce internet-based purchasing. Not only has the technology changed, but also the threat of attack and the linkages between one department (purchasing) and others (administration and central data storage) have now been created. The planner can only plan once she or he has *discovered* that such changes have occurred.

There is also the question of *mindset*. Social scientists such as Hanson (1969) have recognised that our mental models, prejudices and views of the world are "in the seeing from the outset". For example, in a critique of a number of studies of race and intelligence, Gould (1996) found little evidence of deliberate manipulation but many indications of extreme bias in the selections of samples, recordings of data and finally in the interpretation of findings. The findings, for example, of influential scientists including the nineteenth-century anthropologist Samuel Morton and, more recently, Hans Jürgen Eysenck (1952) owed more to their prior prejudicial subjectivity than to true and objective science, asserted Gould (1996). Similarly the scope and nature of BCM will reflect the prior prejudicial subjectivity of those commissioning it and those charged with introducing it. If introduced as a response to a particular problem, it may be more difficult to extend its scope further. Analysts and managers may be unable to consider new scenarios (such as the need for greater digital resilience as demonstrated in Chapter 3) or the impact of new problems upon well-established systems. For example, the response of the British Airports Authority in introducing tight restrictions upon hand luggage and carriage of liquids on British air travellers caused mayhem as baggage handling equipment was unable to cope with the increased quantity of "traffic" and with the small size of the units being transported. This is easy to identify with hindsight but would it have been possible to have employed analysis and scenario planning to develop foresight?

Toft and Reynolds (1997) and Elliott and Smith (2006) have criticised the failure of many organisations to learn from hindsight, let alone foresight. Hindsight refers to a failure to learn obvious lessons from past interruptions. A creative understanding of an organisation, its suppliers and customers, coupled with an ability to consider the lessons of history and alternative scenarios is a difficult to achieve, but is an essential pre-requisite of effective BCM.

One of the first issues facing an organisation setting out to develop a BC plan is who should have primary responsibility for the research, planning, analysis and drafting of preliminary plans. Although the planning process requires a dedicated project manager, it is normally with senior management support. Progress in relation to BC activities should be reported regularly to the top management team (TMT) or appropriate committee. Woodman's (2006) survey indicated that the board is viewed as the most important stakeholder in the process, with 77 per cent of organisations reporting progress back to the main board.

Elliott and colleagues (1999a) suggested that this project management task should not be undertaken by an IT specialist within an IT department. This is because of the original emphasis upon IT within the BC profession (reflecting its disaster recovery roots) and the danger that it will be seen as a technical-only activity. The appointment of an IT specialist may be seen as an indicator that BCP is merely an information technology issue, with little human impact or involvement, and temporary in its nature. As we discuss later, the choice of personnel can provide a powerful signal to staff within an organisation, and stakeholders outside, about the nature of BC and may, right from the start, play a key part in determining the success or otherwise of the process. From previous studies (see, for example, Elliott et al., 1999a) many successful organisations have placed BC within a central department that has responsibility for strategic planning and analysis among other tasks. A useful model includes a steering group to support the project manager. This steering group should include senior and influential staff from different business units or departments.

A further problem which arises from the outset of any planning process, whether strategic, functional or BC-oriented, is the "legacy hindrance". Organisations are complex socio-technical systems which reflect antecedents such as decisions, systems, structures, values and beliefs. The mutual influence of strategy upon an organisation's structure is long recognised (Chandler, 1962) and, despite considerable debate in this respect, structure should remain a focus of attention since it offers one manner in which the organisation can be viewed and, therefore, analysed. The way in which one perceives an organisation can often determine the decisions and actions that are taken (Snyder and Ebeling, 1992; Herbane and Rouse, 2000).

In a BC context (and in practical terms) many organisations find themselves in a "brownfield" planning context. By this, managers involved must recognise that they cannot make sweeping changes to the organisation and its social and technical systems. They must plan in their context. This does not necessarily mean that they should eschew possibilities for a greenfield planning. For example, in the early 1990s when a US bank decided to locate its European headquarters in the UK, it deliberately avoided a building in the City of London where the majority of rivals and suppliers were located, preferring instead a site some distance away. Here it could exploit building designs to accommodate business recovery requirements better and was also less at risk from threats of interruption from transportation strikes and indiscriminate terrorist activity. The FSA (2005) noted that few financial sector organisations had primary and recovery sites outside the M25, representing a huge concentration and potential vulnerability. Some other organisations rely on luck. When fire destroyed a B&Q superstore, a British DIY retailer, it was fortunate to find replacement premises available less than 100 metres away. Hence, the challenge facing planners resulting from brownfield and greenfield situations is not dissimilar to those which emanate from business process redesign (Hammer, 1990; Mumford and Hendricks, 1996).

The perception of failure may also influence the discovery process that precedes the development of BC plans. In some organisations, failure is considered to be a positive side-effect from which discovery and subsequent improvements can be effected. Kumar and colleagues (2000) recount that Sony's failure in the development of products such as the 2-inch diskette produced avenues to the development of games consoles. Equally, planners should be aware of symbolism that failure can bring. The plan could be blamed, or specific individuals could be blamed. The failure itself is more nebulous and without a thorough understanding, and could lead to little, if any, improvement should similar circumstances arise in the future (see Box 4.1).

Box 4.1 Who's to Blame? What's to Blame?

On 5 May 2000, computer servers and email systems were shut down. The "love bug" virus spread from South East Asia as companies in different countries logged on. Primarily affected were computer systems using Microsoft Outlook programs and users quickly found that the "worm" had buried itself into hard drives. Struck by the virus, Germco (a fictional name) quickly invoked its plans for widespread virus disruption. The virus type had not been seen before and therefore could not be stopped. Users logged in as usual and, intrigued by the "love letter" opened, the message with disastrous effects for seven working days. A few days later the "inquiry" began. Germco managers blamed the IT division for a lack of systems protection. The IT division refuted this, arguing that user "naivety" generated, propagated and compounded the problem. The solution, it seemed, was a simple one – to update virus software and prevent similar viruses entering the systems in the future. In early July 2000, the email systems closed again for three days. The virus had remained dormant in the in-box of an absent colleague and, upon his return, began to spread. This time, preparedness was not to blame. Instead, a lack of communications and a willingness to change led to the re-occurrence. Staff had not been told how to upgrade their desktop virus software and still continued with the inappropriate practices of using the preview window in their software and opening unusual messages. People's behaviour – specifically a reluctance to learn positively from failure – led to the loss of 4 per cent of the working year.

The experience of Germco indicates the need for continuity management to be an ongoing, iterative process. The lessons from the first
interruption were not heeded. Unsurprisingly, therefore, the preconditions for a subsequent interruption remained in place. Furthermore,
the misdirection of blame can serve as a deflection away from the real
causes of a crisis.

Furthermore, the implication that a systematic and formulated approach
to planning is a rational one does not always hold true. Long established
are studies which suggest that decision making can be distorted through
a phenomenon known as "Groupthink" (Janis, 1983), where individuals
coalesce around the ideas of influential persons in group decision making.

The notions of rationality in managerial behaviour and decision making have been challenged since the early work of Simon (1957) through the
notion of bounded rationality, whereby the individual (or in a collective)
is cognitively impeded due to the inability to process infinite amounts of
information in a limited period of time. This is compounded by the differing perspectives that individuals may have of a situation or environment.
Although this should not be taken to suggest that managers act irration-
ally in decision making, limited rationality presents what Eisenhardt and
Zbaracki (1992: 22) term a "heuristic perspective", whereby aspects of the
decision-making process can be rational, while others are not.

More recently, the view that perceptions influence behaviour (that is,
decisions and actions) has been refined to include a consideration of experiential influences, values and beliefs, and the filtering of information in the
development of managers' perceptions (Day and Lord, 1992; Finkelstein
and Hambrick, 1988). Others have examined the links between managers'
perceptions of the environment and organisational performance (Dutton
and Dukerich, 1991; Thomas et al., 1993), suggesting that there is a clear
link between how managers perceive their organisation and environment
and how they subsequently act to achieve predetermined goals and that
external influences have a greater impact on managers' perceptions of
functional experience and conditioning (Chattopadhyay et al., 1999).
Furthermore, a study by Ashmos, and colleagues (1997) found that senior
managers were more likely to participate in a crisis issue that were labelled
"opportunities" than one that was simply labelled a "crisis". Hence, it is
important how we frame planning for continuity.

In short, those involved in the planning process should be aware of the
limitations of any planning methodology which they employ. Rather than
dismiss the formal planning process out of hand, creative solutions should
be sought. Nonetheless, there are many activities which characterise
BCP (Chapter 5). Prior to that, however, we turn to how planning can be
initiated and maintained.

The interim goal of the planning process is to develop a BC plan (or set of plans) which can be invoked (used) in the event of an interruption. Planning marks neither the start nor the end of the BCM process (Figure 4.1). The ultimate goal of the planning process is to improve the resilience of the business to interruptions, thereby protecting the organisation's operating or trading position.

Basic Strategies Underlying Business Continuity Provision

Figure 4.2 outlines the nature of the basic strategies underlying the BC provision found in companies.

A key barrier to initiating BC will include costs in terms of time, money and opportunity. This is particularly the case with small and medium-sized enterprises (SMEs) (Bird, 2002). For example, Spillan and Hough (2003) suggested that 85 per cent of small businesses in the US did not have a crisis management team and that the experience of a crisis by a small company was the principal stimulus for becoming concerned about organisational vulnerability. Whether these firms had the resources to allay their concerns was a vexed question. Often smaller companies are resource poor and consider themselves unable to devote the financial or human resources to the BC activities examined in this chapter and the next. However, with limited resources SMEs may be more vulnerable to suffering adverse effects from interruptions as Bird (2002) argued. Bird (2002) provided two illustrations of these vulnerabilities.

- A small food processing company's key account was with a manor supermarket chain. A severe flood in its processing facility led to the sewage contamination of their premises. The supermarket required just-in-time delivery which the SME was unable to provide. The result was immediate loss of cash flow and by the time the insurers paid they were out of business.

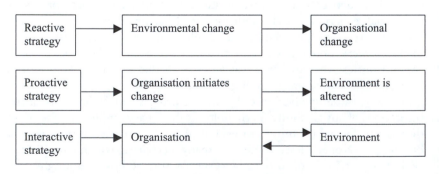

Figure 4.2 Basic strategies underlying business continuity provision.

- A small plastics company lost its main injection-moulding machine in a small fire. The rest of its facilities were unscathed. But the machine was key to every process and the replacement of such equipment took three months. The company employed a subcontractor to fulfil its contracts, and resolved its short-term difficulties. In the longer term it discovered that it had merely introduced its customers to a new supplier to whom they eventually went direct. The company went bankrupt.

Bird (2002) makes a case for such organisations to tailor their BCM efforts to their resources, but also to invest sufficiently to deal with some of the key potential interruptions. For instance, in the US, the Red Cross provides access to basic training for SMEs. The organisation provides a BC guide for companies, as well as an emergency management guide (Red Cross, 2008). Katrina disaster in 2005 supplied evidence of how vulnerable to natural disasters companies may be. It has provided pause for thought about how prepared cities and governments are to deal with events which may or may not be due to global warming.

Should it not be feasible to have an interactive strategy, the organisation should at least be proactive and put in place measures which take into account the range of internal and external factors it might be exposed to. In practice, it is perhaps inevitable that many organisations will, in the first instance, initiate BC provision as part of a reactive strategy to cope with a crisis triggered by a specific event, either internal or external. Some organisations might then move towards being more proactive. It has been found that many finance sector organisations (investment banks and insurance companies) in the UK had experienced some form of interruption prior to setting up a BC unit and capability. These interruptions varied from the secondary effects of bombs and a major fire at a site in Europe to parcel bombs and telecommunications lines being severed by construction equipment during building works. However, since 2000, continuity managers' concerns have extended from a primary focus upon internal issues to a growing awareness of external threats. It is clear, however, following 9/11, bombings in London and Madrid, the 2004 Indian Ocean Tsunami, Hurricane Katrina and the spread of the so-called bird flu (the H5N1 virus), that external threats are increasingly viewed as significant. An outcome of the August 2006 alleged terrorist plot to use liquid explosives on US-bound aircraft from the UK is that rumour and threat can create almost as much business interruption as a real explosion. As the name suggests, it is terror and fear that are the strongest weapons, rather than their tangible manifestations alone. This has implication as organisations decide upon those hazards/threats for which they have a specific plan, since the list of priorities might not be determined simply by the likely losses and probabilities, but the *perceived* losses and probabilities influenced by stakeholders whose awareness may be socially amplified through the volume of media reporting that a specific issue or event attracts (Kasperson et al., 1988).

As the environment changes more rapidly, an interactive BC strategy is best suited to the development of plans to be used in a crisis or disruption. Resource limitations may impede the ability of organisations to take such an approach given the internal, market and macro-environmental pressure placed upon them. It is in this context that for the organisation to develop an interactive BC strategy, the initiation of the planning process be treated as a high priority, for it is at this stage that the remit, commitment and resources for subsequent activities is determined. Consequently, the focus for the remainder of the chapter is the initiation and redefinition of the continuity management process.

The Initiation and Redefinition of Business Continuity Planning

Initiation and redefinition are the stages at which formal strategic decisions are made to undertake, review and evaluate BCM, to set policy, define structures, allocate resources and agree specific projects and monitoring mechanisms. As senior managers become more aware of potential threats, it is probable that initial decisions will be reviewed and further (or fewer) resources allocated as a result. From this, the organisation can establish the objectives and scope of continuity activities and begin to shift the mindset of employees away from recovery to one of recovery *and* prevention.

BCM sets out to change the behaviour of managers and employees. The object is to sensitise everyone to the possibility and impact of business interruption and the need to take active steps to guard against it. The initiation and redefinition stage, with its strategic perspective, is the appropriate arena in which to consider how BC will be managed. Careful consideration of these issues at the outset will facilitate operational management during the implementation stage (Chapters 5 and 6).

Figure 4.3 sets out the BCM process and identifies what must be done to initiate or redefine it. Decisions made at this stage will determine fundamentally the approach, or mindset, adopted by the organisation to continuity management.

Decide Scope and Set Policy

The role of the management board is to decide how broad or constrained the focus of BC provision is to be. This will involve a consideration of the business processes that are to be covered by continuity provision, and the extent to which external continuity services will be used. For instance, the remit of BC activities may be confined to administrative or head-quarter offices for organisations that have emergency management plans for their operations at factory, plant or facility level. A further decision

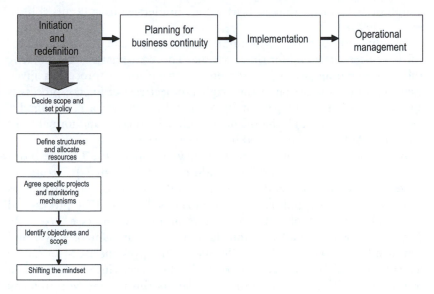

Figure 4.3 Initiation in the continuity management process.
Source: adapted from Elliott et al. (1999a)

involves where the BCM team should be located. This can vary widely from the IT department (which can signal a priority placed on the IT recovery activities) to the human resources or personnel function (which signals an orientation that is influenced more by the recognition that staff are the most important resources in prevention and recovery).

The top management team (TMT) has also to determine the mindset that will drive BCM in a strategic sense. The UK government reiterates this view in its advice to companies:

> Board-level commitment is vital. Without top down direction, support and ownership, success in both the BCM process and activating the BCP will be difficult, if not impossible.
>
> (Power, 1999: 4)

Once the TMT has made these policy decisions, it should issue a clear statement about the importance of BCM, and make sure that it appears in communications channels such as the annual report, the company newspaper and the company intranet. In this respect practice varies widely among different companies. Calor Gas uses human resources managers to drive awareness, J Sainsbury uses its active continuity team, while the Royal Bank of Scotland uses both informal and formal communication forums (including "roadshows", videos, newspapers, and the annual report) to communicate the importance of BC. These organisations acknowledge that the extent to which the TMT is seen as giving BC a high priority affects the ease with which implementation occurs (Elliott et al., 1999b).

Clearly, additional policy recommendations will be made once plans for BC have been drawn up for the first time. This continual process whereby the understanding reached at the end of the planning process is given feedback into a discussion of the original objectives set for the process is an extremely important part of BCM. The best means of ensuring this feedback loop is through the BC organisational structure and formal links with the TMT. This is discussed in the next section.

In addition to the formulation of a policy document, the TMT or board may appoint BC "champions" (in addition to a dedicated BC team) to drive the process at local or departmental level. The role of such champions is to support, in a tangible and practical manner, both the BCP process and the implementation of any planning recommendations (see Box 4.2). These champions should therefore have a certain amount of power and command the respect of their colleagues. This gives the BCM initiative legitimacy, and it can help to persuade the unconvinced of the need to implement BC practices. In the early days of this process, within many organisations the BC function was treated as the last stop for IT personnel before they retired or were made redundant. The assumption was that these employees had technical skills and were well placed to be the guardians of technical systems. As a result, within these organisations the image of BC was damaged and resulted in the low morale in the emergent teams as they were seen as a career cul-de-sac. Despite the technical expertise of team leaders, they lacked critical people management and leadership skills. They lacked experience of interacting in a persuasive and influential capacity. Underpinning their work was the assumption that their plans would most likely never be invoked. An objective, therefore, was to spend as little money as possible on the employees in the BC function. The emergence of BC as a profession is exemplified by the BCI/DRII's ten standards of professional competence (see Chapter 2) and is reflected in Woodman's (2006) survey. Although there are indications of immense progress there remains a long tail of inactivity and disengagement.

Box 4.2 Senior Management Reluctance in Flames

In one organisation based in the City of London, we interviewed executives who admitted to the frustrations they felt at the organisational assumptions about BC that existed in their organisation. They illustrated this with the example of a senior executive who had paid little attention to their efforts to obtain her support – she alleged that there were more important business issues to be attended to. During the conversation however, it became clear that there was a major fire taking place at a bank very close by. In fact, they could see the smoke rising from the building through the window of the office in which the meeting was taking place. This incident was reported widely that evening and could therefore be used by the team to convince the reluctant senior executive of the importance of being prepared.

Source: Elliott et al. (1999a)

Although it would be rare to see a City of London-based firm with no continuity capability today, elsewhere and within some other sectors such reluctance is still commonplace. The example of the frustrated BC manager is instructive, as it is not only in the BCM field that senior managers adopt this type of attitude. An analogy may be drawn with the response of senior managers in large companies to the challenge posed by the internet. Rosabeth Moss-Kanter's (2001a) review of the strategic responses of corporations to the web mirrors the type of attitude and cultural response we observed in respect of BCM. This attitude speaks of mixed messages – on the one hand, senior managers are aware that they have to be seen to be responding to the internet but, on the other hand, they are not entirely comfortable with this and lack a strategic understanding of exactly how this new technology might be exploited for organisational advantage. Moss-Kanter calls such organisations "wanna-dots" and she illustrated how those in charge of online strategy and ventures are set up in a manner which can only lead to failure. In the box below we have used her lessons about how to sabotage online ventures as a blueprint to show how the same process is at work for continuity teams.

Five Ways to Sabotage Business Continuity Management!

1   Recruit IT staff with poorly developed leadership skills and who lack understanding of the potential of business continuity. This often means that a lack of understanding of business areas will translate into a highly technically focused initiative; sadly it also often means that the initiative becomes reduced to essentially a series of lists of telephone numbers and rules on what to do after an incident.

2   Recruit staff who do not have political influence and who do not have well-developed relationships across functions.

3   Sprinkle responsibility for business continuity in an uneven way across organisational functions. (Be inconsistent in which functional or divisional heads have to assume responsibility for business continuity. This way there is much scope for such individuals to shirk responsibility and handle the activity in a sceptical manner.)

4　Form a committee to develop the organisation's policy on business continuity management. Recruit to this committee staff who are already highly committed to many other important projects and do not allow them time to devote to this new initiative. This will ensure that not enough time will be devoted to business continuity and at critical times all you have to do is to produce your lists to satisfy any regulatory requirements.

5　Treat each business unit as a separate entity and do not link rewards into achievements in business continuity. In fact, within business units, do not link reward systems to the team effort at all. This ensures that business continuity is regarded as something that has no value at all to individuals or teams.

Define Structures

It is important that the structure through which BCM is to be implemented is considered at the initiation stage. From observations of company practice (Elliott et al., 1999a; Elliott and Smith, 2006), the structure featured in Figure 4.4 represents a useful model. The key feature of this organisational structure is that it ensures close contact between the BCM team and the board on an ongoing basis. It also makes provision for all business units to "own" their plans and implement these themselves. However, as Woodman (2006) reports, there is much evidence that BCM is still largely focused upon IT, facilities and HR, and to a lesser extent upon functions such as marketing, production and outsourcing. Given the primary value adding nature of marketing and production, this may be seen as a point for concern and reflect the slow pace at which a continuity management mindset permeates organisations.

Allocate Resources

The BC strategy will determine both the financial and the human resources required to facilitate the BC process. To a large extent the commitment made will depend upon the mindset that the board adopts and its assessment of the perceived risks versus the potential business impact that such risks might have. This type of risk assessment will often involve judgements based on historical data. The Financial Services Agency (FSA) (2005) reported that despite the presence of many of the building blocks for effective crisis management, few organisations had provided adequate empowered spending in the event of a major incident.

Some immediate costs will be incurred by the execution of the planning stage of the BCM process. They will be determined by the extent of the planning process, and whether or not external assistance is required with it. In some organisations, external consultants are used to take the BCM

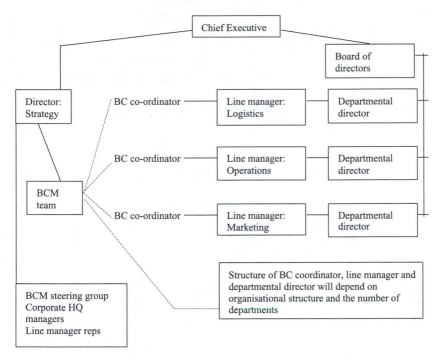

Figure 4.4 Organisational structure model for effective business continuity management.

team through one full cycle (covering the most critical parts of the business) of the planning process. The in-house team will work alongside the consultants and build up a knowledge base. Once a pre-determined period had passed, and the in-house team had been trained, the work is executed internally and external experts consulted only for specialised areas of the process. Such areas may include data vaulting and mirroring, and activities where equipment from a third party may be used (for example, office space and telecommunications). Fixed contract costs for the use of third party "business recovery centres" will often cost tens of thousands of dollars per month and may be subject to a maximum occupation period (up to eight weeks per year including occupation for testing) and minimum contract durations (two to three years). The opportunity cost of service contracts and external consultants (if used as part or wholly for the planning process) is the lost opportunity for in-house resources and a greater level of in-house expertise. In addition to direct salary and service provider costs, BCM carries a number of less obvious costs that should be recognised but, equally, balanced against the value that improved resilience and effective recovery can provide. These include those costs incurred if staff are seconded from a function to support planning, training or testing activities. Added to these is the cost of testing BC plans. A portfolio of testing techniques are available to organisations (Chapter 7) and, as tests vary in their scale and complexity, so too do their costs rise in terms of redirecting staff to recovery rehearsals rather than normal operational duties. Nevertheless, the financial support for BCM should be considered a strategic investment given the strategic consequences that a failure to respond to a crisis might generate.

The issue of knowledge and skills is clearly very important in the planning process – for both the BC team and the coordinators at the business unit level. It is becoming apparent that as continuity management becomes more focused on interruptions that are not solely IT related, all those involved in this area should have the following skills and attributes:

• Good communication skills to enable internal awareness raising.
• External liasion with key stakeholders.
• A thorough understanding of how the business operates as a whole.
• An understanding of the key value adding activities of the organisation.

In a study of the stages that organisations move through as they approach greater IT maturity, Hirschheim and Verrijn-Stuart (1996) found that the skills cited above, rather than technical skills, were the requisite capabilities that enabled IT to be managed for organisational advantage.

The BC team requires (in addition to the above) the following capabilities:

• Strategic analysis and risk assessment skills, to conduct the BC planning stage.
• Project management skills.
• Change management skills, to manage the implementation and operational management stages.
• An understanding of quality improvement management.

Agree Projects and Monitoring Mechanisms

Specific projects must be agreed and a decision has to be taken on how BCM is to be "rolled-out" across the organisation. Figure 4.5 sets out a suggested structure for the control of projects.

The project team should be led by a project manager, drawn from the BC team, who will work as a facilitator and coordinator of working groups. The project team should consist of appropriate staff from the BC team/unit or external consultants, the business unit coordinators and BC champions, and other managers from the business units.

The project team should drive the process through the use of regular progress reports, which should be submitted upwards to the BCM board, and then ultimately to the board of directors. The Central Computer and Telecommunications Agency (CCTA, 1995b) also suggests that project

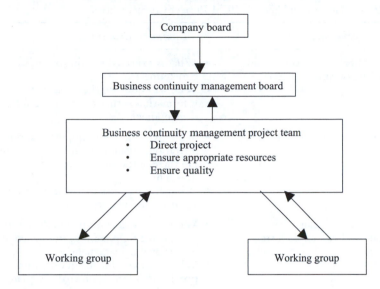

Figure 4.5 Suggested business continuity project management structure.

plans should contain five characteristics which have been applied to the context of initiating a BCM process in Table 4.1.

Initiation is clearly a crucial part of the BCM process, as it determines the cultural environment within which implementation and operational management will take place. BC managers comment on the difficulties that they often experience at the implementation stage with embedding the process within business units. The seeds for success in implementation are sown during the initiation phase. Arguably this is where the organisation's attitude towards BC will be set and it is vital that the issues raised during this first stage of the process be given due consideration. This is the phase of the planning process where the leadership of the organisation will create certain assumptions about the nature of BCM. These assumptions will permeate the entire organisation and establish the mindset or cultural attitude of the organisation towards BCM (Schein, 1992). Furthermore, without an "executive sponsor" for BC, it is argued that insufficient financial and management support will be given to the activity (Fitzgerald, 1995). It is therefore imperative that the planning process, beginning with initiation, be approached in a strategic manner.

Identifying Objectives and Scope

Organisations establish their objectives, which vary in terms of scope and time. The broadest and longest term objective – the mission or vision – is often the best known of those generated by an organisation. The desire to be number one in a market, to reflect social, ethical and environmental

Table 4.1 Generic and Specific BCM Project Characteristics

Generic project characteristics	BCM initiation characteristics
Specific project outcomes and quality assessment criteria	• What is expected within specific timeframes? • Who will evaluate the quality of information gathering, training and plan development?
Start and end dates for each stage	• When will planning, implementation, operational management start and finish? • Do these dates vary by department or division? • What are the dates for testing, going live, auditing and maintenance?
The clear allocation of responsibilities for each stage	• Which departments and employees are responsible for planning, implementation, operational management? • Who is responsible for information provision, information analysis, plan authorship, and plan authorisation?
The identification of important dependencies	• Upon whom are those involved above dependent for authorisation, information or analysis (including legal, regulatory and technical advice)?
Dates for project meetings	• Given project outcomes and date timelines for the commencement and completion of each stage identified above, how is this timeline punctuated with meetings of coordinators, managers and the top management team of the organisation to ensure consistency, clarity and quality in the development of business continuity resources?

values, or to continuously innovate, may seem far removed from BCP. Such objectives do not conflict with continuity management. Without BC provisions, an organisation's vision or mission could be threatened and without a linkage between an organisation's strategy and BC, efforts directed at the latter can be perceived as of lesser importance. However, due regard to the organisation's mission gives rise to the term "mission-critical", referring to processes, resources and people which are most directly associated with the accomplishment of the mission. J Sainsbury uses the organisation's mission statement, and those of its business units, as the starting point for the BCM process. Continuity is thus focused upon the organisation's stated strategy (reported in Elliott et al., 1999a).

For e-commerce companies, information technology is a "mission-critical" resource which ought to receive early attention in a BC sense.

However, such attention is highly variable. For example, a UK-based online travel agency operated for nearly a year without any disaster recovery provisions, only to find that a server failure was the trigger to seek further assistance in protecting the company's systems. Feldman (1998) reported that many US companies failed to manage short-term interruptions (such as to power), the introduction of alternative facilities, develop detailed recovery plans, or continuously evaluate emergency procedures. For predominantly online businesses, the impact of losing critical infrastructure such as telecommunications renders it incapable of taking and fulfilling orders and communicating with clients. When a digger damaged a telecommunications cable in Manchester (UK), one of the country's largest online electrical retailers found itself in a position of losing sales estimated to be in the region of £500,000 for each day of inactivity (Lettice, 2002).

A further "mission-critical" resource is postal and distribution systems. Many companies have partnership arrangements with courier and delivery companies. Accordingly, managers should give due regard to their exposure to an interruption arising with their delivery partners. For example, Petroni (1999) found that the Banca Commerciale Italiana's involvement in a system of inter-bank settlements led to the introduction of continuity planning for information systems in 1992. The objective of this planning was to ensure the objective of "zero downtime" (Petroni, 1999: 104).

The use of Information and Communication Technologies (ICT) is now commonplace. Indeed, companies are now increasingly reliant on shared technology or information from their suppliers, not just in their country of origins, but overseas as well. Table 4.2 shows the use of ICT for purchasing operations, using a variety of technologies, including the web, email, extranets and electronic data interchanges. From the table, we can see that there are high rates of usage of such technologies across all sectors and across many industrialised nations, and thereby discern the potential vulnerability of such systems to interruptions. Furthermore, as companies move towards lean models of production and just-in-time stockless production, the need for continuity in the supply chain is increasingly critical as companies tend, no longer, to have large warehouses of stock available to continue operations in the event of a disruption at a supplier's facilities.

Beyond the broad remit and purpose of the mission or vision, organisations set detailed objectives because they provide a foci for action, generate benchmarks which serve as a control system, and enable managers to evaluate performance over a specified period. In addition, specific goals have been argued to improve the motivation of the individual to attain a predetermined level of proficiency (Locke, 1968). This is particularly important for BCP in organisations where the activity is new and/or where the planning is being undertaken by a project manager whose responsibilities vary more widely than simply BC. It is therefore advisable for organisations to set goals for BCM. For instance (Elliott et al., 1999a)

Table 4.2 Technology and the Supply Chain – an International Perspective

Country	Businesses ordering supplies online (%)	Businesses' online orders (%)	Businesses making online payments (%)	Technologies used to order goods from suppliers online (%)			
				E-mail	Web	Extranet	EDI
UK	45	14	28	77	85	9	18
France	21	13	7	55	61	18	27
Germany	45	24	20	82	85	13	13
Italy	28	14	10	88	61	7	7
Sweden	50	21	23	73	89	16	12
US	53	28	19	72	91	20	18
Canada	43	24	21	83	87	22	17
Japan	15	45	6	62	56	14	40

Source: Compiled from UK Online for Business (2000)

reported the BCM objectives for several UK and international companies (Table 4.3).

In each case a clear rationale existed, reflecting organisational priorities and resources. What you will also notice is that the objectives shown in Table 4.3 vary in terms of the organisation's experience and approach to BCM. The protection of mainframes reflects a disaster recovery philosophy (Chapter 1) whereas the protection of the head office marks the organisation's attempt to slowly introduce BCM, starting with the most important building. The most experienced company (the bank) has extended its BCM to the entire organisation, including the smallest of its branches. Objectives can also be phrased not only to refer to what is included and protection but also to encompass the philosophy of the company's approach to BC. King (1997: 17) found that the objective of one US credit card company's BC resources was to "make sure that the customer doesn't see anything they shouldn't . . . [and] making sure what could become a disaster doesn't become one". For this company, it is about maintaining the credibility of "business as usual" in the event of a disruption.

The objectives of BCP will influence the scope of planning activities. "Scope" refers to the staff, systems, facilities, business processes, suppliers and stakeholders to be included within the analysis and subsequent plan (see Box 4.3). The assurance of continuity has extended, in recent years, in scope from buildings, computers and information systems (a "facilities" focus) to include people and business processes – from hardware to "think-ware" or human capital. As the bombings and transport strikes of the

Table 4.3 Examples of BCM Objectives

Company type	BCP objective
Public authority	Protect mainframe systems
Energy supply company	Protect head office functions
Water company	Maintain supply to customers
Bank	Protect head office and branches
Automotive manufacturer	Supplier continuity
University	Continuity of teaching activities

early 1990s in the UK have indicated, there is little value in having buildings and working information systems if staff cannot access them. However, the FSA (2005) reports that an imbalance between IT and "people" resilience, with the latter remaining a point for concern within a number of organisations.

Box 4.3 Using Objectives and Scope as Foundations for Planning

Standard Chartered Bank, an international financial services company, manages the continuity management process from its Singapore headquarters. The company has formally defined the scope of continuity management activities as follows:

> To develop a BC plan for the main business units so they will be able to resume effective operations within an acceptable time-frame in the event of a disaster.

It continues by defining the meaning of a disaster in the context of the bank's operations:

> A sudden, unplanned, calamitous event, which results in a great amount of damage or loss. Any event which prohibits the bank's business units/critical business functions from gaining access to their premises for a period of a week or more.

From this, a series of objectives have been developed from the scope noted above:

- Provide for the safety and well being of people in the branch at the time of the disaster.

- Establish management succession and emergency powers.
- Identify critical businesses and supporting functions.
- Minimise immediate damage and losses.
- Resume critical business functions in temporary premises.
- Return to normal operations when the primary facility is restored.

The objectives can be seen to complement and support the scope of BCP. Furthermore, having established this series of objectives, continuity managers at Standard Chartered developed a number of assumptions designed to ensure that planning activities and investments would be focused to meet the most likely continuity needs:

- No access to the affected building for seven days.
- No more than one building will be affected concurrently by a disaster.
- Disaster occurs at the most vulnerable time for each function.
- IT recovery plan or disaster recovery plan is in place and tested.
- Only critical business functions are recovered and the less essential business functions can be postponed.
- Alternative staff and replacement equipment are available within planned timeframes.

In establishing scope and objectives for BC, it is apparent that this organisation recognises that in the event of a disaster or interruption it may not be possible to recover all operations immediately and simultaneously.

Source: Heng (1996)

Preliminary Steps

Where an organisation has no BC plans in place, it is advisable for a preliminary brief on the objectives, scope, investment requirements and timing to be prepared at this stage. This briefing document (or draft BC policy) should identify the following important themes which are necessary for the successful completion of the first BC plan:

- the objectives of the process;
- its scope;
- board level champion;
- involvement of third parties (suppliers, stakeholders);

- the intended level of detail and sophistication of the analysis;
- timing, including a realistic draft timetable;
- likely costs;
- budget.

It is essential that the rationale for introducing and retaining BCP, in addition to the briefing document, be communicated as fully as possible to all concerned. The involvement of as many people as possible will make it more effective. At this stage the involvement of staff from around the organisation is sought and negotiated. Problems of securing their input should be resolved, with board level support if necessary, as soon as practicably possible. This requires that the BC project manager possesses not only access to a senior executive but also relatively high status and good quality communication and negotiation skills. Such skills are particularly important since planning teams often work best if they comprise participants from different business areas (information systems, human resources, facilities, etc.) rather than comprise solely from one functional area (Herbane et al., 1997). In Chapter 1 we noted that the predecessor of BCP, disaster recovery planning, was dominated by practitioners with IT backgrounds.

Shifting the Mindset

Once the objectives and scope have been decided, a worthy step is to develop an understanding of the type of crisis which an organisation could face: that is, those which could reasonably be expected to occur. This is an important activity since there is a need to develop parameters of the organisation's exposure to interruptions or crises and associated needs. In addition, an understanding of the types of potential disruptions can be used to develop scenarios which are important for plans and their testing.

It has been argued that organisations themselves incubate the potential for accidents or business interruptions (Greiner, 1972; Perrow, 1984; Pauchant and Mitroff, 1992). That is, while the final trigger might be an uncontrollable external element (for example, earthquake, terrorist bomb), the weaknesses that permitted such a trigger to cause a crisis are within the control of the organisation that experienced the failure.

For example, lax management, poor procedures and a lack of appropriate investment were cited as key causes at Bhopal in 1984 (Shrivastava, 1987a) and at Chernobyl. The organisational crises triggered by the IRA's City of London bombs were largely determined by internal factors – the degree of centralisation, hardware and software back-up routines and out-of-hours staff communications. A gas explosion or earthquake might have had similar effects. Following the Bishopsgate bombing, the National Westminster Bank's data transfer routines were cited as a key factor in its ability to maintain operations. Conversely, the routines of the Hong Kong and Shanghai Bank Corporation did not facilitate a quick return to normality. The trigger, created by the bomb, only caused crises for some organisations (Herbane, 1997). Deutsche Bank in New York City, similarly had preparedness provisions in the form of a mirror site in central New Jersey when their New York offices were adversely affected during 9/11. The building, at 130 Liberty Street, Lower Manhattan, was not directly hit by the terrorist planes, but was extensively damaged by debris that cut across its north façade (LMDC, 2007). Different business models within an industry may also influence the impact of any common trigger upon a particular company. For example, Virgin airline was especially hard hit by the dramatically more rigorous security checks introduced in August 2006 because it is essentially a long haul carrier and is more heavily concentrated in Heathrow and Gatwick airports – two of the worst affected. "Competitors" with a greater short haul and airport coverage, such as BA and the budget carriers such as Ryanair and Easyjet, although affected, incurred fewer proportionate costs. For example, Virgin was forced to send empty planes across the Atlantic to collect stranded passengers. O'Leary (2006) of Ryanair and Harrison (2006) of Easyjet were reported as claiming that the greater resilience of their airlines was due to their model being based on quick aircraft turnarounds, efficient use of resources, direct selling, etc.

The critical issue here is that the trajectory of many organisational crises (and in most cases the success of recovery efforts) are influenced by events, decisions and actions that precede the crisis. While such causality may seem to be a statement of the apparent, planners should be aware that much can be learned from an examination of the events, decisions and actions that led to a crisis, and set into place measures which reduce these or similar malevolent events, decision and actions occurring in the future. The Virgin example highlights the importance of understanding how alternative business models may leave a particular organisation more or less exposed than its competitors, in particular circumstances. In addition to examining crises faced by the organisation in the past, it is often useful to learn from the experiences of others (see Box 4.4). Such learning is illustrated shortly from the experiences of Perrier. You will recall that a critical difference between disaster recovery and BCP is that the latter balances its focus upon both prevention *and* recovery.

Box 4.4 Crisis Management Strategies – The Airline Industry

Tragedies in the airline industry demonstrate the importance of preparedness in the event of a disaster. In September 1998, Swissair Flight 111 crashed near the coast of Nova Scotia. Within an hour of learning of the crisis, the regional vice-president, Walter Vollenweider, was answering press questions at New York's JFK airport. Furthermore, a 24 hour call centre was brought immediately into use and information, media and counselling services were offered during the aftermath of the crisis. Months after the incident, families and affected parties had access to their own "care-givers" employed and trained by Swissair to ease the post-crisis phase.

Swissair, having faced a crisis, recognised that not only was the immediate crisis recovery important to the company, its image and its stakeholders, the longer-term actions of the company would add to those upon which it would be judged.

The ValuJet crash of 1996 highlighted the importance of the pre-crisis phase and how the use of third parties in the provision of a service can lead to a crisis. SabreTech Inc. had been used by the airline to undertake routine maintenance. During the course of these activities it was alleged that maintenance employees were poorly trained and that (subsequent to the crash) the company had made a misleading statement in respect of SabreTech's improper handling and loading of oxygen canisters attributed as the cause. Since little was seemingly done to mitigate against the potential for a disaster to occur in this instance, the post-crisis phase of the crash led to the first criminal prosecution against the company and employees of a company associated with a maintenance failure. As Chapter 2 indicated, the widening of corporate liability along supply chains will increasingly require a more proactive, interactive strategy towards continuity provision.

Although the company has not faced a major incident involving fatalities, another airline which recognises the importance of being seen to be prepared, responsive and responsible in a crisis is Virgin Atlantic. The company has in place a website area that can be brought "online" in the event of disaster. The web page (www.virgin-atlantic.com/emergency) presents the following text:

> A Virgin Atlantic aircraft has been involved in an accident: The plane was flying from X(PLACE)X to X(PLACE)X on X(DATE)X. It took off from X(PLACE)X at X(TIME)X local time. The flight number is VS X(NUMBER)X.

> We are already working closely with emergency authorities involved and are channelling all our efforts into collecting information about the accident.

The existence of such a provision may not be unexpected. However, it indicates that the company is not complacent in terms of its safety record since its foundation.

Each of these short illustrations show (to varying degrees) the preparations that companies within the same industry have in place in the event of a crisis. They are (albeit partial ones) measure of the degree of crisis preparedness in place within organisations. Although selected by us, they also indicate a particular concern with how to respond to a crash. Recent events indicate that airlines may face many other types of crisis more frequently.

For example, in August 2003 BA was hit hard by a baggage handlers' strike at Heathrow, at a cost of an estimated £8 million per day (Morgan, 2003). The strike was triggered when BA sought to introduce a new staff monitoring system and may be seen as part of ongoing industrial relations difficulties for the organisation. BA's handling of the dispute was criticised by PR experts and City analysts alike:

> It doesn't matter whether unions are to blame or not. They don't have the brand the public recognises. BA does and it is the one that gets damaged.
>
> (Morgan, 2003: 16)

In late July and August 2005 BA was once again the focus of significant media attention when a key supplier of food and drink on its aircraft, Gate Gourmet, experienced major industrial action. Ryan (2005) reported that BA staff engaged in a wild cat strike in support of the 650 Gate Gourmet workers who had been sacked. The immediate impact was upon 70,000 passengers, although the dispute continued for months with many flights departing with no provisions. Media views were that "Once again, BA seemed to have been taken completely by surprise. And, yet again, no contingency plan appeared to have been in place" (Ryan, 2005).

Although it is hoped that a crisis will not occur, a continuity management approach necessitates a focus on the preparation and prevention in addition to recovery.

Sources: Parris (1999); Carrington (2000); Schneider (2000); Morgan (2003); Ryan (2005)

Smith (1990) proposes that a crisis comprises three stages (see Figure 4.6). Based on this, the stages can be conceived of as the before, during and after phases.

The pre-crisis stage refers to the period in which the potential for failure is incubated. In the years and months before an incident occurs, decisions will be made that make the organisation more or less vulnerable to crises. Such decisions might include (in)appropriate staffing levels, the timing and frequency of back-up routines, the discrediting or ignoring of internal and external safety reviews, or a focus upon profit to the detriment of safe working practices.

The second stage refers to the immediate organisational handling of an incident and includes the immediate period of the crisis, between the crisis

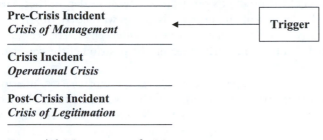

Figure 4.6 Three stages of crisis.

Source: adapted from Smith (1990)

taking place and the resumption of operations or activities. Clearly, this period will vary according to the nature of the crisis itself and the ability of the organisation to respond. In the next chapter, BC plans are shown to include details of which operations should be resumed, in which order and when (for example, 1 hour, 4 hours, 24 hours, 3 working days, etc.). The period following the advent of a crisis has been called a "glide path" (Fitzgerald, 1995). This analogy has been used because aircraft will vary in their ability to glide based on environmental conditions, design, load and pilot skills. Similarly, organisations may, following an interruption to their operations, be able to continue their operations albeit for a short period of time. In general terms, the so-called "glide path" connotes the manner and speed with which operations are recovered.

The third, and final, stage refers to the period in which an organisation seeks to consolidate and then reposition itself (see Box 4.5). Of course, stage three provides feedback into stage one as organisations may or may not learn from their experiences.

Box 4.5 Perrier and Tylenol – A Contrast of Approaches

In 1990, Perrier recalled 160 million bottles of its sparkling mineral water when traces of benzene were found during tests. However, nobody died or suffered illness as a result of drinking Perrier water. Perrier's handling of the crisis may have cost them an estimated £2 billion in terms of managing the crisis, product recall and lost market share. Contrast this experience this with Johnson & Johnson when their painkilling drug Tylenol was maliciously laced with cyanide in two separate incidents, two years apart. A total of eleven people died in the two incidents. The threat might have been averted had Johnson & Johnson switched from a capsule to a contamination-proof tablet form sooner – they did so immediately after the second incident. The impact for Johnson & Johnson was lesser in severity than for Perrier, with little impact to the company's market share and retention of the product's position as market leader. In these two instances, the impact of the post-crisis phase was vastly different – the apparently more threatening crisis (which involved deaths to customers) did not significantly threaten the position of the company affected.

Why the different experiences? A large part of the explanation concerns the pre-crisis preparations of the two companies. Where the media found Perrier to be aloof and secretive with the media, Johnson & Johnson had an open approach with good media relations. Where Perrier seemed slow to respond to their crisis, Johnson & Johnson responded quickly and positively. Their strong and popular public image allowed them a third chance when Perrier was denied a second. Our conclusions are that the outcomes of the crises were determined by the preparations of these companies for crisis and their ability to respond quickly and positively. Johnson & Johnson had healthy relations with the media, a good understanding of their customers and as a result recovered quickly. The unhealthy relations between Perrier and the media acted as a powerful force that prevented Perrier from mounting an effective response to their crisis.

Having considered the "process" of crisis using Smith's (1990) model, the next step in the planning process is to identify the types of crisis which an organisation is likely to face. It is, at this point, where planning for BC begins in earnest.

Summary

Having examined the regulatory and legal pressures which increase the need for organisations to introduce or improve continuity management, this chapter introduced a BCM process which comprises of four stages: intimation, planning, implementation and operational management. The chapter continued by focusing upon the first stage of initiation.

Three basic strategies underlying BC provision have been introduced. These suggest differing approaches and attitudes towards the way in which an organisation can influence and be influenced by its environment in the event of a crisis or interruption. The recognition of which strategy an organisation has or should adopt will influence the resource requirements and investments necessary to improve the protection against crises and the effectiveness of recover activities.

Initiation comprises of seven steps. It begins with the need to set the scope and policy of continuity management. Without this, there is the danger that the organisation may be too ambitious in attempting to introduce continuity management into the organisation. Once the remit BCM has been established, organisations need to decide how the continuity activities will be integrated into the prevailing structure. The formal coordination of BC is vital since if it is to be more than merely IT disaster recovery, it may be advisable to position the activity as a general business function. As the chapter noted early on, it is only with the wide and full participation of employees that continuity management can achieve its full potential.

Once structural issues have been resolved, clearly defined resources, projects and responsibilities need to be attached to BC activities. The latter is often achieved through monitoring and communication mechanisms such as project teams and coordinators. Once established, the preliminary steps towards planning can be undertaken.

The preliminary steps for planning include the development of a draft BC policy and the wide communication of its existence and content to employees. Once this is in place, one final step is required – a shift the mindset.

We ended the chapter by "shifting the mindset" that we may have of crises and disasters by examining a three-stage process of crisis. By adopting a crisis management perspective on BC, a greater acceptance of the role of prevention in addition to recovery will likely arise. Having completed an examination of how planning for BC is initiated, the next chapter introduces the second stage of the BCM process – planning for BC.

Study Questions

1   How would you encourage a small business owner to introduce continuity management?
2   Using the web, look at how the mineral water market has changed since the Perrier crisis. How is market share distributed?
3   Using the web, examine how the airline industry has evolved since the emergence of the budget airlines. What is the impact upon the vulnerability of different types of airline?
4   Find an example of a crisis which has occurred recently. You may wish to use electronic databases to search for information using keywords such as "crisis", "strike", "product recall", "interruption", etc.

   a   What evidence can you find to support Smith's three-stage model of crisis?
   b   What was the outcome of the crisis for the organisation concerned? You should try to look for financial performance and stock price changes, and changes to the senior management team.

Further Reading

Barton, L. (1993) "Terrorism as an international business crisis", *Management Decision*, 31 (1): 22–25.

Clair, J.A. (1998) "Reframing crisis management", *Academy of Management Review* 23 (1): 59–76.

Kotheimer, C.J. and Coffin, B. (2003) "How to justify business continuity management", *Risk Management*, May, 50 (5): 30–35.

Meisinger, S. (2006) "Crisis management and HR's role", *HR Magazine*, February, 51 (2): 12.

Mitroff, I., Pauchant, T., Finney, M. and Pearson, C. (1989) "Do some organisations cause their own crises? The cultural profiles of crisis-prone vs crisis-prepared organisations", *Industrial Crisis Quarterly*, 3 (4): 269–283.

Schiano, W. and Weiss, J.W. (2006) "Y2K all over again: How groupthink permeates IS and compromises security", *Business Horizons*, 49: 115–125.

Smith, M. and Sherwood, J. (1995) "Business continuity planning", *Computers and Security*, 14 (1): 14–23.

5 Continuity Analysis and Planning

Introduction

Since the first edition of this book was published the importance of BC has become clearer. The expectation that organisations should consider BC routinely comes from many sources: suppliers, government, communities and publics increasingly expect it; customers may demand it; insurers require it; and governments encourage it. Within the so-called Audit Society (Power, 1997), many stakeholders almost demand that organisations are able to demonstrate compliance with standards and benchmarks, else risk losing custom. The importance of being seen to do the right thing cannot be underestimated, as evidenced by the growing popularity of benchmarking (Green, 2006). Where the last chapter was concerned with establishing and reinvigorating the process of continuity management, the focus of this chapter is upon planning for BC. This requires analysing an organisation's capabilities and resources as well as the business environment in which it operates. It also calls for BC practitioners and managers to think creatively about potential interruption scenarios and their possible impacts upon activities and stakeholders.

In this chapter, we argue that creating the right mindset is essential for successful BCM. Taleb (2007: xvii) recounts that before the discovery of Australia, old world beliefs were that all swans were white, "an unassailable belief as it seemed completely confirmed by empirical evidence". The surprise of the early explorers who first glimpsed the black swan can only be imagined. In considering potential business interruptions Taleb (2007) uses the metaphor of the black swan as a warning to over dependence upon experience as the sole guide in a complex and rapidly changing world. For Taleb "black swan" events are outliers, outside our regular expectations; there is no easy way of dealing with the black swan problem. In terms of the planning process, it emphasises the importance of balancing the rigour of the systematic analytical process with a more creative, multi-perspective, iterative and questioning mindset. This cuts to the heart of the planning process, not least in the importance of employing different methods for data collection. For example, using focus groups as part of a business impact analysis is likely to yield richer insights than relying solely upon a structured questionnaire in which it assumed all questions are known from the outset. In terms of mindset, Elliott and colleagues' (2005) study of crises in the services sector identified a shift from an orgo-centric to customer-centric perspective. In the latter perspective the customer is the focus and service recovery becomes central to business recovery. Successful recovery also requires paying attention to many stake-holders. BC analysts must avoid being swayed by the terminology which may imply a particular set of priorities and seek to keep an "open mind" throughout the entire process of analysis and preparation. The process of BC *management* is iterative and incorporates testing, maintenance and embedding the process, which are the focus of later chapters. The objective of this chapter is to provide an overview of some of the methods which organisations can use during the BCP process.

As a starting point, although the plan is a key output from the planning process, it should be seen as part of the learning process with the goal a more effective capability to respond than production of the document itself. Possessing a plan must not be confused with a real BC capability, which may emerge from the related processes of planning, testing and exercising. Any plan must be seen as a guide for action in the event of an interruption. Brevity and adaptability are likely attributes of the best plan. Local authorities in the UK County of Gloucestershire won awards for their BCP processes in March 2007; when floods struck the Gloucester-shire in July 2007, these award-winning processes failed (Pitt, 2008; Elliott and MacPherson, 2009). Planners should be aware that the value of the plans they produce will be determined by the manner in which they guide responders through the recovery process.

Planning within the Business Continuity Management Process

Figure 5.1 portrays the BCM process introduced in Chapter 4. Since this chapter is concerned with planning for BC, you will observe a planning flowchart connected to the second step, showing the sequence of activities that are typically used to generate a BC plan (Figure 5.2). The value of the activities is often determined by the degree to which planners think about what is the most appropriate method of analysis. Thus, while a wide variety of frameworks and models exist for this purpose, our objective is to identify and explore the key steps required to generate BC plans. Central to the process is a Business Impact Evaluation which draws together the analysis of the organisation and its environment. From this analysis a risk assessment profile can be developed which, combined with scenario planning, leads to the generation of the plan.

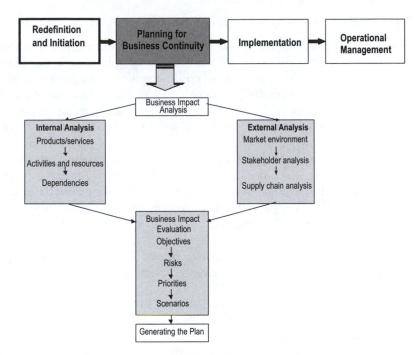

Figure 5.1 The business continuity management process.

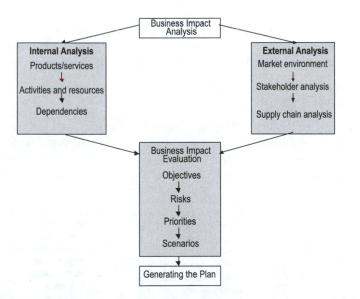

Figure 5.2 Business continuity planning flowchart.

Source: adapted from Elliott et al. (1999a)

Frameworks for Identifying Priorities and Crisis Types

Preparing and planning for the unexpected, in a dynamic world, offers one of the primary difficulties for the planner (or planning team). The desire to arrive at a "definitive" list of crises which the organisation might face could prove to be counterproductive. Why? The natural question of "what interruptions or crises could we face?" may lead to an unstructured list similar to that shown in Figure 5.3. The list presented is, quite clearly, by no means exhaustive.

The next step might be to attempt to create specific recovery provisions for each. However, this would lead to planning being determined by the length of the crisis list rather than the needs and priorities of the organisation. Three key ways to distil a long list of crises into a more manageable and practical format are:

1   *Classification techniques* to categorise threats according to their type and source. Similarities may be precursors to the development of generic responses.
2   *Risk analysis/rating approaches* (such as Annual Loss Expectancy) to rank threats in terms of the relative threat that each hazard or incident presents to the organisation.
3   *Arbitrary approaches* in which managers use judgement, bias or personal experience to determine threat priorities.

Establishing priorities is vital as these provide focus for plans and will influence the order of recovery activities to ensure that the most critical functions, processes and outputs (product/services) are restored first.

Classification Techniques

Mitroff and colleagues (1988) developed a framework for classifying types of resources according to *where* the crisis is generated and *which* systems are the primary causes (Figure 5.4).

Although developing contingency for every eventuality is impractical,

Adverse weather	Hostile merger or acquisition	Reputation crisis
Bribery and blackmail	Illegal activities	Product injuries
Computer breakdown	Industrial action	Product tampering
Computer failures	Kidnapping	Sabotage by outsiders
Computer 'bugs'	Loss of important staff	Sabotage by staff
Currency fluctuations	Major industrial accidents	Suicide bomber
Fire	Military coup	Supplier crisis
Floods	Oil shortage	Telecommunications failure
Flu pandemic		Terrorism
Global warming		Web fails

Figure 5.3 An unstructured list of crises and triggers.

Crisis Typology
Technical/Economic

Major accidents	Natural disasters
Product recall	Aggressive takeover
Computer failure	Social breakdown
Internal	**External**
Sabotage	Product tampering
Occupational health disease	Terrorism
Fraud	

Human/Organisational/Social

Figure 5.4 Generic crisis typology.

Source: Mitroff et al. (1988)

this matrix provides a starting point for a creative brainstorming session which provides a means of identifying the range of interruptions an organisation might experience. Rather than deal with individual incidents, "families" of crises may be clustered together and provide a focus for preparations. For example, a number of BC professionals complained in 2007 of the high profile given to preparations for a possible flu pandemic; this was seen as just one possible trigger resulting in loss of staff and thus usually already identified and prepared for. It is the impact of an interruption upon an organisation and its stakeholders that is relevant, not the nature of the interruption itself. Thus the consequences (or interruption to business) of fire, flood, earthquake and explosion may be similar and thus require only one type of preparation. Taking the analysis one step further, even triggers positioned within different cells may have similar impacts, requiring a similar type of response. For example, in Figure 5.4 injuries arising from a defective product, equipment sabotage by employees and product tampering by outsiders are each positioned within different cells but need to invoke product recall plans. Hence, analysis of clustered threats using classification techniques should be a two-stage process involving (i) within-cluster analysis of shared attributes and responses, and (ii) across-cluster analysis of shared attributes and responses. Although the categories and crisis types identified in the generic model could relate to any industry, it should be adapted to create a matrix directly relevant to each organisation and industry. Figure 5.5 provides examples from a holiday travel company.

From Figure 5.5 it is evident that some types of crisis are common to most organisations; for example, computer viruses, strikes and loss of key staff. However, others may be more relevant to certain industries so that

Technical/Economic

IT breakdown Computer virus	Fluctuating currency rates
Internal	**External**
Industrial action Sabotage Lose key staff	Customers affected by: Civil unrest Traffic accidents Natural disaster Third party failure

Human/Organisational/Social

Figure 5.5 Crisis typology: holiday travel company example.

Source: Adapted from Mitroff et al. (1988) and Elliott et al. (1999a)

travel companies may be concerned with fatal coach crashes, the kidnap of customers or tourists being affected by events such as the Indian Ocean Tsunami (2004) or civil unrest as in Myanmar in 2007, Thailand, 2008 and India in 2009. Following Hurricane Katrina, there were widely circulating stories of tourists forced to take cover in the New Orleans Super Dome where they were, allegedly, threatened with rape and beatings. Although the stories were exaggerated, Smith-Spark's report suggests that there may have been some truth underlying the claims (Smith-Spark, 2005). Providing support to customers must have tested the plans of many tour operators who might not have envisaged such a widespread "interruption" in the world's richest country. Third party failure refers to the dependence that all travel companies usually have on other organisations to supply (in part) the final service, ranging from hoteliers, air carriers to coach excursion companies. In this example, the matrix builds upon the categories identified in the generic model and produces crises relevant to the travel industry.

The matrix may be used as a framework from which potential crisis triggers and their consequences are considered. A word of caution should be noted at this juncture. As with all models and frameworks, these are merely tools with which to think about situations and problems. Many such models are, by their very nature, one-dimensional and may not reflect the impact of time and the subtle relationships between two or more factors. For example, Stucke and Straub (2005) reported that after 9/11 a number of businesses had plans for recovery anticipating the loss of infrastructure but took no account of a loss of personnel and expertise. Although events of the scale of 9/11 are rare, a growing literature has dealt with the issues surrounding the preservation of corporate knowledge when employees leave (see, for example, Beazley et al., 2002).

While it will be virtually impossible to prevent natural disasters, it may be possible to limit the impact of such triggers. Such events may be exacerbated by human factors, first noted by Hardin (1971). For instance, the impact upon humans of the 2004 Indian Ocean Tsunami was influenced by the concentration of populations in vulnerable conurbations and was further compounded by the absence of early warning systems and the collapse of communication systems. In May 2006 more than twenty-four Asian and Pacific countries engaged in testing new Tsunami alerts and safety drills, illustrating how the identification of potential threats may lead to developing resilience. The flooding of New Orleans in 2005 and Gloucestershire in 2007 were only problematic because of the investment in human activity in these vulnerable areas.

Another approach to classification techniques is based upon intention and impact: that is, the degree to which an individual or group sought to generate an interruption for an organisation. Karakasidis (1997) addresses this issue by suggesting that not only should the cause–effect relationship be examined, but also intention. This is shown in Table 5.1. When Firestone tyres were implicated in a series of road accidents and the organisation was under a significant threat, a key group of employees chose to take industrial action, recognising the vulnerability of their employer (Blaney et al., 2002). Digitalisation provides further opportunities for stakeholders who may choose to exacerbate a situation. Russia was alleged to have launched cyber-war on Estonia in early 2007 following a dispute concerning a war memorial (Traynor, 2007). Within the UK, the 7/7 bombings highlighted how the general public were in a position to shape news coverage when the event was described by Bell (2006) as "the tipping point for mobile phone video and picture use; the interest sparked in 'citizen journalism' reverberated around every newsroom in the country." A deliberate web campaign to embarrass P&O into providing high levels of compensation was orchestrated by some passengers, using cell phones and web-based communications as a vehicle to express themselves when an outbreak of the Novo virus occurred on P&O's cruise ship *Aurora*. This was much to the annoyance of other customers (Elliott et al., 2005).

Once again, there is value to be gained in seeking to identify similarities in the impact that crisis types may have. In the case of Table 5.1, bombs and fire differ in their intention but may lead to similar impacts in terms of denial of access to an organisation's facilities. Similarly, vandalism and power loss may differ vastly in terms of intention but lead to the same result – loss of functionality within a facility (that is, the inability to use electrical equipment).

Risk Analysis/Rating Approaches

One of the biggest difficulties with the term "risk management" is that it encompasses or describes a wide variety of techniques and roles – often

Table 5.1 Intention and Crisis Types

Crisis Classification: Impacts

Cause	Impact
Intentional crises	
Bomb	Building evacuation, search, diffusion of device, declaration of safety, return to normal
Data disclosure/corruption	Deliberate theft or disclosure, programme code manipulation, virus
Extortion	Hostage taking, ransom demands, product tampering
Industrial action	Lockouts, go-slow, work to rule, processing delays
Vandalism	Loss of equipment and ability to process customer orders
Unintentional crises	
Communication service loss	Failure of phone network and exchange, possible damage to equipment
Disease/epidemic	Closure of company facilities, quarantine, staff/customer contamination
Fire	Internal/external cause leading to fire damage, and secondary damage due to water and smoke
Power failure and electrical faults	Power surges, sags, spikes, loss of voltage, insufficient power to back up systems

Source: adapted from Karakasidis (1997)

entirely separated from each other. Accordingly, we have financial, operational, strategic risk – each with their own practices, techniques and functional homes within analyses such as actuarial science, enterprise risk management and value at risk. Similarly, there is no broad agreement about whether risk management analysis is part of BCM or whether BCM is a part of risk management. Our approach is to incorporate risk analysis within the BCP process and to develop BCM as a way in which operational and strategic risk management are undertaken either as a stand-alone activity, or as a complementary/integrated element of a broader risk management system. For operational purposes, our definition of risk is based on the word's etymology from the Italian "risico" (danger) to indicate an uncertain outcome which has a negative impact.

Risk analysis/rating approaches can be useful in cases where there is adequate company specific information to fulfil the requirements of a systematic analysis. Risk management is integrated into BCM in two ways. First, BCM as a process and as a capability serves to define, identify and address dangers (risks) facing the organisation. Second, risk analysis can be integrated within the planning process to provide systematic and analytical insights to inform priorities, vulnerabilities and requirements. At the start of the BC planning process, risk analysis offers a useful way of identifying the priorities that the organisation should concentrate on given finite time and resources. In the latter parts of the planning process – specifically during the Business Impact Evaluation – the assessment of risk is made in the light of the preceding analysis of the organisation's recovery resources and experience to give a more contextually accurate assessment that specific risks present. It is worth noting that risk analysis is a well established discipline in its own right; our coverage of risk is limited to how it may be usefully deployed within BCM and that it is polemic in its own right (see Box 5.1 Risk as a social and personal construct).

Within BCM, risk analysis is about insight rather than prediction alone. As an old Chinese proverb recounts, "when men speak of the future, the Gods laugh". A cautious but informed application of risk is therefore required. The essence of quantitative risk analysis is the assignation of numerical values to represent the key determinants of the level of risk that an event hazard presents. Generally, these values will refer to the frequency or likelihood of the event occurring and the impact or cost that the event would have. The function of the two values (frequency/likelihood and impact/cost) is known as the EV – expected value – approach (Jablonowski, 2006). The EV approach provides a metric with which to rank a long list of hazards or events for which the two contributory values (frequency/likelihood and impact/cost) can be ascertained.

Originating in the National Bureau of Standards' Federal Information Processing Standard 65, *Guideline for Automatic Data Processing Risk Analysis* (National Bureau of Standards, 1979), annual loss expectancy (ALE) was originally intended to evaluate information technology risks. Since then, ALE has received wider attention for those wishing to undertake systematic quantitative risk analyses (for example, Broder, 2000; Soo Hoo, 2000). As an extension of the expected value approach, ALE produces not only rankings but also clusters of hazards which can be instructive in a number of ways. Figure 5.7 shows how ALE can be calculated based on known frequency and costs to determine the value of i (impact) and f (frequency of occurrence), which can then be applied to a developed ALE formula which takes the following form:

$$\frac{10^{(f + i - 3)}}{3}$$

Thus, a hazard that occurs once every 100 days and with a cost or loss on each occasion of £10,000 would have an annual loss expectancy of £33,333. In the broadest sense, this is the annual impact or cost of this specific hazard.

Considered alone, the figure of £33,333 calculated above is relatively uninformative. When, however, it is compared with other threat types for which an ALE figure has been computed, it becomes more illuminative. Furthermore, as we shall see shortly, ALE calculations can be used in

Impact (i)		Frequency of occurrence (f)	
£10	let $i = 1$	Once in 300 yrs	let $f = 1$
£100	let $i = 2$	Once in 30 yrs	let $f = 2$
£1,000	let $i = 3$	Once in 3 yrs	let $f = 3$
£10,000	let $i = 4$	Once in 100 days	let $f = 4$
£100,000	let $i = 5$	Once in 10 days	let $f = 5$
£1,000,000	let $i = 6$	Once in 1 day	let $f = 6$
£10,000,000	let $i = 7$	10 times per day	let $f = 7$
£100,000,000	let $i = 8$	100 times per day	let $f = 8$

Impact rating formula $\quad = \quad \dfrac{10^{(f+i-3)}}{3}$

e.g. Threat type A:

$\quad$ *Impact* $= 4$ *and Frequency* $= 4$

$\quad$ Impact rating $\quad = \quad \dfrac{10^{5}}{3}$ $\quad$ (i.e. 4 + 4-3)

$\qquad\qquad\qquad\quad = \quad$ £33,333 $\quad$ (100,000/3)

Figure 5.6 Calculation of annual loss expectancy.

Source: adapted from Broder (2000: 22)

investment adequacy considerations. The comparative value of ALE metrics can be seen in Table 5.2 in which a list of hazards and threats has been subjected to the ALE formula set out in Figure 5.6. The resultant ranking serves to cluster together hazards into five discernible tiers of priority. This overcomes the problem that "being unable to distinguish between high-frequency, low-impact events and low-frequency, high-impact events" (Soo Hoo, 2000: 4). The comparative ALE shows that three threats rank highest in terms of ALE: denial of access to building (>1week), Distributed Denial of Service (DDoS) attacks and missing back-up or data theft. While having a low impact value (which could mean that this type of threat may be considered to be *present* but not strategically *important*), the cumulative DDoS attacks over an annual period revealed by the ALE highlight that it is a threat that – in terms of occurrence and impact – should be treated no less seriously than the loss of a building for a week or more, or the loss of back-ups and data (with its regulatory, legal and reputational consequences). For the BC manager, thought should be given as to how well placed an organisation is to respond to such threats and whether and how the impact and frequencies could be ameliorated.

In the lower tiers (tiers 4 and 5) in Table 5.2, threats such as damage to telecommunications capability and external power supply loss are, at first glance, out of position given the importance of these resources to the

Table 5.2 Comparative Annual Loss Expectancy

Threat type for a facility in Central London	Impact value (i)	Frequency of occurrence (f)	ALE	Priority tier
Denial of access to building (>1week)	7	3	3333333	1
Missing back-up/data theft	7	3	3333333	1
Distributed denial of service (DDOS) attacks	2	8	3333333	1
Transport strike	5	4	333333	2
IT outage caused by hardware failure	5	4	333333	2
Fire (permanent loss)	7	2	333333	2
Building contamination/infection	6	3	333333	2
Postal/courier strikes	6	3	333333	2
Software errors	6	3	333333	2
Denial of access to building (<1week)	5	3	33333	3
Falling trees	5	3	33333	3
Gas leakage (no fire)	5	3	33333	3
Lightning strike	4	4	33333	3
Burglary	4	3	3333	4
Bomb threat	5	2	3333	4
Damage to telecommunications capability	5	2	3333	4
External power supply loss	2	4	333	5
Flood	3	3	333	5

functionality of a building. Surely these should be a higher tier of threat and thus a higher priority for BCM? Instead, the lower ranking is due to greater resilience to failure in terms of telecommunications equipment (and the availability of wireless alternatives which mean that a complete loss of voice and data functionality arises infrequently) and the use of back-up emergency generator systems to reduce the reliance on utility companies to expedite restoration of power supplies. Such an analysis highlights that, in many instances, organisations can influence the impact that a threat may present even if they are unable to reduce or prevent its occurrence. Moreover, the analysis may differ vastly between organisations given their different endowments of resources, skills, experience coupled with differing locations, products, services and activities. Hence, a risk analysis will necessarily benefit from a more detailed analysis of the organisation's resources, processes and activities and this is why risk analysis forms part of the business impact evaluation phase of the planning process considered later in this chapter.

One further benefit of ALE calculations is that they can facilitate investment adequacy decisions. The idea of ALE takes the probability of an event and the loss caused by that event and generates an annual figure for its loss. By producing an annual figure, a comparison can be made against investments in prevention and/or recovery from that event in terms of annual expenditure. In so doing, the comparison between ALE and BC budgets represents a simple test for investment adequacy.

For example, consider a business interruption threat such as the loss of power to an organisation's head office. Historical data, a facilities audit and expert advice indicates that there is a 10 per cent chance (in annual terms) or probability of 0.10 that there will be a power loss to the building in any given year in a ten-year period – in other words, once every ten years. Should a power loss arise, operations would be interrupted for 48 hours. This interruption would include restoring power, resuming and checking systems, and dealing with the backlog of work. The duration of the interruption incur costs and losses totalling £1,000,000. Accordingly, the ALE is 10 per cent of £1,000,000. The resulting ALE of £100,000 per annum is then compared with investment, planning and maintenance costs over the same period. So, for instance, if the total costs of installing uninterruptible power supplies are £20,000 per annum over the ten-year period and the annual costs of staff training, recovery plan development and testing, and system maintenance are £5,000 per annum over the ten-year period, the annual cost of this countermeasure for the power loss hazard is £25,000 compared with a potential loss of £100,000 in the same period.

The ALE approach demonstrates the potential insights that can arise from a risk analysis even in its simplest form but such a quantification of risk is not without its problems. For instance, could the event happen more or fewer times than the probability or frequency indicates and where does this leave us? Might it happen at all? Is the effect of a hazard linear: that is, are the losses that arise spread equally over the period of interruption; are the greatest losses in the early stages of an interruption (for example, 80 per cent of the cost/losses incurred arise in the first eight trading hours of a 48-hour power loss because after a day, processes can be switched to an alternative site)? Are there alternative responses which cost less relative to the current probability, or cost more but in so doing reduce the likelihood of the event arising? How do in-house and outsourced solutions compare? Time horizons are also problematic in risk analysis. Using a short period of observation (in order to ascertain the frequency of an event) could mean that a catastrophic event might not happen. In analysing too long a time horizon, the conditions which led to the level of impact at the start of the observation period may no longer apply since resources, resilience and provisions may have changed significantly. As planners, do we have the full picture in order to see the total number of occurrences and how far back can we go before the collection of observations becomes irrelevant? In addition, imperfect knowledge means that we may not be able to quantify the frequency or certainty of a major event, perhaps calling into question the extent to which resources and attention should be directed to addressing the manifestation of the event. A fatalistic approach to risk might be exhibited in the decision to "do nothing" given the possibility that the event might not happen. In contrast, a precautionary approach to risk might be exhibited in the decision to "do something" given the possibility that the event might happen. Furthermore, the *reasonable man* argument – whereby it is unreasonable for the costs of coun- termeasures to exceed the cost of the interruption – highlights the dangers of an organisation carrying out an exercise in which it takes (at worst) "act" or "ignore" decisions. The consequences of such a decision in legal terms could become problematic in instances where a known preventable threat or hazard has been the subject of such an assessment.

So where does this leave the use of ALE? The level of analysis within ALE is that of specific threat types, their likelihood, impact and response. At the very least it draws attention to whether, given the scale and scope of a hazard, an organisation should increase its resource allocations to improve its resilience to the threat. A comparison of the ALE figures between hazard types – for example, power loss, building loss, distributed denial of service attack, data loss – might illuminate instances of where a specific threat type faces underinvestment in countermeasures relative to the threat that it presents to the organisation in comparison with other threats. Using ALE or EV is a starting point but by no means the only one and neither is the end point in risk analysis. It is, however, an illumin- ating distillation of the critical variables in risk analysis and is a basis for managing risks by understanding them (albeit not fully).

Box 5.1 Risk as a Social and Personal Construct

One of the principal difficulties with probabilistic risk analysis such as expected value or annual loss expectancy is the assumption that the understanding of risk is factual rather than perceived. Hansson (2005) argues that risk assessment should not only include cost and frequency but also other factors such as the degree of intention, consent, rights, agency, duties, equity and agency as determinants of risk. These highlight the context of the individual person or organisations within a risk assessment landscape.

Löfstedt and Frewer (1998) have argued that assessments of risk may be socially constructed and socially amplified. The social *construction* of risk refers to the idea that assessments of risk cannot be definitive or absolute. Both the assessment of risk and the choice of actions in relation to a risk are judgements made under conditions of uncertainty and are influenced by factors such as fear, ignorance and experience. Perceptions of risk may be *amplified* such that other individuals and groups may influence the perceived level of risk that a hazard presents to such an extent that it is distorted beyond the actual risk that it would present; for example, the influences of millennialism (the year 2000 effect), disaster pornography (whereby the more visual an event is, the more media coverage it receives (Alexander, 2000)) and terrorgoating (whereby the association of an event with terrorism amplifies the level of concern that it attracts (BBC, 2002)).

Slovic (1998) suggests that expertise and choice may influence an individual's assessment of risk. In the case of an "optimistic bias", an individual may believe that they can intervene or control a hazard, thereby lowering the risk. Others, however, may not share the same capabilities or belief. The same might apply to organisations. The notion of "revealed preferences" suggests that risks are more acceptable (and thus may be rated less undesirably) if they may generate a benefit: that is, it is worthwhile "taking the risk". Consequently, voluntary risks (such as driving or skydiving) will be perceived to be more acceptable than involuntary or less avoidable risks (for example, pesticide use in food production or genetic modification). Slovic (1998) also points out that lay-persons rate risks differently from experts. In the relative absence of technical or statistical knowledge lay-persons subconsciously classify risks into those which are a "dread risk" (heavily influenced by fear of the risk) or "unknown risk" (heavily influenced about uncertainty about the risk). This brief vignette further highlights the presence of risk analysis as an imperfect science in an imperfectly understood world. Since risk as a social and personal construct (coupled with some of the shortcomings that surround the quantification of probability and impact), there may be differences in the boundaries between acting and ignoring risk – the point at which a risk (known as a *de minimis* risk) is so inconsequential that it is beyond concern or no risk at all.

Arbitrary Approaches

The third approach which could be used to decide upon on threat priorities is based on heuristics – namely, judgement, bias or personal experience. In this case, a team of managers may ask the question "What are the most important threats about which we should be concerned?" The resulting discussion may lead to the identification of a small number of threats that set the priority planning scenarios for BCM. For instance, a manufacturing firm may decide upon its BCM priorities based on the following influences:

- The factory is located in the landing approach path of an international airport.

- The company is highly reliant on component suppliers for which there are no immediate alternatives.
- An adjacent factory was razed in a fire a short time earlier.

Note that the determining factors are not necessarily a factual indication that the three hazards are the most threatening to the company's facilities.

In identifying the causes of crises, organisations should seek to understand how they may make themselves more vulnerable to external events. Despite the fatalistic connotations of the term "disaster", such incidents are rarely unpredictable or unavoidable. There is much that organisations can do to reduce their exposure to crises as the introduction of tsunami early warning systems suggests. However, while a focus upon prevention makes sense, it will never be a completely successful approach, so identifying the range of crisis types facing an organisation represents an important step in the process of BCM. The major objective of the analysis stage is to examine the potential risks that the organisation is exposed to and to consider strategies for reducing that risk as part of a BCM process.

Business Impact Analysis

The business impact analysis (BIA) is a critical part of the planning for BC. Meredith (1999: 139) described it as forming the "backbone of the entire business continuity exercise". This technique represents the fundamental analysis of an organisation's resources and its vulnerability to loss or damage. This process will determine priorities which in turn influence many of the financial commitments to BC provisions. For the British Standards Institute (2006), the BIA is a key to securing a full understanding of an organisation: its key products and services and the activities that create and support them. The role of the BIA is to determine and document the impact of any disruption to activities, and an outcome of the BIA will be an understanding of the likely financial and operational consequences of an interruption. The focus of the BIA should always be upon a specific business process, which might be defined as a group of business activities undertaken within an organisation and it is recommended that analysts should identify the overlap of resources, processes, systems and technologies by mapping their shared use across the functions, departments and divisions of the organisation. Such activities may occur within or between departments. Such business processes might be function based (for example, marketing or personnel) or not (for example, quality management which often spans more than one function). The CCTA (1995b) recommend using strategic planning or business process re-engineering documents to identify such business processes.

Business Impact Analysis: Preparations and Methodology

The business impact analysis might begin with a focus upon identifying the purpose of an organisation and how it adds value for its customers of clients. Is value driven by efficient processes as in commodity businesses, by linking research and development to new product development or is the focus upon client protection? The focus upon value creation and then the activities and resources which support it is a key first step in the BIA and ensures it avoids simply listing what we do or what we own. The next step is to consider mission or time-critical processes, resources and activities. A useful list of these has been suggested by Jackson (2001):

- personnel;
- facilities;
- technology platforms (that is, all computer systems) and software;
- data and voice networks and equipments;
- vital paper records;
- vital electronic records.

Some of the key functions and processes that organisations should focus upon include payroll, order and data processing, customer service and support, accounting, communications (voice and data), technical support (IS and customer-led), production scheduling and purchasing (Pabrai, 2005).

A further alternative is to use value chain analysis as a means of mapping out processes (Porter, 1985). The focus of value chain analysis is to separate primary and support activities and to recognise that it is the linkages between them that often add value. Value chain analysis reinforces the view that a key objective of BC is not to simply protect particular activities but also the linkages between them which result in core capabilities.

Widely acknowledged as the originators of the BIA (albeit with a technical focus), Strohl Systems recommend that the BIA process should involve the following nine steps:

1   Define assumptions and scope of project for which BIA is being conducted.
2   Develop a survey or questionnaire to gather necessary information.
3   Identify and notify the appropriate survey recipients.
4   Distribute the survey and collect responses.
5   Review completed surveys and conduct follow-up interviews with respondents as needed.
6   Modify survey responses based on follow-up interviews.
7   Analyse survey data.
8   Verify results with respondents.

9   Prepare report and findings to senior management (Strohl Systems, 1995: 2–11).

The emphasis of Strohl Systems upon surveys and questionnaires does not mean that such data collection instruments need lack variety. Since Strohl Systems first published their guidance, the practice of the BIA from the early 1990s has included a wide range of methods. For example, Honour (2006) reports that organisations employ a range of data collection methods:

- Software   23%
- Survey/questionnaire   23%
- One-to-one interviews   19%
- Interviews and survey questionnaire   18%
- Workshops/focus groups   8%
- Interviews and workshops   5%
- Interviews, workshops and survey   2%

The exclusive use of prescriptive software and surveys suggests that the creators of the data collection instruments know all the questions to ask. Semi-structured interviews, focus groups and workshops allow for dialogue and permit new insights to be gained from reflection. Closed tools such as software and surveys are contrary to the open-mind needed to consider, creatively, threats and impacts. The mindset of an organisation will also heavily influence the outputs of a BIA. For example, a customer-centric organisation may seek to focus upon the impacts upon customers and other stakeholders. Orgo-centric organisations will be preoccupied with their own problems. Pauchant and Mitroff (1992) argued that inner-oriented organisations were likely to be more prone to crises than those that recognised their position within a wider social and commercial system or network. For example, a customer-centric recovery plan might mean that an airline takes the almost unpalatable decision to place its customers on a rival's flights to ensure that they reach their destination. Firestone actively elicited supplies from Michelin, and deliberately not Goodyear, in their response to the so-called Ford–Firestone crisis of 2002.

The content of the interview schedule or questionnaire will differ for each organisation and each business process. The objective of such interviews is for the BCM team to gather data from line managers and other staff. The content should cover the generic categories outlined below:

- range of potential crises;
- business unit objectives;
- descriptions of key processes (flowcharts etc.);
- resource needs;
- reputational context;

- key stakeholders;
- linkages and dependencies with other business units;
- linkages and dependencies with suppliers, customers and other agencies;
- legal issues;
- consequences of being out of action for different time periods (for example, 1 hour, 8 hours, 24 hours, 1 week);
- prioritisation of core and other activities;
- minimum resources required to restore key activities;
- seasonal trends or critical timing issues.

At J Sainsbury the starting point for the BIA is the retailer's mission statement, which cascades down to strategic business unit level (Elliott et al., 1999b). Although not listed above, a clear sense of an organisation's key strategic objectives and stakeholders should also be kept in mind throughout the analysis process. The headings above (which lead to related questions) should be adapted to meet the needs of the organisation – be it public or private. The objective of such questions is to stimulate the interviewee to think about risk and how change in any of these broad categories might affect business processes and, ultimately, customers. An advantage of focus groups is that they can provide an opportunity for participants to build and enrich initially incomplete accounts, or else to express differences of opinion (Wilkinson, 2004). Within the context of exploring linkages and dependencies, richer insights may emerge from the interaction of participants. Proformas similar to that shown in Figure 5.7 provide a helpful way of ensuring consistency of data collection. Hence, each of these categories should be used to define situations which could have an impact on business for specific periods of time. The analysis should concentrate on those impacts most likely to occur and where the potential for damage is greatest. Managers should be encouraged to quantify impacts where possible, although not exclusively – this may involve financial impact or less easily quantifiable impacts such as loss of credibility, loss of quality of service or product. An alternative rating approach is suggested by Pabrai (2005) using the classifications of "critical", "essential", "necessary" and "desirable" from the most to the least important resource ratings respectively.

A critical consideration is the duration of impact. How long could the interruption last? To ensure an effective BIA, organisations should consider the full range of internal and external factors.

Business Impact Analysis: Determining Initial Recovery Priorities

An example of how the results from BIA can be presented and interpreted is given in Tables 5.3 and 5.4. Table 5.3 identifies a number of resources that are used in an organisation's headquarters building (known as build-

BIA Proforma

Date:	Role of function/department:
Time:	
Interviewee:	
Position:	

Links to other departments:

Systems/resource usage and dependency:

System/ resource (name etc.)	Purpose of system/ resource (relationship to dept)	Usage (how often and by who?)	Impact of loss (what could we not do?)	Degree of loss (halt or slow down the process) 1, 2, 5 days

Figure 5.7 Business impact analysis proforma.

ing A). In each case, the chart briefly explains the impact of the lost resources in terms of what could not be done and how the impact changes over four time periods (less than a day, after 1 day, after 2 days and after five days. For clarity, you will notice that the resources are listed in the order of their importance as determined by how important and how soon the resource is required.

Since the building does not have any fully automated processes, the analysis identifies human resources as the most critical resource due to the high and immediate impact from their loss. From a practical perspective, the analysis may also have identified the minimum staffing resource required to resource recovery teams for each of the departments and functions in the building. The second vital resource is the building. The building is mixed purpose and has both customer and corporate activities accommodated within it. The analysis raises the question of whether single or multiple alternative locales are necessary to provide places to restore activities in the event of a denial of access scenario. The third resource, known as "Accosoft", is the company's proprietary accounting system. The analysis identifies that the impact of losing access to this is high from the onset of an interruption. It is high for two reasons. First, all departments within the building use this software. Second, for most departments, the impact of the loss of this resource is high within the first day of an interruption. It is also an important resource since there are dependencies on this from sales personnel, company branches and credit search agencies.

The maximum acceptable downtime for data systems and networks is less than one day because all departments within building A require connectivity to central servers for client and investment data. Stand-alone computers would not be able to operate fully without this connectivity. Vital electronic records include individual client records, including incoming and outgoing payments and are deemed to be highly important, as are vital paper records such as customer enquires and documents, and contractual information. Although mobile telephone/VOIP alternatives suffice for intra-building contact (assuming functionality remains), the presence of a call-centre within this building means that the loss of the building would effectively close off the business to incoming new and existing client contact. In terms of the loss of the company's archive database, total loss would clearly be catastrophic if it were not available off-site in back-up form. However, in terms of the day-to-day operations of this building, the lack of access to this resource would only become a concern at about five days after an interruption.

In our example, since the company does not presently use email as a principal form of communication with clients, it is deemed to be less of a priority than telephony functionality as necessitated through the presence of a call centre in building A. However, as the organisation develops its electronic commerce activities, email will clearly become more important and therefore it will require a more immediate restoration in the event of its interruption. This highlights the need for planning activities to take place on a regular basis to capture and respond to changes in the way that resources are used and the changing relative importance of resources. In the case of other resources that are present within building A (resources Ω, Σ, θ and β) concerns about the loss of these resources and their restoration would only be warranted after two days (unless one department was specifically and especially dependent on its restoration). In relative terms, resource β is the least important resource but should process λ (which might take place in another important building) become more important because of a seasonal peak or milestone in the year such as the end of a financial period, the impact rating of resource β would be elevated.

Table 5.4 shows how BIA is extended into functions and departments (this is one example, but there would be a similar exercise undertaken for each function within the building). In this case, the figure lists the resources used within the "Customer Management Department" within

Table 5.3 Worked Business Impact Analysis 1

Business area	Resource	Impact from loss of resource	Impact within 1 day	Impact after 1 day	Impact after 2 days	Impact after 5 days
All departments in building A	Personnel	Lack of human recovery resources	H	H	H	H
	Building A	Loss of accommodation for both HQ activities, the central information systems facility and a call centre	H	H	H	H
	"Accosoft" Accounting software	Staff cannot access investment accounting data	H	H	H	H
	Data networks and equipment	Loss of connectivity between information systems	M-H	H	H	H
	Vital electronic records	Cannot provide client and operational records	M-H	H	H	H
	Vital paper records	Information for operational decisions and activities is inaccessible	M-H	H	H	H
	Telephones	Customer contact impeded	M-H	H	H	H
	Archive Database 1	Staff cannot access and update client portfolios	L	L-M	M	M-H
	E-mail	Unable to communicate electronically with other departments	L	L	L-M	M
	Resource Ω	Unable to [. . . context-specific explanation . . .]	L	L	L-M	L-M
	Resource Σ	Restricted access to [. . . context-specific explanation . . .]	L	L	L-M	L-M
	Resource θ	Staff cannot [. . . context-specific explanation. . .]	L	L	L	L-M
	Resource β	Process λ cannot be completed	L	L-M	L-M	L-M

Table 5.4 Worked Business Impact Analysis 2

Business area	Resource	Impact from loss of resource	Impact within 1 day	Impact after 1 day	Impact after 2 days	Impact after 5 days	Restoration order	
							Resource	Activity
Customer Management Department	Accosoft Accounting software	Staff are unable to access customer files	M-H	M-H	H	H	1st	ii
		Staff are unable to expedite payments	H	H	H	H		i
		Staff are unable to set up new files	M	M	M-H	M-H		iii
		Unable to deal with queries from other departments	L	L-M	M-H	H		iv
	Data networks and equipment	Unable to [. . . context-specific explanation . . .]	M	M-H	M-H	M-H	2nd	i
		Staff cannot [. . . context-specific explanation . . .]	M	M	M-H	M-H		ii
		Restricted access to [. . . context-specific explanation . . .]	L	L	L-M	L-M		iii
	Vital electronic records	Unable to [. . . context-specific explanation . . .]	M	M	M-H	M-H	3rd	i
		Staff cannot [. . . context-specific explanation . . .]	M	M	M	M-H		ii
		Restricted access to [. . . context-specific explanation . . .]	L	L	L	L-M		iii
	Vital paper records	Unable to [. . . context-specific explanation . . .]	M	M	M	M-H	4th	i
		Staff cannot [. . . context-specific explanation . . .]	L	L	L	L		iii
		Restricted access to [. . . context-specific explanation . . .]	L	L	L	L-M		ii
	Telephones	Unable to [. . . context-specific explanation . . .]	M	M	M	M	7th	i
		Staff cannot [. . . context-specific explanation . . .]	L	L	L	L		iii
		Restricted access to [. . . context-specific explanation . . .]	L	L	L	L-M		ii
	Archive Database 1	Unable to [. . . context-specific explanation . . .]	L-M	M	M	M	8th	i
		Staff cannot [. . . context-specific explanation . . .]	L	L	L	L		iii
		Restricted access to [. . . context-specific explanation . . .]	L	L	L	L-M		ii

Email	Unable to [. . . context-specific explanation . . .]	M	M	M	M-H	M-H	5th	i
	Staff cannot[. . . context-specific explanation . . .]	L	L	L	L	L		iii
	Restricted access to [. . . context-specific explanation . . .]	L	L	L-M	L-M	L-M		ii
Word processing software	Staff are unable to access templates and regulatory reports	M	M	M	M	M-H	6th	i
	Staff unable to produce ad hoc documents	L	L	L	L	L		iii
	Staff unable to produce correspondence/Covering letters	L	L	L-M	L-M	L-M		ii
Resource Ω	Unable to [. . . context-specific explanation . . .]	L	L	L-M	L-M	L-M	9th	iii
	Unable to [. . . context-specific explanation . . .]	L	L-M	L-M	L-M	L-M		ii
	Unable to [. . . context-specific explanation . . .]	M	M	M-H	M-H	M-H		i
Resource Σ	Restricted access to [. . . context-specific explanation . . .]	L	L	L	L	L	10th	iii
	Unable to . . . [. . . context-specific explanation . . .]	L	L	L	L	L-M		ii
	Unable to [. . . context-specific explanation . . .]	L	L-M	M	M	M		i

building A. Additional detail for each resource has been identified in terms of the impact of the loss of the resources, indicating that each resource has more than a single role within a department. Furthermore, the figure shows how the importance of these context-specific uses for each resource will vary. The outcome of this more detailed analysis of the impact reveals not only the restoration order of the resources (1st, 2nd, 3rd, etc.) based on their overall importance in terms of immediacy and importance of use but also the order in which activities should be reinstated once the resource are operational once again (i followed by ii followed by iii etc.). For instance, after staff and facilities, the "Accosoft" accounting system is the most important resource within this function. In the event of the loss of this resource, once restored, the order of activities which should follow should commence with the expedition of payments to clients, followed by the reinstatement of access to customer files (which is necessary to allow the call centre to handle queries) and the creation of new files for customers. Once underway, queries from other departments can be honoured.

The approach suggested here is but one way to use BIA. In contrast, Gluckman (2000) suggests that BIA should be the foremost analysis which leads to the final generation of the BC plan(s). However, the position and role of BIA in this process echoes the view of Lee and Harrald (1999: 188) who concluded that "in order to carry out the [BIA] efficiently, it is first necessary to identify business functions/processes".

BSI (2006) emphasised more generic outputs in their recommended BIA. The aim of the BIA is identified as determining and documenting the impact of a disruption upon activities. This should include:

- assess over time the impacts arising from a disrupted activity;
- establish the maximum, tolerable period of disruption for each activity:
  - o the maximum period within which an activity should be resumed;
  - o the minimum level each activity should be performed at once resumed;
  - o the length of time by which "normal" operational levels have resumed;
- identify interdependencies.

The BIA offers a preliminary analysis of some of the idiosyncrasies of every organisations' resources, systems and operations. The next step is to build upon this through a systematic analysis of an organisation's operating environment and a detailed examination of its outputs, activities and dependencies. The final three aspects come to form the internal analysis.

Internal Analysis

Internal analysis is needed to understand the nature of an organisation's operations and how these influence the recovery priorities that will be a central part of BC plans. This analysis should be undertaken in three ways and in the following order:

- Products and services
- Activities and resources
- Linkages and dependencies.

The rationale behind this is to begin the analysis at the level of the product or service, the most direct contact with the customer. From this, the concern is with how a company's products or services share resources, since an interruption may have greater effects due to such sharing. In so doing, the analysis should answer three important questions:

- What does the organisation do?
- Who and what is involved in the creation of products and services?
- How are our activities linked?

Products and Services

Since BCM is concerned with an organisation's survival and the protection of its strategic objectives, the first stage of the internal analysis involves the identification of its products or services. In the case of a public sector organisation, an analysis of the major (often statutory) responsibilities of the organisation should be identified. This starting point indicates what is likely to be affected by a business interruption (products and services) and who will be affected (customers).

The portfolio of products or services produced by an organisation is a further consideration. Key issues to identify are:

- The number and variety of products and services.
- The market shares of individual products and services (where appropriate).
- The revenues and profits of individual products and services (where appropriate).
- Temporal issues (for example, seasonality, daily, weekly sales patterns).

This information helps to identify those products and services which, in the event of a crisis, would have the greatest impact on organisational performance and survival. A firm with a narrow product range is more vulnerable to threats from product contamination than those with a diverse range of interests, or those with a very narrow geographic sourcing pipeline – as many China-dependent companies have discovered in 2007 (DeWoskin, 2007) when food and consumer product companies recalled pet food and toys.

Consider the example of two well-known companies: The Coca-Cola Company and Pepsi Co International. The former is reliant upon the carbonated drinks market to a greater degree than Pepsi Co, which has diversified into restaurants and snacks. A threat to the carbonated drinks market would have a greater impact upon Coca-Cola than Pepsi Co. For example, bans on carbonated drinks in schools in California and India have affected Coca-Cola's marketshare and revealed its exposure as one with a narrow product portfolio. In California its launch of the Dasani water brand has helped reduce the impact. However, in the UK, Dasani was soon withdrawn after its launch. The water source for Dasani UK was the mains supply to Coca-Cola's factory in Sidcup, Kent, where it was subject to three stages of filtration and the addition of calcium chloride (Lawrence, 2004). Unfortunately for Coca-Cola one of the UK's most popular TV comedy series had seen the two main characters earn a fortune by bottling tap water and selling it as natural spring water, only to see their new empire collapse when their secret emerged. As Lawrence stated, Coca-Cola's problems worsened when it was discovered that their additives created a potential carcinogenic:

> So now the full scale of Coke's PR disaster is clear. It goes something like this: take Thames Water from the tap in your factory . . . put it through a purification process, call it "pure" and give it a mark-up from 0.03p to 95p per half litre; in the process, add a batch of calcium chloride, containing bromide, for "taste profile"; then pump ozone through it, oxidising the bromide – which is not a problem – into bromate – which is. Finally, dispatch to the shops bottles of water containing up to twice the legal limit for bromate (10 micrograms per litre).
>
> (2004: 21)

Current products are likely to provide the main focus for analysis but new products should also be evaluated within the BIA, especially to assess the impact of new product introductions and strategies that involve a move into new product or geographical markets. Such changes in the future may significantly alter an organisation's dependence on current products and markets, thereby reducing the salience and relevance of current continuity provisions. By considering such issues, continuity planning provides a contingency for the future. An organisation's product or service roadmap will indicate the timings of key product and service introduction over the course of a number of years and may indicate whether the rollover from one product to another is simultaneous (new and old product are sold at the same time) or sequential (old product stock is exhausted at the point of the new product's introduction). Clearly, the latter makes for a more acute situation in the event of a crisis such as a product recall or launch/ production delay.

Faced with growing complexity in the manufacturing requirements for the Xbox360, Microsoft developed a real-time visibility system into its supply chain. This has enabled it to better manage its strategy of out-sourcing key manufacturing operations, providing the means by which it can retain tight control over suppliers and contract manufacturers to ensure that they meet service level agreements (SLAs) for on-time delivery and component quality (Microsoft, 2006). As with the car industry's use of "e-build", one clear outcome has been to reduce the likelihood of assembly problems and errors which could lead to a costly product recall (Kochan, 1999). Here new technology not only improved product quality but also helped mitigate against the costly and litigious threat that may follow a product recall (Chapter 2).

Analysis of the organisation's product portfolio is insufficient, on its own, to assess the impact of an interruption. Products may be very similar or share resources in ways that are not immediately evident. An under-standing of how they may be linked is achieved by looking at activities and resources.

Activities and Resources

Once the profile of products and services is known, the analysis should progress to an identification of all resources which contribute to the prod-uct. These include those activities and resources which lead to the devel-opment, manufacture and sale of the product. By working back from the final product or service, all key resources leading to the final output should be identified. The types of resources that should be considered include:

- intellectual property;
- physical manufacturing equipment;
- information technology;
- transportation, storage and logistics assets;
- telecommunications systems;
- financial resources;
- employees;
- buildings;
- subsidiaries or divisions which produce components, parts or materials.

The contribution of each of these resources will vary according to the nature of the organisation's business. For instance, an online bank such as Nexity will rely to a far greater extent upon IT and communications (telephones) than a manufacturer of electronic goods. Online banks with few ATMs will also find themselves dependent upon third party outlets and possessing fewer bargaining counters. Similarly, a physical goods manufacturer would be vulnerable to disruptions arising from fuel shortages, port blockades and haulage company industrial actions than a web-based financial services. The degree to which these resources contribute to the final product or service will determine the provisions that are chosen for their continuity.

One way in which to assist this activity is to look at which business units are involved in creating a product or service. In addition, the role of outside suppliers or channels (as in the case of the competitors who Nexity is forced to rely on to provide access to its customers' cash) should be examined. The greater the number of in-house departments and/or suppliers that are used in a product or service, the wider the scope for an interruption to occur. This does not necessarily mean a greater likelihood of interruption, simply that there are more links in the chain that could fail.

Linkages and Dependencies

The final stage of the internal analysis is to consider the whole chain together. The purpose of identifying the dependencies is to determine how an interruption in one part of an organisation could affect the ability to supply goods and services (see Box 5.2). Dependencies are important linkages in which one activity must be preceded by another. If an activity fails, all other activities that are dependent upon it will also fail. For example, the provision of consumer goods on supermarket shelves requires the production and transportation of each unit from a factory to the supermarket. Within this process there are many dependencies and potential points of failure. Thus the process is dependent upon the availability of raw materials, processing equipment and lorries to transport the finished goods. Dependencies are not simply physical exchanges in a production environment, they could take the form of *information* dependencies (such as a university's timetabling department requiring enrolment data from faculties in order to produce personalised timetables for students), or *decision* dependencies in which a decision or authorisation is required in order for another process to proceed (such as an application for personal finance).

Box 5.2 Functional Dependencies

Dependencies	*Examples*
Operations management and production	Production of components must precede assembly of finished product.

Information and communication technologies (ICT)	Online banks depend upon securing access to ATMs from competitors and are more heavily dependent upon utility and software service providers and equipment providers. Increase in air flights tightens coupling in flight corridors placing greater demands on technology and staff.
Marketing (shared brands, marketing and promotion)	Coca-Cola perceived to be contaminated leads to fears that other soft drinks may also be harmful to consumer. Tread separation on Firestone tyres fitted to Ford cars raise questions about full range.
Distribution channels (type, number and mix of wholesalers/retailers)	Increasing concentration of power in large retailers in many European markets (for example, Wal-Mart, Carrefour, Tesco, Aldi, J Sainsbury).
Purchasing and procurement (raw materials and components from suppliers)	Carrefour review purchasing guidelines for genetically modified foods. Industrial action at Gate Gourmet, suppliers of airline food, interrupt provisioning of BA flights for months.
Logistics (whether in-house or otherwise)	Toyota requires suppliers to use helicopter delivery to maintain JIT schedules.
Organisational support activities (such as legal, finance)	Increased regulation of financial services requires regular and ongoing review of day-to-day activities else face punitive fines.

Within this stage of the internal analysis, it is important to develop links with operational planning in order to ensure that future investments are properly examined. For instance, new investment in IT or automation may radically alter employee skills requirements, training, supervision and functional structures.

External Analysis

Without reference to the external environment, BCP will be severely limited. By better understanding of how external groups may interact with an organisation, tangible improvements can be made to BC provisions. Indeed, Mitroff and colleagues' (1988) typology of crises explicitly recognised the external environment as a potential source of crisis triggers. Recognising this, Sheffi and Rice (2005) identified that UPS invests in its own weather forecasting service which sometimes outperforms the "National Weather Service" in its accuracy. A detailed understanding of the natural environment is clearly vital to UPS. Additionally, Smith's (1990) crisis of legitimation implies that the response of an organisation to an interruption, and the way that it is seen (or otherwise) to act appropriately, by rivals, customers, regulators and other observant parties is an important dynamic. In December 2006, unflattering comparisons were drawn between London Heathrow Airport's treatment of passengers stranded because of thick fog and those in Denver, Colorado, who were snow bound. In both cases the trigger emerged from adverse weather conditions, but one airport responded in a way that was seen as positive and the other did not.

The Market Environment

The position of a company's product or service in a market will influence the impact of an interruption. It may be argued that a product with a low market share and few dependencies may suffer a lesser impact from a crisis than one with a high market share and high degree of dependency. Market position may also contrive to alter the level of impact that an organisation suffers. Market position, relative to that of a rival, can be considered in two ways:

- actual market share;
- image.

In the case of Perrier (Chapter 4), the dominant position of the company as market leader in the mineral water market was irrevocably damaged. In terms of image, Mercedes-Benz recalled its all-new A-Class vehicle in 1997, shortly after its launch, and suspended deliveries for three months at an estimated cost of £100 million (Prowse, 1998). This blow to the company's image arose from a product that had yet to establish any market share. Ironically, the company had recalled a far larger number of their existing luxury car models for component replacements. Moreover, the A-Class recall highlights the effects of a crisis across an entire organisation. In a two-month period as the crisis unfolded, Mercedes-Benz's parent company (Daimler-Benz) saw its share price fall by 32 per cent (Olins and Lynn, 1997). The melamine contamination of Chinese dairy products in late 2008 saw more than 54,000 infants seeking medical treatment and a number of deaths, adversely affecting the international reputation of this nascent industry.

Next, those involved in the planning process should consider how the market position (market share and image) could be affected by the onset of a disaster. Could it delay a new product launch, erode the company's market position or adversely change the company's image? In terms of the effect on company performance, these products or services and their dependencies should be a priority for BC protection.

A commonly used tool for analysing an organisation's environment is the so-called PEST analysis – an acronym that has been stretched in Table 5.5 to include the physical environment and geographical themes, and competitors' activity. Used primarily as a tool in the process of strategic management, it provides a checklist of potential environmental forces. The purpose is to identify those factors that might increase the potential for crisis or hinder an effective response. The purpose of such considerations is to develop a sensitivity to environmental influences.

The market analysis should identify key customers in terms of their strategic and financial value and the service level agreements that the organisation has agreed with them in advance (relating to delivery, continuity of supply, etc.). This analysis can be extended to consider the relative market share position of rivals who could benefit from an interruption so

Table 5.5 PEST Applied in a Business Continuity Context

Category	Examples
Political	Environmental policy, training provision, ICT initiatives, food hygiene regulations, industry watchdogs
Legal	Regulation/legislation relating to: Health and safety Product liability Negligence Hazardous substances Security and information Food processing Building and construction Intellectual property
Economic	Fiscal and monetary policy
Environmental and geographical	Floods, pollution, drought, earthquakes
Social	Pressure group activities Consumer watchdogs Cultural and social changes (religious observance, ethnicity, etc.)
Commercial	Actions of competitors – legal or illegal
Technological	New products (recall of faulty products) New processes (moves towards paperless office environments)

that their activities can be monitored. Finally, there is an opportunity to learn from rivals' experiences of crisis, including how they responded to customers and other stakeholders. Finally, should a close rival encounter a crisis, it may be used as an exemplar to highlight the need for BCM to employees.

Stakeholder Analysis

The concept of stakeholders acknowledges that no business is an island and that business interacts with society in a number of different ways. This notion is not new. Dill (1958) noted the manner in which outside parties could bring their interests to bear upon an organisation's managers and vice versa. It makes good business sense for organisations to be aware of their stakeholders as their interests and the satisfaction of their needs may determine business success. The objectives of an organisation will be circumscribed by the extent to which relationships with stakeholders such as suppliers, bankers, shareholders or customers are successfully managed. Nowhere is this more important than in BCM, since their response to the organisation in the post-crisis phase will have an impact on the success of recovery efforts and, ultimately, survival of the company (see Box 5.3). Stakeholders such as government, local government, industry authorities and business support groups are useful in a crisis and plans may require modification in the light of a stakeholder analysis.

Stakeholders are those individuals, groups or organisations who have an interest, direct and indirect, in an organisation. More importantly, stakeholders possess power that can be wielded to support or to thwart organisational change. An organisation's stakeholders may be divided into "primary" and "secondary" groups.

Primary stakeholders are those who have a direct and often economic stake in an organisation, usually in the form of a transaction of resources, finances or services. Figure 5.8 illustrates the range of different stakeholder groups that constitute primary stakeholders. These are usually the most obvious groups and those with whom an organisation has the most contact.

Secondary stakeholders include those organisations or individuals who are affected, indirectly, by the activities of the organisation. Figure 5.9 represents these. Professional bodies, competitors, pressure groups and local authorities all form part of this group of stakeholders. Clearly, they all have very diverse objectives and their influence over the organisation will also differ greatly. The use of the term "secondary" is not meant to indicate that these groups have a lesser impact on organisations. Far from it – for example, local government may wield significant power over where businesses might be sited and the green movement have in recent years been very successful in getting corporations to consider environmental issues.

Crises involve many different stakeholders and it may not always be clear which the key ones are. Any crisis response must take into consideration

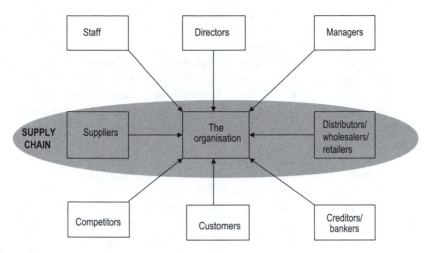

Figure 5.8 The organisation and its primary stakeholders.

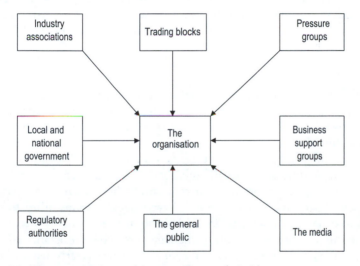

Figure 5.9 The organisation and its secondary stakeholders.

the diversity of stakeholder involvement and need if management efforts are to be effective. Mitchell and colleagues (1997) suggest that stakeholder salience results from the interplay between the relative power of a stakeholder, perceptions of its legitimacy regarding an issue and the urgency in terms of criticality and time sensitivity an issue posed for it. This results in a variety of potential stances for stakeholders before and during a crisis. The value of considering these three influences is that it provides a means by which the shifting salience of stakeholders may be identified and potentially predicted. It encourages us to identify the latent power or legitimacy and may be used alongside scenario planning.

When Firestone tyres, fitted to Ford's Explorer motor vehicle, were implicated in a large number of fatal accidents, both Bridgestone and Ford sought to deflect blame for the event away from them. On 6 August 2000, a US Federal agency raised concerns about the safety of the tyres and the Ford Explorer. Sears Roebuck, a distributor, immediately stopped sales of suspect tyres. Ford announced a voluntary recall on 9 August, some three days after the official concerns on 11 August. Ford identified a range of possible causes, including an earlier strike in the plant where Firestone tyres were produced and design flaws in the rubber coating on the tyres, firmly placing responsibility for the failure upon Firestone. The United Steel Workers Union threatened Firestone with strike action, selecting a moment of peak vulnerability for the employer. Lawyers were quick to offer their services on a "no-win-no-fee" basis. Goodyear, a competitor of Bridgestone, was quick to exploit their vulnerability with a number of tactical movements of stock and prices. The media was quick to highlight the conflict between Ford and Firestone and to provide coverage of consumer and consumer group concerns. In this example there was no single event as is often assumed; this escalation resulted from the accumulation of many incidents which combined to create crises for those concerned (Elliott, 2005).

Internal Stakeholders

Equally, the crucial role of internal stakeholders in implementation of a BCM process, is being recognised. At a broad level, employees or managers form one category of direct stakeholder. However, rarely do they form a monolithic whole in terms of aims and objectives. Organisations are political in nature and various departments or functions will regard continuity management differently. Board members and other senior managers are regarded as more important than they might have been in the past. The company board and other directors have a legal responsibility to ensure the survival of the organisation. This is often one mechanism that might be used in support of continuity management where resistance to implementation is encountered. Such recourse to power clearly has to be used sparingly and wisely. But in those organisations where the culture is not supportive of planning for preparedness, it is often virtually impossible to effectively implement BCM programmes without the support of an internal coalition – be it the board or other groups that carry power.

Box 5.3 Stakeholder Analysis and Continuity Planning

For example, Thames Water in the UK has used stakeholder analysis to enhance the understanding of how an incident will have different repercussions upon different groups. In the past, a burst water mains was seen as a question of identifying the fault and repairing or replacing it, whereas, at present, the company has invested time and effort into identifying different types of stakeholders and their needs. For example, a detailed database will inform Thames Water quickly whether vulnerable groups (such as an elderly person's residential home) are affected by a burst water main pipe or whether a business customer's processes requires large volumes of water. The database provides the central point for the collection of information that relates to the varying needs of users and the likely impact of a failure on them and Thames Water. Internally, the development of staff training in handling events has distinguished between the needs of line managers and operational staff. Stakeholder analysis has been used in a diagnostic way to discover the range of needs of the diverse groups of people that surround it. By identifying groups (such as pressure groups) that have no direct stake in the organisation, potential problems can be anticipated and, possibly, avoided.

Source: based on Elliott et al. (1999a)

The planning team should conduct a thorough stakeholder analysis of the organisation, similar to that used by Thames Water. This can then form the basis of a discussion between business units and the BCM team about potential strategies that might be used to manage key relationships. Indeed, Ramprasad and colleagues (1998) argue that a systematic stakeholder analysis can help to ascertain the organisation's recovery priorities and can also act as a valuable theme by which to communicate the importance of BC and re-educate sceptical managers and functions. A framework for stakeholder analysis should consider:

- who the organisations stakeholders are;
- the goals of stakeholders with regard to the organisation;
- the likely reaction to, or effect of, the range of interruption types that could be encountered;
- ways in which stakeholder relationships can be managed during an interruption.

In one local authority, involvement in planning new facilities highlighted to the BCP team the importance of planning officers. They had not previously specifically considered this group as necessarily constituting an important stakeholder but realised that a co-operative relationship might be advantageous should they require planning or siting permission in the future. The professional body for this group is one that is now consciously targeted as a networking organisation.

The concept of stakeholders and its value for BCM is not a distant and abstract one. No organisation is self-sufficient and each organisation will depend to a greater or lesser extent upon a range of different stakeholder groups. The key is to identify the key relationships, especially those which might not be immediately apparent. As Shell discovered when it sought to dispose of the Brent Spar oil rig in the North Sea, it may be the least obvious stakeholder groups that can exert tremendous power. Greenpeace, through clever use of media images and an essentially emotional argument, forced the giant Shell, and the UK government, to back down over the issue of oil rig disposal. An environmental activist now advises the Shell board on environmental matters. In their campaign against the testing of chemicals on animals, activists targeted the banks and suppliers of the Huntingdon Life Sciences laboratory to achieve their objectives.

Without due regard to the role that stakeholders play in enabling companies to carry out their activities, crises can be exacerbated. When, in early 2000, it was discovered that staff working at the Sellafield reprocessing plant owned by British Nuclear Fuel Ltd (BNFL) had falsified safety records, the company faced public humiliation, internal and external inquiries, a damaged reputation and the loss of future business, including £4 billion from Japan's Kansai Electric alone (Jones et al., 2000). Following the immediate crisis arising from falsification activities, the company announced that it would compensate Kansai Electric with a payment of £40 million and would re-take possession of the polemic shipment of mixed oxide. Seemingly near to the conclusion of the crisis, the re-possession of the shipment would itself widen the membership of the stakeholder group pertinent to the crisis, as concerns were raised by the USA and Pacific, Central and South American states over the dangerous cargo which could pass through or near their territorial waters. To compound the situation, the Japanese government has moved its energy policy towards "greener" sources following the BNFL incident, local opposition and a nuclear accident at Tokaimura in September 1999 (Rahman, 2000).

Despite the dynamic and unexpected manner in which stakeholder relationships develop, it is important for organisations to retain their attention upon the day-to-day relationships between an organisation and its direct stakeholders. For example, stakeholder relationships are a constant reality within an organisation's supply chain (Bursa et al., 1997).

Planning for Supply Chain Interruptions

We have previously noted that, as stakeholders, suppliers are clearly influential to the degree to which they can exert their bargaining power over customers downstream in the supply chain (Porter, 1980). Thus, planners' attention should also be directed to the potential risks that their organisations' face from its suppliers, in spite of having well developed internal BCM.

A stark illustration of the varying degrees of vulnerability that a company has when its suppliers encounter continuity challenges can be seen in the case of a fire which destroyed a Phillips Electronics factory in

Albuquerque, New Mexico, in March 2000. Both Ericsson and Nokia were reliant on semiconductors from the plant for their mobile phone handsets and the combination of fire damage to equipment and the complete smoke contamination of stocks interrupted supply of these components. While Nokia was able to switch to alternative sources of supply for these vital components, Ericsson found itself without a supply to continue production, resulting in a halving of its market share and a $400 million loss for the financial year (Klay Management Ltd, 2003; Canadian Underwriter, 2005).

Supply chain issues, such as purchasing and product development, have traditionally fallen under the remit of purchasing and procurement departments. Increasingly, the role of the supply chain in BC has grown, given that the tight integration of companies along a supply chain often comes to form a source of competitive advantage (Chadwick and Rajagopal, 1995). Sheffi and Rice (2005) advocate a more strategic approach in order to develop resilience. They identified that there may be marked differences in the warning signs from the immediate onset of a tornado to winter fuel shortages in Europe (2006/7) or growing industrial unrest. They also note the varying lengths of time from onset to real impact, whereby system redundancy may cushion the immediate impact. Over reliance upon one supplier may be seen as the result of strategic myopia, an expensive mistake for IBM in using one software supplier in the early days of the PC. Sheffi and Rice (2005) developed a matrix for assessing an organisation's supply chain vulnerability in terms of probability of interruption and its likely consequences, in a manner that is reminiscent of an expected value approach. For example, McDonalds is cited as being at low risk of threat from terrorism given its distributed nature; also, its use of franchisees makes it relatively impervious to industrial action. However, an outbreak of mad cow disease could affect its entire operations. Indeed, sales of UK McDonalds were hit in the early days of the BSE scare. Organisations should be aware of their reliance upon a single supplier for components, materials or energy requirements. The effects of this may be seen following a fire at the Longford natural gas processing plant in Australia. The 1998 incident cut supplies for over a week and restrictions lasted for several months. As a consequence, both Toyota and Ford were forced to close their plants, with Toyota estimating losses of AUS$10 million for each day of non-production (Tilley, 1998). Sheffi and Rice (2005) recommend that organisations spread the risk of supply or, alternatively, develop very deep relationships with key suppliers. Further, they recommend organisations consider building redundancy into their systems to facilitate flexibility. Retailers may use Christmas distribution centres as "emergency centres" for the remainder of the year. Although this begs the question of what might happen should a crisis strike near Christmas!

A key issue concerns decisions about how to manage customer demands in the event of a disruption. Arguably Dell's agile supply chain enabled it to better deal with the aftermath of the 1999 Taiwanese earthquake than competitors such as Apple (see Martinson and Elliott, 1999; Stirpe, 1999). A key issue for manufacturers is to properly assess the trade offs between lean and agile supply (Womack et al., 1990). What is key is that organisations can anticipate potential problems and plan to manage their resources flexibly in the event of an interruption. A current research project at the University of Liverpool is exploring how "informal" networks, a form of social capital, provided the foundation for the quick recovery of rail services following a 2007 rail crash at Lambrigg in the North of England. Of particular interest is the use of informal networks that appear, in some cases, to rival the effectiveness of formal contracts and arrangements. However, the ability of organisations to recover will depend upon strategic decisions taken a long time before any interruption.

In BCP, there are essentially two types of suppliers: *operational* suppliers, those day-to-day companies which supply goods or services for production or service provision activities, and *recovery* suppliers, which are companies whose services are used in the event of business interruption. These services include hot or cold sites (buildings furnished with hardware, software, data and telecommunications specific to a company's requirements – also known as "business recovery centres"), data mirroring (the real-time off-site storage of important computer data), salvage (physical building search and recovery), and telecommunications (for alternative phone and data lines, and emergency call centres). You will recall that the assessment of third party requirements offered by recovery suppliers formed part of the purpose of the BIA seen earlier in this chapter.

Returning to our focus upon operational suppliers, the BC planner should be cognisant of the analogy of a chain being only as strong as its weakest link, which is valid in the context of the supply chain and BC. Operational suppliers could cause a business interruption in several ways:

- industrial action halting production;
- faulty components are supplied which lead to a product recall;
- cessation of trading (bankruptcy and receivership);
- fire or flooding in the suppliers premises;
- failure of computer systems.

For instance, in mid-1997 a strike at the largest of the US delivery services, United Postal Service (UPS), brought the company's deliveries of domestic and commercial parcels in the US to a halt. The industrial action severely affected mail order companies' ability to deliver products on time to customers. In particular, Gateway, a personal computer manufacturer that sells directly to customers, suffered substantial disruption to its business during the lengthy duration of the strike as around half of its shipments were made by UPS.

As Gateway's sole distribution channel had been interrupted, a tangible impact was seen on its mid-year earnings at a time when it was seeking to consolidate its European expansion strategy. When the company's third quarter earnings did not meet stock market analyst's forecasts, the company's share price fell by 8 per cent. Dell, Gateway's major rival had only 20 per cent of its deliveries made by UPS and reported revenue growth in line with expectations. Many other PC mail-order rivals used Federal Express as a delivery partner and were, consequently, less affected (CNN, 1997).

Many organisations, through projects to deal with the Year 2000 computer problem, have turned to the supply chain to identify further possible sources of interruption. Increasingly, organisations have introduced sophisticated links through technology for ordering, payment and information interchange that are vital to the logistics and production process, such as electronic data interchange (Kcrmar et al., 1995) and more recently the internet. Weiner (1995) highlights some of the major risks associated with the interruption of systems shared with suppliers (Table 5.6)

Despite the connotations of looking merely at suppliers, customers should already have been considered in the stakeholder and external analyses, since a business interruption which halts production will lead to a supplier being unable to trade. With large stocks and cancelled deliveries from a major customer, a supplier could easily find its own production halted quickly.

Auditing the Supply Chain for Business Continuity

The audit of the supply chain comprises two steps: identification of critical suppliers and an evaluation of suppliers' BCM provisions. The first involves

Table 5.6 The Impact of Interrupted Suppliers

Type of impact	Reason for impact
Loss of independence	The company is unable to fulfil its customers' orders
Loss of confidential/sensitive information	Proprietary information could fall into the wrong hands
Increased exposure to fraud	Unauthorised transactions/invoices could arise following the loss of data
Loss of audit trail	Particularly where no paper copies of document exist
Software failure	Purchasing and scheduling systems which rely on EDI information could subsequently fail
Legal liability	Due to an inability to fulfil contractual obligations with trading partners.

Source: based on Weiner (1995: 56)

the identification of supplier and buyers, highlighting those which are most important. Several factors will provide a suitable indication (Table 5.7). For buyers, this includes what is bought from the organisation, the value of output sold to the buyer, and the proportion of output sold to the buyer. In addition, any collaboration with buyers in terms of distribution, retail and marketing should be considered. Furthermore, through the purchasing department, it should be known whether there are alternative buyers available in the event of a lengthy (or permanent interruption in the case of a retailer going bankrupt, etc.). The identification of critical suppliers may also be achieved thought the use of systematic comparative analyses such as BIA, which examines each supplier or buyer rather than in-house resources.

Secondly, an evaluation should be made of the provisions which these organisations (buyers and suppliers) have in place in the event of a disruption. These will include:

- the level of interaction between the organisations (IT, staff, resources);
- whether they have BC plans in place;
- the nature of recovery contingencies that may be in place, if no formal BC plans exist;
- how long plans have been in place;
- who are the main BC contacts in the organisation;
- whether reference is made to the organisation by its buyers/suppliers' BC plans;
- how often plans are tested and revised;
- whether the buyer or supplier evaluates its buyer/suppliers' BC plans.

Table 5.7 Generic Supply Chain Audit Questions

Downstream (buyers)	*Upstream (suppliers)*
Information source → sales department	Information source → purchasing/procurement sales department
What is sold to the organisation?	What is purchased from the supplier?
What value of output is sold to the customer?	What is the value of goods supplied?
Where are they located?	Where are they located? Are they located within our facilities?
What collaboration is there in distribution, retail and marketing?	How important are the goods/services supplied (are they essential)?
Are alternatives supplies/suppliers available?	Is the supplier a partner in research and development?
How quickly could the customer switch to another source of supply?	Are alternatives supplies/suppliers available?

The selection and evaluation of recovery suppliers should be treated with equal rigour, although given the specific nature of the service provided certain issues should receive a higher priority. There could be nothing worse than for a recovery supplier not to be able to offer its full service to an affected company (which is contractually agreed in advance) in the event of an interruption.

Business Impact Evaluation

The final steps in the planning process involve drawing together the preceding analyses into a cohesive whole in order to begin the process of preparing the actual BC plan. The business impact evaluation (BIE) re-evaluates the initial objectives, set at the outset of the BCP process, and assesses the risk against those objectives. It determines the priorities for business resumption and BC investments. Thus it should incorporate an assessment of the resources that each business unit and function requires to resume at an appropriate time. Of course such analysis may provide many alternative "resumption scenarios" and the business impact evalaution concerns the stage at which these are identified and considered. The BIE comprises of four analyses: first, the BC objectives are refined; second, risks are re-evaluated; third, priorities for business recovery are established; and fourth, business interuption scenarios are developed.

Objectives

In order to have feasible and testable objectives, those which have been identified prior to the BIA should be refined in order to elucidate the minimum required level at which each function or business process can operate. These revised objectives may include reference to time. For example:

- Customer contact must be re-established within two hours.
- Invoicing must be resumed within one week for major customers and return to normal within two weeks.
- Delivery suppliers must recommence within 4 hours.
- Telephones must be operational within 30 minutes.

Through the incorporation of greater detail into these objectives, a further sequence of events and timings can be devised and incorporated into the draft BC plan.

Risk Assessment

Risk assessment is the term used to describe the process of gauging the most likely outcomes of a set of events and the consequences of those outcomes. At a personal level, informal assessments of risk are a more or less continual mental process from crossing the road, judging when to contribute to a meeting, buying goods and so forth. The risk management discipline has sought to formalise risk assessment in an attempt to reduce the effects of personal bias. A limitation is that, where complex systems are concerned, identifying all possible outcomes and consequences is extremely difficult. It has been argued that any attempt to quantify risk will fail because no matter the degree of sophistication of the mathematics, all risk assessment is inherently value laden. Nevertheless, a structured approach to risk assessment is better than none (see Box 5.4). But a good understanding of the aims and objectives of such a process is more important than a detailed statistical knowledge. It is also worth noting at this point that a risk analysis may already have been undertaken in order to identify priorities for the BC process and that the risk analysis undertaken at this point may be an extension of this analysis based on the knowledge derived from the BIA. At this point a much improved understanding of the threats, impacts and vulnerabilities should be available than at the start of the planning process where only the threat type might be known (since impact is influenced by vulnerability and vulnerability is determined by the organisation's resources).

Box 5.4 Risk Assessment Questions

- What hazards, potential failures or interruptions face the organisation?
- What would be the effects of particular failures on the organisation? Our business partners? Our customers? The local community? Our staff? And so forth.
- What is the likelihood of each failure or hazard occurring?
- Do we do enough currently to identify and prepare for such events?
- Is the risk acceptable? To the organisation? Our business partners? Our customers? The local community? Our staff? And so forth.
- What could be done to control the level of risk or to prepare for a failure?
- What should the organisation do?
- What constraints are there?

A simple matrix is commonly used to categorise risks and hence to prioritise remedial actions is shown in Figure 5.10.

A development of the matrix approach in Figure 5.10 can be seen in the Australian/New Zealand Standard for Risk Management AS/NZS 4360

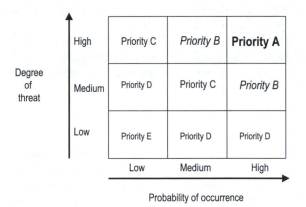

Figure 5.10 Risk assessment matrix.

(1999) introduced in Chapter 2. This approach to risk analysis includes five phases establishing the context and need for risk management, risk identification (sources), risk analysis (consequences), risk evaluation (importance: acceptable or not?) and risk treatment.The identification of risks according to their likelihood and consequence incorporates generic proposals for their treatment according to their severity. Where risks are rated as extreme, immediate action is required. High risk require action but less immediately. Moderate threats may require a more limited response or can be monitored until such time as they become high or extreme. Low threats can be treated with routine procedures.

Priorities and Scenario Planning

The determination of resumption priorities is not an exact science. In many cases, particularly where there is a lack of historical data to draw on, BCM managers find that they have to base their analysis on past experience and judgement. However, a systematic BIA and BIE will offer a clear understanding of the most effective way to implement the necessary steps to undertake recovery activities.

Companies often find that, where leading edge technology is used, due to the lack of appropriate data to draw on, they have to make use of what historical data they have, together with the experience of highly skilled functional experts and BCP managers.

The involvement of experienced BCM personnel is particularly important to facilitate a realistic determination of priorities. Elliott and colleagues (1999a) recount how at a UK bank, the BCM team was actively involved in this part of the planning process. The company also instituted a structure that enabled BCP managers to appeal to higher authorities should individual functions not arrive at sensible priorities. This acts as further evidence to highlight the need to have an effective structure to enable implementation of the BCP (Chapters 6 and 7).

Conducted well, the BIA and the subsequent BIE allow the development of plans that reflect the best and most sensible balance between BCM investment and the exposure to risk. The resulting strategies should be based upon the information generated by the BIA.

Scenario Planning

While BC planning is an activity undertaken for the present, its value will generally only be realised in the future when a plan is invoked and an organisation is able to recover more swiftly and easily than might previously have been the case. Nonetheless, without an understanding of how the organisation and its markets, stakeholders and supply chains may change, the assumptions that are made today may not be valid tomorrow. While the BC planning process has, so far, focused on the past and present, it is equally important to address these future changes. The problem that arises, however, is finding a way to look at the future analytically. To do otherwise would make such efforts purely speculative. Scenario planning is an approach that can be usefully employed for this purpose. It has its origins in wider business planning (Leemhuis, 1985; Kassler, 1995; Moyer, 1996) but it has been shown to generate further value in the context of BCP (Herbane and Rouse, 2000).

Scenario planning recognises the uncertainty that faces organisations. It has developed as an alternative method of planning in circumstances where predominantly quantitative analysis cannot adequately deal with high levels of uncertainty. Its value in BCP cannot be underestimated. In essence, a scenario is a narrative of a major event in the future, its implications for an organisation and an understanding of the major changes that are needed for managers to confront the future. What differentiates scenarios from speculation is that they are carefully considered, internally consistent and are based on knowledge, expertise and experience (see Box 5.5). Scenario planning should be used to explore the most important threats that have been identified in the preceding risk analysis. Scenarios are often used as a context within which plans are tested (Chapter 7).

The key to successful scenario planning is participation. Without it, the scenarios will not benefit from a wide variety of experience from contributors. In the context of BCP, the following questions could be used in scenario planning:

- How would a change in government in a major overseas market affect BC?
- How would BC change if a supplier is acquired by another company?
- How would a major product recall affect the company?

- How would a change in government affect the funding of an organisation in the public sector?

In each of these cases, there is a great deal of uncertainty and variety in the outcome. For example, a change in the governing political party could lead to a major swing in policy. Equally, minor changes may only occur.

Box 5.5 Scenario Planning at Artem Plc

Artem Plc (a fictional company) is a manufacturer of plastic packaging used by the manufacturers of cleaning products (bleach, etc.). Currently its markets are UK and EU based, although it intends to enter the US and South East Asian markets in the next five years. With a presence in these new markets, Artem will be in position to provide higher returns to shareholders and achieve growth through strategic alliances and take-overs of smaller companies in the industry. Artem is uncertain of how a product recall could affect the organisation. Scenario planning has led to two main scenarios.

The first scenario occurs prior to the company moving into the new markets. The company's plastic bottles are recalled from customers (cleaning product producers) due to an anomaly in the manufacturing process. In order to recover from this crisis, the company has to re-deploy substantial resources to deal with enquiries from customers, identify the cause of the product defect, improve processes and to compensate customers who have to find alternative suppliers. Consequent to the immediate crisis, Artem has to pay heavy fines levied by Health and Safety bodies in UK and EU countries and pay for increased insurance premiums. Furthermore, with a tarnished reputation, the company encounters major difficulties in establishing local distribution and sales agreements with third parties in the new markets. The loss of sales and the fall in reputation leads to the abandonment of the market entry strategy. Artem Plc's share value falls substantially and the company becomes the target for a hostile takeover.

The second scenario occurs having entered the US market. The company's products are affected by one of its customers recalling its bleach products after a split in the bottles causes bleach to spray onto customers' hands leading to several injuries. The reaction of the bleach manufacturer is to (erroneously and publicly) blame the packaging producer (Artem Plc) for the split in the plastic bottle. The attention of the public and the regulatory authorities turns immediately to Artem Plc, which finds itself the subject of several lawsuits. In addition, several other buyers in the US market have suspended orders pending an official enquiry into the incident. The incident leaves the company with rapidly falling sales, a tarnished reputation and facing several lawsuits which it must set out to defend (although it is clearly not culpable). A year later, the bleach manufacturer finally admits that the bleach contained in the damaged bottles was the result of faulty production which made the bleach far more corrosive than normal, although it still claims that the plastic bottles should have been more resilient. Artem Plc now decides that the only way in which it can restore its image and lost sales is through litigation against the bleach manufacturer for lost revenue and libel. Some eight years after the initial incident, the company successfully concludes litigation and receives substantial compensation. However, Artem's intended strategy of growth through alliances and acquisitions has been severely impeded.

While both scenarios are quite different, the common themes are BCM related. The product recall exposes the organisation to a wide variety of risks which cannot be precisely foreseen.

The scenario planning process for BCP comprises six stages. First, the identification of participants is undertaken. These might include employees throughout an organisation, suppliers, buyers, industry experts, trade associations and government agencies. Second, data are collected from participants in the form of a questionnaire or interview. Participants are asked to consider the central question and related themes such as:

- How quickly changes are expected to happen.
- The impact of the changes on the organisation.
- The impact of changes on similar organisations/rivals.
- Steps that can be taken to prevent or reduce the impact of the scenario arising.

The answers are normally structured in the form of a questionnaire to ensure comparability of the (often large) number of responses.

The third stage entails the analysis of responses. The planner should then aggregate the responses in order to identify common themes and issues in the responses, and identify variations in the responses. Once the analysis is complete, scenario planning marks the fourth stage. From the responses, scenarios should be written in the form of a narrative, starting from the precursors to the scenario event (that is, what are the signs that it may happen?), the event itself and the aftermath and implications for the organisation. In many instances, more than one scenario may be written, reflecting the degree of uncertainty.

The scenarios that have been developed require validation to ensure that they reflect the views of participants and contain a logical and feasible narrative. Hence, the penultimate stage normally involves group seminars charged with scrutiny of the scenarios which have been devised. This scrutiny serves to evaluate whether the assumptions underpinning the scenarios are correct, raise awareness of the impact of the scenarios arising and stimulate discussion of the ways in which the organisation should have provisions in place to deal with the scenario(s). Finally, the scenarios should be integrated into the BC plan. Many organisations' BC plans will contain a section labelled "scenarios". In other cases, rather that provide the lengthy detail of the scenario, a short summary is provided (see Box 5.6).

Box 5.6 An Example of a Summarised Scenario

Access to Yorkshire building is lost due to:

- Building collapse in vicinity
- Utility leak (gas/water)
- Anti-capitalist demonstrations
- Closure of vicinity by police
- Malicious hoax

Outcomes of the scenario:
Computer and telecommunications systems are available but activities need to be located to the hot site (invoke part 2 of the plan)

Or:

All resources within the building are not available/damaged (invoke part 3 of the plan).

Summary of the Planning Process

Scenario planning is the penultimate stage of the planning process. Each of the proceeding stages have been designed to systematically gather information and develop knowledge about the nature of the organisation and its BC requirements. These are summarised in Table 5.8.

The final stage is the development of the plan itself – the document(s) to be used in the event of a crisis.

Table 5.8 Summary of the Planning Process

Stage of planning process	Purpose
Identifying objectives and scope	*Recognise* why and where BC is needed
Identifying the causes of crisis	*Anticipate* and evaluate a range of interruptions
Business impact analysis	*Assess* the balance between investment and exposure
	Evaluate outputs, resources, linkages and dependencies
	Understand the external influences on BCM
Business impact evaluation	*Balance* internal and external analyses
	Consider the likelihood and consequence of crises
	Incorporate future changes into today's plans

Generating the Business Continuity Plan

The development of a BC plan does not mark the end of the BCM process. It marks only a small part of it. The emphasis of BCM is upon management. However much attention is placed on plans, they can often lead to the misbelief that an organisation has good BC practices in place. It is the improvements provoked by the plans for business resumption that are the real indicators of their worth. Any plan than arises from the planning stage of the BCM process is a reflection of the quality of input.

Plans do not exist to show the merit and exactitude of the planning process from which it was borne. Plans exist to:

- help to establish the severity of an incident;
- coordinate human resource requirements;
- guide people in a systematic way through the recovery process;
- demonstrate to stakeholders that an organisation's business recovery arrangements are suitable;
- guide the process of testing (Chapter 7);
- improve confidence in the BC process;
- provide a focus for the planning process which is the real source of all learning;
- help challenge, where apt, current operational practices and assumptions.

However many plans are in place within an organisation, in order for them to be effective they must be *achievable, testable* and *cost-effective*.

Organisations can generally determine the content of plans in two ways. The first is to use specialist software that provides a template (often adapted). This offers a comprehensive and consistent structure with which to work. The second is an organic approach developed in-house. In these cases the BC manager devises a structure developed from the internal and external analyses and may be influenced by a variety of publicly available sources. Every organisation has a different style of plan. Some organisations tend to combine several documents together, while others retain them as separate, but related, documents. Whichever approach is taken, the essence of a plan is to systematically guide recovery teams through the stages of incident recognition, invocation, damage assessment, staff callout and recovery or restoration activities.

In addition to how well developed BCM is, factors such as organisational structure and size, geographical location, the number of departments and the variety of product sold will determine whether an organisation has many or few plans. The term "plan" in a BC context often refers to a series of inter-related documents which are broadly found within the following categories:

1 The "general" BC plan.
2 The call-out lists.
3 The timeline of recovery.
4 Functional BC plans.

Whichever combination of documents an organisation chooses to devise, they must be considered to be "live". Without regular maintenance and testing, their usefulness in a real crisis may be severely limited.

The General Business Continuity Plan

Effectively the reference work for BCP within an organisation or large function and its size and use will vary between organisations. In some organisations, the general BC plan will effectively be the document to which reference is made during an interruption. In others, factors such as size and structure will lead to the development of functional or departmental sub-plans which are implemented by smaller groups. However, as Smith notes "Sub-plans for individual departments . . . need a coordinating 'top' plan to prevent conflict of interest and misuse of resources. A priority should be to incorporate measures to contain the crisis, ensuring continuity of function and a speedy return to normality" (1996: 27).

Table 5.9 shows the relationships between the planning activities and specific sections of the plan.

The general plan forms the basis from which call-out lists, timelines of recovery and functional policies are devised. Tables 5.10 and 5.11 show some of the structures that plans may adopt.

The first example (Table 5.10), the document structure serves as a broader reference "manual" for the BC procedures that the organisation has

Table 5.9 General Plan Content and Relationship with the Planning Process

"General BC plan": Section name	Source of information: Analysis/planning activity
The organisation's goals and objectives	Objectives and scope
BCM policies	BIE – objectives
Identification of which business areas have BC plans	BIE – risk assessment
Terms of reference, i.e., what constitutes a crisis that would lead to invocation of plans	Frameworks of crisis types and scenario planning
Priorities of business operations	BIE
Immediate resumption	BIA, BIE and priorities
Intermediate resumption	BIA, BIE and priorities
Late resumption	BIA, BIE and priorities
Scenarios (including the "worst case")	Scenario planning
How simultaneous interruptions are dealt with	Scenario planning
Resources and deployment	BIA
Off-site facilities	BIA and supply chain analysis
Composition and structure of the crisis management team	Objectives and scope
General recovery procedures	BIE
Plan maintenance and testing	Discussed in Chapter 5
Contracts and agreements with third party suppliers	BIA and supply chain analysis

Table 5.10 Sample BC Plan Structure (A)

"Investment operations: ********* Bank Plc"

Section number and title	Contents
Section 1: Overview	Objectives Terms of reference BCM policies Identification of critical tasks Continuity of management Resumption of normal operations
Section 2: Recovery procedures	Declaring the "zero hour" Initiating call tree/cascade call: criteria and report of unreachables Arrangements for transport to alternate facilities

	Establishing emergency command centre
	Inventory of equipment and matched against requirements:
	Office equipment
	Telecommunications
	Vital records and supplies
	Terminal hardware
	Computer equipment
	Software
	Set up and testing of equipment
	Establishing telecommunications
Section 3: Operating requirements and reference	Call tree, initiator and recovery team details
	Alternative location specification (workspaces)
	Proximity requirements
	Dependencies on other groups
Section 4: Plan maintenance and testing	Identifying changes to plans
	Amending current "live" plan
	Authorisation of changes
	Testing
	Pre-defined scenarios
	Frequency and type
	Announced
	Unannounced
	Walk-through
	Live
	Evaluation
	Measurement criteria
	Procedures and review
Section 5: Forms, logs and general reference	Restoration logs
	General supply requests
	Contacts
	Telecommunications
	Service agreements
	PR guides
Appendices	BC plans for departments and functions
	Call-out lists
	Timelines of recovery
	Functional policies

Source: based on Elliott et al. (1999a)

in place. Reference is made to the general objectives of the BC plan and to the ongoing testing and auditing (which we consider in Chapter 6). In addition the plan details the types of equipment that are necessary to carry out recovery activities (Section 2) and contractual relationships that the company has with recovery suppliers (Section 5). The second example (Table 5.11) is focused more towards the activities and organisation involved in practical recovery efforts. Issues such as objectives, testing and third party relationships are not included. This does not mean that the company has chosen not to include these within the plan. Instead, it

Table 5.11 Sample BC Plan Structure (B)

"International operations: ********* Plc"	
Section number and title	*Contents*
Section 1: Introduction	1.1 Control Levels and Escalation 1.2 Incident Response 1.2.1 Duty Emergency Team 1.2.2 Incident Response Group 1.2.3 Emergency Management Board 1.2.4 Business Continuity Team 1.2.5 Front Line Team 1.3 Command and Control System 1.3.1 Gold, Silver, Bronze Hierarchy 1.4 Associated Documents
Section 2: Definition of terms used in this document	Explains the terms used in the Section 1 of the plan and other relevant terminologies.
Section 3: Plan index	Index to general BC plan and functional plans.
Section 4: Plan detail	Timelines of recovery.
Appendix 1	Emergency Services Incident Information
Appendix 2	Duty Emergency Team Membership
Appendix 3	Incident Response Group Membership
Appendix 4	Emergency Management Board Membership
Appendix 5	Procedure for Call Out of Incident Response Group Call-Out Script
Appendix 6	Evacuation Inside the Building Leaving the Building At the Assembly Points
Appendix 7	Maps and Plans
Appendix 8	Local and National Government Contacts

recognises that much of this information may not immediately be required in the event of an interruption. Accordingly, rather than having one single "plan" which documents all aspects of BCM, this plan is focused on the structure and organisation of recovery activities following invocation. Plan structure B is much more practical in nature and comprises two parts. In the main sections, the user navigates from the procedure required at the start of an incident through to call out and assembly of recovery teams. Once the damage assessment is complete, teams are assembled at the appropriate location (which could be off-site in the case of a denial of access incident). Users then proceed to the plans that are required from the damage assessment in order to restore or replace resources and processes that are known to require attention. The plan's appendices also tend to contain practical information rather than information that would be superfluous in an invocation and which might serve to make the document less easy to navigate.

Their differences are, primae facie, that of focus. Ultimately, however, it is the testing process that will determine the usability of the plan under circumstances of an interruption. Elements which are common to both plans and all practical plans are call-out procedures (which systematically call staff to the recovery location) and timelines of recovery (which direct the recovery process). We now turn to each of these important elements, starting with the call-out procedure.

Call-Out Procedures

Often found as an appendix of departmental or functional plans, the call-out procedure provides a systematic way in which to call out employees in the event of a business interruption outside office hours. Also known as a "cascade call", the objective is to call out essential personnel in the most efficient manner possible. Any variation to the contrary will affect the ability of recovery efforts to take place effectively. Such lists have to be constantly revised to incorporate changes to personnel, roles and responsibilities, and home telephone numbers. The call out should be designed to bring the appropriate employees to work on business recovery at the appropriate time. A predetermined call-out script should include a security check, information about when and where to attend, and reminders to bring ID and not to talk to the media without authorisation. Plans can stand or fall by virtue of call-out procedures. If too many staff are called out, valuable time is wasted in deciding which staff to retain, and which to send home to await further instructions. Equally, too few may be available for call out due to personal details being out of date, incorrect or responders unable to arrange transportation or childcare at the time of a call out.

Good links between BC managers and human resource departments are essential to the success of call-out lists. Perhaps the most critical relationship, however, is between the BC department and the line managers who should be responsible for ensuring that cascade lists are kept up to date; call-out lists have to reflect the dynamics of the organisation's staff through arrivals, departures, promotions and restructuring, etc.

Timelines of Recovery

The general plan identifies the priorities of business operations which are incorporated into a chronology of events from the time that an incident takes place (known as the "zero hour"). Listed in sequence are the activities required to resume normal operations. The BIE provides the list of priority tasks which should be completed as quickly as possible. The levels of recovery for prioritised tasks are known as recovery time objectives (RTOs), recovery milestones (RMs) or recovery point objectives (RPOs). RTOs are based on the priorities for resumption from BIA and then BIE, an understanding of dependencies from the internal, external and supply chain analyses and worked through or known procedures to move, restore or replace a resource, process or activity. The concepts of RTOs, RPOs and RMs are often used interchangeable to denote recovery activities that must be accomplished by a predetermined time following the zero hour (the time of invocation). The predetermined time is identified from an understanding of dependencies, service level agreements in the supply chain, stakeholder needs and restoration lead times (that is, how quickly a resource of process can physically be restored in practice). These elements constitute the maximum acceptable downtime or "outage tolerance" for a resource or process. Distinctions between RPOs and RTOs have been articulated with the former referring data and the latter to processes (Rider, 2003).

The timing of an activity's recovery is determined by its strategic importance to the organisation as informed by the BIA. Often, these priorities are agreed at board level to ensure that resumption is truly based upon a highest priority first. Activities which require immediate resumption are those critical to the survival of the organisation. The next priority would be activities which could have an effect upon the longer term position of the organisation. Following the resumption of these priorities, activities which restrict customer service or hamper administration should be recovered. The approach taken will vary according to the organisation and the type of interruption. For example, Lee and Russo (1996) suggest that the response to an interruption has two phases. The response phase deals with bringing the situation under control (such as stabilising a leak, restoring power, recalling products) and the recovery stage which follows deals with returning operations to normality (repairing and preventing the leak, upgrading or introducing back-up power systems, and rectifying the recalled product's design). Where an organisation's plans to be structured in such a manner, it would be appropriate for this to be applied to recovery time objectives.

Clearly, each crisis will have different effects, but the timeline will clarify the priority and timing of critical activities. An example can be seen in Figure 5.11. There are two critical features: the chronological order of activities from the time of the incident (spanning from one to twenty-four hours), and the sequence of activities which should be undertaken within each time period. For example, within the first hour of the incident, there is little to be gained if staff are informed (and subsequently called out or otherwise) but the staff help-line is not available. Equally, within the third hour of the incident, recovery suppliers are informed that their services

	RTO to be achieved within time after invocation (hours)								
	1	2	3	4	5	6	7	8	24
Tick when completed	☑	☑	☑	☑	☑	☑	☑	☑	☑
Inform BC manager	☐								
Establish staff help-line	☐								
Inform staff of incident	☐								
Inform staff of incident and tell them to be on standby	☐								
Await Recovery Team (RT) approval to invoke plan		☐							
Establish customer/supplier help-line		☐							
Conduct preliminary assessment of damage		☐							
RT go-ahead to invoke functional plans if needed		☐							
Identify staff requirements		☐							
Inform senior management of incident		☐							
Invoke contingency service agreements			☐						
Attend recovery site			☐						
Request critical staff to attend site			☐						
Inform non-critical staff to remain at home and await further instructions				☐					
Hold situational report meeting				☐					
Set team objectives				☐					
Assess state of work in progress				☐					
Call up back up tapes or records				☐					
Inform linked departments					☐				
Informed linked departments of new arrangements					☐				
Inform customers and external suppliers					☐				
Initiate delivery of contingency agreements:						☐			
Equipment						☐			
Stationary						☐			
Telecommunications						☐			
Mail service						☐			
Prioritise new work						☐			
Test new equipment							☐		
Resume critical activities								☐	
Inform non-critical staff of progress								☐	
Prepare schedule for return to full capacity (Including the clearance of any backlog)									☐

Figure 5.11 Example structure of timelines of recovery.

will be required and therefore the recovery team is expected to arrive. Then, staff called to the recovery site can be managed and directed upon their arrival.

Organisations can use alternatives to the method shown in Figure 5.11; for instance, by using flowcharts. However the sequence of events is organised, employees involved in recovery should be aware of what they ought and ought not to be doing. This can be communicated to employees through awareness raising, meetings, testing and documentation. A free phone number, with a changing message, may also provide a means of easily communicating with staff during a crisis.

Functional Business Continuity Plans and Recovery Strategies

At a functional or departmental level, organisations may choose to develop individual continuity plans. For instance, the timelines of recovery for an

IT department could differ widely to that of a production department. It is therefore prudent to develop recovery-timelines for each. Such department-specific RTOs (similar to Figure 5.11) will be found in the general plan, but the department's BC plan will contain a greater level of specific detail on how the department will recover its operations. Functional BC plans may take another form, which recognises the specialist assistance that it can provide in the event of an interruption elsewhere in the organisation.

The human resources or personnel department may be deployed in an interruption situation to liaise with employees that are not immediately required, ensuring that employees are paid and overtime payments are promptly processed and that extra expenses (for transportation and food) incurred are dealt with quickly. It may also provide counselling facilities or coordinate contact between staff and third parties in this regard. A further role may involve managing the release of confidential employee information via the PR department to the media (in the event of fatalities or injuries) and to provide continuance in its obligation to the availability of documents required by law (for example, for industrial tribunals etc.).

The public relations function will adopt the role of interface between the organisation and the public. Its functional BC plan with pay particular attention to protocols for the release of authorised verbal, printed or electronic information to the media, organisation of PR briefings and dealing with unsolicited media enquiries. Moreover, a crisis media centre will also require advance planning and organisation, the detail of which should be explicit within both the functional BC plan and the general BC plan.

In the event of an interruption which does not directly affect the sales department, the sales function BC plan should aim to ensure that existing and future sales are not jeopardised. Therefore, the critical activities are to maintain contact with customers, establish a customer database in alternative locations (if necessary), provide and resource a help desk for customers, ensure the continuity of sales in progress and payments, and ensure the availability of documents required by law (for example, contracts, etc.).

Similarly, the purchasing, procurement or logistics functions should focus upon parties within the supply chain, but in this instance the focus should be on those from which deliveries of goods and services are required. Important activities with the functional BC plan may involve contact procedures to suppliers in order to divert or suspend deliveries, BC of electronic ordering or payment systems and the provision of documents required by law (for example, vehicle licensing, etc.).

The Health and Safety department has an obvious role in the management of an incident involving hazards, accidents and evacuations. In addition, where the recovery process moves to another location, the department will be involved in ensuring the compliance of alternative premises with due regard to statutory provisions. Similar to sales and personnel functions, documents required by law will have to be made available and post-incident reporting will often represent the mainstay of the department's activities. The facilities (or property/premises) function will play an important role in providing an emergency centre (food, drink, toilets, etc.), ensuring security, and liaising with emergency services and local authorities.

The functional BC plan associated with legal departments will include provision for activities such as the preparation of insurance claims, liaison with other functions to determine the scope for litigation, preparation for product or company liability litigation and the ongoing pursuance of industry and regulatory requirements. Often, it is the legal department which has the longest role in the post-recovery phase, due to the initiation of legislation against the organisation in the aftermath of a crisis.

Box 5.7 Product Recall Strategies

Product recalls may arise due to accidental design, testing and assembly failures, or as a result of a deliberate campaign of malicious product tampering (Chapter 2). Specific provisions for a product recall may include the following:

- Early warning systems – are high levels of complaints and repairs monitored to identify trends and warning signals before it is too late?
- Recall classifications – how are resources shared which might influence the scope of a product recall?
- Recall decision – who is authorised to take the decision to recall the product (if voluntary)?
- Corrective action – what options are available – refund, replacement, repair or retrofitted correction?
- Recall level – where and how far along supply chain are we required to recall the product?
- Traceability – what systems does the company have to identify affected batches or model numbers and to locate defective products?
- Notification – what systems and media will be used to inform supply chain partners and customer of the product recall?
- Response rates – what proportion of total production has been retrieved?

No single function can produce a product recall plan alone. The requirements listed above necessitate the involvement of several functions to monitor, implement and respond to product recall developments. Variations in the requirements for product recall plans will differ by industry and location (for instance, the US

Consumer Product Safety Commission an enforce recalls as can local authorities under The General Product Safety Regulations 2005 in the UK). Siomkos and Kurzbard (1994) have associated the type of response from an organisation in relation to a product recall with the customer's perception of danger and future purchase decision. The "super effort" response, in which the company makes it very easy for the customer to return or replace the product is likely to lead to the most positive outcome in what, invariably, is an uncertain situation for a company facing media and customer scrutiny.

In the case of a malicious product tampering incident, many elements of a general recall plan can be used but the criminal dimension of the threat means that the responses may differ in a number of ways. First, there will be a need to liaise with law enforcement agencies and this may involve a line of investigation in which suspects include employees as well as outsiders. Second, it may be difficult to provide detailed information to the media given that the incident may lead to criminal proceedings. Such constraints need to be communicated clearly to the media since otherwise the company may be presented as being uncooperative. Third, once the cause of the sabotage (tampering with the product and packaging or tampering with equipment) is known, steps will be required not only to remedy the shortcoming but also to communicate this to consumers to reassure and rebuild confidence in the company, its products and brands.

Source: based on Abbott (1992); Siomkos and Kurzbard (1994)

Tucker (2006) identified a number of generic recovery strategies that organisations should consider as they set out to re-establish and restore activities:

- Business recovery centre strategy (availability and use of hot, warm and cold sites).
- Office relocation strategy (to other owned building or new rented facilities).
- Home-working strategy (reduce reliance on immediate relocation).
- Switched telecommunications strategy (using cellular/mobile phones).
- Outsourced manufacturing strategy (to overcome extended recovery of facilities).
- Materials purchasing strategy (including buying materials from competitors to fulfil orders).
- Data systems protection strategy (a central part of a company's BCM).
- Alternative systems strategy (move from automated to manual or vice versa).

- Human resources strategy (change shift patterns to speed up recovery).
- Reciprocal agreement strategy (with partners or rivals).
- Equipment hire strategy (to provide access to office or manufacturing equipment, vehicles, mobile phones, etc.).
- Production scheduling strategy (to determine new production priorities).
- Resource reallocation strategy (to identify the scope to shift resources to deal with the most urgent recovery priorities).
- Purchase recovery strategy (to ensure the swift delivery of large volume purchases of equipment).

The development and implementation of functional BC plans and generic recovery strategies recognises that a portfolio of plans and strategies may be required rather than one overall plan. As we pointed out earlier, while plans are a tangible output of the BC planning process, they are only as useful as their relevance in the event of a crisis. Learning from the planning process may be as important as the plan itself.

Summary

Planning for the future is well established. Indeed, the twentieth century marked the birth, adolescence and maturation of many planning techniques which have influenced the BC planning process. There is a critical difference however. General business planning (strategic, operational or marketing) is underpinned by the expectation – indeed, the hope that – the scenarios (the future) contained within the plan will arise. In contrast, the BC planning process differs in its expectation and its hope – that the plan will not be used. This is not a mandate to disregard the importance of the plan, but rather to consider the impact of not having a well formulated BC plan in place.

In this chapter we have explored the individual stages of the planning process. The planning process is derivative of organisations' widely differing approaches and should be tailored to meet the idiosyncrasies of an organisation's structure, processes, people, industry and stakeholders. Without this, the likelihood of poor planning and poor plans is heightened.

Critical to the planning process are knowledge and participation. Without the two, those who are best served to inform the plan and its procedures will remain under-utilised, and those who will be required to implement the plan in the event of an interruption will have little ownership of the processes which they are to follow. We have sought to emphasise that we consider interactive forms of data collection as a vital complement to the more structured but more closed approaches usually adopted. Although the process identified above may be seen as systematic, we contend that planning remains more of an art than a science.

As we made clear early in this chapter, planning and plans do not mark the end of BC activities. It is the pivot between planning and the ongoing management of increased resilience from and response to business interruptions. In the next chapter, we address how such management is enacted in organisations, specifically with how the changes which necessarily accompany BC are implemented, both strategically and operationally.

Study Questions

1   Visit the websites of an organisation that has recently encountered a crisis. What do these companies have to say about their stakeholders?
2   What are the problems associated with the methodology of risk assessment?
3   Write down some examples of resources that are shared widely across organisations.
4   Identify a small number of examples of how the PEST factors could increase the potential for crisis.

Further Reading

Alexander, D. (2000) "Scenario methodology for teaching principles of emergency management", *Disaster Prevention and Management*, 9 (2): 89–97.

Herbane, B., Elliott, D. and Swartz, E. (2004) "Business continuity management – time for a strategic role?", *Long Range Planning*, October, 37 (5): 435–457.

Johnson, W. H. and Matthews, W.R. (1997) "Disaster plan simulates plane crash into high-rise building", *Disaster Prevention and Management*, 6 (5): 311–317.

Keown-McMullan, C. (1997) "Crisis: when does a molehill become a mountain?", *Disaster Prevention and Management*, 6 (1): 4–10.

Le Coze, J. (2005) "Are organisations too complex to be integrated in technical risk assessment and current safety auditing?", *Safety Science*, 43 (8): 613–638.

Macgill, S.M. and Sui, Y.L. (2005) "A new paradigm for risk analysis", *Futures*, 37: 1105–1131.

Morwood, G. (1998) "Business continuity: awareness and training programmes", *Information Management and Computer Security*, 6 (1): 28–32.

Pitt, M. and Goyal, S. (2004) "Business continuity planning as a facilities management tool", *Facilities*, 22 (3/4): 87–99.

Ringland, G. (2006) *Scenarios in Public Policy*, Chichester: John Wiley & Sons.

Smallman, C. and Weir, D. (1999) "Communication and cultural distortion during crises", *Disaster Prevention and Management*, 8 (1): 33–41.

6 Embedding Business Continuity Management

Introduction

Where the focus of Chapter 5 was with analysis and planning for BC, this one is concerned with embedding related processes and change management. The old adage, "plans are nothing, planning is everything" has been attributed to many great leaders, including Churchill and Eisenhower, and reflects the view that the investment of time and capital in plan creation is of little value without using "learning" from the process as a platform from which to adapt, flexibly and aptly, to changing environments. This is as true of BC as it is of planning in general. This chapter is primarily concerned with the issues of change management and, in particular, with considering how BC processes may be embedded throughout an organisation, the third stage of our model of effective BCM, shown in Figure 6.1. In Chapter 1 the evolution of BCM was charted from its disaster recovery roots to the current day. It was suggested that the auditing mindset was a response to a series of financial scandals occurring during the early 1990s. This mindset has developed into the modern focus upon benchmarking and standard setting. It is not enough to do BC, it is vital to be seen to be doing it in an accepted way. Increasingly, the practices of BC have become institutionalised and associated knowledge codified. Organisations are "porous" (Chesbrough, 2003) and interlinked and do not practice BCM as islands. Information sharing is a constant and practitioners understand the importance of proactively seeking out information that can be shared. The validity of such information may be subject to the forces of institutionalisation and, as Meyer and Rowan (1977) argued, the rational drivers of innovation may come to be replaced by emotional ones as the importance of being seen to do what is considered right comes to replace acting in a considered way. The typical manager, short of time, is all too willing in many cases to accept the advice of experts or adopt "industry standards" with limited questioning.

When freak rainfall affected the UK during 2007, the county of Gloucestershire was badly hit, with transport infrastructure severed leading to 10,000 motorists stranded, some 6,000 homes and businesses flooded,

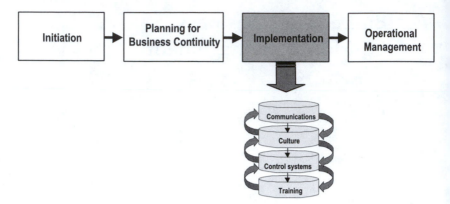

Figure 6.1 Business continuity management as a business process.

25,000 homes without electricity for two days and water supplies to 135,000 homes and 7,500 businesses cut for from twelve days to twenty weeks. Three people died in Gloucestershire, raising questions about the county's preparedness. Yet Gloucestershire had won awards for its emergency and BCP, it had achieved Beacon Status and was seen as a model of best practice. Yet after the flooding, Garnham (2007) identified a number of limitations of its preparedness including:

- Lack of consultation with key agencies in developing emergency plans.
- Vulnerable location of the Emergency Management Service Emergency Response Centre in an underground bunker that was prone to flooding. The Centre had to be relocated during the crisis event.
- Failure to identify single points of failure, such as water treatment works, and prioritise apt response.
- Poor communications between agencies.

The "award winning" process did not appear to be fit for purpose when faced with the acid test of a major event, yet had provided a model of best practice for other organisations and may act as a cautionary tale to avoid complacency and to question, always, expert advice. In Chapter 5 a framework for analysis and evaluation was put forward, which we suggest, if followed in a critical and reflective spirit, should result in valuable and useful insights. As with any such process however, "garbage in will result in garbage out" (Elliott and Johnson, 2008a). Assuming that the understandings derived possess some validity, this chapter is concerned with their translation into apt behaviours, in both preparing for and responding to interruptions.

In Chapter 5 the BC process was depicted as a sequential process to suggest a logical progression from project set up, through analysis to implementation. This reflects the systematic process for analysis recommended.

However, in practice the BCI's and BSI's depictions of the BC lifecycle captures the essence of an ongoing, iterative, never ceasing process (see Figure 6.2). The BSI's (2007) BCM lifecycle depicts BCM programme management at the centre of the organisation and four core activities, starting with understanding the organisation, determining strategy, developing and implementing response and finally moving to exercising, maintaining and reviewing activity. These four activities are iterative and are located in a particular organisational context within which BCM has been embedded. This "embeddedness" is at the heart of making organisations resilient and we will explore the aspects of organisational life that make this possible.

Embedding BC into the organisation presupposes effective implementation. Two elements provide the key to securing effective implementation. First, an organisational structure is required to ensure clear lines of authority, control and communication. Second, the creation of the organisational conditions for effective implementation (communications, culture, and control and reward systems and training). The first part of this chapter places the discussion within the wider context of organisation studies, with a brief review of the literature associated with change management and organisational culture. The second part reviews a number of practical issues associated with building a flourishing BCM process. While "audit"-driven approaches (see, for example, BSI, 2007a, b) provide a useful checklist of "things to do", the logical and sequential approach that it suggests is rarely possible. Such approaches fail to capture the messy complexity of organisational life, which arises from a diversity of factors including changing contexts, internal politics, faulty assumptions and the

Figure 6.2 The business continuity management lifecycle.

Source: adapted from BCI (2007b)

bounded rationality of managers. Successful BCM requires effective change management.

Change Management

Two fundamental theoretical perspectives to change management may be identified (Clegg, 1992; Wilson, 1992;[6] Collins, 1998). The first places great emphasis upon structural approaches to change and includes concern with organisational design and organisation–environment linkages. This perspective places less emphasis upon human activity and how individuals make sense of the world. Instead, it emphasises the importance of *getting* the logic of the change strategy right, persuading people of that logic and designing appropriate structures and control systems for the next steps. Such an approach involves a minimum of three stages:

- analysis
- choice
- action.

Such an approach suggests that the management of change may be dealt with in a logical, rational manner. Once a chosen change strategy emerges from the analysis and selection process, the central task for the "change agent" is to convince individuals and groups of the need for change.

A second approach combines behavioural studies derived from inter-personal and social psychology and cultural studies, which regard organ-isational climate, ideologies and beliefs as pre-eminent (see, for example, Deal and Kennedy, 1982). As Johnson and Scholes (2008) have argued, ultimately the success of strategic change depends upon the extent to which people change their behaviour. Change is thus concerned with their beliefs and assumptions and the processes in their organisational lives. In some instances, managers are perceived as possessing superhuman qualities that enable them to alter the thinking of colleagues, subordinates and customers. While not dismissing the need for planning, proponents of this view emphasise the importance of securing the commitment of individuals to change.

These two perspectives are not mutually exclusive but reflect trends within the study of change management (Worren et al., 1999). Indeed, following an examination of these two dominant approaches, a hybrid model is suggested – one that seeks to combine the rationality of planning approaches with the "humanistic emphasis" of behavioural approaches.

Wilson (1992) provides a four-celled matrix, characterising approaches to change management (see Figure 6.3). The matrix is founded upon two dimensions: planned–emergent change and process–implementation of change. Models of change which assume that change can be planned for in advance will differ radically from those which have been developed from

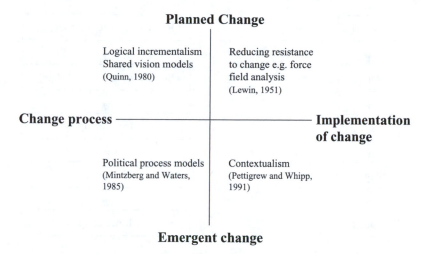

Figure 6.3 Approaches to organisational change.

Source: adapted from Wilson (1992)

the premise that change emerges from the interplay between a myriad of variables. While much can be gleaned from pursuing a logical process of analysis, there are dangers that the difficulties of achieving change will be underestimated. The process–implementation dimension is less clear as represented by Pettigrew and colleagues' (1989) attempt to span the two in their work. For Wilson (1992) the distinction between process and implementation is that the latter focuses on the management of individuals, while "process" is concerned with the critical examination of the context, history, motivations and movement of change. For our current purposes it is sufficient to note these contributions and move on to consider using the change management literature from a practical perspective. More detailed reviews of the change management literature can be found in Wilson (1992) and Collins (1998).

Planned Change

Planned approaches follow a predetermined path through analysis of change, identifying likely consequences and developing the means to overcome resistance. Forces for and against change can be shown in terms of a force-field analysis. Lewin (1951) held that organisations existed in a state of equilibrium created by the interplay between opposing forces. This results in a state not conducive to change. Change, argued Lewin, required the "unfreezing" of the existing state of affairs, the intended change to be enacted, and then the new *status quo* to be refrozen (as shown in Figure 6.4).

The concept of force-field analysis underlies many planned change approaches (see, for example, Kotter and Schlesinger, 1979; Dunphy and

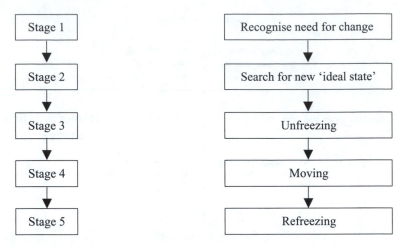

Figure 6.4 Lewin's force-field analysis.

Table 6.1 Example of Force-Field Analysis for Business Continuity Management

Forces for change	Forces acting against change
BCM part of good management	Economic downturn
Customer–supplier relationships (Mutual dependencies in supply chain)	Partner intransigence
Growing reliance upon technology	BCM a none core activity
Customer expectations: client focus	Too little time
Experience of interruption	Individual not team incentives
Corporate governance	Complacency about change
BS 25999	Other priorities
Board commitment	BCM not my job
Insurer requirement	BCM an expense not an investment
Change normal	No reward for BCM success

Stace 1987; Plant, 1987) and its use is widely advocated in strategic management textbooks. Table 6.1 shows an example of force-field analysis applied to an organisation implementing a BC process. The forces for change include external and internal pressures. These may represent forces specific to an organisation (for example, experience of a crisis) as well as generic stimuli such as industry or national and international standards of expectation. Forces acting against change are usually concerned with the individual organisation, including its belief systems, operating norms, reward and control systems (see Table 6.1). A later section of this chapter examines Johnson and colleagues' (1997) cultural web and it is suggested that elements of these two tools may be combined to provide an insightful analysis.

The success of planned approaches to change depends on accurate identification of the best way forward and anticipating barriers to change. In their adaptation of a force-field analysis Kotter and Schlesinger (1979) identified self-interest, misunderstanding, lack of trust, different assessments of the need for change and low tolerance as the most common reasons for resistance to change. All may be present, to differing degrees, within one organisation or even within an individual. For example, misunderstanding or different assessments of the need for change may be reinforced by self-interest.

Selecting the means for overcoming resistance will depend on a correct diagnosis of the cause(s). Dealing with resistance can encompass, at one extreme, coercion; although inevitable when managing change that is urgent and important (for example, during a turnaround situation), it may encourage resistance where urgency does not provide much needed legitimacy. Elliott and colleagues (1999b) have argued that the successful embedding of a BCM process requires line managers to assume responsibility for the process. As Kotter and Schlesinger (1979) noted, coercion is not effective as a means of securing a long-term change in beliefs.

Change management's relationship with BC is not just with managing interruptions, but also with enhancing an organisation's capabilities for preventing and responding to potential crises.

In summary, the advice emanating from planned approaches is that successful change efforts will be those where choices are internally consistent and fit the key situational variables. Table 6.2 combines a traditional force-field analysis with a range of options for overcoming resistance. Burnes (2004: 342), drawing upon extensive empirical data, argued that, in

Table 6.2 Planned Change

Forces for change	Forces against change (Kotter and Schlesinger)	Strategies for overcoming resistance (Kotter and Schlesinger)
External • economic • political • social • competitive • legal Internal • experience • board • strategic • decision	• Differing perceptions • Self-interest • Misunderstanding • Mistrust • Different assessments • Low tolerance for change	• Education • Communication • Participation and involvement • Facilitation and support • Negotiation • Manipulation • Coercion

spite of the prescriptive planning approaches offered by the gurus, "most managers are driven by expediency and operate in a responsive mode". Whatever the appeal of planned approaches, and it is our view that they may provide a valuable source of data and a process to aid reflection, they do not act as a mirror of practice. The management of change within organisations is more complex and messier than is often suggested in textbooks. Although Burnes (1996: 322) proceeds to critique emergent approaches to change management, it appears from a close reading of his work that he is dealing with a simplistic view of the emergent nature of change.

In our usage of the term, the emergent properties of change refer to their human and organisational behavioural origins. In other words, successful change management depends on changing the values, beliefs, attitudes and thus actions of individuals and groups. Planned approaches may assist in determining the nature and extent of required change. Emergent approaches emphasise the important human element that will determine the success of any change management programme and it is to this that we now turn.

Box 6.1 Means of Embedding Business Continuity

Some organisations delegate responsibility for BC from a dedicated team to line managers. A common pattern emerged from these organisations. Education and communication played an important role in raising the profile of BC and informing managers of why they should take it seriously. Thus, short training programmes, regular newsletters and ongoing informal contact created the platform from which effective BCM was implemented. Potential resistance to change was further reduced by encouraging participation and involvement. For example, the Royal Bank of Scotland and J Sainsbury included staff from a range of business areas within their BC teams. Such secondees contributed to the process by bringing in differing perspectives and by acting as ambassadors for BC when their period of secondment ended. A further source of resistance to change concerned a possible lack of expertise in the area of BCM. While secondees provided one means of spreading expertise, BC teams provided ongoing support, coordination and encouragement. In one USA-based bank, the BC team possessed an almost evangelical zeal in terms of combining education, communication, encouragement and, as a last resort, cajolement, to ensure that line managers treated continuity seriously. In some other banks, the individual reward systems appeared to act against the taking of continuity seriously. For the successful dealer, like the top football player, if the team fails, they can simply transfer to a new one and possibly earn even higher rewards.

Source: Herbane et al. (1997); Elliott et al. (1999b)

Writing in 2009, it is clear that J Sainsbury retains an effective BC capability, one which has resulted in competitive advantage in the face of major interruptions triggered by extreme weather. In both cases, rapid recovery ensuring continuity of service resulted in advantage over rivals not so well prepared to respond to interruption. Equally noteworthy is the persistence, in some organisations, of viewing BCM as a one-off project, conducted by a project officer and shelved as soon as the plan is prepared (Elliott and Johnson, 2008a).

Emergent Change Management: Creating a Vision for Change

Approaches to change management, which emphasise its emergent nature, are particularly concerned with managing the process and less concerned with implementing a detailed plan. Key issues concern organisational politics, culture and setting a sense of vision. As many authors have noted, change management is all about modifying individual and organisational behaviour. This section draws on the strategic management literature and considers how managers might handle the change process.

Effective change management requires a clear sense of purpose that is well communicated throughout an organisation. Many successful organisations have a clearly expressed sense of vision. For Komatsu, the Japanese bulldozer manufacturer, the sense of vision was to encircle Caterpillar, symbolised as ©. Komatsu's strategy was to build market share slowly by targeting small customer segments who were not fully satisfied by Caterpillar, and to build market share incrementally, thereby avoiding a head-on clash that would have been too risky for Komatsu. For Microsoft, "Windows software on every desk" proved irresistible until it was observed that this suggested office workers and computers. It is now "Windows everywhere" reflecting a drive towards any viable technical platform. In Figure 6.5 the vision may be seen as setting the parameters for the stream of decisions in an emergent strategy.

With regard to BCM, preparing a vision statement may fulfil two important roles:

- First, the very process of formulating a short, sharp statement of intent should help clarify for the BCM manager, other line managers and senior executives, the essence of continuity management. For some, BC may concern only technical or information systems problems, for others it may include many forms of operational risk. The speedy refund and compensation paid to passengers on the cruise ship *Aurora* in April 2000 may be seen as a consumer-oriented approach to BC. The redefining of BCM to incorporate protection of brand, stakeholder and value-adding activities reflects the growth of a broader view of it.

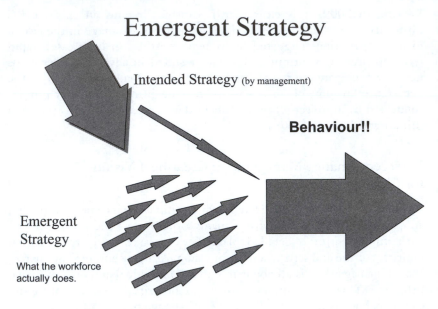

Figure 6.5 Deliberate and emergent strategies.

Source: adapted from Mintzberg and Waters (1985)

- Second, such a statement should provide a valuable communication tool for raising awareness across an organisation and to staff at all levels. To be effective it must not only be easily understood but also must combine relevance with simplicity and thus impact upon an organisation's culture. All staff should be made aware that, even where a dedicated BC team exists, it forms a part of everyone's job.

An apocryphal story tells of an international bank invoking its BC plan and assembling its senior management team. Unfortunately none had the necessary skills to access the relevant databases; this was a task usually delegated to a secretary who was not included within the continuity plan. Continuity management is the preserve neither of senior managers nor of a dedicated team; effective continuity depends on successfully harnessing the energy and interest of staff at all levels. The role of the vision statement is to communicate clearly to all staff.

From our earlier discussion it will be clear that organisational culture has tremendous influence over organisational, and thus individual behaviour. The long-term success of organisations such as HP-Compaq, GE, Disney and more recently Ryanair has been explained in terms of their distinct cultures. For some, the customer service ethos has been key, for others innovation. Whichever, long-term success has been achieved by the development and ongoing support of what Peters and Waterman (1982) described as shared values and which we define as culture.

Culture

Culture, stated Hofstede (1990), has acquired a status similar to strategy and structure within the management literature. Pauchant and Mitroff (1988) suggested that culture is to the organisation as personality is to the individual. Many models of culture (see Table 6.3) agree that it may be thought of as combining a number of distinct layers, some hidden, including individual beliefs and assumptions coming together in the form of shared values and operating norms and, ultimately, consistent patterns of behaviour. More specifically, Mitroff and colleagues (1989) suggest that:

> The culture of an organisation may be defined as the set of rarely articulated, largely unconscious beliefs, values, norms and fundamental assumptions that the organisation makes about itself, the nature of people in general and its environment. In effect, culture is the set of "unwritten rules" that govern "acceptable behaviour" within and outside the organisation.
>
> (1989: 271)

Culture provides an important element of the context in which change occurs. Effective change requires that new behaviours be learned. Learning occurs within a "structure of meaning" that is broadly shared, and Levitt and March (1988) suggested that such structures need to be sufficiently flexible to permit some change in operational procedures, although in practice:

Table 6.3 Alternative Models of Organisational Culture

	Schein (1992)	Pauchant and Mitroff (1988)	Williams et al. (1989)	Hofstede (1990)	Trompenaars (1993)
Description	Multi-layered	Onion	Lily pond	Onion	Onion
Surface level	Artefacts, creations	Plans	Behaviours	Symbols	Observable reality in language etc.
	Structures and processes				
		Organisation structure		Heroes	
				Level 3	
				Rituals	
Partly visible level	Espoused values	Assumptions and beliefs	Attitudes and Values	Values	Norms and values
	Strategies, goals, philosophies				
Invisible level	Basic underlying assumptions	Individual beliefs	Unconscious beliefs		Core assumptions about existence

participants collude in support of interpretations that sustain the [organisational] myths. As a result, stories, paradigms and beliefs are conserved in the face of considerable disconfirmation and what is learned appears to be influenced less by history than by the frames applied to that history.

(1988: 324)

Similarly, Starbuck and colleagues (1978) observed that organisations sought to "routinise" the means by which they had become successful and in so doing became internally focused and concerned with efficiency. In an analysis of man-made disasters, Turner (1976, 1978; Turner and Pidgeon, 1997) argued that all organisations developed a continuous culture closely related to their tasks and environment, and that there was a developmental tendency for a "collective blindness" to important issues:

> This is the danger that some vital factors have been left outside the framework of bounded rationality. When a pervasive and long-established set of beliefs exists within an organisation, these beliefs influence the attitudes of men and women inside the organisation. They affect decision-making procedures and mould organisational arrangements and provisions so that there is the possibility of a vicious self-reinforcing circle growing up.
>
> (1976: 388)

A basic barrier to embedding BC processes concerns cultures, which, it is argued, are resistant to change. The rhetoric of continuity may be spoken but either this falls on stony ground or it slowly percolates to the substrata of the organisation. Culture represents the ground and provides the context for change. As with change, there are different views about the concept of "culture". Two alternative perspectives are put forward in the next two sections.

The first, drawing from a psychoanalytical base, explores in greater detail Pauchant and Mitroff's (1988, 1992) crisis-prone to resistant continuum. The second section presents a normative model of culture. Although its theoretical grounding is limited, it is argued that it can provide useful insights into the many facets of an organisation's culture.

Crisis-Prone or Resistant: Onion Model of Culture

People and groups within organisations may employ a range of reasons and strategies to resist change, even when events highlight inadequacies in systems, procedures and beliefs. The failure to invest in railway infrastructure during the 1990s created a dangerous context as indicated by the accidents at Paddington in 1999 and Hatfield in 2000.[7] The lack of early warning systems across much of South Asia, despite awareness of threat from history, contributed to the deaths of approaching a quarter of a million people in 2004. This tragedy prompted efforts to put right this gap, drawing from the experiences of Japan and Hawaii which, recognising the threat, had such early warning systems already in place (Aglionby, 2005). The failure of an award winning system in Gloucestershire, identified at the start of this chapter, acts as a warning against complacency. Indeed, there were echoes of the criticisms around preparedness in the aftermath of the devastation wreaked by Hurricane Katrina.

Pauchant and Mitroff (1992) suggest that individuals, alone and collectively, employ a range of defence mechanisms or faulty rationalisations that support resistance to change, whether it be outright non-action or commitment to a particular course of action as in the cases of Gloucestershire and during the pre-Hurricane Katrina phase. The greater the use of such defence mechanisms, the more prone to crisis an organisation will be. For example, that the world may be warming seems beyond doubt, yet resistance to change continues. Underpinning this resistance may be outright denial, or disavowal that if it happens, it will not be too serious and warmer summers would be welcome in Northern Europe, or the experts will find a solution or through projection whereby the route to prevention is through controlling economic development in the developing world. Pauchant and Mitroff (1988, 1992) concluded that organisations might be placed on a continuum from crisis-prone to crisis-prepared according to the prevalence of defence mechanisms. The place of an organisation upon such a continuum would be determined by assessing a combination of factors:

- organisational plans and behaviour;
- organisational structures;
- collective beliefs and assumptions;
- individual beliefs.

These four groups of factors were depicted as an onion model of crisis management (see Figure 6.6).

Box 6.2 Learning from the UK Rail Industry

The UK railway industry had undergone dramatic change during the 1990s but it might be argued that little progress had been made. There is evidence that faulty organisational communications hindered the transmission of warnings to key executives and that Railtrack and the rail companies were focused on improving efficiency and their utilisation of resources. A culture focused on economic efficiency and faulty organisational communications combined to provide the underlying causes of the crash. They were manifest in greater debate about the precise nature of improvements to be made to track infrastructure, disagreements regarding the sources of investment, difficulties in prioritising investment, the fragmentation of control over repair and maintenance through growing use of subcontractors.

At Paddington, concerns over the position of signal 109, partly obscured by other fixtures and bright sunlight at certain times of the year, were not heeded. At Hatfield, plans to replace faulty tracks had been made but not acted upon.

Before the Paddington and Hatfield crashes, "cost-benefit analysis" indicated that sophisticated train warning systems were too costly. The deaths of thirty-four people in the two incidents altered the statistics and provided the political will for change.

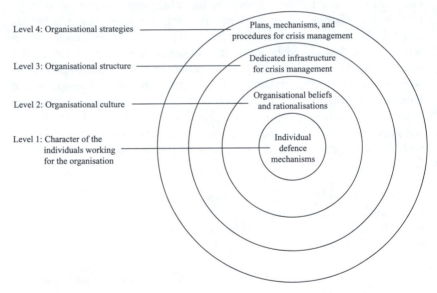

Figure 6.6 Onion model of crisis management.

Source: Pauchant and Mitroff (1992)

This model provides a framework for considering discrete areas requiring management attention during a programme of change. The inner layers refer to individual and group beliefs and assumptions – the focus of behavioural studies of change management. The outer two layers refer to structures, plans and actual behaviour, and provide the focus for the advocates of a planned approach to change management. These tangible elements reflect the beliefs, values and assumptions of the core. The onion model suggests that the effective management of change requires attention to both elements. Mitroff and colleagues (1989: 273) suggest that there is: "extreme overlap and interpenetration between the various factors that compose the levels such that it is extremely difficult to say at times which circles are true subsets of which".

Core Beliefs

At the heart of the onion model lie core beliefs. For Pauchant and Mitroff (1988, 1992) three key factors provide a basis for an organisation's crisis proneness:

- the degree of self-centredness;
- the degree of fatalism;
- the nature of defence mechanisms.

The degree of self-centredness is closely related to an organisation's ability to consider a range of points of view. A stakeholder perspective is akin to a system's perspective: it acknowledges the importance of other groups and their viewpoints, providing a greater basis for understanding. An outer orientation, associated with crisis resistance, may be expressed in terms of seeing beyond traditional organisational boundaries, thereby facilitating a greater understanding of the environment. Crisis-prone organisations had a narrower view of stakeholders, failing to see that they were part of a wider system. An example might be a travel company that perceives a faulty aircraft as a technical problem rather than as an interruption to its customers. When travellers are delayed for lengthy periods, a customer-oriented airline will provide refreshments, telephone facilities and, if necessary, accommodation. When BA's systems failed to cope with the opening of Terminal 5 at London Heathrow, the company was widely criticised for its poor service continuity, with elderly passengers left without refreshments for many hours as the airline's staff failed to cope with the scale of the interruption.

Fatalism, observed Mitroff and colleagues (1989), reduces guilt and responsibility and acts as a justification for doing nothing. At its most basic, the view that disasters are freak accidents or caused by some other external agency reduces the perceived control that any organisation has over them. Such a view will have a strong influence on the amount of time and resources that are invested in crisis prevention and preparation. The president of Exxon insisted that the *Valdez* accident was an "act of God that could not have been prevented"; he failed to acknowledge twenty-nine previous oil spills that shared many similarities (Pauchant and Mitroff, 1992).

Defence mechanisms, argued Pauchant and Mitroff (1992), are employed to "distort external reality" to such an extent that individuals can avoid having to deal with complicated, potentially threatening situations (see Table 6.4). Crisis-prone organisations were approximately seven times as likely to use these devices as crisis-prepared ones. Fixation, the

Table 6.4 Defence Mechanisms

Level 1: Defence mechanisms	Explanation
Denial	Expressed refusal to acknowledge a threatening reality or realities
Disavowal	Acknowledge a threatening reality but downplay its importance
Fixation	Rigid commitment to a particular course of action or attitude in dealing with a threatening situation
Grandiosity	The feeling of omnipotence. "We're so big and powerful that nothing bad can happen to us" (Mitroff and Pauchant, 1990)
Idealisation	Ascribing omnipotence to another person
Intellectualisation	The elaboration of an action or thought. Pauchant and Mitroff (1992a) argue that intellectualisations frequently involve distorted schemes of reasoning to justify a particular course of action
Projection	Attributing unacceptable actions or thoughts to others
Splitting	The extreme isolation of different elements, extreme dichotomisation or fragmentation

Source: adapted from Mitroff et al. (1989); Pauchant and Mitroff (1992)

unquestioning pursuit of a particular course of action, represents an almost complete absence of double-loop learning.

> Single-loop learning asks one-dimensional questions to elicit a one-dimensional answer. For example, a thermostat which measures ambient temperature against a standard setting and turns the heat source on or off accordingly. Double-loop learning takes an additional step, or more often than not, several additional steps. It turns the question back on the questioner. . . . In the case of the thermostat for example, double-loop learning would wonder whether the current setting was actually the most effective temperature at which to keep the room and, if so, whether the present heat source was the most effective means of achieving it. A double-loop process might also ask why the current setting was chosen in the first place.
>
> (Argyris, 1994: 78–79)

For BCM the over-emphasis upon IT interruptions might provide one example of single-loop learning. Similarly, denial and disavowal provide some justification for executives doing nothing – the "it couldn't happen here syndrome", or if it does, "it won't be very serious". Grandiosity and idealisation reflect a view that someone (us or another agency) will be sufficiently powerful to deal with all eventualities. The scale of events such as triggered by the Tsunami of South Asia, Hurricane Katrina and New Orleans or the Italian earthquake of 2009 stretch the resources of rich and poor nations alike. Yet, as we argued in Chapter 5, organisations are dependent upon each other as never before. As individuals we are also connected as never before and viruses, whether virtual or biological, may spread quickly. The increasing scarcity of key resources creates the potential for further interruptions. Fuel supplies from Russia to the Ukraine and countries during the Balkans in the winter of 2008–9 highlighted the dependence of Europe upon Russian gas supplies. Rising fuel prices and shortages of diesel placed greater latent power in the hands of tanker drivers, seen in industrial action. Such triggers seem far removed from individual organisations, yet their impacts may be significant and demonstrate the impotence of even governments to deal with. Individually and together, the presence of these defence mechanisms provides a strong indication of the (in)effectiveness of organisational learning.

Defence mechanisms may lead to the distortion and manipulation of information as individuals acting in groups make use of vagueness, ambiguity, inconsistency and withholding data to obscure errors and make them uncorrectable. Hirokawa's (1988) analysis of the Challenger disaster described how defence mechanisms acted as powerful blockers to the collection, analysis, discussion and exchange of information between engineers employed by the designers of the Space Shuttle and NASA representatives.

In summary, defence mechanisms act as powerful barriers to change. At their most extreme (denial) they block out any attempt to collect information. More subtly, they permit the distortion and misinterpretation of information and reduce the effectiveness of learning. Denial and disavowal may be employed by organisations to ignore potential environmental threats. Pauchant and Mitroff (1992) argue that inner-oriented organisations were more likely to ignore external threats. More significantly, their lack of environmental awareness was reflected structurally and procedurally in the lack of any mechanisms for scanning the environment. This may raise the probability that warning signals are not interpreted accurately and this inner orientation may also act as a barrier to learning from the experience of other organisations.

From a change management perspective, assumptions regarding these issues will create not only ideological barriers to change, but also influence the transfer of knowledge into action by determining the allocation of resources in the form of time and money devoted to a particular area (Elliott and Smith, 2006). Thus, assumptions about the nature of the organisation will play an important role in determining the importance given to issues such as BC. An organisation that believes itself "omnipotent" will choose not to devote time or money to BC. Change may be constrained through lack of time to consider the relevant issues and through the lowly status of its internal champions.

Cultural Web Analysis

Cultural web analysis (Johnson and Scholes, 1997) provides a simple tool for painting a rich picture and thereby gaining some insight into the nature of culture within a particular organisation. An example of a cultural web for a university is shown in Figure 6.7. Such analysis, if it is to be meaningful, requires input from many members of staff; indeed, a useful way of using the tool is to use it as the focus for discussion so that differences and similarities in perception may be examined.

The *stories* told in organisations help shape behaviour by communicating the unwritten values. They indicate what is important. An apocryphal story told at Disney Corporation is of a car park attendant who checks the temperatures of the car engines of senior executives at 7.15 a.m. each day. If the engine is too warm, the executive is fired – because it means that the executive has recently arrived. The story is told to reinforce the view that to get on at Disney you have to work hard and get in early. Staff at IBM claim that the initials stand for "I've been moved" or "I've been married"; success at IBM means giving your all to the company. *Symbols* are a powerful communications tool. The extravagance of corporate entertainment and sports sponsorship of organisation such as AIG and RBS might be seen to symbolise an approach to business, one reflected in recent difficulties. In many Japanese companies, all staff (including executives) wear the same

Stories	Power Structures
Remote vice chancellor communicates via annual DVD/pod cast	Extreme centralism (tail wags the dog)
Win major research or consultancy funds	Hidden power of technical support
Eccentric staff	Rivalry in fight for resources between departments
Approach to customer service likened to a cornered rat	
Symbols	**Control and Reward Systems**
Professorships, PhDs, MScs etc.	Research success
Jargon	Tight budgetary controls
Parking space	Avoid complaints in teaching
Expensive equipment	Communications – 'it's on the intranet'
Rituals and Routines	**Structures**
Teaching comes first	Vertical hierarchy,
Complicated bids for funding	Little inter-school communication
Work alone, little team spirit	
Paradigm	
Low-cost educational provider	
Maximise non-teaching income	
Excellent external programmes, poor internal ones	

Figure 6.7 Cultural web of a university.

type of overall to symbolise the importance of teamwork. *Rituals and routines* provide a powerful, socialising influence. Routines may include never leaving before the boss or everything stopping for the doctor's walk around the ward in a hospital. *Power* is located throughout the organisation, and not just at the pinnacle of the hierarchy. A school's lunchtime supervisor can go on strike; an aggrieved technician can sabotage essential laboratory equipment; an IT technician can plant a virus-bomb – each can disrupt the smooth running of an organisation. Power does not always reside in the most obvious place. The changes in the funding of UK universities led to changes in *reward systems*. The sub-prime mortgage crisis of 2007 and 2008 could similarly be traced to the reward systems in the US mortgage industry. Finally, *structure* may act as a facilitator or as a constraint. The rigid bureaucracy is likely to struggle to adapt to dynamic changes in its environment.

The framework can be used to assess where an organisation is and where it wishes to be. It identifies a number of the softer issues that must be managed if change management is to be effective.

Applying Cultural Analysis to Organisational Change

Cultural web analysis provides an opportunity for those involved in continuity planning to identify barriers and aids to change. A number of stages may be envisaged (shown in Table 6.5). The first stage refers to a state in which it is perceived that there is no need for change and that there is a high degree of fit between an organisation and its environment. Within studies of crisis (see Turner, 1976, 1978, for example) a significant happening is usually required to create the recognition that change is necessary. For IBM, Marks & Spencer and Citi Group, major losses forced a strategic review and refocus. The scale of these losses and the obligation to report them publicly required these companies to change their strategies. IBM and Marks & Spencer sought changes in style, process and market focus. Triggers may arise from the environment too. Bombs at the World Trade Centre and in London highlighted vulnerabilities, as did the love letter virus which demonstrated the growing reliance of international business on email communications. Most recently the failure of web connections in North Africa, Middle East and Asia (http://www.cnn.com/2008/WORLD/meast/01/31/dubai.outage/index.html) blamed on damage to undersea cables in the Mediterranean Sea reminded governments and companies that our communications technology is still dependent on vulnerable physical resources.

The second stage occurs as pressures for change build. Where companies report significant losses within one year it is usual to find a longer, underlying trend of falling profitability that was ignored or played down. Warning signs might include changing customer preferences, new product or process developments. With regard to BCM, warning signs might include ongoing difficulties with a group of suppliers, low staff morale with high absenteeism, problems experienced by competitors, intermittent failures or difficulties experienced by suppliers and competitors, unrest in the Middle East, etc.

The third stage is the trigger, a turning point at which it is recognised that change is needed. The nature of this event will depend upon the sensitivity of each particular organisation. For example, some bottled mineral water producers have yet to introduce a despatch control system that would enable them to identify stocks on supermarket shelves quickly in

Table 6.5 Cultural Readjustment

Stage	Description
1 Initial beliefs and norms	Perceived harmony between organisation and environment
2 Incubation period	Events indicating need for change unnoticed or misunderstood because: <ul><li>of erroneous assumptions</li><li>rigidities of beliefs</li><li>perceptions</li><li>of a reluctance to fear the worst outcome</li><li>of difficulties of handling information in complex situations</li></ul>
3 Trigger	Felt need for change
4 Flux and unfreezing	Information collected and interpreted within managerial mindset Political testing of support for options
5 Cultural readjustment	Definition of new well structured problems and appropriate changes in light of newly acquired knowledge Stories shape attitudes and beliefs BCM seen as an integral part of sound business
6 Active Learning and refreezing	Communication of knowledge and of new expectations to target personnel and/or organisations Knowledge filtered through culture, communications and structures of organisational personnel. New symbols reflect change Questioning of organisational norms and operating procedures Organisational cultural readjustment occurs Cultural readjustment process triggered by perceptions re the symbolic importance of "precipitating event" Propensity of an organisation to learn determines effectiveness of learning process

Source: adapted from Lewin (1951); Turner (1976); Elliott and Smith (2001)

case of a product recall. The estimated $2 billion cost of Perrier's 1990 recall was clearly not seen as providing sufficient warning. Responding to a spate of product tamperings, Heinz have "tamper-indicating" bottle tops on their baby food ranges.

Depending upon its severity, an incident will trigger a state of organisational flux as alternative models of response are examined. This is stage four and fits closely with Lewin's unfreezing stages. The degree of search will depend upon the perceived importance of the imbalance between the current state and the desired state. This stage of analysis will be influenced by the interplay between various interest groups, each with its own peculiar view of the need for change whether founded upon self-interest or upon a different assessment. Identification of these diverse interpretations is vital to securing the success of the change management process.

From this flux will emerge a growing consensus on the nature of change required. This fits closely with Turner's (1976, 1978; Turner and Pidgeon, 1997) cultural readjustment. Active learning (Toft and Reynolds, 1997) refers to the effective translation of change into new operating norms and practices. This fits with Lewin's notion of refreezing, although the growing literature concerned with learning organisations may argue that refreezing is an outdated notion in a constantly changing world. Refreezing, to be effective, requires communication of how and why change must occur; the processing of this knowledge by groups and individuals; and finally, the absorption of the new knowledge through its translation into new or adapted behaviour.

Cultural web analysis has been identified as a tool which may assist in the change process. It may be used to identify a current profile, including barriers to change, with a desired profile to aim at. Figure 6.8 depicts an "ideal" cultural web for effective BCM.

Box 6.3 Cultural Web

The stories reported by BC managers often include events that had initially triggered the continuity process. For some it was a personal experience of floods, the bombings of the City of London, Mumbai, Madrid or the World Trade Centre in New York that had caused the senior management to consider continuity management. In South Africa, a history of political tension was key. In the travel industry, kidnapping, terrorism or air crashes triggered interest in BCM in smaller and medium-sized travel organisations.

The symbols associated with BCM also provide indicators of its status. For example, who does the BC manager report to? Is it to the head of IT, audit or to the director with responsibility for strategy? The reporting structure will not only make more or less difficult the task of communications but also symbolise whether or not BCM is seen as a strategic issue. A direct or easy link to the board will indicate real interest, as will the presence of a board-level champion. Recent events such as the financial crisis spurred by the sub-prime mortgage industry implosion affords us an opportunity to peek at structure and reporting relationships in companies (*Wall Street Journal*, 24 January 2008). Risk management as a function had apparently shifted to a lower stature and importance in most investment banks as the US benefited from the lending boom, and while Wall Street companies enjoyed financial prosperity post-2001, risk managers lost their positions on executive boards and were not allowed as much air time to voice their concerns.

Rituals and routines may be concerned with the extent to which BCM forms a part of the day-to-day management of an organisation. Is continuity routinely considered in the design stages of new products and services, as is increasingly the case with Japanese car manufacturers Toyota and Nissan? Do discussions of strategy routinely include a BC perspective? Are line managers responsible and resourced for the BCM process or is it left to a specialist team? In short, is BCM seen as an extension of sound management practice or is it a bolted-on process that touches the organisation only partially?

Power and control are closely linked with the preceding two categories. The hierarchical structure provides the formal context in which the BC manager operates. If formally a part of the IT department, then barriers may be created between the BC manager and other parts of the organisation. In some organisations, the lead BC coordinator is viewed as a "special projects officer" – a well-liked member of staff who had provided good service to the company but not seen as sufficiently dynamic for more important work. We saw the contrary too. The selection of a manager for BCM sends out powerful signals regarding its perceived importance and thus influences the likely support or interest of line managers who have many tasks to occupy their time.

Reward and control systems influence organisational behaviour. To ensure that BC receives adequate middle management attention requires that it forms a formal component in their appraisal. The nature of the measurement will also be important. For example, is performance measured on the readily observed production of new plan documents or on the less tangible measures of effectiveness, of gaining real commitment from line managers and enhancing organisational resilience to interruption? The latter is clearly more difficult to measure but arguably more important. Better an approximate answer to the right question than an accurate answer to the wrong question.

Structure provides the means by which individual efforts are coordinated and orchestrated into an organisational whole. It provides the conduit along which formal communications run. The range of communication tools includes formal meetings, interviews, training, newsletters, short presentations, testing and informal links. Effective communication in support of BCM requires a combination of these that is appropriate to each organisation at different stages of development.

> We look at the types of people we are dealing with and we will tackle them depending on what they are, so we study them for a while. We learn what their life is like, what they do, what their role is in the organisation and what kind of skills and what type of people are doing this job. You therefore cannot come up with a standard "stand up and tell them that this is the way in which you are going to do contingency" because it won't work like that. You have to look at them and understand what they are like and hit them with the right kind of story. We've become very inventive, haven't we? (both respondents laugh).
>
> (BC managers quoted in Elliott et al., 1999b: 52)

Further means of communication might include the recruitment or secondment of staff from the business to work within the BC team. This ensures input from the business and, after the secondment, it secures continuity ambassadors around the organisation. Staff recruited to BC might be usefully drawn from general business or professional backgrounds to ensure a rich combination of skills and knowledge that can be vital to a creative team.

As the Government Centre for Information Systems (CCTA) (1995a) handbook emphasises, the establishment of a successful BC initiative requires the awareness of the board of directors and senior managers and then the real and physical acceptance of key managers and staff. In preceding chapters, we have identified the important role played by external factors in triggering an organisation's interest in BCM in the first place. Bombs, viruses, floods and fires come to mind as obvious examples. These triggers may play an important role in raising the profile of BC.

However, as the Home Office (1997a, 1997b) handbook, *Bombs: Protecting People and Property*, indicates, terrorist incidents are few and far between in the UK. When they occur they attract considerable interest and possibly divert attention away from the routine interruptions that have a higher probability of occurring. Effective BCM should be concerned with anticipating and preparing for internal and external, technical and human threats. Despite its focus upon facilities-type interruptions, the CCTA handbook recognises the threat inherent in the failure of key suppliers.

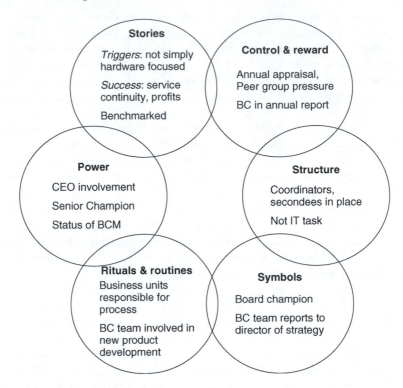

Figure 6.8 Cultural web for business continuity.

BCM is thus about maintaining competitiveness, not the physical infra-structure that supports a firm. As such, it needs to be embedded through all the activities of an organisation, if resilience is to be real.

Awareness without commitment is meaningless. This was highlighted by the broad awareness of the so-called millennium bug or Year 2000 problem. Despite the offer of free government training, the take-up rate of small and medium-sized enterprises was minimal (Williams, 2001), an observation as relevant today as it was then (Elliott and Johnson, 2008a). The first step in extending BCM beyond the bounds of a dedicated team is to secure the commitment of key personnel. We have discussed above the reasons why resistance to change may be present, and we have considered alternative means by which these may be overcome. From the evidence collected it appears that participative approaches combining communica-tion, education, support, encouragement and finally cajolement have proved to be the most effective. Any successful change strategy must meet the complexity of organisational behaviour that it seeks to influence.

We have also considered cultural approaches to change management. It is our opinion that the issues covered support the continuance of BCM as a discipline once the initial launch is completed. As with Human Resource

Management, a specialist department may exist to provide specialist support, but it is our view that BCM is the responsibility of line managers and their staff. Its ongoing consideration requires that it forms a part of the organisation's culture in the shape of values, beliefs and operating norms. To further reinforce this type of behaviour requires that control and reward systems support efforts in this area, otherwise it will quickly be relegated to the group of "should do, but don't have time for" duties.

Finally, for change to be managed effectively a number of key issues need to be addressed. First, it is important that a clear view exists within an organisation regarding the desired changes. Second, change requires both awareness and commitment from key personnel. Third, contextual issues must be identified and addressed. Each organisation will require its own pattern of change management, possibly following similar designs to other organisations, but the fine detail must match organisational idiosyncrasies. Fourth, cultural constraints, although often hidden, must be uncovered and addressed. Failure to do so is the equivalent of papering over the cracks. How do organisations create the preconditions for effective BCM?

Creating the Preconditions for Effective Business Continuity Management Implementation

Overcoming resistance and securing commitment to BCM are key conditions to the success of the implementation process. The importance and influence of middle managers in determining the successful implementation of BC cannot be overestimated. This is in effect the realm of the organisation where much of the organisation's culture is determined. In the BSI's BCM lifecycle this would form an important component of the "Understanding the Organisation". Such understanding is pinned upon four vital components: communications, culture, control and reward systems, and training. The cooperation of middle managers is required to ensure that these four components are put in place.

Communications

Middle managers play a key role in shaping communications; they are often the main conduit for information within an organisation. The mechanism used by many companies to ensure that information about BCM does not get "stuck" at this level is a system of "departmental" coordinators who work with the BCM team. These coordinators may act as champions of BCM within front-line departments, or they may simply provide a formal day-to-day point of contact between the BC team and line managers. Swartz and colleagues (1995) identified that the role of the coordinator was often imprecisely defined, with real responsibility remaining with the BC manager. Many respondents reported difficulties in securing the full commitment of line managers, citing in particular the higher priority given to achieving business objectives. Within many organisations, preparing for a business interruption was seen as a luxury, unless there was an obvious motive such as the threat of terrorism (Elliott et al., 1999a) or a desire to secure BS 25999 accreditation (Elliott and Johnson, 2008a).

In "better-practice" organisations (Herbane et al., 1997), the BC team typically consisted of a small, multi-disciplinary group which reported good relations and regular contact with a group of coordinators drawn from all levels of their business. For instance, at the Royal Bank of Scotland, close contact and a reported high regard for one another enabled the BC team to work with different business units in the development and implementation of new products. The Royal Bank of Scotland BC manager emphasised that his team always sought to persuade and negotiate with managers should they have very pressing business objectives at a particular moment in time. "Better-practice" organisations utilised a combination of methods, carefully targeted to communicate the relevance of BC throughout their organisations (see Table 6.6). These methods included formal reporting requirements as well as the development of informal peer pressure and company intranet sites. The range of media, as well as the deliberate

Table 6.6 Communications Methods Used to Support Implementation

Organisation	Communications mechanisms
Automobile Association	Coordinators play key role in transmitting information
	BCM policy document and guide circulated to all staff
	Presentations by BCM manager to board and business continuity forum
British Telecom	Intranet and Emergency Planning Quality Council
	Peer pressure as BCM is regarded as "part of the job"; coordinators
Calor Gas	Board briefed every three months
	Company magazine used to communicate progress
	Ongoing communications with business units via coordinators
Royal Bank of Scotland	BCM structure ensures close contact with strategy development
	Quarterly report to board
	Liaison meetings with project members
	BCM policy statement
	Company video on corporate security issues
	BCM Quality Assurance manager feedback to line managers
	Video and "roadshows" organised by BCM team
	Peer group pressure

Health Trust A (teaching hospital included)	Business continuity plans prepared by dedicated team in liaison with line departments
	Briefing seminars
	Deliberately selected team members with strong communication skills
Health Trust B	Business continuity plans prepared by dedicated team in liaison with line departments
	Briefing seminars
J Sainsbury	BCM is developed from clearly identified objectives for each business unit. BCM planning and preparation process includes regular meetings of the steering group with each director signing off the review and plans for her/his own section
	BCM and emergency procedures forms part of induction process for all new staff
	Regular articles within in-house journal publicise the work of the BCM team; staff credit card-sized emergency instruction sheet
	J Sainsbury intranet bulletin board
	Board simulations
	Regular tests and exercises
	Awareness raising seminars for all head office staff
	Tests are circulated via intranet
Sunderland	Each department has a nominated officer with responsibility for risk management. The process of identifying and preparing for risk is fed back to the relevant committee and departmental management team
	Emergency plan documents are distributed to key officers in an accessible format
	The success of the authority in a number of risk management areas has created a number of success stories
Thames Water	New event management procedures form a part of standard practice for Thames Water. The risk identification and management process is regularly reported to the board
	Event management card is distributed to all operational staff to clarify emergency procedures and philosophy; regular seminars

Source: adapted from Elliott et al. (1999a)

search for new and better ways to communicate the importance of BC, distinguished better from mediocre or poor practice.

Communication plays a number of roles in developing an effective BC process. At one level it raises awareness and informs staff of the need for crisis preparation. At J Sainsbury, an in-house journal article depicted an office complex destroyed by a bomb. The picture was accompanied by a short statement that summarised the aims of the new BC team as:

> to develop a BC plan to form part of an ongoing management discipline to ensure that if a similar fate befell J Sainsbury that the impact to the business would be minimised.

This combination of words and picture helped raise the profile of BC and demonstrate its value. That message was continually repeated through a variety of media to staff and through the induction process to new appointees.

A second key role for communications is continually to remind staff of the ongoing relevance and value of BCM. J Sainsbury regularly provides progress reports through intranet sites, seminars and in-house journal articles. A permanent reminder of emergency procedures is carried by all staff in a credit card-sized leaflet, a widely used practice elsewhere. The Royal Bank of Scotland employed regular liaison meetings to update project members who communicate with staff within their own business units.

A third role for effective communications concerned the process of collecting and disseminating data during the analysis stages. Line departments and managers know most about their business, and the BC team knows most about continuity processes. Good communication is essential if the parties are to work well together. The clarity of data collection forms and questionnaires is one aspect of good communication. In a number of organisations face-to-face meetings or focus groups were the primary vehicles for collecting data permitting two-way communications. Another aspect of clear communication is a clear sense of the purpose and scope of the process, which helps line managers to identify the information required from them quickly. Similarly, good processes for monitoring and updating staff contact lists will also ease the BC process. Today several software tools and digital media have made this task much more easily manageable. The approach to communications is clearly linked to the issue of organisational culture.

Culture

Organisational culture, as discussed earlier, refers to the deep-seated values and beliefs that members of an organisation hold about their approach to BC. In a number of organisations that had prepared BC plans, while there was evidence of new structures, there was little evidence of any change in the core organisational assumptions, even though some new structures had been put in place. In "better-practice" organisations, the development of BC had led to a deeper re-evaluation of core assumptions. This had resulted in a process that not only sought to protect the integrity of their systems but also extended to a concern for protecting their customers and other stakeholders. In a number of other organisations, line managers saw BC as someone else's problem and expected that someone else (for example, the BC team) would rescue them should an incident directly affect their area. This view seemed to be typical where the focus of BC was internal and upon hardware.

The recognition of internal and external dimensions to the BCP process was also characteristic of "better-practice" organisations (Herbane et al., 1997; Elliott et al., 1999a, 1999b); here there was evidence that plans were developed in partnership between the BC team and front-line operatives. As a result, business units, rather than the BC team, appeared to "own" the planning process. Thus, at BT, sales staff who interfaced with government and corporate clients saw the value of BC: "We have good plans and processes that have been tested and they [sales staff] can utilise this in talking to customers . . . use it as a differentiator to point to things we do."

At Thames Water, a database was used to identify vulnerable residents and businesses in order that the full implications of a service interruption could be recognised quickly. In one case, a burst water main flooded a large garden two days before it was to be used for a wedding reception. Thames Water called in a contract team that restored the garden and ensured that the reception was not spoilt. Although not an everyday event, this was held to typify the growing customer orientation of Thames Water's preparation for emergencies. Indeed, Thames had not publicised the incident because they thought that others might see it as a cynical public relations exercise. The story, however, is repeated within Thames as a symbol of its growing customer orientation and to reinforce the view that events are not just technical in nature. Instead, an interruption's severity is measured by the impact upon customers. Thames Water now uses the term "service continuity" to emphasise a customer-first philosophy.

In the examples given above, of BT and Thames Water, the so-called BC approach was adopted by operational staff and became, quite simply, "the way in which they do things". It had entered their culture.

Achieving Cultural Change

Achieving desired cultural change is a difficult and lengthy process requiring education, communication, participation and leading by example. In particular, an approach to changing organisational culture to incorporate a new priority for BCM might include:

* the development of a clear BC purpose or vision;
* communication of this and a published action plan;
* visual depiction of the relevance of BC;
* awareness-raising newsletters;
* ongoing seminar programme;

- supporting and guiding people towards the acquisition of knowledge and confidence;
- BC team members working alongside operational staff and line managers;
- beginning with people in key positions (opinion formers);
- chief executive or other champion to provide symbolic support;
- providing effective leadership.

Lou Gerstner, chief executive of IBM, decided that all directors, including himself, would spend 50 per cent of working time with customers to demonstrate IBM's new customer orientation. Fred Hassan, CEO of the pharmaceutical company Schering-Plough, is similarly developing a reputation for focusing on the sales force in the companies that he has turned around (Stewart and Champion, 2006). The visible commitment of the CEO and/or a senior board member as champions of BC at organisations such as Sunderland City Council and the Royal Bank of Scotland was highly effective. J Sainsbury employs a system of clearly stated objectives for all business units, including the BCM team, as a means of communicating to team members and internal customers the aims of each unit. The regular review of these objectives encourages staff frequently to think about why they do what they do. BC at J Sainsbury is thereby clearly focused upon business objectives and priorities.

Previous research indicates that effective BC requires the specialist team to play a leading, guiding and supportive role while operational units take responsibility for the BC plan itself. Thus, although BC skills are clearly essential for members of the specialist team, change management skills are also required.

Control and Reward Systems

Adjusting control and reward systems can lead to changes in individual and organisational behaviour. The persistent abuse of pensions-selling reflects the difficulty in changing the behaviour of financial services sales representatives when a large proportion of their salary is commission based. Control and reward systems are the mechanisms by which an organisation makes its requirements of employees explicit. Such systems reinforce operating norms and practices and culture. A performance management system, which cascades an organisation's top level objectives down through successive layers of managers and front-line staff, may be one useful method of communicating goals, such as the need for effective BCM.

If BC is to receive adequate middle management attention, the individual's performance in this area should be regularly reviewed, as part of their normal performance appraisal. The results of such an appraisal may, formally or informally, feed into pay decisions. Evidence indicates that those organisations which use BC to add value, use BCM objectives in performance appraisal.

The way in which performance in BC is measured is also important. On the one hand, the production of new plan documents is readily observed and easily measured. Alternatively, less tangible measures of effectiveness – gaining real commitment from line managers and enhancing organisational resilience to interruption – are more difficult to measure yet arguably more important. Where BC forms a component of the appraisal system for line managers and operational staff, it indicates that BC is an important part of day-to-day practice and not a separate activity. BCM becomes not just a technique to be applied to particular functions but also consonant with the business approach.

Comparing two approaches to quality management illustrates the differences between standard and better practice. Quality control inspections are an after-the-event, weeding exercise that seeks to prevent faulty goods from reaching customers. It is expensive because it can lead to high wastage levels and requires expenditure on an inspection team. A Total Quality Management (TQM) approach works from the starting point that quality is everyone's job and sets a target of zero defects throughout the value chain. This reduces wastage and eliminates the need for an inspection team. Quality inspection is bolted on while TQM is embedded within the organisation. A range of tactics employed by organisations in promoting BCM is shown in Table 6.7.

Training

As a new and evolving discipline, BC training provides an essential source of up-to-date knowledge and skills. The training needs of BC managers and operational staff differ. It appears that BC teams acquire skills and knowledge in the following ways (Elliott et al., 1999a):

- as a result of internal training by BCM consultants – in particular the process of acquiring skills by working alongside such consultants;
- through external BC training delivered by external BC consultants.

Training seeks to develop relevant skill sets covering such areas as those identified within the BCI's ten standards (BCI, 2001). Although these standards reflect the "hardware focus" origins of the Institute, they identify a key part of the range of activities that a BC team may be expected to undertake. Thus research has indicated that BC practitioners consider expertise in areas such as strategic analysis is essential preparation to their work. This reflected a concern that BC could become both insular and too technical in its focus. A sound grasp of strategy would encourage the practitioner to consider the role of BC activity within the broader objectives of an organisation. For example, the Royal Bank Scotland used tools

Table 6.7 Control and Reward Systems Used to Support BCM Implementation

Organisation	Formal mechanisms
Automobile Association	Ownership placed with business unit managers
British Telecom	Appraisal system used for all management staff involved
Calor Gas	No formal mechanisms – rewards are intrinsic rather than extrinsic
Royal Bank of Scotland	Formal appraisal system not used but de facto use of BCM as a key result are for business unit coordinators Quality manager recognises coordinator contribution through formal letter to line manager Peer group pressure
Health Trust A (teaching hospital included)	Business continuity (Millennium Bug project) a key element of the appraisal for key administrative staff
Health Trust B	No formal mechanisms
J Sainsbury	BCM policy explained via company newsletter BCM formally part of induction process; intranet site "Buddy" scheme between head office and store managers to be used to improve communications regarding BCM Reports to company secretary
Sunderland	Formal appraisal of staff with responsibility for risk management; forms an element of chief officer performance measurement
Thames Water	Appraisal planned. Performance indirectly assessed through review of event handling; peer recognition of contribution of new event management procedures

Source: adapted from Elliott et al. (1999a); Elliott and Johnson (2008a)

and frameworks covered on conventional Master of Business Administration courses in its BCP processes. The use of such general business tools supports a broad view of BC and helps to ensure that preparations are not simply restricted to hardware and facilities. Effective BCM also requires training in the relevant tools and frameworks, outlined in Chapters 4 and 5.

Operationalising BC also requires skills in corporate communications, change management and business process understanding, to name but a few. Effective BCM is a way of thinking as much as a set of tools. The good driver will have a good understanding of the highway code and know what each pedal and lever does. But on its own this understanding does not make a good driver; competent and excellent driving reflect an attitude of mind. This is based on sound principles, of course, but it is the way in which the skills and knowledge are put into practice that distinguishes the good from the mediocre and bad driver.

In terms of training for other staff, a range of practices currently used are shown in Table 6.8. These range from formal skills training in aspects of managing specific technology, to more informal, on-the-job training which is, in the main, provided by the BCM team. While some of these organisations do not directly engage in providing training, they are often invaluable sources of information. For instance, these bodies might have special interest groups, which focus on specific aspects of BCM that would enable practitioners to share experiences and knowledge in a safe and knowledgeable environment. Such groups also share information more directly through members sharing practice in their companies. Much learning can transpire in this way. Other forms of more direct collaboration are clearly feasible. For example, there is evidence that, within specific sectors,

Table 6.8 Training Practices Supportive of Business Continuity Management

Company	Practices
Automobile Association	In-house training in use of software and data collection Post-test evaluations
British Telecom	Live exercises (major "lift and shift" exercises) Tabletop testing
Calor	Training of steering group and continuity manager by external consultants
Royal Bank of Scotland	Tabletop testing On-the-job training for coordinators Consultants train continuity team
Health Trust A (teaching hospital included)	Desk-top checks with external suppliers Business continuity team "downsized" 31/03/2000
Health Trust B	Not tested, disbanded 01/01/2000
J Sainsbury	Plan testing for each business unit High-profile media handling training event Tabletop exercises New staff briefed on BCM as a part of induction.
Sunderland	Officers with risk management responsibility sent on relevant external courses
Thames Water	Tabletop exercises Continuity team members attend university conferences and higher education courses

Source: adapted from Elliott et al. (1999a)

organisations are starting to engage in a sharing of very expensive physical resources. For instance, two organisations requiring a hot or cold site to be available might collaborate to share the facility and hence reduce costs.

Another purpose of training, and one which moves away from rehearsal and testing, is to develop adaptive capacity. As conceptions of what is BC have evolved, the notion of resilience has gained in prominence. Despite its inclusion in current definitions of BC, Elliott and Johnson's (2008a) exploration of BCM practice found little evidence that it was actively nurtured. However, work on high-reliability organisations and growing interest in supply chain resilience suggest that consideration of such capacity may become central to BCM practice in the future.

Resilience

In a review of how different disciplines use the concept of resilience, Elliott and Johnson (2008) identified a number of definitions of resilience. For Sutcliffe and Vogus (2003), resilience refers to the maintenance of positive adjustment under challenging conditions. From a materials science view, it is the ability to absorb energy in the elastic range (Nash, 1998: 5). Engineers emphasise characteristics of return time and efficiency (Folke et al., 2003). Moving towards socio-ecological systems, resilience is the capacity of a system to absorb disturbance and reorganise while undergoing change so as to still retain the same function, structure, identity and feedbacks (Walker and Meyers, 2004). Without a social or human element in systems, interpretations of resilience seem to focus on absorbing stress or disturbance with an ability to persist or recover (Elliott and Johnson, 2008a). Introducing a social or human element broadens the scope of resilience to include an ability to reorganise in the face of change. More recent conceptions of organisational resilience tend to extend the concept beyond "bouncing back" and include aspects of sustaining *and* developing, adaptive capacity, and learning and transformation (Lengnick-Hall and Beck, 2003, 2005). Resilience appears on one hand to be an ability to absorb shocks and recover from interruptions, a view that reflects Meyer's (1982) study of how hospitals adapted to an unexpected doctors' strike. Here the term "resiliency" was used to refer to an organisation's ability to absorb a discrete environmental jolt and restore prior order. On the other hand, resilience is an ability to positively adapt to change and transform experiences or situations to advantage, and emerge stronger and more resilient from doing so, as did Sandler O'Neill & Partners.

Sandler O'Neill & Partners, formerly of the World Trade Centre (South Tower), lost almost 40 per cent of staff as a consequence of the attack, including two-thirds of the management committee, the majority of their physical assets and records and significant losses in social capital, including relationships, tacit knowledge and understandings, income and equity. Temporary offices were found and trading resumed the week following the attack. Within one year the company was doing better than ever with record profits and revenues and new highly desirable lines of business (Freeman et al., 2003). How was Sandler O'Neill & Partners able to recover and what is its relevance to BC?

Before reflecting further upon Sandler O'Neill & Partners we will consider further some of the literature relating to organisational resilience. Although many organisations adopt anticipatory approaches to dealing with interruptions, Wildavsky (1988) argued that anticipation is only effective in coping with risk when predictions are highly probable and policies serve to avoid or mitigate outcomes. He suggested that organisations seek a balance between anticipation and resilience as the most beneficial strategy for coping with risk. The anticipation component might comprise formal BCP. The resilience component is the capacity to cope with unanticipated dangers after they have become manifest. At the root of resilience would seem to lie notions of adaptability, self-organisation, innovation and creativity – elements identified in Weick's depiction of the Mann Gulch Fire (Weick, 1993). A central question posed by Elliott and Johnson (2008a) is what conditions enable these characteristics? For Sutcliffe and Vogus (2003), resilience develops over time from continually handling risks, stresses and strains, where an entity not only survives or thrives by positively adjusting to current adversity, but also, in the process of responding, strengthens its capability to make future adjustments. Taking this view, resilience is not only manifest in response to adversity but is inherent in an organisation's ongoing development. Lengnick-Hall and Beck (2005: 705) refer to "resilience capacity" defined as a blend of cognitive, behavioural and contextual properties. As an organisation develops resilience capacity, they argued, it interprets uncertain situations more creatively (cognitive resilience) and therefore is better to conceive of both familiar and unconventional activities (behavioural resilience) that take advantage of relationships and resources (contextual resilience).

Organisations with *cognitive resilience* encourage ingenuity and look for opportunities to develop new skills. Cognitive resilience results from decision-makers' ability to intelligently analyse and respond to a discontinuity and comprises two elements – constructive sense-making and a strong ideological identity. Constructive sense-making is the reciprocal interaction of information seeking, meaning ascription and action. For example, following the 9/11 attacks, Sandler O'Neill were able to re-engage a mass of retired people and ex-workers, including many volunteers, to fulfil important roles knowing that these people had a good working knowledge of the company's business. The body amassed represent Weick's (1993) virtual role systems and contributed to opportunistic restructuring of departments. According to Freeman et al. (2003), a key reason for the successful effort was a feeling of moral purpose in response to terrorism.

The strong moral purpose may have been an "enactment" of strong ideological identity, the second element of cognitive resilience.

Behavioural resilience relates to the interactions and activities that allow organisational members to respond collaboratively to a discontinuous disruption in ways that promote advantageous organisational transformation. It comprises two elements: a complex and varied action inventory, which enables an organisation to take actions that deviate from their norms; and functional habits (rehearsed routines that seek multiple sources of information when uncertainty increases). Implicit in both these elements is a mindset that exploits the utilisation of slack or redundancy, rather than seeking "one size fits all" or "best practice" approaches to solving (what may be) complex problems. It may be because only one of the managing committee survived the attack, having one senior manager made rapid decision making easier, such as the appointment of key staff to take on roles such as communications. Relatives and other volunteers supported Sandler O'Neill by taking on routine administrative and clerical tasks.

Elliott and Johnson (2008a) identified behavioural resilience in the response to the Virgin train derailment in Cumbria (2007). Rapid response and reconstruction of the crash site was greatly aided through the collaborations of a pool of contractors or "community of practice", who, although included competitors, were able to work together to achieve communal objectives. These collaborations are an outcome of contextual social capital and networks.

Contextual resilience is the setting for integrating and using cognitive and behavioural resilience, and is composed of connections and resources – deep social capital and a broad resource network. Social capital has been defined as the networks, norms and social trust that facilitate coordination and cooperation for mutual benefit (Putnam, 1993). Both deep social capital and a broad resource network may be recognised in Sandler O'Neill's resilience following the 9/11 attacks. Freeman et al. (2003) describe Sandler O'Neill as a tight-knit firm – many employees' families were best friends. The organisation was also known as a "relationships" firm on Wall Street. Post-event help from good relationships came in the form of competitors helping with work load and cutting Sandler O'Neill into deals; a supplier providing temporary office space; and past clients remaining loyal to the firm.

Along with an ability to absorb shocks and recover, modern conceptions of organisational resilience recognise the additional abilities for "improvement", "developing customised responses" and "improvisation". Each of these latter abilities represents an underlying capacity for organisational learning, to become stronger and more resilient for dealing with future events. While some events can be anticipated and arrangements put in place to manage those events, there may also be unanticipated events. This is where organisations with these additional qualities or abilities may be more likely to influence positive adjustment under challenging conditions.

Summary

This chapter has identified those elements that, when successfully managed, will aid the development of effective BC processes. Our concern has been to argue that effective BCM requires a cultural change. Effective continuity management is not a bolt-on process but an integral part of sound management. As human resource managers should aim to facilitate the day-to-day efforts of line managers and their staff, the effective BC team should play the role of championing and communicating good practice, providing expert support and ultimately working through line managers. There is no simple recipe but this section has identified the importance of:

- alternative communications strategies;
- suggestions on cultural change;
- control and reward systems used by organisations;
- sources of training;
- providing a clear structure for BC.

It is evident that generic change management strategies may be employed to ensure the effective implementation of BC. Where this has been recognised, "better practice" has emerged as a consequence. We finished the chapter with brief reference to the concept of resilience and discussed its growing relevance for BCM. This provides the focus for ongoing research at the University of Liverpool, UK, which is particularly concerned with exploring how social capital within networks may be exploited to build resilience. BCM is still very much on journey and is not the finished article as the new standards might suggest.

Study Questions

1 Draw up a cultural web analysis of two organisations with which you are familiar. What are the key differences between them? How would these differences influence the development of BCM?
2 Identify five successful organisations. How clearly do they articulate their vision?
3 What are the key issues for a large organisation introducing BCM to consider with regard to creating the effective preconditions for successful implementation?
4 How might these differ for a smaller organisation?

Further Reading

Barney, J. (1986) "Organisational culture: can it be a source of sustained competitive advantage?", *Academy of Management Review*, 11: 656–665.
Bryman, A. (1989) "Leadership and culture in organisations", *Public Money and Management*, autumn: 35–8.

Casse, P. (1991) "Deciding on change: what and how?", *European Management Journal*, 9 (1): 18–20.

Hassard, J. and Sharifi, S. (1989) "Corporate culture and strategic change", *Journal of General Management*, 15 (2): 4–19.

Sheffi, Y. and Rice, J.B. (2005) "A supply chain view of the resilient enterprise", *MIT Sloan Management Review*, 47: 41–48.

7 Operational Management

Testing, Exercising and Incident Management

In early 2008, a British Airways' Boeing 777, flying from Beijing to London, crash landed at Heathrow Airport. Remarkably there were neither fatalities nor serious injuries. The 152 crew and passengers escaped with minimal minor injuries. Willie Walsh, CEO of BA, praised his staff for their calm and orderly management. The happy outcome appeared to reflect the results of much training and simulation, an acid test of the efficacy of all the planning that had gone on before. Passengers later spoke of the calm efficiency of the staff and the speed at which the evacuation took place (BBC, 2008). Further plans swung into action as planes were diverted, priorities allocated, evidence collected and disappointed non-flying passengers directed towards alternative or no arrangements. The apparently smooth operations raised few eyebrows; after all we've come to expect effective BCM, even if many organisations still fail to deliver.

Some fifteen-plus years earlier, Commercial Union's City of London headquarters were affected by an IRA bomb (Commercial Union, 1995). A crisis management team meeting was convened at 7.30 the following morning. Some years previously, Commercial Union had prepared detailed disaster plans for computer installations, datacom systems, hardware, software and telecommunications, with general plans for premises. After all, its advertising catchphrase was "Don't make a drama out of a crisis".

The headquarters was badly damaged. Three people had died and another sixty-seven were injured. Had the bomb exploded earlier, the casualty list would have much longer. Commercial Union staff could not gain access to the building for some days as the emergency services sought to make the premises safe and, where appropriate, collect forensic evidence.

The bomb had badly damaged the headquarters and the network nodes and telephone switchboard contained within it. This loss affected other Commercial Union sites and initially the crisis management team was unable to make either outgoing calls or receive incoming ones. The establishment of new communication facilities was a top priority.

The senior management team was divided into two: one to deal with ongoing business issues, the other to deal with the incident. The business team advised key staff that they intended to have business as usual by

Monday. Outlining their response afterwards, Peter Ward reported that during the early stages it was martial law: "We couldn't afford to have a committee meeting to decide who should go where and who didn't like going there. It was a question of allocating space and telling people where they were going." The intense time pressures required decisions to be made quickly regardless of cost. Replacing the switchboard and network nodes was simply too important to be hindered by an extensive tendering process. Commercial Union was anxious to live up to its catchphrase and not to make a drama out of a crisis.

Commercial Union's response was widely considered as a model of good practice and was circulated among the growing BC community. As this community matured, the scope of its interests extended from considering facilities to incorporate employees – a wide range of stakeholders including customers.

In May 2000, when P&O's £200 million cruise ship *Aurora* sailed out of Southampton on its maiden voyage, 1,800 passengers were aboard. Within twenty-four hours the cruise was over and the *Aurora* was heading back to port. It had simply broken down. The *Aurora*'s passengers were described by P&O as "bitterly disappointed". Anxious to compensate passengers and to avoid extensive negative publicity, P&O quickly offered a generous compensation package, including a full refund and the offer of a free cruise of an equivalent value. The compensation package cost P&O's insurers an estimated £6 million but was successful in controlling negative publicity. Jill Turner, 37, from Bishop Auckland, Co. Durham, said: "There was a general feeling that there should have been more rigorous sea trials before the voyage. People are disappointed but the compensation package is very generous." The quick and generous response removed uncertainty, pacified customers and prevented greater harm to P&O's reputation. Indeed, the speed of response may have enhanced it (Perry, 2000).

Three years later the *Aurora* was at the centre of another incident when there was an outbreak of the Novo Virus (a cause of diarrhoea and vomiting) among passengers and crew (see Elliott et al., 2005: 52). An international crisis was triggered (see, for example, Vasagar and Tremlett, 2003; Searle et al., 2003). The range of stakeholders affected included almost 600 passengers and crew who were confined to cabins; the remaining passengers and crew unaffected by the virus who were confined to the ship as Greek and Spanish authorities refused the ship permission for passengers to disembark in their territories (a decision reinforced with the threat of force); P&O, the cruise ship owners and their shareholders; the lawyers who sought to contact *Aurora* passengers with a view to encouraging litigation; the world's media; and arguably potential future customers. Time pressures were evident in that the cruise was intended to last for seventeen days with specified stops around the Mediterranean Sea. The scale of the virus outbreak required further medical personnel and resource than was available on board the ship (Dolan, 2003). The scale of the outbreak and the impact of the decisions by the Greek and Spanish authorities widened the scope of the interruption, which appeared to take P&O by surprise. This created high levels of ambiguity and uncertainty for P&O as the company sought to deal with the immediate health problems and interruption to the cruise while the scope of the political and media-induced crises was more difficult to manage. Greek port authorities refused permission for docking at Athens and the Spanish government closed its border with Gibraltar to *Aurora* passengers. The media crisis was further exacerbated by the ease with which passengers could use modern technology to communicate with family, friends, lawyers and the media, creating another layer of uncertainty. P&O's credibility came into question as some passengers criticised the company for its slow and tardy response. The media re-examined past virus outbreaks on P&O cruise ships, thereby questioning the company's ability to learn from previous incidents. Although ostensibly a crisis triggered by the cumulative impact of many passengers and staff catching a virus, the scale and scope of the crisis were greatly exacerbated by other stakeholders and by the extensive media scrutiny, fuelled, in part, by the desire of some customers for compensation (Hamilton, 2003).

These four incidents reflect the changing context of BCM. BA's seemingly smooth running incident response was no more than what was to be expected, while Commercial Union had been widely praised. The second Aurora incident identified not only the multiplicity of stakeholders to be considered during a drawn out incident but also the influence of new communication technologies and customer "pathogens" exacerbating the crisis situation.

As BC matures, its emphasis may shift from preparing for dealing with relatively well-structured interruptions, triggered by a loss of facility as at Commercial Union, to the "creeping," ill-structured interruption experienced by P&O during the second *Aurora* incident. It is more difficult to pin point the start and end of such incidents and to predict the range of stakeholders involved. The Ford–Firestone "crisis" discussed in earlier chapters, or the potential emergence of avian flu pandemic or the interruptions posed by the problems of "peak oil" resulting in reducing the supply of a key commodity, pose a much greater challenge than the more traditional bread and butter of BC.

It is evident that more attention has been given to the planning dimension of the BCM process than to that of implementation (see, for example, Ginn, 1989; Strohl Systems, 1995; Hiles and Barnes, 1999). Plans provide a tangible output while effective preparations only become evident in the event of an organisation invoking its continuity plans. Vodafone (2007) cite Niven, Vodafone's head of internal communication, reflecting upon the company's response to the flooding of its headquarters in July 2007. Niven highlighted the importance of options within the plans; for example, how the emergency tannoy system was disabled and staff relied upon text and email. The combination of text and intranet also proved vital to communications with staff after the main building had been evacuated and personnel stayed at home. As the majority of staff had already been provided with mobile phones and web access, home working for a few days was easily achieved. Proud of their response, Vodafone produced a glossy brochure describing it.

The aim of this chapter is to provide an overview of, and introduction to, the key issues associated with incident management. Successful management of an incident is the decisive test of the efficacy of the BC process (see Figure 7.1). It represents the culmination of the organisational pre-crisis efforts – although effective incident management can be summed up in a two-page article, if you believe some authors. It is our view that there is no simple, quick fix or prescription. Effective management of an incident is dependent on sound preparation, correct data in contact lists and a flexible attitude and plan. Earlier chapters have dealt with analysis, planning and testing which may provide a sound platform from which to manage an incident. Pauchant and Mitroff's (1988, 1992) seminal work has indicated that while some organisations are prone to crises, others are more resistant to interruptions. They argue that the plans prepared, and actual response, will be shaped by core organisational beliefs and assumptions. Resilience and resistance may be developed through the identification and examination of potential failures, understanding their implications and preparing for an effective response. The focus of this chapter is on incident management.

There is an expectation that organisations should possess the capabilities to manage major incidents (Cameron, 1994). Within the UK, the loss of the Piper Alpha oil rig provided an important stimulus for the development of crisis management teams, as it highlighted the limitations of much that had passed as accepted practice (Smith, 2000). Moore and Lakha (2006) identify that numerous investigations into disasters have highlighted deficiencies in continuous training and exercising of staff. While agencies such as the UK's Home Office (1997a, 1997b) and the

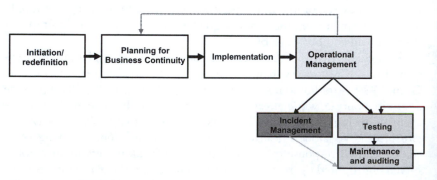

Figure 7.1 BCM as a business process.

Government Centre for Information Systems (1995a, 1995b) have published guidelines, Smart and Vertinsky's (1977) seminal work also remains highly relevant. Responding in part to the events of 9/11 and 7/7 and others which highlighted vulnerabilities, the HM Treasury, Financial Services Authority and Bank of England initiated a benchmarking review of all significant finance sector organisations in the UK to determine their resilience and response capability to potential threats. A key element of this review was a sector-wide exercise. A reported weakness of this exercise was the absence of other stakeholders, such as key suppliers and utilities – a limitation easily remedied. Such partial exercises are clearly valuable but they are incomplete and may not truly replicate the conditions of a real incident.

Handling an incident places specific demands upon an organisation and is usually characterised by complexity and dynamism, requiring organisational and communications structures to fit. Time is likely to be of the essence, a view reflected in ten Berge's (1990) *The First 24 Hours*, which seeks to provide advice on how to manage the first elements of a crisis. Within the aerospace industry an immediate emergency management phase deals with the most pressing rescue and containment. This is closely followed by what is labelled the crisis management phase, in which the focus switches to a broader perspective where the impact on the organisation and its stakeholders is considered and managed and the foundations are laid for the final phase of business recovery. Moore and Lakha (2006) offer a similar definition of these two terms. When BA's Boeing 777 crash landed, cabin crew followed drill and ensured the speedy evacuation of the plane. Airport emergency services were also mobilised to the crash site and the incident was managed effectively. Behind the scenes BA and BAA BCM plans were activated and decisions made on prioritising and diverting other flights, given this interruption to normal operations. Within less than three hours, evidence of BA's moving into a crisis management response may be seen in the briefing given by CEO Willie Walsh to the press.

Of course the number of phases and their duration will be determined by the character of the incident itself. Thus the "critical" period for Ford and Firestone (2000) and Perrier (1990) extended over a number of weeks. In these cases, the recall of product (tyres and mineral water respectively) took place over a period of days, while crisis management efforts stretched over weeks. Crisis management teams are not required simply for twenty-four hours but for the entire lifetime of an incident.

Turner (1976; Turner and Pidgeon, 1997) argued that organisations incubate the potential for major interruptions themselves. Although particularly concerned with major disasters investigated through the public inquiry process, Turner's model (see Table 7.1) has a broader applicability for business interruptions of all types.

Table 7.1 Turner's Model of Crisis

Crisis stage	Description
Initial beliefs and norms	Notional starting point
Incubation period	Ignore warnings and complaints
Trigger incident	Precipitating event
Onset	Focal crisis
Rescue and salvage	Immediate response
Cultural readjustment	Organisational learning

Source: adapted from Turner (1976)

Box 7.1 Missing the Warning Signals

A car manufacturer seeks to employ a minimal stock system, a variant of just in time, and a contract to provide good quality components at a competitive price is agreed with relevant suppliers. Initial beliefs and norms refer to the stage at which the contract is agreed and seen to work. However, imagine a scenario in which the supplier of a key component begins to miss supply deadlines or provides sub-standard parts. At first, the car manufacturer's buffer stocks disguise the problem and, while managers are aware of difficulties, they take no action. They ignore the warning signs because they have many other demands on their time. Then, a significant supply shortfall occurs. Fortunately, the car manufacturer is able to bring forward some planned maintenance and avoids a major problem. Somehow, over a period of a few years many potential minor interruptions are dealt with or avoided by "muddling through". The difficulties are never significant enough to warrant a questioning of the supplier contract. Partial unreliability is excused because of a long-term business relationship and competitive price.

   Then the motor industry enters the growth part of its economic cycle leading to increased demands. The supplier that had been unable to deal with demand properly at its previous level is faced with a sudden surge in demand for the components that it supplies. Despite having given assurances to its customers of its ability to increase production quickly, it is unable to do so. All the warning signs had been there before. Its difficulties had been caused by obsolete production processes, lack of investment in new technology and a demoralised workforce looking for employment elsewhere. Entry into the growth stage of the business cycle placed more pressure on the production process at a time when employees could find employment elsewhere more easily. This is the trigger that causes a crisis for both supplier and car manufacturing customer. The success of rescue and salvage will be dependent, in large measure, on the quality of continuity plans prepared prior to the "incident"; for example, the identification of alternative sources of supply or components. Cultural readjustment refers to a post-incident stage in which the car manufacturer might reconsider its methods of supplier recruitment, monitoring, discipline and management.

An incident of the type depicted in Box 7.1 was chosen to emphasise that the methodologies discussed in this chapter are not solely concerned with major accidents involving fire, death and explosion. It is possible that the shortage of a key component might have damaged, significantly, the competitiveness of a large car manufacturer which would have required a coordinated response to manage an interruption to production, distributors, other suppliers and, ultimately, to customers. Increasingly, BCM is gaining a customer focus as organisations are increasingly expected to provide a continuous uninterrupted service.

In this chapter we are especially concerned with crisis management teams building on the seminal work of Smart and Vertinsky (1977). The chapter then progresses to an examination of major incident management structures chosen by some organisations. A natural progression is to consider, albeit briefly, the nature of stress and its potential for hindering an organisation's response to crisis. As stress arises from a perceived imbalance between an individual's capabilities and demands, we consider how organisations may test and maintain plans and processes while building individual capabilities. We conclude with a consideration of the communication aspects of major incident management.

Crisis Management Teams

Teams are considered to be important because, generally, they outperform individuals although, as Janis's (1982) groundbreaking work identified, teams are still fallible. In essence, Janis's notion of groupthink argued that groups might come to consider themselves invulnerable, and be intolerant of those views which counter those of the established group through a combination of faulty rationalisations, negatively stereotyping dissenters and pressuring those within the group who express doubts. The time pressures associated with crisis contexts were seen as especially conducive to groupthink, which might be manifest in a refusal to consider alternative courses of action. Vaughan (1996) applies Janis's ideas to the case of the Space Shuttle Challenger. This potential for the vulnerability of crisis decision units has also been identified by Smart and Vertinsky (1977), who were concerned with malfunctions affecting the quality of information processing and decisions. Raiffa (1968) identified four types of decision error:

- rejecting a correct course of action;
- accepting a wrong solution to a problem;
- solving the wrong problem;
- solving the right problem, correctly, but too late.

Errors may arise from the poor quality of the information available, the cognitive abilities of the group and the "fidelity of objective articulation and trade-off evaluation" (Smart and Vertinsky, 1977: 642). These will manifest themselves in the emergence of groupthink, rigidity in problem-solving, the distortion of information and a reluctance to adapt to new circumstances or to implement solutions quickly. Such errors rarely occur in isolation and some authors have identified organisational cultures according to the way in which they deal with safety information (see Table 7.2). A practical question for organisations to consider is "To what extent do we possess a pathological culture?" The characteristics of a pathological culture will include the employment of the defence mechanisms identified in the last chapter. Such organisations make themselves more prone to crisis. With hindsight, it is possible, usually, to pick out warning signals of impending failure. Union Carbide not rectifying a number of safety difficulties at their Bhopal plant in the years preceding the 1984 disaster; Barings had identified deficiencies in their risk control procedures following a 1994 fraud but, as their treasurer observed, regarding the implementation of remedies, "There was always something else that seemed more pressing" (quoted in Reason, 1997: 39).

A summary of the remedies to these potential difficulties includes:

Table 7.2 How Different Organisational Cultures Handle Safety Information

Pathological culture	Bureaucratic culture	Generative culture
Don't want to know	May not find out	Actively seek it
Whistleblowers are "shot"	Messengers listened to if they arrive	Messengers are trained and rewarded
Responsibility is avoided	Responsibility is compartmentalised	Responsibility is shared
Failure is punished or hidden	Failures lead to local repairs	Failures lead to far-reaching reforms
New ideas are discouraged	New ideas often present problems	New ideas are welcomed

Source: Reason (1997)

- encouraging alternative viewpoints through creative problem-solving techniques;
- rotating team members;
- including outside experts;
- protecting minority points of view;
- developing better information collection techniques;
- formally creating a devil's advocate role;
- encouraging expression of concerns or doubts;
- developing flexible operating procedures;
- establishing contingency plans;
- holding crisis simulations;
- building network of trusted, potential coordinators in line departments (adapted from Smart and Vertinsky, 1977).

Implicit in Smart and Vertinsky's analysis is the development of the critical team. A recurring theme within the literature (with regard to teams in general and crisis management teams in particular) concerns variety and balance. Belbin (1981) observed that management teams commonly consist of members holding particular appointments. They are appointed to fulfil a particular day-to-day role, perhaps as head of finance or personnel or operations. As a senior management team, suggests Belbin, they may be no more than a random collection of individuals possessing "as wide a spread of human foibles and personality characteristics as one might expect to find in the population at large" (1981: 132). The basic criticism of such an approach is that no effort is made to select and design teams to promote greater effectiveness, they are simply composed of people holding particular positions within an organisation. Belbin's (1981) much applied approach suggests nine key roles for individuals within teams, arguing that a balance between these roles is key to ensuring team success. Put simply, Belbin argues that the psychological characteristics of the individuals comprising a team will be a key influence in determining their effectiveness.

Similarly, crisis management teams (CMT) are often created by drawing in personnel to represent parts of the organisation (Anderson, 2007) or to provide specific skills or knowledge (Elliott, 2008). For example, different business divisions may be represented or individuals with particular knowledge such as legal, information systems, human resources or corporate communications may be appointed to a CMT. Given the stressful demands of a crisis, greater attention may be required to the personality characteristics of potential members (Smith, 2000). As Anderson notes, a person's role within a crisis team may differ significantly from their usual day job and the demands of a crisis may mean that the effective steady state manager is less competent in dealing with complex and dynamic events. Where a significant amount of attention has been focused upon leaders and crisis (see, for example, Flin, 1996; Smith and Elliott, 2007), there has been less attention given to the competencies and skills of a CMT – a key gap in the literature (see Anderson, 2007). Anderson's (2007) study identifies seven non-technical competencies for members of CMTs:

- decision making and judgement;
- situational awareness;
- leading and motivating others;
- team work;
- creative and innovative thinking;
- information gathering;
- self-confidence.

Although these seven competencies are posited on limited empirical evidence, albeit supported by an extensive literature review, the presence of these seven "competencies" would, from a common-sense perspective, appear to increase the chance of a CMT acting effectively. The notion of considering competence from a team perspective is an interesting one and Anderson argues that failure to do so may lead to overconfidence. Elliott (2008) from a cross-sectoral study identified the importance of careful selection of CMT members and avoiding the temptation to select on the basis of an individual's seniority within an organisation. The skills and competencies that make an effective normal operations manager may differ from those required for a crisis context. Taking Carley's (1991) work, which argued that personnel should be recruited from a range of backgrounds and knowledge bases, it may be seen that the membership of a CMT should be decided on the grounds of non-technical competence and appropriate specialist knowledge.

Further, the effective crisis management team, it is suggested, incorporates processes and people for continually questioning decisions and information, and has in place the mechanisms, personnel and communication channels to support quick and effective implementation. The nature of criticism is not that of the awkward individual but that of devil's advocate. In practice, a careful balance must be maintained between an open mind and procrastination.

Another area of research dealing with effective groups and teams suggests that improving performance may be gained through greater interactiveness and cohesion. Seven main factors are identified by McKenna (cited in Smith, 2000), including shared attitudes and goals, time spent together, degree of separation from other groups, the degree of perceived threat, the perceived rewards for the group, difficulty of entry to the group, the location of the group and its impact upon interaction. Where Belbin (1981), Smith (2000) and Anderson (2007) emphasise the importance of careful selection of team members based on personality and competence, McKenna's (1994) work suggests the importance of bringing CMTs together through training and exercises to develop interaction and cohesiveness by nurturing shared goals and attitudes, spending time together and establishing the team as a distinct entity. A closely related issue concerns structure and it is to this that we now turn.

Configuration

Not all structures are as effective in providing a platform for the characteristics of an effective crisis management team. Mintzberg (1983b) argued that organisational success required a fit between structure and environment. From his analysis, Mintzberg identified a range of organisational structure types, five of which are shown in Figure 7.2.

A simple and stable environment provides the right conditions for an organisational programme, the so-called "machine bureaucracy". Lack of change and simplicity of environmental demands permits control through strict procedures. Within this predictable context, nothing new happens so the workforce are not permitted to deviate from plan; they have no need as all has been anticipated and all eventualities prepared for. Organisational success follows the ruthless pursuit of efficiency. Examples include large manufacturing plants, IBM's focus upon sales in the 1980s and British banks during the 1960s and 1970s. All activities, in these examples, were tightly controlled. Arguably, these mechanistic approaches, and the insu-

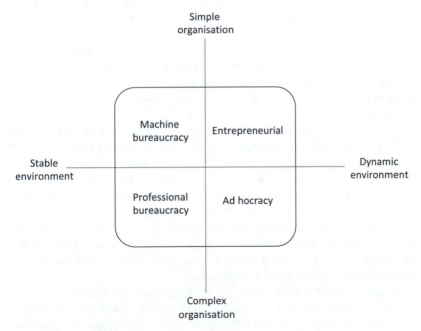

Figure 7.2 Configuration–environment–organisational fit.

Source: adapted from Mintzberg (1983b)

larity associated with them, played a major part in a failure to read the warning signs of environmental change. IBM placed too much emphasis on the mainframe to the detriment of the personal computer; British banks were slow to innovate in terms of customer service and in their use of new technology; flexible manufacturing units threatened large manufacturing plants. The machine bureaucracy is not well suited to crisis management as its structures and procedures are likely to slow down and confuse any response to a dynamic and complex situation. There will not be time to work through an organisation's usual processes. An effective crisis management team is unlikely to flourish within a bureaucratic context. Perversely it may seem, a drilled response may be an effective means of ensuring an effective, immediate emergency response; for example, when there are few options and limited time, as during the Heathrow crash landing. The drill of the aircraft cabin crew ensured that certain processes were put into action to evacuate passengers. Almost without thought, a drilled response was successful in ensuring an orderly evacuation, as BA's crash landing pilot observed afterwards: "As British Airways flight and cabin crew, we are trained on a regular basis to deal with emergency situations, we have procedures to follow and everyone knows their role" (Burkhill, 2008).

The entrepreneur flourishes in a context combining simplicity and dynamism. With no need to consult, he or she can respond quickly to change. The small firm is the typical example of this organisational form. Many entrepreneurs describe their work as fire-fighting. They have the advantage of being able to respond quickly should they need to. Typically, one person can make a decision. However, the individual cannot hope to deal with the same degree of complexity as an effective group. There is also the danger that, within the entrepreneurial context, there will be insufficient scope for the leader to be questioned, preventing the development of the "critical team".

The professional bureaucracy occupies a context combining complexity with relative stability. Complexity is dealt with by professionals who receive extensive training before commencing employment; for example, health, education, public service professionals, engineers. These professionals are sheltered within a bureaucracy that provides the organisational means by which stability is managed. Inevitably, professional associations may play a major part in regulating behaviour and influencing operating norms as may be seen in the case of the medical profession. Thus, internal procedures and external pressures may slow down decision making, undermining any effective crisis response.

A further organisational type, Mintzberg labels the ad hocracy, consists of small groups of highly trained individuals working together; for example, a research and development team or management consultancy. A collection of highly skilled people enable it to deal with complexity, while its small size and network structure permit rapid decision making, facilitating a quick response to environmental change. Smart and Vertin-sky's (1977) model crisis management team fits closely with Mintzberg's ad hocracy.

The final pure type is the divisionalised form in which Mintzberg recognised that the large size of firms often meant that one company might incorporate a number of these types. Of course, each of the five is a pure type and, in practice, it is likely that an organisation will show a tendency towards a particular type rather than adopt it as a pure structure.

What is the relevance of structure to continuity? Structure will condition the types of response to the environment that an organisation can make. In times of rapid change, bureaucracy tends to stifle change causing the structure to be out of fit with its environment and thereby limiting effectiveness. Although drill may be of value in effecting an immediate emergency response, it is less likely to be as useful as the event and its consequences unfurl. Vodafone emphasised the importance of options given the unexpected emergence of the interruption triggered by the flooding of their headquarters, requiring a considered rather than drilled or planned response (Vodafone, 2007). Similarly BA was criticised by some passengers for their poor communications and over concern with security with regard to the handling of the survivors (Tamburro, 2008).

It is not suggested that organisations configure themselves as an ad hocracy, just in case. Managers, however, must be aware of their usual configuration and the difficulties that may be posed when dealing with a major interruption. A critical question concerns how personnel, used to tight order and prescription, may be encouraged and empowered to deviate and use their initiative in the event of a major interruption. This is the purpose of command-and-control structures, which should incorporate a clear sense of ultimate objective with flexibility in how that may be achieved.

Box 7.2 Machine Bureaucracy

An extreme example concerns the fire service. Although dealing with our day-to-day crises and what we would consider to be the complexities and dynamism of house fires and road traffic accidents, the fire service has developed a drilled response to such incidents. When it arrives at an incident, each fire fighter knows exactly his or her specific task. Deviation from the drilled response requires authority from a supervising officer, who retains a note of all such deviations in order that the lives of other fire-fighters are not placed in jeopardy. Put another way, the fire service operates in a very machine bureaucracy manner. For a large proportion of incidents, such a style works well. However, when faced with a major incident that bears little resemblance to those practised by fire-fighters in training, deviation from the plan is required. The supervisor will be inundated with requests for permission to deviate from the plan and will become overloaded with information. Effective emergency response is in danger of breakdown at this point, as the structure fails to cope with the demands of the environment. Such a breakdown affected the fire service at Kegworth in 1989 and the police at Hillsborough in the same year (see Elliott and Smith, 1993). Structure provides the context in which strategy is implemented. If it does not fit with its environment, then the strategy will at best be hindered, at worst fail.

Command-and-Control Structures

In addition to the day-to-day structures required to implement BCM, a command-and-control structure for managing major incidents is needed. Many companies utilise a three-tier structure as advocated by the Home Office (1997a, 1997b) and the Government Centre for Information Systems (1995b). This mimics the structure used by the British police service, who label the three levels bronze, silver and gold system (respectively tactical, operational and strategic). This structure emerged from an attempt to encourage consistency between the emergency services and thereby minimise confusion when dealing with an incident (Flin, 1996).

The purpose of the three levels is to ensure that an organisation's response to an incident is effectively coordinated. Bronze (operational) corresponds to the normal operational response provided by the emergency services where the management is of routine tasks. The immediate response to an incident is likely to be managed at this level. When the emergency services deal with a major incident, the "bronze commander" is likely to lead a front-line team. Silver (tactical) refers to the command level, which seeks to identify priorities and allocate resources accordingly. During a major incident, it is likely that the silver commander will take charge of managing the incident itself. The role of the gold (strategic) group and commander is to take an overview, to arbitrate between any conflicts at silver level and to assume responsibility for liaising with the media and key stakeholder groups. The "gold commander" is not expected to participate in the detailed management of an incident (adapted from the Home Office, 1997a, 1997b) (see Figure 7.3).

Box 7.3 World Trade Centre, 1993

The New York World Trade Centre (WTC) was one of the tallest buildings in the world with twin towers, each with 110 storeys. The WTC was a major commercial building with over 1,000 businesses employing more than 50,000 staff.

McFadden (1993), reporting for the *New York Times*, recorded that the bomb blast "knocked out the police command and operations centers for the towers, which rendered the office complex's evacuation plans useless". Many of those who walked down scores of flights from the upper reaches of the trade centre towers said there had been no alarm bells and no instructions from building personnel or emergency workers. While little panic was reported, witnesses said confusion reigned in the darkness of crowded stairwells, where smoke billowed and unknown dangers lurked below.

The immediate impact of the explosion was to leave an estimated 50,000 people in a building, parts of which were burning, with little power for light and with none of the 250 elevators working. The scale of the interruption had taken the WTC's management team by surprise. A knock-on effect was that, with so many firms experiencing an interruption, there was a surge in demand for disaster recovery services, a surge that could not be readily met by supply.

Dean Witter, which employed 5,000 staff in the WTC, invoked contingency plans and made use of access to alternative office space in New York.

Source: McFadden (1993); Hiles and Barnes (1999)

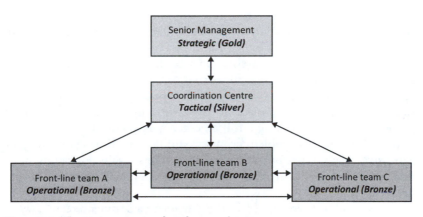

Figure 7.3 Three-tier command-and-control system.

The applicability of such a framework to the emergency services is relatively clear. However, its suitability for a wider range of organisations is less obvious. For this reason we devote the remainder of this section to an examination of how this framework was adapted to meet the requirements of a global bank (see Figure 7.4). The key word is "adapted"; all organisations are unique in terms of structures, cultures, personnel and location, to name four factors. Any contingency plans should be developed with that uniqueness in mind.

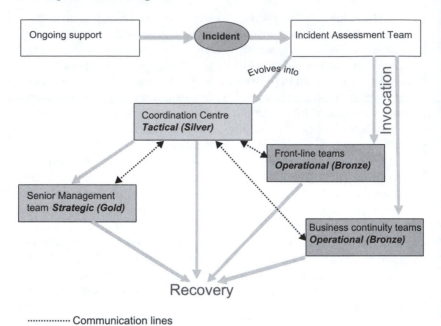

Figure 7.4 Incident management.

The three levels identify a minimum of three roles to be undertaken when managing an incident. In smaller organisations one team or individual may perform these distinct roles. Two further roles have been added to the framework for the international bank. The first is the "ongoing support box", which identifies the activities that deal with the day-to-day interruptions that face organisations of all types. For example, most organisations have systems in place to deal with maintenance and routine problem-solving – invoking a full emergency response every time a computer fails or another problem occurs would be both time-consuming and expensive. Many types of interruption may be initially logged as minor difficulties and it is likely that internal help desks will be called upon to deal with them first.

The second additional tier is the "incident assessment team", which consists of business managers, both those affected by an interruption and managers drawn from the relevant support services from IT and facilities through to personnel. In the event of an interruption, this team should undertake an initial assessment and determine the most suitable response for an organisation. Determining when a minor interruption requires the activation of a full-blown incident response is not always straightforward. A major fire or systems failure may be obviously serious, but often the significance of an interruption may not be immediately evident. In some organisations this role is undertaken by a duty manager who alone makes the decision whether to escalate or not.

Figure 7.5 represents a matrix that can be used to assess the severity of an incident. It is not intended to provide a quantitative tool but rather a checklist of key issues. This particular example was developed for a large financial sector organisation and should be adapted to meet the needs and priorities of a particular organisation. The matrix shows that when an incident occurs, an incident assessment takes place to determine the type of predetermined response that is necessary. In this case, three scenarios have been identified, each of which differ in terms of their severity and impact. System rating refers to the importance of a particular IT system. Tier 1 systems are business-critical, essential for trading and for regulatory compliance. Tier 3 might include stand-alone packages whose loss poses no more than an inconvenience. Regulatory impact was a key criterion for the bank, given the increasing requirements for financial sector organisations to demonstrate probity. Recovery timeline refers to the predicted length of the interruption. Where expense concerns the tangible cost of dealing with an interruption, financial impact deals with the consequences of an interruption. For example, the failure to respond to an incident quickly may lead to the loss of key customers who move their business elsewhere. Deadline impact identifies the vagaries of the calendar for all businesses. There are in most industries busy and lean times. Interruptions at critical times may have a dramatic effect. For example, one British university experienced a breakdown in its telephone systems in the period following the publication of A-level results, its busiest recruitment time. A toy retailer may experience the loss of critical systems during the six weeks before Christmas.

The final row indicates the type of response required by an incident. Few incidents warrant the active and ongoing attention of a senior management team. Working processes already exist to deal with these. Every organisation can determine the most appropriate level of response to an incident.

	Interruption	Incident	Major Incident
System rating	Tier 3	Tier 2	Tier 1
Regulatory impact	No Regulatory Issues	Minimal Reulatory issues	Significant Regulatory Matter
Recovery timeline	Up to 2 hours	Between 2 and 24 hours	1 day or more
Invocation Expense	£10k	£100k	£1m
Financial impact	Potential loss of £	Potential loss of £x2	Potential loss of $£^2$
Dealine impact	Routine	Regular milestone approaching	Key deadline approaching
Appropriate recovery mechanism	Normal Procedures	Normal Procedures I	Major Incident Plan

Figure 7.5 Incident severity assessment matrix.

Following its evaluation, the incident assessment team will activate bronze, silver and gold teams to meet the needs of the organisation. The tool is best used as an aid to decision making rather than in a simple quantitative way.

Bronze Tactical

Business recovery teams include specialist support teams (for example, IT, premises, personnel) and business unit teams (that is, those performing primary activities). To use a military metaphor these are the troops on the ground combining the sappers and engineers with the fighting platoons. Following an interruption, it is likely that support teams will seek to prepare suitable accommodation, information systems, and transport and subsistence arrangements. Business units will seek to establish agreed levels of service in key activities to important customer and stakeholder groups. Financial organisations may focus upon "triple A rated clients", utilities might concentrate upon vulnerable groups or vital industrial plants – such priorities having been identified during the stages of analysis.

In summary, BC plans exist at business unit and team level, identifying what is to be done in the event of short, long and uncertain interruptions. These might include, for a large investment bank, switching to manual systems, reducing levels of trading to key customer accounts or ceasing trade completely.

Silver Operational

Within Figure 7.4 the role of the "coordination centre" is to coordinate the BC teams from both primary and secondary teams. Members of the silver team, although dependent upon the demands of a particular event, are drawn from a pool of senior operational managers. Its primary task is to ensure that the bank's response to an incident is effectively coordinated and that the bronze support and business teams are deployed in the sequence most appropriate to the needs of the bank. For example, if an organisation is forced to relocate to an emergency site with accommodation for fewer staff than the regular building, decisions will need to be made about which staff will be relocated and in what priority order. At this level, the silver team will need to identify corporate priorities and the order in which business units are restored to agreed levels of service. Each team may consider itself the most important, requiring the silver team to determine what meets corporate objectives most effectively.

Gold Strategic

Consisting of an organisation's most senior executives, the role of this team is to deal with strategic issues emerging from an incident. At their most basic, these issues are concerned with ensuring that incident response does not spill over into areas of a business unaffected by a particular incident. Dealing with a major incident may require significant expenditure. The senior management team will be responsible for such authorisation. Another vital task is for high-level media and stakeholder representation; for example, BA's CEO Willie Walsh's high profile after the crash landing at Heathrow hours after the accident and in the following days, not least in hosting a press conference for the pilot team who were credited with averting a major disaster. Potential threats to confidence in BA and the Boeing 777 were nipped in the bud and it is possible that the credit given to the pilots and BA's emergency drill may have enhanced the company's reputation. The senior management team provides a port of last resort for issues that cannot be resolved by the coordinating centre. However, it is not expected to have an active role in the operational coordination of responding to an incident.

Although the bronze, silver and gold incident command structure has been adopted by a number of organisations, there is no single way of organising for a crisis. The idiosyncrasies of organisations will require structures reflecting their different needs. BT's structure, for example, sets out responsibilities at the centre and in the regions. There is a two-tier hierarchy with supporting documentation explaining roles, levels of authority and checklists for the main incident manager and the forward control manager, who have key functions. Regional coordinators also have a clear understanding of what their role is and how they fit into the overall command-and-control structure. Everyone concerned will have received some training; exercises are run regularly and participants will draw on their experience of real invocations. Currently, all operational managers at Thames Water may, in theory, be called upon to act as an "event manager" (that is, to manage crisis incidents of differing severity).

Figure 7.6 depicts how one multinational company organised its two-tier structure when faced with a major business interruption. The brief of the executive management team is to coordinate activities on two fronts – crisis management and mitigation – that encompass external communications with media and regulators, as well as internal communications with support functions in the organisation.

The brief of the business management team is to coordinate the business recovery teams for the business units. The recovery teams have a focus on the supply chain and will work to a recovery plan to maximise contact with customers, suppliers and other relevant stakeholders. The particular arrangements for handling incidents or crises vary between organisations. What they share, however, is a recognition of the need for teams to specialise in a controlled way. There is a need for strategic, tactical and operational activities to be separated in some way. The detail may differ from industry to industry and from scenario to scenario, but there must be some means of ensuring a coordinated response.

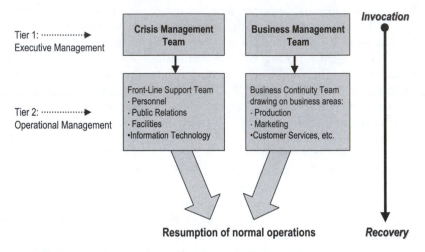

Figure 7.6 Example command-and-control structure to manage incidents.

Alternatively, one international retailer has designed a crisis team structure as a central hub around which functions revolve with responsibility for specific activities. Thus corporate communications deal with all requests for information and media handling, logistics and marketing deal with the customer interface and maintaining supply, the retail directorate with managing the scene of the incident and liaising with the emergency services, facilities with structural issues and HR with people issues. The structure is communicated in a series of bubbles in place of the more hierarchical depiction of the three-tier model so commonly employed. The means of communication emphasises a flexible approach to incident response.

Effective teamwork, leadership and contingency planning are all essential ingredients of effective crisis management. Inevitably, a disproportionate amount of research effort has focused upon incidents involving many injuries or multiple fatalities. Such incidents lend themselves to research as they come into the public domain. There are resulting dangers that crisis management is perceived to be a discipline restricted to such events, or that managers within other industries fail to learn the lessons. Flin's (1996) comprehensive analysis of incident command provides a short analysis of a range of multiple fatality accidents from stadium disasters and fires to airplane crashes and concludes that these:

> were all situations in which incident commanders were faced with extremely difficult decisions, characterised by ambiguous and conflicting information, shifting goals, time pressure, dynamic conditions, complex operational team structures and poor communications. . . . Despite the broad spectrum of incidents types and conditions . . . there is sufficient commonality in the roles of various incident commanders

to merit an integrated examination of their selection, their training . . . coping with stress, decision-making and team management.

(Flin, 1996: 37)

Strip away the colour labels of the Home Office's (1997a, 1997b) incident
command structure and we are left with the recognition that there are at
least three distinct, basic roles to be undertaken during any incident. For
the emergency services, there is an implied assumption that dealing with
incidents is their *raison d'être*. For commercial organisations, incident management is, hopefully, a rare event and team members will be less practised
at it. The role of the crisis management team for the commercial organisation will also be to remove the burden of dealing with an incident from
routine operations; in other words, it will seek to ensure that unaffected
parts of the business will be able to continue trading. Because incidents
will occur rarely and be associated with high levels of uncertainty, individuals may find incident management a stressful experience and it is to a
consideration of this that we now turn.

Decision Making under Stress

Defining Stress

Major incidents are likely to prove a stressful experience for people, threatening health and potentially hindering an organisation's response. The
study of stress and crisis decision making has provided the focus for many
studies yet still it seems that:

> The concept of stress is elusive because it is poorly defined. There is no
> single agreed definition in existence. It is a concept which is familiar
> to both layman and professional alike; it is understood by all when
> used in a general context but by very few when a more precise account
> is required, and this seems to be the central problem.

(Cox, 1978: 1)

Cox's (1978) view is as apt today as it was when it was first written.
Within the academic literature, there are various approaches to the study of
stress, each with its particular definition of the term. Cranwell-Ward (1990)
identified two broad approaches from her study of stress in management:
those that related to the *causes* of the stress and those that related to the
effects induced by it. A third approach is the transactional model, defined
below (Cox, 1978; Fisher, 1986; Brown and Campbell, 1994). The transactional or interactional model of stress is developed from the work of
Lazarus, Cox and their colleagues (Cox, 1978; Lazarus, 1966, 1999; Lazarus
and Launier, 1978; Lazarus and Folhman, 1984): "the physiological and
psychological reaction which occurs when people perceive an imbalance,

between the level of demand placed upon them, and their capability to meet those demands" (Cranwell-Ward, 1990: 10).

This definition is close to the one used by Cox in his observation that:

> Stress . . . can only be sensibly defined as a perceptual phenomenon arising from a comparison between the demand on the person and his ability to cope. An imbalance in this mechanism, when coping is important, gives rise to the experience of stress, and to stress response. The latter represent attempts at coping with the source of stress.
>
> (1978: 25)

This interactional model posits that an individual interacts with his or her environment and that, while the environment can affect the individual, the individual can also affect the environment. In both cases, there is seen to be an imbalance between the demands placed upon the individual and their perceived abilities to cope with these demands. Both groups of authors emphasise the continuing nature of this process and both emphasise the role of cognitive appraisal in determining the perceived imbalance and therefore stress. For Lazarus (1978), the evaluation process occurs in two stages. The first stage, or primary appraisal, occurs when the individual first evaluates the event or demand and focuses upon the negative outcomes that can result from the interaction. The secondary stage occurs when the respondent seeks to evaluate the potential responses that can be made to the negative outcomes that were previously determined.

Stress and Incident Management

Given the difficulties associated with managing crisis incidents, the notion of stress and increasingly more specifically post-traumatic stress disorder (PTSD), as a potential impairer of individual and thus organisational performance, is becoming an important consideration (see, for example, Elliott and Smith, 2000).

Within the study of crises, prominence has been given to PTSD, although it must be pointed out that occupational stress has increased in importance for human resource managers. A number of studies have been concerned with the traumatic experiences of military personnel or emergency services staff acting in the role of rescuers (see, for example, Elliott and Smith, 2000). PTSD emerges from an experience of an event outside the usual bounds of experience, such as threat to oneself, loved ones, home, or close involvement in a major incident. Symptoms may include re-experiencing the trauma, avoiding stimuli associated with the trauma and persistent increased arousal in the form of:

- thoughts or feelings
- activities or situations

- psychogenic amnesia
- lack of interest
- detachment or estrangement.

The implications for effective incident management by individuals experiencing some or all of these symptoms are obvious. Yet few organisations consider stress when creating continuity plans, despite the evidence that staff will tolerate the dislocation associated with crisis incidents for a short period only. This toleration may well be determined by factors such as pre-incident culture and the extent to which an organisation's support staff are called upon to commit more time and energy to their employer than usual. This has implications for all operational staff but, more critically in this context, for staff participating within crisis management teams. As we have seen, major incidents will be characterised by uncertainty, lack of information, time pressures and a tendency towards rigidity in decision making. Within such a context, organisations must ensure that the most appropriate individuals are selected and managed effectively.

The types of incident that come quickly to mind are fires and explosions but these represent the tip of the iceberg. The failures of information systems, prolonged transport breakdown and failures of suppliers will also create uncertainty within time constraints. Although little research has been undertaken, it seems probable that the blockade of UK oil refineries during September 2000 will have caused high levels of uncertainty for a range of organisations. For retailers, demand rose sharply at a time when supply to stores was difficult (Mellish, 2000).

Box 7.4 Employee Mobility

An insurance company owns two main offices in France: one near Paris, another at Lyon. In case of the loss of either office, it plans to switch staff to the other one. As the two cities are more than 300 km apart, the plan assumes that staff are able to spend the week away from their homes. Not only will working routines be affected, but so will domestic arrangements. Anecdotal evidence suggests that, while employees may be willing to accept such a major upheaval for a very short period, their patience will be short lived.

In another case, an organisation was forced to relocate its staff, temporarily, from a West End office to the East End of London, disrupting the daily routines of hundreds of staff. The organisation reported higher levels of absenteeism and, subsequently, higher turnover.

When Commercial Union's headquarters was severely damaged in 1992, the management team quickly recognised that enthusiasm for a two and three-quarter hour journey to the temporary headquarters, each way, each day, changing trains twice en route, would soon wane, however dedicated its staff were. To support staff it gave regular updates on progress, to reassure them of concern for welfare. Commercial Union also agreed to reimburse any additional travel costs incurred; flexi-time arrangements for staff were introduced including the possibility of days off.

Stress and the Individual

At a basic level, an individual's response to stress appears to be dependent upon two factors. First, an individual's personality characteristics may modify any response to stress. Training and experience may play a vital mediating role, indicating that organisations must consider methods of developing staff skills. In the case of J Sainsbury's handling of the oil blockade and the extra demands placed upon staff, the existence of a clear process played a key role. Staff had rehearsed responses to similar scenarios (that is, panic buying at the millennium) and could rely on a process that was familiar to them and to colleagues (Mellish, 2000). The second factor concerns the nature of the traumatic experience itself and the recovery environment. An individual's perception of the nature of an experience will be key because, as Lazarus argues, only an individual can describe a particular event as stressful to himself or herself. However, it seems clear that certain situations are more likely than others to lead to a negative "stressful" response, almost irrespective of individual characteristics. Organisational crises, characterised by lack of information, uncertainty and limited time for decisions, are just such situations. The duration of an incident may also play a part. Mellish (2000) identifies the role played by the "Dunkirk Spirit" in J Sainsbury's crisis response. Had the incident been prolonged that spirit might have been broken.

Evidence has suggested that previous exposure to some of the hazards encountered may also reduce the perceived threat, and thereby reduce the experience of stress (Warr, 1990). Fire-fighters are exposed to heights and smoke-filled rooms, pilots to water-filled simulators; indeed, the use of simulated crisis exercises within organisations of all types (discussed later) might be seen as one useful means of preparing staff for handling an incident (Elliott and Smith, 2000).

A number of possibilities for organisations emerge from these studies. Effective intervention may include three basic groups of practice:

- the identification of "hardy" individuals during recruitment, selection and training;
- staff development to raise individual capabilities and thereby reduce the perceived threat of a situation;

• providing a supportive recovery environment.

The first is difficult, both politically and practically, and may be interpreted as placing blame upon the individual. Further, while it may have relevance to the emergency services, the notion that a hardy personality is a requirement for many other jobs might be challenged. The second and third groups recognise management's role in this area and avoid individual blame. The effects and duration of the symptoms of PTSD will be critical factors in impairing organisational effectiveness. Counselling via a detailed debriefing has long been advocated, particularly for the emergency services. However, recent research has suggested that in some cases debriefing has the effect of forcing individuals to re-live traumatic events with dire consequences (Raphael et al., 1995; Rick and Briner, 2000).

Managers and supervisors should be trained to identify the symptoms of psychological distress and to provide immediate support, including the monitoring of individuals who may be potentially at risk from the effects of stress and PTSD. Most practically, the evidence is (see Elliott and Smith, 1993, 2000) that training plays a major role in preparing staff for incident management, in terms of raising their capabilities and readying them for the demands of crisis management. The HSE (2001) has provided much guidance on the causes of stress at work and, while their concern is with occupational stress, their findings have some relevance for our subject.

The HSE checklist provides a useful means of summarising this section. There is a danger that stress is considered to arise from fire, explosion or threat to life. It will do so in some cases, yet stress may arise from more mundane scenarios. Role ambiguity, excessive demands, poor relationships and a perception of lack of control may cause stress on a daily basis. These are more likely to arise at times of crisis and should therefore be considered by continuity managers. Key considerations include ensuring that excessive demands are not placed on staff, even during times of crisis. While the "Dunkirk spirit" may come to the fore initially, fatigue may break it. The uncertainty associated with interruptions of all sorts will increase the likelihood of role ambiguity. Training can play a major role in reducing the threat of role ambiguity and in identifying the demands placed upon any particular role. An advantage of the HSE's checklist of factors is that it provides an indicator of how stress may arise.

Box 7.5 Causes of Stress

Key causes of occupational stress and their remedies:

1   Poor management culture.
    Improved by:

- commitment to promoting the health of employees;
- value and respect for employees;
- support for staff raising problems about their work.

2   Excessive demands upon staff.
At a manageable level of demand:

- staff are able to cope with the volume and complexity of the work which is scheduled so that there is sufficient time to do allocated tasks;
- people are not expected to work long hours over an extended period.

3   Lack of control.
People feel in control when:

- they may influence how they do their work;
- control is balanced against the demands placed upon them.

4   Poor relationships.
Good relationships evolve when:

- there is good communication, with employees understand what's expected and employers react to any problems being experienced by the employees;
- employees are not bullied or harassed.

5   Poor management of change.
Good change management will be characterised by:

- an organisation communicating the reasons why change is essential;
- an organisation having a clear sense of purpose;
- the organisation having a timetable for implementing change, which includes realistic first step;
- the organisation ensuring a supportive climate for employees.

6   Lack of training, support and failure to take account of individual factors.
Examples of good practice:

- employees receive adequate training to do their jobs;
- employees receive support from their immediate line management, even when things go wrong;
- the organisation encourages people to share their concerns about health and safety and, in particular, work-related stress;
- the individual is fair to the employer – they discuss their concerns and work towards agreed solutions.

7   Role ambiguity.
    Examples of where people understand their role are when:

    - they know why they are undertaking the work and how this fits in with the organisation's wider aims and objectives;
    - jobs are clearly defined to avoid confusion.

The Health and Safety Executive (HSE) is working towards standards of good management practice in these areas.

Source: adapted from HSE Guidance (2001)

We have argued that the planning process is more important than the plan and that testing, maintenance and auditing are vital elements of this. They can ensure that personnel develop relevant skills and are exposed to the potential stressors of a real business interruption. Recovery can be complex and unpredictable and stress is an important factor to consider since situational awareness can be affected. The quality of situational awareness can be improved through the regular testing of plans (Paton, 2003).

Testing, Maintenance and Auditing

BCM depends on up-to-date information within plan documents, which provide the basic tools for effective interruption response and will provide better preparation for staff involved in incident response. Mintzberg and Waters' (1985) view of strategy as "a pattern in a stream of decisions" or strategies "as patterns or consistencies in such streams" recognised that a distinction must be made between what organisations intend to do (as set out in plans, be they strategic or continuity plans) and what they do. Strategy is distinguished between those actions that were intended (planned) and those which emerged (realised). For plans to shape behaviour fully requires absolute certainty and does not allow for the bounded rationality of managers.

As discussed in Chapter 6 (see Figure 6.5 for a depiction of Mintzberg and Waters' emergent properties of strategy), intended strategy refers to the plan. The many arrows refer to the behaviour of individuals and teams, which, cumulatively, add up to the organisation's behaviour. Marks & Spencer's long-standing reputation for customer service provides a good example. That reputation is founded on every interaction between members of staff and customers. Together, these interactions prove the decisive test of customer service. Achieving this consistently requires selecting and training the right staff, maintaining a positive disposition, systems and processes for handling difficulties and a real top management commitment. Each arrow may be thought of as representing one interaction and the successful retailer must ensure consistency in millions of such interactions every week – no mean feat. In the context of continuity management, these arrows may be thought of as sheep and the continuity management team, using their plans, may be thought of as the sheep dog, steering the flock towards safety. The metaphor of the sheep dog is useful as they are well trained but are also flexible, able to adapt to differing circumstances. The purpose of the plan is to help managers steer a safe course in response to an interruption. The purpose of testing, auditing and maintenance is to ensure that plan documents can support this, rather than to impose a bureaucratic stricture on the BC process. The imposition of a bureaucracy would impede an organisation's response and make the context worse for individual managers.

Operational Management of Business Continuity

In this section, the assimilation of BCM into day-to-day management is considered. This is the fourth stage of our framework (see Figure 7.1) – operational management. Note that there are links back to planning since testing and invocation provide opportunities for learning. Regular testing offers the opportunity for continuous improvement. The operational management of BCM falls broadly into two areas: testing, and maintenance and auditing.

Testing

BC plans are living documents and one of the greatest sources of nutrition is the process and activity of testing. Since the purpose of BCM is to restore "business as usual", plans need to most closely resemble the current nature of the business, its operating context and historical, known and contemporary challenges (as identified through risk analysis). Hence testing should not be considered to be the end of the BCP process but a natural transition between multiple phases of planning (as indicated by the return to the activity of planning following the operations management phase in Figure 7.1). Plans have to be achievable and testable. They are not a wish list (as might be some strategic plans); they are practical guides for action, including assembly, organisation and recovery efforts for processes and facilities following the invocation of a plan.

Testing is a generic term for a number of activities that are designed to evaluate whether BC plans direct business resumption efforts as expected. It is designed to be scheduled and systematic in order to assess their viability under conditions of an interruption.

As Doemland (1999) observed, the purpose of testing and auditing is to ensure the continuing readiness of a plan. Contact information is a particularly good example, as such data may become dated quickly, making plans dependent upon such databases worthless.

There are four basic premises for testing:

- ensuring the organisation can walk before it tries to run;
- reducing complacency – the "we have a plan" attitude;
- improving maintenance and auditing;
- maintaining awareness.

With suitable preparation, testing can also provide an opportunity for an organisation to:

- determine adequacy of Service Level Agreements (SLAs) with third-party providers of services (such as emergency telecommunications, business recovery centres and data storage);
- test communications through the use of role playing and simulations with senior managers and BC coordinators;
- offer a context for practical training and evaluation and build situational awareness capabilities at individual and group level;
- dispel incorrect assumptions about recovery provisions, conditions, tasks and roles;
- provide a safe and supportive context in which to practise responses to interruptions.

Clark and Harman (2004) have suggested that "the notion that the more one practices, the luckier one gets is seldom more true". They also add that business recovery efforts are often compounded where organisations have interconnected activities such as production in one country or time-zone and distribution or HQ functions in another. Importantly, testing provides a way of reducing uncertainty, as to both what could happen and how an organisation will react to recover business activities. Testing provides a benchmark for the BCM process in terms of how successful initiation was, the appropriateness of planning for BC and the degree of success in overcoming resistance to change. Testing provides an opportunity to shift the view of BCM as being a theoretical necessity to being a practical one by extending involvement throughout an organisation. The planning process (see Chapter 5) should have determined the type and frequency of tests. A key difficulty is that testing will be subject to the range of demands facing an organisation.

Preparing for Tests

Before a test, the BC manager must decide what is to be tested and how it is to be tested. This involves two decisions: setting the context and setting the scope of response. Setting the context for the test in the form of a scenario (perhaps one identified in the planning process) is intended to address specific causes of interruption and to trigger the invocation of plans.

Typical scenarios may include:

- loss of a key supplier;
- threat to reputation;
- loss of key customer;
- failure of a major competitor;
- chemical or hazard spill;
- information systems shutdown;
- logistics interruption;
- loss of a building (totally, temporarily, indefinitely);
- denial of access caused by location within an exclusion zone caused by others;
- loss of utilities (power, telecommunications, water);
- product recall or malicious product tampering.

Setting the scope for the response refers to the frequency of testing (quarterly, yearly, etc.) and whether tests are announced or unannounced. Announced tests serve to evaluate the procedures within a plan. Unannounced tests are designed to evaluate whether employees can respond to an unexpected event and implement plans as originally intended. As Doemland (1999) notes, such tests may also provide a means of assessing an individual's capacity for decision making under stress. Ramsay (1999) also adds that surprise tests motivates those with a formal role in a BC team to be constantly familiar with the location and content of plans. Generally, announced tests are undertaken more frequently. Setting the context and scope of the test is important because it underpins the expectations and criteria against which the efficacy of the test will be assessed. One problem with unannounced tests is that stakeholders may not realise that the event is a test until some substantial time has elapsed. This was starkly illustrated at Nairobi Airport in August 2002 when the world's media began reporting the crash of a Boeing 737, resulting in the death of seventy-six passengers and crew. Emergency workers, airlines and government officials became involved while unaware that what they believed was true was in fact an exercise that the Kenyan police authorities thought would raise situational readiness and awareness (Mwende, 2002)

Lewis (2005) has identified a number of factors that are often ignored or omitted from BC plans and which thereby impede their implementation (whether in testing or real invocation). These included:

- failure of telecoms equipment to water damage;
- employees unable to attend because of childcare, personal or transportation problems;
- assumptions that the company will be a priority to its suppliers (including utilities);
- unavailability of important paper resources (such as purchase orders and cheques);
- unavailability of keys;

- obsolete links with, or information for, emergency services.

Mitts (2005) suggests that the involvement (consultation and/or participation) of local emergency service in BC plan testing is also beneficial by adding further realism to tests. This arises by promoting a more outward-looking perspective on recovery activities since, in many instances, understanding how emergency services act and think, and understanding how other organisations in close proximity would respond in similar or the same circumstances is necessary. Other pre-test considerations include the scope of departmental and employee scope of test, the anticipation of hazards, physical and geographical boundaries, the degree of realism and budgetary constraints (Mitts, 2005).

Types of Tests

A variety of different tests are available – each varying in terms of their processes, participants, frequency and complexity (Figure 7.7).

Desk check tests are the simplest and most frequent form of tests. The author of the plan simply checks the contents of the plan to ensure that information, such as named employees and telephone numbers, are up to date. In addition, the desk check should consider whether the plan reflects

Type of Test	Process	Participants	Frequency	Complexity
Desk check	Check the contents of the plan as a precursor to maintenance	• Author of plan • Another manager (verification)	High	Low
Walk-through	Carry out an extended desk-check to check interaction and roles of participants	• Author of plan • Main participants		
Simulation exercise	Incorporates associated plans: • business plans • buildings • communications	• Main participants • Observers • Co-ordinators		
Function testing	Moves work to another site. Recreate the existing work from the displaced site	• Employees in a business area • Hot site suppliers • Observers • Co-ordinators		
Full test	Shutting down an entire building and relocating work	• All employees in a building • Hot site suppliers • Observers • Co-ordinators	Low	High

Figure 7.7 Types of business continuity tests.

the organisation's operations as they currently stand. If, for example, a department has taken on new responsibilities within an organisation, this may necessitate revisions. The rapidity of organisational change influenced by staff turnover as well as environmental shifts requires a regular, if not ongoing, monitoring of business unit responsibilities. Some organisations carry out desk checks with two persons in order to ensure that the limitations of a single person's knowledge does not hamper the verification of the plan.

Walk-through (also known as a "talk-through" given that it is often still desk-based) exercises are similar to desk checks in their execution but involve all named participants (which will vary between plans and organisations). The participants are brought together to role play their defined resumption procedures alongside those of others. In this way, issues such as the timing of activities, reporting lines and coordination between incumbents can be verified. Often, the walk-through is undertaken to meet a specified disruption scenario. From these exercises, BC coordinators can initiate maintenance to ensure that coordination is enhanced when the plan is invoked in a real situation.

Simulation exercises widen participation to all those who are to be involved in business recovery. Such tests are conducted with prior notice to all employees concerned. In this type of test, an interruption, such as a building fire, provides a scenario in which employees do not have access to normal facilities and must recreate the working environment in an alternative location. In addition, role plays are used to ensure that BC activities such as customer services, public relations and legal affairs can operate under simulated conditions of a disaster. Throughout the exercise, a team of observers is responsible for recording how recovery activities were undertaken, whether they conformed to procedures laid down in plans and whether problems or omissions in the plan become apparent. Since a simulation exercise is designed to test the integration of plans from the zero hour to seventy-two hours or more, often a system of "accelerated time" is used, whereby the simulation requires all steps to be completed in a quarter of the time normally required. Where this approach is taken, activities are not "completed" but "acknowledged", whereby the personnel responsible will simulate the procedure in the correct order and register its "completion" with the manager responsible for coordinating the overall recovery process (normally the BC manager).

Function or operational testing is limited in scope to one or two departments or functions. In such a test, normal facilities are closed and employees must recreate their working environment in an alternative location, such as another company building or at the premises of a third-party supplier. The purpose of these tests is to ensure that a function can be recovered to another location in the time-scale set in the BC plan and to ensure that sufficient resources are available to resume adequately a minimum level of service. For instance, a function test may reveal that employees were able to move a telephone sales department to an alternative site quickly, only to find that insufficient telephone lines and computer terminals were available. During the test, observers are in place to note such anomalies and areas for improvement.

Full or live exercises are the most extensive, realistic and expensive form of test. Consequently, they are normally only undertaken on a yearly or bi-yearly basis. This is the largest-scale test and involves the invocation of the main BC plans and functional BC policies to deal with a scenario, which normally involves a move to another site where operations are to be resumed and organisational preparedness is evaluated. Live exercises differ from other tests because participants are not given prior notice of the invocation. Accordingly, this ensures that, as far as is possible, the test is the most rigorous that could be achieved without facing a real disaster. The dependencies and links between different plans are a focal point of this type of testing. For example, individual plans may have timelines of recovery that are, in isolation, consistent and coordinated. In a full test, it may be the case that variations in the timelines of recovery between different functions conspire to hamper recovery efforts.

In addition, the full test raises organisation-wide awareness of the impact that a disaster could have. When an entire facility has to invoke its plans and cease normal operations, this is the ultimate test of whether the two most vital recovery resources – plans and personnel – can work together effectively. Only then can BC managers and coordinators fully evaluate the effectiveness of pre-planning, decision making, coordination and awareness-raising. Normally, senior management approval is required before such tests can take place and the timing of these events may coincide with quieter periods in the calendar (although a successful resumption during a quiet period could be misleading).

Testing Schedules

As plans become more complex and the number of plans increases as the scope of BCM expands, both a greater variety of functional teams will become involved and a greater degree of integration between teams will become necessary to reflect the human resource team requirements should an interruption arise in earnest. This gives rise to multiple iterations of testing activities over an extended period of time and these should be organised through a schedule of testing. In the same way that a plan should be tested before it tests the organisation, the testing schedule should consider the most appropriate times to test plans while minimising disruption and maximising learning opportunities. An example of a testing schedule is visualised in Figure 7.8.

In the example seen in Figure 7.8, the testing schedule is designed to generate momentum as the company tests its plans in four different ways and on six different occasions in a five-month period before the annual live

Type of Test		Jan	Feb	Mar	Apr	May	Jun	Jul	Aug	Sep	Oct	Nov	Dec
Desk check	Maintenance ⇨	■						■			■		
	Testing ⇨	■						■			■		
Walk-through	Maintenance ⇨		■			■			■			■	
	Testing ⇨		■			■			■			■	
Simulation exercise	Maintenance ⇨			■						■			
	Testing ⇨			■						■			
Function testing	Maintenance ⇨				■						■		
	Testing ⇨				■						■		
Full test	Maintenance ⇨							■					
	Testing ⇨							■					

Figure 7.8 An example of a testing schedule.

test in July. Each test leads to some form of maintenance activity – ranging from confirmation that current plans are fit for purpose, to revisions that are to be tested within the next three months. Differences in the size of bars denote the magnitude (in terms of the commitment of human, physical and financial resources) to the test type rather than (necessarily) the time taken to undertake the test and maintenance. In the example shown, the rationale for the timing of the tests in the calendar year reflects an identification that the operational peak for this organisation (which could be a retailer) is in December and the operational trough is in July. The annual test is scheduled for July and there is no testing activity in June to provide some free time or slack to ensure that lessons from preceding tests are embedded within BC plans in advance of the annual full test. The remaining months have a balanced allocation of testing activity in which desk-checks inform subsequent walk-through tests and these, then, inform simulation and function tests (each of which take place half-yearly). While the organisation tests at its quietest periods, the scenario that would be deployed would involve a worst-case scenario of an interruption occurring at the busiest time of year.

Post-test Evaluations

The post-test evaluation should be conducted by the BC managers, coordinators and independent observers (where used). With specific reference to the plans and bearing in mind the context and the scope of response, the following issues should be considered:

- Did the plans help or hinder recovery efforts?
- Did people deviate from the plan and, if so, what was the effect of this?
- Were recovery time objectives (RTOs) achieved?
- Where and when did delays occur?
- What did staff do well?
- What did staff do badly?
- How did the expectations differ from what actually happened?
- Were functional policies or plans integrated sufficiently to achieve recovery?
- What are the priorities for change?
- Is there a paper or audit trail?
- How should changes be implemented?
- Could the observation process be improved?

Questionnaires can be used to gather information from participants and to demonstrate that the users of plans have some input into how they are formed, developed and presented. In addition, questionnaires can be valuable for measuring attitudes towards BCM over time. If questionnaire surveys are carried out regularly, this provides important information to the BCM team about changing attitudes towards BCM. The results could highlight that the barriers to change (see Chapter 6) have not been removed, prompting improvements to training, communication and control-and-reward systems. Depending on the outcome of the post-test evaluation, maintenance and auditing will follow.

Complexity, Crisis Management Teams, Training and Exercising

A key assumption is that testing and exercises will increase the probability of successful incident management. In our earlier discussion of crisis management teams (CMTs), it was argued that the performance of teams might be enhanced through the careful selection of members and design of team structures (Belbin, 1981; Smith, 2000; Anderson, 2007) supported by the use of simulations to develop cohesiveness and interaction (McKenna, 1994). Paraskevas (2006) argues that a complexity approach will further enhance the effectiveness of an organisation's crisis response. NECSI provide the following over view of a complexity approach.

> The study of complex systems is about understanding indirect effects. Problems that are difficult to solve are often hard to understand because the causes and effects are not obviously related. Pushing on a complex system "here" often has effects "over there" because the parts are interdependent. This has become more and more apparent in our efforts to solve societal problems or avoid ecological disasters caused by our own actions. The field of complex systems provides a number of sophisticated tools, some of them concepts that help us think about these systems, some of them analytical for studying these systems in greater depth, and some of them computer based for describing, modelling or simulating these systems.
>
> (NECSI, 2008)

Paraskevas' (2006) discussion is concerned with the case of a hotel chain experiencing multiple reports of a food-borne crisis across its portfolio of five star hotels and resorts. The chain, located within one Mediterranean country, utilised detailed standard operating procedures across its units and operated central purchasing of all foodstuffs. Following the events of 9/11, the chain had established crisis management procedures and protocols for CMTs. As the scale of the outbreaks became apparent, plans were activated and crisis task forces dispatched; these were over seen by a central crisis coordinating cell. Despite these preparations, the presence of a media relations plan, advice from two consulting organisations, and prior training and simulation the chain's crisis efforts did not have the expected results. For example, while the news did not reach the media, a key account was lost early during the crisis (Paraskevas, 2006). Substantial amounts of monies were paid out in compensation, pending possible legal action from guests and operators and an unspecified further blow created further reputational damage.

In reviewing their performance, the CEO's confidence in the plan was tested:

> We had conducted a simulation exercise only five months ago. The scenario was similar but not in such scale. Nevertheless, we all felt confident that although it was a highly unexpected situation, the plan was designed with such a crisis in mind and we would be able to deal with it effectively. We did not expect that some people would not be able to cope and that some others would react in such a negative manner.
>
> (CEO, reported in Paraskevas, 2006: 898)

Another member of the senior executive reported that the level of detail in the plan had misled the chain in terms of assuming preparedness "what looks good in paper does not really work in practice". For Paraskevas:

> One important insight of seeing crisis response as a complex co-evolving system (CCES) is that evolutionary processes and processes of self-organisation may lead to a multitude of new order situations which are not necessarily all optimal.
>
> (2006: 898)

For example, despite the "impressive" amount of detail in the plans, some managers needed it but others did not. Further, the intensity of crisis differed from site to site, requiring a consistent rather than uni-form approach – an important if subtle distinction (see Elliott et al., 1997). For Paraskevas (2006) the case challenges a paradigm of crisis planning that emphasises a static and detailed approach in place of one that focuses upon "dynamic adaptability". In other words, creating a team which can successfully interpret a changing situation and adapt solutions to meet the needs as they evolve. Reporting much soul search-ing after the event, a member of the senior executive confessed to a widespread belief that by simply investing in crisis planning and simu-lations they would achieve a high level of crisis preparedness. However, this respondent continued:

> The mere existence of CMPs does not mean that the entire chain is "crisis prepared". We were like a head detached from the rest of the body. We should make sure that we create a common mindset throughout the chain in terms of what a CMP means and what it is here to do.
>
> (Executive Committee Member, quoted in Paraskevas, 2006)

Paraskevas (2006) reports that the rigorous crisis plans were stifling and constraining and may have prevented managers from exercising their judgement. Such a mechanistic approach shares much with the response of the police at Hillsborough, whose mechanistic response was a key cause in the crisis of 1989 in which ninety-six spectators died (see Elliott and Smith, 1993). In earlier simulations Paraskevas (2006) reports how a manager was unwilling to risk a promotion and deviate from the plan having been reprimanded for doing so during an earlier simulation. Another felt her hands tied by the detailed plans and another site manager reported being unable to deal with key account guests as responsibility for these had been allocated to a central team that was located centrally and thus unable to respond quickly. The "paper" ideal of a central team to provide special support to key accounts was in practice a key weakness, especially at remote sites where there was a delay in a response from this team. Given the relatively short incubation of the effects of the contamination, the dispersed location of sites and the limitations of only two central key account teams, an effective response could simply not be achieved on a crisis of this scale across the entire chain. Paraskevas concludes that:

> The management of organisations should view crisis response not as a procedure but as a living system within their organisation and enable this system to achieve its purpose, which is not the solution of a problem but to create the conditions that enable the solution of multiple problems.
>
> (2006: 902–903)

Indeed, the case points to the potential for complacency arising from the creation of crisis plans and structures. Although these may be useful, crisis preparedness will emerge from mature attitudes towards crisis and an understanding that plans may not meet every eventuality and that adaptive structures supported by an apt culture are vital to ensuring effective response. Paraskevas' description of the chain's preparations for crisis seems to have more in common with a "drilled" response, which though apt for certain contexts is unlikely to be suited to the demands of crisis event.

Maintenance and Auditing

Maintenance is a generic term for a number of activities that are designed to evaluate whether BC plans are up to date: that is, their relevance. Maintenance, like testing, should be undertaken regularly to ensure that plans accurately mirror the organisation's structure and operations. As a plan is only as effective as its most recent test, so too is it as relevant to organisational needs as its most recent maintenance. Maintenance can be triggered in two ways: testing (as above) or periodic reviews.

The BC manager and those at a departmental or functional level responsible for ensuring that plans are not out of date undertake periodic reviews. In many ways, periodic reviews are similar to desk-check tests, and in some cases this type of test will be used as the most regular form of maintenance.

Auditing is a generic term for a number of activities that are designed to evaluate whether BC plans are appropriate: that is, meet the specific needs of a changing organisation. This activity has wider connotations and implications, and may require a new BIA and BIE (Chapter 5). If testing has shown that plans have failed to meet major recovery objectives, a fundamental review of provisions may be required. In particular, where an organisation has grown in such a way that it now has new information systems, departments, facilities, or has been involved in merger or acquisition, maintenance will be insufficient to ensure that plans are appropriate. With the introduction of the new BS 25999 it is probable that there will be greater demands of auditing as means of evaluating BC practice.

Business Continuity Management as a Continuous Organisational Process

Plans are live documents. If they are not sustained, improved and, when necessary, changed, the investment in BCM will be wasted. Moreover, if a plan is perceived to be of little help both during tests and in real invocations, support for BCM will falter. BCM often starts as a minor project with little investment yet with major strategic importance; a failure to engage support from the organisation will increase the barriers to change BCM intends to reduce. Moreover, BCM should be considered to be more than a project, which implies a small-scale temporary activity. Few organisations can invest in BCM on a large scale at start-up, but this does not mean that, as time passes, BCM should not become a normal part of every activity within an organisation. This is why we refer to BCM as a process: it is ongoing, continual, organisation-wide and normalised.

Continuity Plans

There can be no simple prescription for the content of BC and major incident plans. At one level, the major incident plan is concerned with the coordination of an organisation's response to a significant interruption. It provides a process for activating those mechanisms required to ensure that the continuity response is conducted in the best interests of the entire organisation. At another, the major incident plan will probably be a short document identifying roles and responsibilities of the strategic, tactical and operational groups as well as indicating where key information is located. Detailed plans will lie at the operational level, for each business unit, team or support function. Personnel may have plans for a range of alternative scenarios, from outlining support for staff in the event of a major relocation following the loss of a building, through to using last month's BACS payroll data in the event of a loss of current employee information.

Crisis Communications

How might corporate image and reputation help or hinder an organisation's crisis response? The wealth of material dealing with crisis from a communications perspective indicates that its importance is well understood (see, for example, Stone, 1995; Regester and Larkin, 1997). It is not the purpose of this chapter simply to repeat what is available elsewhere. The books identified above provide useful prescriptions for crisis communications and further recommendations are made in the further reading list at the end of this chapter. Rather, we intend to consider some of the broader issues concerned with crisis communications. The underlying philosophy of our approach is that sound preparation builds resilience. Nowhere is this truer than with regard to crisis communications. An organisation's historical context, expressed in the form of the established corporate reputation, can be seen as a crucial factor in determining the efficacy of crisis communications. As Shrivastava observed:

> Crisis communications is not a short-term, one-shot public relations effort, or a one-way transfer of pertinent information from organisations to the public. Instead it should be viewed as establishment of permanent long-term communicative relationships with multiple internal and external stakeholders. Communication implies not only the transfer of information, but an exchange of information and underlying assumptions, and discourse aimed at reaching a common understanding of issues.
>
> (1987b: 5)

This reputational context will be determined by the fit of crisis communications with a number of factors including:

- ongoing marketing communications;
- relationship with the media;
- history of previous incidents (expressed in terms of the affected organisation and its broader industrial sector);
- previous experience of successfully dealing with events;
- stakeholder relationships;
- organisational culture and structure.

Ongoing marketing communications refers to branding, advertising and promotional issues. Perrier water's close association with "naturally pure" was struck an almost fatal blow when it was contaminated with benzene.

Perrier was perceived as a secretive, awkward organisation with poor media relations preceding the crisis. Cunard was vilified for its tardy handling of passenger complaints when its expensively refitted luxury liner was not ready in time for a cruise. Disgruntled passengers received extensive media coverage damaging the company's image. Contrast that with the plaudits received by P&O when affected by a similar problem. In May 2000 P&O's brand new, £200 million cruise ship *Aurora* limped back into port after breaking down one day into her maiden voyage. *Aurora*'s 1,800 passengers were bitterly disappointed at the cancellation of their once-in-a-lifetime holiday cruise. Clearly, maintaining customer confidence in this luxury market demanded a quick, super response. Passengers were quickly offered a full compensation package, which included a refund on their ticket as well as another free cruise of an equivalent value costing P&O's insurers an estimated £6 million.

Reputation may be damaged when stars paid to endorse particular brands are implicated in a scandal. When O.J. Simpson was alleged to have murdered his wife, Hertz Rent A Car ended a ten-year-long advertising campaign featuring the sportsman. Michael Jackson's paid endorsement of Pepsi terminated shortly after he was alleged to have been involved in impropriety. Star endorsement in such scenarios is double edged with negative associations potentially replacing positive ones.

Effective crisis communications, it is suggested, can be nourished by a reservoir of goodwill, built up with the media and customers alike. Such resources cannot deal with a crisis on their own, but they can provide a powerful platform from which to launch an effective crisis communications strategy.

Effective communications requires getting the right message to the right stakeholder group. During the pre-crisis stage, this requires that organisations identify:

- who their stakeholders are;
- what problems the crisis causes for them;
- what their initial perceptions of the organisation are;
- the best means of communicating with them;
- the message or information that they require.

Increasingly, utility companies maintain detailed databases of customers so that they can quickly identify the likely consequences of an interruption. Such databases may include at-risk groups, be they elderly residents, young families or major industries requiring significant resources. Some databases record when groups may have been affected by previous interruptions, or where influential environmental groups or politicians are located. From a self-interested point of view, this provides a useful warning of public embarrassment. Such monitoring requires significant investment and commitment. A growing dimension of marketing concerns the development of relationships within industrial and consumer markets (Egan, 1995b). Relationships are increasingly seen as the key to success and it may be a truism to say that most relationships founder when truly tested. An increasing amount of evidence suggests that strong loyalties can be developed where there is a long record of assistance during crises.

The means of communicating must be closely linked to the content and purpose of a message. For example, personal telephone communications is the mode chosen by hospital trusts to communicate with patients who have received the wrong treatment or have been treated by a medic with an infectious disease. A personal touch is important and the target group is well defined. Product recalls of consumer goods are usually handled via the print and broadcast media, depending upon the threat of the difficulty and the likely public interest. Radio may be used for urgent, local warnings such as major pollution scares. During winter, local radio is often the best source of information on the effects of snow. It is difficult to be prescriptive as the demands of every interruption will differ. Further advice can be found in Regester and Larkin (1995) and Lagadec (1993). Despite uncertainty about the precise nature of a crisis that might arise in the future, organisations can develop predetermined elements of crisis communication. For instance, specially prepared websites known as "darksites" can remain hidden from public view until such time as the organisation needs to make information about an accident, recall or incident available (one such example is that of Virgin Atlantic as seen in Box 4.4 Chapter 4). In the event of an invocation, information can be brought online quickly since information about company policy, legal issues and media contacts have already been approved by senior management, legal advisers and BC managers. Equally, the media and customers will check an organisation's website and may rely upon it as a continuous source of current information as the incident unfolds and develops. Snellen (2003) proposes that darksites should contain general organisation or company information in major languages about products or services, company safety policies and track record, frequently asked questions and multimedia. At a functional level, darksites are emblematic of a BCM approach to crisis management – prepared in advance of a crisis, using digital technology and understanding the informational needs of important stakeholders.

Summary

This chapter has sought to provide some insight into the key issues associated with incident management. The ad hocracy has been put forward as the model crisis management team. Carefully selected, well-trained, multi-skilled and able to draw on up-to-date documents, the crisis management team needs to retain some flexibility. Distinction between gold, silver and bronze level activities highlights the different roles needed to manage with an interruption effectively. Other key issues during the operational crisis stage concern staff, health and welfare, and effective communications. Change will affect different staff in different ways and supervisory staff must be aware of the symptoms. Similarly, those with a coordinating role must consider ways of either reducing the burden upon individuals or else implement practical steps to support staff. Although crisis communications are seen as a key part of response, it has been argued that pre-crisis investment in this area will reap rich rewards. Training, maintenance and auditing will play a key role in exposing staff to potential stressors, raising capabilities and identifying communication needs. They help ensure that the best possible support is available to staff called upon to deal with an interruption. They also provide an opportunity for staff to experience in some way the possible stressors of incident management. This, as we have argued, will reduce the negative aspect of stress. Finally, we have considered, briefly, the essentials of communications management. In this, we have sought to emphasise that good communications is built up from firm foundations and is unlikely to appear out of the ether following an interruption.

Study Questions

1　a　What are the different types of test?

　　b　What are their advantages and disadvantages?

2　What are the elements of an effective crisis management team?

3　How might stress influence decision-making capabilities?

Further Reading

Alesi, P. (2008) "Building enterprise-wide resilience by integrating business continuity capability into day-to-day business culture and technology", *Journal of Business Continuity & Emergency Planning*, 2 (3): 214–220.

Barnett, C. (2003) "Crisis communications now: three views", *Tactics*, January, pp. 15–16.

Dilenschneider, R.L. and Hyde, R.C. (1985) "Crisis communications: planning for the unplanned", *Business Horizons*, Jan/Feb, 28 (1): 35–40.

Elliott, D. and Smith, D. (2000) "Opening Pandora's box", in S. Cole, D. Smith and S. Tombs (eds) *Managing in the Risk Society*, Cambridge: Kluwer.

Flin, R. (1996) *Sitting in the Hot Seat*, London: John Wiley.

Friedman, M. (2002) "25 ways to perfect your press release", *Tactics*, July, np.

Gashen, D.J. (2003) "Crisis – what crisis? Taking your crisis communications plan for a test drive", *Tactics*, May, pp. 12.

Goodman, M.B. (2001) "Current trends in corporate communication", *Corporate Communications: An International Journal*, 6 (3): 117–123.

Guilbert, A. (1999) "Crisis communications", *Ivey Business Journal*, November/December, pp. 78–81.

Gustin, C. (2003) "Avoiding the seven sins of crisis communications", *Electric Perspectives*, July/August, pp. 5–6.

Johnson, D.G. (2003) "Crisis management: forewarned is forearmed", *Journal of Business Strategy*, March/April, 14 (2): 58–62.

Johnson, V. and Pappas, S.C. (2003) "Crisis management in Belgium: the case of Coca-Cola", *Corporate Communications: An International Journal*, 8 (1): 18–22.

Lindstedt, D. (2008) "Grounding the discipline of business continuity planning: What needs to be done to take it forward?", *Journal of Business Continuity & Emergency Planning*, 2 (2): 197–205.

Love, G.J. and Anderson, M.R. (2008) "Exercise management: new thoughts on an old process", *Journal of Business Continuity & Emergency Planning*, 2 (4): 349–356.

Moore, T. and Lakha, R. (2006) *Tolley's Handbook of Disaster and Emergency Management*, London: Butterworth-Heinemann.

Morwood, G. (1998) "Business continuity: awareness and training programmes", *Information Management and Computer Security*, 6 (1): 28–32.

Puchan, H. (2001) "The Mercedes-Benz A-class crisis", *Corporate Communications: An International Journal*, 6 (1): 42–46.

Ramsay, C.G. (1999) "Protecting your business: from emergency planning to crisis management", *Journal of Hazardous Materials*, 65: 131–149.

Ressler, J.A. (1982) "Crisis communications", *Public Relations Quarterly*, Fall, 27 (3): 8–11.

Samansky, A.W. (2002) "RUN!: That's not the crisis communications plan you need", *Public Relations Quarterly*, Fall, 47 (3): 25–27.

Senior, A. and Copely, R. (2008) "Deploying a new system for recording and managing information during an emergency to aid decision making", *Journal of Business Continuity & Emergency Planning*, 2 (3): 267 –270.

Seville, E., Brunsdon, D., Dantas, A., Le Masurier, J., Wilkinson, S. and Vargo, J. (2008) "Organisational resilience: Researching the reality of New Zealand organisations", *Journal of Business Continuity & Emergency Planning*, 2 (3): 258–266.

Sheth, S., McHugh, J. and Jones, F. (2008) "A dashboard for measuring capability when designing, implementing and validating business continuity and disaster recovery projects", *Journal of Business Continuity & Emergency Planning*, 2 (3): 221–239.

Smallman, C. and Weir, D. (1999) "Communication and cultural distortion during crises", *Disaster Prevention and Management*, 8 (1): 33–41.

Truitt, R.H. and Kelley, S.S. (1989) "Battling a crisis in advance", *Public Relations Quarterly*, Spring: 6–8.

Vaid, R. (2008) "How are operational risk and business continuity coming together as a common risk management spectrum?", *Journal of Business Continuity & Emergency Planning*, 2 (4): 330–339.

Walch, D. and Merante, J. (2008) "What is the appropriate business continuity management staff size?", *Journal of Business Continuity & Emergency Planning*, 2 (3): 240–250.

Wigley, S. (2003) "Relationship management in a time of crisis: the 2001 Oklahoma state university plane crash", *Public Relations Quarterly*, Summer: 39–42.

8 Reflections on Past and Future

Introduction

In the opening chapter we presented our view of the evolution of BCM. In the first edition of this book we had suggested that a value-based approach to BCM, concerned less with compliance or technology failure and more with the needs of the business itself, would emerge. We may have been optimistic and there is evidence that the audit-based approach has been remarkably persistent (Krell, 2006; Elliott and Johnson, 2008b). We recognise that audit may play an important role in raising the profile of processes such as BCM but have a concern that compliance rather than effective BC becomes the focus. In Chapter 1 we introduced the notion of BCM as a capability, reflecting the development of a resource-based view of competitive advantage. Strategic capability is related to the competences with which activities are undertaken, resources are available to an organisation and the overall balance of resources, units and activities and how these are managed. The objective of a BCM capability is to provide effective prevention and recovery for the organisation, while maintaining competitive advantage and value system integrity. Running throughout this book, however, is the view that BC concerns more than information systems security; although the ubiquity of information systems and our dependence upon it has often made this a focus for continuity efforts. The typology of crisis introduced in Chapter 4 provided some insight into the potential range of interruptions and we have also argued that plans may suit more than one trigger or type of interruption. For example, Mellish (2000) described how Sainsbury's activated their plans for dealing with the so-called millennium bug when faced with a fuel crisis that was caused by a blockade of UK oil refineries. More recently many organisations have reported the value of BC plans when faced with the potential threat of a pandemic (Elliott and Johnson, 2008b). Similarly, many companies, among them Deutsche Bank New York, Salomon Smith Barney and Morgan Stanley in New York City, were able to benefit from continuity preparedness on that fateful morning of 9/11 (Risk Management, 2002). The concern of this chapter is with the future, with the challenges facing

BCM and to argue that it is a strategic concern – that the needs of the business should drive all BCM consideration. In this, our analysis has to be both "outside-in" and "inside-out". Our starting point is to consider the challenges that companies will face due to developments in the political, economic, social and technological environments. However, organisational culture and structure, resources and people will, together, shape resilience. We consider the internal and external environments because these elements provide important "push" and "pull" factors for continuity management.

Globalisation, the devastation triggered by natural disasters on every continent and, arguably, the rise in international terrorism such as the events of 9/11 provide a new context for continuity management. Technologically the internet provides a vital dimension for many of the changes that together form a "postmodern" world. We then proceed to consider a range of other political and social factors. In Chapter 1 we suggested not only that BCM has constantly evolved but also that this process continues. This chapter considers a range of themes, divided into the main political, social and economic issues that will provide push factors in the evolution of BCM.

Interest in reputation management, for example, has grown rapidly as organisations recognise that poor images can be beamed around the world instantly. News of the credit crunch and the major losses suffered by some of the world's largest banks spread quickly, triggering an almost calamitous collapse in consumer confidence and the first run on a UK bank (Northern Rock) for more than one hundred years. The rise of consumerism and activism has also been fuelled by new technologies, whether hackers target Microsoft's software or employ technology to organise campaigns. These themes do not provide an exhaustive list but draw on our anticipation of the most important and imminent developments that organisations should be aware of.

Globalisation and Business Continuity Management

Globalisation represents the single most important opportunity and obstacle for business (Ghemawat, 2008; Wiersema and Bowen, 2008). It is an important variable to consider when companies plot strategy and, as Wiersema and Bowen argue, forces firms to consider global expansion as a legitimate competitive move such that scope economies and location differences in national competencies can be exploited. Quoting Porter (1986) and Kogut (1983) they remind us that:

> Interregional differences in factor costs may necessitate a complete reorganisation of the firm's value chain activities, including where to locate different activities as well as re-evaluating whether certain activities should be undertaken internally or outsourced.
>
> (Wiersema and Bowen, 2008: 118)

The rise of economic "megaregions" demonstrate that globalisation exerts both a "centrifugal" *and* a "centripetal" force on economic activity (Florida, 2008). Hence, we see the rise of megaregions as defined in which most of the world's economic activity, population concentration and innovation occurs. Forty such megaregions have been identified (Florida, 2008). Florida's concept of a megaregion is based on research done at the University of Maryland on light-based economic activity (for more discussion of this see http://www.cissm.umd.edu/papers/display.php?id=135) that reveal these clusters of economic activity. Examples of such megaregions include the Boston, New York and Washington corridor in the US; London and the Leeds, Manchester, Liverpool and Birmingham corridor in the UK; finally, the Shanghai, Nanyang and Hangzhou triangle in China. Megaregions are areas where the light-based regional product, a measure of economic productivity, equals an annual $100 billion.

Whether one subscribes to Florida's theses or not, the data is compelling and resonates with the experience of economic trends. Globalisation has spawned a countervailing force towards pockets of concentration, with clusters of similar types of economic activity taking place in particular locations. For instance, sourcing raw materials for manufacturing, including the manufacturing itself, can be found in specific regions in China, call centres in India, and biotechnology manufacturing in the US and Europe.

> The mistake is to see globalisation as an either-or proposition. It's not. The key to finding competitive advantage in this new economic landscape lies in understanding that the world is both flat and spiky: Economic activity is dispersing and concentrating at the same time.
>
> (Florida, 2008: 19)

Hence, although Friedman and Kaplan (2002) theorised that globalisation is mediated by the underlying computer and communications technologies that enable companies to operate in a seamless manner in both space and time, coupling together countries, markets and finances, the strategic decisions that companies make with regard to use of resources and capabilities should not be overlooked. As a globalised world flattens, some parts of the world also benefit from a much greater concentration of economic resources, competences and power. What are the implications for BCM? At a strategic level – at the level of the board – companies should therefore understand what this new economic landscape means and how best BCM capabilities may be developed in the future. There is already evidence that some large investment banks are selecting specific regions of the world to locate aspects of their BCM infrastructure based upon security and capability concerns.

The opportunity that globalisation creates is well illustrated by the case of the Nasdaq[8] stock exchange in the US. The company was founded in 1971, well before the dawn of the internet, as a commercial medium but with the foresight that a stock exchange need not necessarily be based on the conventional idea of having a physical trading floor (Greifeld, 2006). An exchange merely needed access to computers and telecommunications equipment to conduct its trading. Then, connectivity with its customer base could be on both east and west coasts of the US (two of the examples of the megaregions that exist in North America), while today Nasdaq can operate around the world, courtesy of online trading technology and the internet as an interface with its stakeholders.

However, globalisation brings with it a myriad of challenges, one of which is the extreme stock price volatility and uncertainty that accompany tightly coupled systems, as evidenced in the rapid spread of the so-called credit crunch. The internet and Web 2.0 means that transparency is forced onto companies not only in the form of pricing (Sinha, 2000) but also with the conduct of business more generally. This even applies to the trade relations of countries. Witness the case of China's relationship with Sudan and Zimbabwe, discussed in Box 8.1.

Box 8.1 China and Imperialism in the Age of the Internet

It was predictable that during the 2008 China Olympic Games activists would focus attention on the less salutary aspects of China's governmental relations with a range of issues – the genocide in Darfur being but one of these. A glimpse of this was to be had during 2007 and the massacre of monks involved in a protest against Chinese rule of Tibet. A number of online news organisations run by activists ensured the international community would hear a more objective view of events. However, not expected was an expose of the relationship the Chinese had established with the dictatorship of Zimbabwe, Robert Mugabe and the ruling Zanu-PF party. During April 2008, shortly after the conduct of parliamentary elections, which appeared to have been won by the opposition party (the Movement for Democratic Change), a ship containing arms bound for Zimbabwe docked at the South African port of Durban. When it became evident that the arms were destined for use by Mugabe's government, the dockworkers' union refused to allow its members to unload the cargo. The South African government intervened by ordering the shipment to be unloaded and transported to Zimbabwe, but a High Court injunction forced the ship to set sail for an alternative port to unload its consignment of arms. Several other African governments joined the call for the arms not to be allowed to reach Zimbabwe, where it would be used for repressive purposes. The event has added to the embarrassment of the Chinese government in the run-up to the Beijing Olympics and there was evidence that the shipment of arms would be returned to Beijing.

Source: McGregor and Russell (2008)

We could add to Richard Florida's assertions that the post-9/11 world has seen a backlash against the "flattening" of the world. Indeed, security and economic concerns have led to concerns that the "pace of economic globalisation was moving too fast" (Davis, 2008). Additionally, security concerns have led governments to exert greater control over the ostensibly borderless internet such that it has been described as "balkanised" (Wu and Yoo, 2007).

At the company level, globalisation creates strategic issues that companies have to confront. At the level of corporate strategy, the board has to be clear about the direction of a company. However, this is a challenge at a time of fundamental change and when those who comprise the board do not have a deep knowledge of the new technology and its capabilities. Skapinker (2000) points out two issues of strategic concern to boards. The first is how to value companies – old methods do not work any longer, particularly when companies that have not made a profit have such huge and volatile valuations, evidenced by Freeserve, which was sold by its parent company for a much lower figure than its original valuation. Today this company no longer exists. Witness the case of eBay acquiring the communications company Skype for $4.3 billion in 2005 (Maurer, 2007) and today contemplating the sale of the company due to the lack of success eBay has had in using Skype to add value for shareholders.

The second issue concerns how conventional companies should respond to the commercial challenges brought about by technological change. As we discussed in Chapters 1 and 3, the age of Web 2.0 and social media present both big opportunities and challenges. Many companies are pondering how best to exploit social media in a manner that is consistent with strategy and company culture. This is a very vexing issue. Of course, we need only look back at the advent of the internet itself for a highly analogous situation where companies were also facing Handy's (1990) boiled frog scenario – how best to embrace discontinuous change! During the late 1990s, Moss-Kanter (2001b) found two patterns of company behaviour regarding exploitation of the internet. "Pacesetters" embraced the internet early as a commercial channel. Alternatively, "Laggards" described companies unable to support change processes internal to the organisation that would move employees to embrace the internet as another point of contact with consumers. Many large companies reported that they had spent substantial sums of money on internet sites without deriving any benefit. One company reported spending $100 million on 1,000 websites without any quantifiable benefits (Moss-Kanter, 2001b). The issues that inhibit action to embrace the internet will clearly vary across industries and for different companies. Some may experience resistance internally from constituencies such as a company sales force (Moss-Kanter, 2001b), who regard new channels as a threat. On the other hand, franchisors may experience resistance from franchisees who might regard the internet as a threat to sales at "brick and mortar" sites; for example, the reaction of the franchisees to the launch of the Body Shop website (Body Shop International, 2000). Finally, established organisations have to be cognisant of the balance of power within their industry. Today retailers increasingly wield power in fast-moving consumer goods industries, requiring caution from manufacturers who are intent on establishing their own websites as part of a multi-channel strategy. Large retailers may retaliate should a manufacturer wish to sell direct to the consumer.

New technologies have thrown up incredible opportunities (economic growth through technological change and productivity increases), extreme uncertainty and many challenges. How companies respond to these will depend upon the fundamentals that are in place in the organisation. We refer here to the corporate and competitive strategies they adopt, with a central place in those given to principles of crisis management and BC in formulating corporate strategy. Directors clearly play a crucial role in determining that these issues are dealt with from a continuity perspective. Yet, few if any companies today have BCM[9] represented at board level, even though the current conditions provide a strong case for such representation (Elliott and Johnson, 2008b). Of note there is the fact that, as the difficult economic environment continues, with multiple cases of bankruptcy and loss of company values, companies are finding it increasingly difficult to obtain affordable Directors' and Officers' (D&O) insurance (Felstead, 2007). The value-based mindset, discussed in Chapter 1, indicated that some organisations have attempted to better integrate BC by ensuring a structural link to the board via a senior director. In better practice companies, it was not unusual to find that BC managers would be invited to brief the board on specific strategic issues (Herbane et al., 1997). Furthermore, companies that can demonstrate the development of a BC capability might be well placed to negotiate with insurance carriers on the costs associated with D&O insurance.

Globalisation and the increasing business-based nature of BC require that BCM becomes a transnational activity analogous to R&D in sectors such as telecommunications and pharmaceuticals. This implies that plans from different regions should be as integrated as the operations they seek to protect. Full consideration would need to be given to the those regions of the world economy that Florida refers to as "flat" and "spiky" and which of these would best serve as locations where BCM competences are located in line with the human and locational resources to be found in such regions. Accordingly, BC planners will need to be aware of organisational, cultural and national differences for plans to maintain their potential. For truly global companies, there is a rationale for companies to consider how best they might use the competencies developed in a particular location globally to support the total continuity effort of the company. Indeed, were a company very successful at inculcating a BC capability, and if this were in line with company strategy, such a capability could be the basis for becoming a provider for other companies with a similar need but lacking the capability. With the development of cloud computing, we are starting to see the emergence of centralised data storage facilities by companies such as Google and Yahoo. Cloud computing allows the development of software by using the storage capacity offered by major companies such as Google or Amazon. Individuals or companies can then pay for usage of the applications in the "cloud" as they use time on the server (Hogge, 2008). The security implications of such choices would also need to be considered.

E-continuity

In Chapter 1 four different BC mindsets were identified. It was argued that, during the early years of the twenty-first century, BC would become "normalised" in certain types of environment, becoming an integral part of the management task. It was also argued that practice would be influenced by an organisation's experience of interruptions, organisational culture, management style and approach to technology and strategy. Thus, some organisations would develop a more sophisticated approach to continuity management than others. A continuum of practice was put forward, bounded by polarities of either "standard practice" or "better practice", depending on the scope of preparations and how embedded BC had become within the organisation. This model was developed from earlier research (see Herbane et al., 1997). The term "better practice" was employed to emphasise that, despite the suggestion of polarities, there was no intention to suggest that the best practice of 1997 constituted an end-point. Figure 8.1 provides a modified version of the BCM continuum that considers how the internet will force organisations to modify their BCM focus, progressing from a disaster recovery focus through a value-based continuity focus, to an e-continuity focus. This will be driven primarily by a realisation that there is no end-point in pursuing organisational preparedness. Indeed, the philosophy of continuous improvement and the learning organisation have been used as an analogy for the learning that needs to occur about BCM. The field is in its infancy and the possibilities are endless.

"E-continuity" refers to the provision of BCM services to e-business sites as well as the virtual networks, which they spawn. Indeed, it is salutary that the Year 2000 problem effectively became a non-event in most countries, only to be replaced by disruption to e-business sites in early January 2000. What both businesses and consumers suddenly discovered was that, once your main supplier's site was targeted and shut down, your own business could not operate – "e-continuity" is being driven by changes in

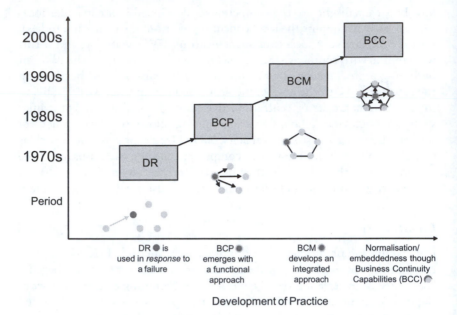

Figure 8.1 From disaster recovery to e-continuity.

economic sectors as fundamental as those experienced during the industrial revolution.[10] Indeed, the internet exposes the fact that no organisation can exist on its own, a fundamental concept in crisis management thinking.

Figure 8.1 illustrates how, as organisations become more reliant on virtual networks, the focus of BCM has to shift, in an appropriate way, to capture the networked nature of business. Thus, strategic analysis has to take into account virtual value chains and external networks. No longer will it be appropriate to focus solely upon staff within the organisation but intra-organisational teams will have to be considered; a virtual systems view will need to replace thinking about conventional organisational boundaries and continuous improvement focus needs to be considered both up and down the virtual value system.

Providing Continuity for Virtual Value Chains

A key issue for BC will be the provision of continuity for virtual value chains. The virtual value chain refers to the new opportunities for value creation, facilitated by developments in Web 2.0 (see Box 8.2). It has been argued that business on the internet creates a "market space" in addition to the normal marketplace in which business transactions take place (Rayport and Sviokla, 1995). Rayport and Sviokla present the case of a virtual value chain, which runs parallel to the value chain that defines the conventional activities of the company. Three conditions are necessary before the virtual value chain can yield value.

- First is that companies have to use information systems to coordinate the activities in their conventional value chain in such a manner that those activities become *visible* as a process.

- Second is that of *"mirroring capability"* in which physical activities are substituted by virtual ones, creating the infrastructure of the virtual value chain.

- Third is the creation of *new customer relationships* – it is during this stage that real value can be added by revolutionising product offerings.

Kodak, a household name in consumer photography and applications, is grappling with the transformation of the core of the company such that it secures the continued existence of the company in the age of Web 2.0 and social media. We turn to a short case that illustrates the difficulties involved in this transmutation.

Box 8.2 Kodak

The Kodak Eastman Company was created in 1879 with the invention of a dry plate by founder George Eastman for photographic reproduction. Throughout its long history the company has innovated new products and processes to become one of the leading companies in traditional photographic film products. However, despite continuing efforts in the latter part of the twentieth century to invest in R&D in traditional media as well as electronic imaging, the company found itself embattled in its attempts to move from traditional photography to digital photography. Several CEOs came and went, recruited from inside the company, as well as from companies outside of the traditional photographic and imaging sectors. The company continues to attempt to stem losses and the decline of sales in its core businesses. By 1999 Kodak had shrunk its global workforce by nearly 20,000 and such job losses may continue well into the future should restructuring efforts fail.

For a company that commands the brand recognition and respect that Kodak does, the lack of success in embracing digital technologies and bringing these to market successfully (and profitably) is a bitter pill to swallow. The company has worked diligently over the last five years to correct this by actively embracing digital solutions to imaging. Some of this has come out of Kodak's labs but also through acquiring small, entrepreneurial ventures such as Ofoto and Design2Launch that enable consumers to access photographic and print services through the internet.

Sources: Gavetti et al. (2005); Datamonitor (2007)

Continuity plays a role in all aspects of the three conditions of building a virtual business, but particularly during the stage of establishing customer relationships. This is when customers are receiving a product or service that has utility. A break in continuity during this phase of the virtual value chain destroys value for both the client company and the provider of the virtual service. During the stage where visibility is established, client organisations are not themselves affected should a website not be accessible. Similarly, where a company still provides a service through conventional channels, the client organisation has the option to consume the service through such channels. Such options may not exist in the final stage of establishing new customer relationships. This leads us to consider the implications of some developments in e-business and the resultant challenges likely to flow from these – in many cases we do not have definitive answers yet as digitality, social media, virtuality and business have only recently started to dance together and the rules of consumer behaviour online are currently being established.

Implications of the Growth of E-business

The new economy is exemplified by the rapid take-off of e-business. By e-business we mean that there are effectively three processes of importance. Consumers usually experience the sales side of e-business – be this in the form of business-to-consumer or business-to-business sales. However, to enable sales, the e-company has to acquire raw materials, and transform these into saleable goods. On the purchasing end of e-business, a key activity emerges in the form of managing the supply chain in such a manner that efficiency is maximised across the entire chain, but particularly in logistics and distribution. On the sales side, customer relationship management becomes essential, calling for new electronically based administrative tools and a call centre through which to make all this possible.

The main strategic risks that are associated with doing business on the internet have been divided into the following (Clemons, 2000). First, structural risk arises from business models that do not heed industry structure and profitability in certain industries or sectors. Thus, we know that in the toy business, profit margins range between 35 per cent and 40 per cent but that this is known to be too low to sustain the structure of online toy companies when their investment in e-business technology, advertising, warehousing and fulfilment costs are factored into their business model. This business model conundrum, faced by retailers, such as e-Toys and Amazon.com in the early years of the commercial application of the internet, is now being experienced by companies who have embraced Web 2.0 service companies such as Facebook.com and MySpace.com. Many successful companies, including Amazon.com found that it took many years of funding the acquisition of customers to win market share. We are witnessing a repeat of this with social networking sites. Additionally, the interactivity of the Web 2.0 companies empower customers to become active participants in determining consumption of services but also in how data about their consumer behaviour is utilised to monetise web applications.

Risk is also present in that online retailers have less latitude with pricing as the web makes both costs and pricing much more transparent than would conventionally be the case, forcing retailers of consumer goods to sell at cost or below the optimum price (Sinha, 2000). Indeed, the troubled e-Toys discovered that it would be more profitable for them to launch a range of own-label toys that would yield around 75 per cent margin. Alas, this lesson was not sufficient to save e-Toys from bankruptcy. In 2001 the company filed for bankruptcy and was acquired by KBToys. Subsequently, due to competitive pressures in the toy industry, KBToys sold e-Toys to equity investors and the company was renamed eToys Direct.

Channel risk threatens established relationships within a value system (Clemons, 2000). Most companies make use of distribution networks to reach the consumer. We are all aware, through making use of intermediaries such as travel agents, that many such organisations are threatened by the existence of online sites owned by the airline companies themselves, who increasingly sell directly to the consumer. Conversely, if you wish to run an online company, it is imperative that your supply chain is robust. For example, the difficulties that characterised fulfilment services at the ToysRUs.com warehouses in the US during December 1999–2000 caused a strong reaction against the company. Once customers' holiday packages did leave the warehouse many still did not reach their destination promptly. The negative publicity and consumer reaction to this incident forced ToysRUs to reconsider their strategy and they outsources fulfilment to Amazon.com.

Sourcing risk involves over-dependence upon one or a few critical suppliers. This may also be associated with the transfer of critical information to a strategic supplier (Clemons, 2000) that may decide to start up in competition. Finally, risk of strategic uncertainty arises when trends are misread or misunderstood and preparations are made on incorrect assumptions. A good example again comes courtesy of Kodak. The company had its first digital warning shot during 1981 when Sony first announced the development of a digital camera. At the time Kodak had similar technologies that could have been developed and eventually marketed. The company's difficulties in responding comprehensively to this external threat have been interpreted variously; Tripsas (2009), writing about Polaroid's similar difficulty in adapting to digital technology, suggests that the company and its management suffered from both organisational and cognitive inertia. They suggest that, particularly in circumstances where technological change requires the development of a new "dominant logic", managers in industries where rapid change is experienced often have difficulty adapting mental models that positions that company to compete effectively. Rapid technological change makes strategic uncertainty a more likely event for online business than for conventional companies. How to determine the future behaviour of buyers in the online world makes it difficult for companies to respond. Overall, therefore, it is clear that e-business requires a completely new set of strategic capabilities which may usefully draw their inspiration from the tools and techniques of BCM. We discussed some of these tools in earlier chapters, but of note would be the requirement to employ staff with an understanding of the behaviour of customers (business or consumers) in a virtual setting.

In terms of security, e-business raises an interesting conundrum for organisations: as IT infrastructure becomes more complex and organisations more networked, it becomes sensible to outsource the design and management of e-business solutions to specialists but place at a slight distance the control over security. Such a situation played itself out on Wednesday, 5 April 2000 when the London Stock Exchange (LSE) did not open for trading until 15:45, creating havoc on the last trading day of the tax year (BBC, 2001). The incident apparently arose because of technical problems inside the electronic share dealing system itself; the then chief executive of the exchange, Gavin Casey, admitted the following day that they did not fully understand what had caused the outage. The LSE outsources responsibility for the computerised system to Andersen Consulting, who worked through the night to correct system errors. It appears that two of the processing systems were not synchronised and that this could have been induced by the sheer volume of trade generated the previous day by the dramatic swings and volumes of trade in the US market. Data were corrupted and the exchange could not make use of incorrect share information. Even the back-up systems were not useful as they relied upon the same corrupted information (*Financial Times*, 2000a: 8).

The LSE outage demonstrates how tightly coupled technological systems have become today, and how much more vulnerable companies will become because of the convergence of technology. Over the next decade e-business and globalisation will be major influences on continuity management.

Supply Chain Issues

In making an analysis of the supply chain changes that might occur due to the internet, we are less concerned with the strategic content of these changes than with the implications of such changes for security. It is clear that an important security issue becomes who owns which part of the converged telecommunications chain, and who is responsible for safeguarding its integrity. Where there is increasing convergence between electronic systems of companies and their suppliers, there is a greater need for collaboration in respect of managing the continuity of business systems. All organisations making use of such technology will become a part of the total system and will therefore become exposed should systems fail.

This situation is one which is already fairly commonplace in the financial sector, where, with some companies, there is already a new mindset with respect to the system security required to complement the new means of conducting business (Krell, 2007; Herbane et al., 1997). It is now accepted by investment banks that, should they wish to do business with another organisation and there are convergence implications, they have to submit to inspections of their BC or contingency arrangements before contracts are even considered. Krell (2006) cites the example of the New York Stock Exchange, which requires listed companies to provide an annual update to their continuity management plans. Additionally, in the US, provisions under the Sarbanes–Oxley Act drives compliance via a strengthening of internal procedures. Such provisions will only grow as technological change intensifies.

Security and the Internet

In Chapter 3 we discussed at great length the need for companies to develop digital resilience when we looked at the expansion of the web as a metasystem. We considered in that chapter the issues this might raise in terms of the threats resulting from the external environment as well as internal weakness that, when combined with the web as a metasystem, could potentially lead to system and organisational vulnerability. Furthermore, we noted a number of high-profile security incidents that led to major or complete interruptions in services to consumers between the publication of the first and second editions of this text. During the early years (mid-1990s to early 2000) of the expansion of online business, the rush to be first and establish an advantage over competitors meant that security considerations were relegated, often only to be considered at a later date. Regretfully, this has often proven to be an extremely costly choice. The Computer Security Institute in the US and the San Francisco Federal Bureau of Investigation's Computer Intrusion Squad surveyed US companies during 1999 and estimated that financial losses due to "cybercrime" doubled to more than $226 million during that year (*Financial Times*, 2000b). Approaching 74 per cent of the 600 organisations polled had suffered some financial loss due to computer crime. The nature of the computer crimes were also of interest (sabotage, theft of proprietary information and financial fraud) when one considers that these crimes were committed from both *inside* and *outside* the organisations (*Financial Times*, 2000b: 4). The most costly of these, however, appear to be those committed using the internet as a channel, with several highly visible e-business companies suffering huge losses in early January 2000. Such losses continue to be a problem for companies today, even as our learning about the issue has grown, with the Universities of Iowa and Virginia (Gaudin, 2007) and the University of Missouri (Semelka, 2007).

Building Organisational Resilience

Although technology is a vital part of an organisation's internal and external context, it sits with social processes. The need to build resilience through both technology and people within an organisation was raised in Chapter 3 and returned to in Chapter 6. Elliott and Johnson (2008b) report perspectives from different fields, and suggest some discrepancy as to the meaning of resilience. In organisation studies, perspectives of resilience have referred to an ability or capacity to absorb strain and preserve, *or improve*, despite the presence of adversity (Sutcliffe and Vogus, 2003: 96), or the capacity to cope with unanticipated dangers after they have become manifest, learning to bounce back (Wildavsky, 1988: 77). More recent conceptions of organisational resilience tend to extend the concept beyond "bouncing back" and include aspects of sustaining *and* developing, adaptive capacity, learning and transformation (Lengnick-Hall and Beck, 2005). Key to developing that capacity is an organisation's people – its human capital.

A new generation of employees has started to enter our workplaces, and continuity management will have to consider their place in the strategy and the BCM puzzle. It has been a key contention of this book that continuity management has to consider the place of the human element as a critical component of building organisational and digital resilience. Surveys conducted of the behaviour and expectations of members of the millennials demonstrate a generation at ease with technology, and with radically different career expectations compared to baby boomers, Gen X and Gen Y employees. We are currently in the year zero with respect to how millenials will deal with computer security issues. Organisations such as the Pew Research Trusts (www.pewinternet.org) have started to conduct research on the behaviours of teens online, particularly with regard to how they treat security on the web (Pew Internet and American Life Project, 2007); however, how and whether this behaviour as consumers online will translate into similar behaviour once they are part of a workforce remains an unanswered question at present.

The 9/11 tragedy enabled researchers to draw some conclusions about how some companies were able to absorb the shock of the event, primarily through its people. Elliott and Johnson (2008b), drawing on Freeman et al. (2003), cited the example of Sandler O'Neill & Partners, formerly of the World Trade Centre (South Tower). Losing almost 40 per cent of their people, including two-thirds of the management committee, and the majority of physical assets and records, the company was able to survive and thrive. Despite massive losses in relationships, tacit knowledge and understandings, income and equity, the company moved to temporary offices and began trading again the week after the attack, and within one year the company were doing better than ever with record profits and revenues and new highly desirable lines of business (Freeman et al., 2003). Others examples where organisations appear to have transformed crises to advantage include Odwalla Inc. in 1996, where a young girl died from drinking apple juice contaminated with E. coli bacteria, and Johnson & Johnson's Tylenol poisoning crisis in the 1980s which led to the death of seven people in Chicago. Both of these events were managed in a way that not only dealt effectively with a tragic situation, but also enhanced organisational core capabilities enabling them to thrive (Lengnick-Hall and Beck, 2005: 3). The challenge is to understand why and how some organisations manage to thrive and enhance core capabilities when faced crisis and others fail, or at best return to equilibrium.

Building organisational and digital resilience in an age of open innovation is one of the most challenging activities facing organisations today. As described in Chapter 6, organisations today are porous in nature, with information increasingly spilling out in a variety of ways, and primarily through its employees. Information also ingresses into the company and clearly companies may benefit in those cases where knowledge can usefully be shared about practices in BCM elsewhere. Those with insight will seek a means to capture such ingress of information to systematically exploit such information for competitive advantage. Of note here is that BCM employees should be encouraged to participate in professional forums through which such external learning can take place. Conversely, where disgruntled employees have access to increasingly mobile technology and information, procedures would have to be established to build preparedness to deal with loss of data.

Of course the discipline of BCM has become more sophisticated since its early days of disaster recovery in the 1970s. As we conjecture in Chapter 1 on where the practice is headed, BCM will become more business-based and will be approached as a discipline to deal with a broad range of operational risks. To date, this has been implicit as we witness the view that BC practitioners are well placed to support boards of directors in controlling the group of operational risks identified by the Institute of Chartered Accountants in England and Wales' guidance notes for *Implementing Turnbull* (Jones and Sutherland, 1999). It is clear, however, that sharp differences may still exist in the minds of BC practitioners about what their role should be. Given the youth of the discipline, this is to be expected. On one side are those who emphasise the recovery of the technical systems aspect of BC. Such a mindset can be seen from the glossary of terms in Doswell's (2000) guide to BCM. This "nuts and bolts" or technology approach is concerned with identifying potential points of failure and preparing contingency plans to recover them in line with corporate objectives. An alternative, augmented, approach incorporates the "nuts and bolts" but is not driven by them. Instead it focuses upon value and BC and is driven by business objectives.

BC has evolved, within some organisations, from a focus limited to technology to a much broader, value-based approach. The latter has not replaced the former; rather it has evolved from it. The core elements remain but have been augmented in a number of ways. Where the technology phase was driven by IT personnel, the value-based phase is characterised by its employment of staff from a range of business disciplines. Where the technology phase is located firmly in the IT or information systems department, the value-based approach places responsibility for continuity management with line business units, supported by a dedicated BC team. This symbolises that continuity management is not an IT or facilities issue alone, but is concerned with continuing value-adding activities. A higher profile and closer links to the core business activities arguably ensures that continuity management can be invoked to deal with any interruption.

The perceived link between internal BCM and external reputation management is characteristic of the value-based approach. Chapter 7 referred to the example of P&O's rapid response to compensate customers aboard the cruiser *Aurora* and limit damaging publicity. The importance of reputation management grows all the time, a feature of the media society (Pilger, 1998). The corporate re-brandings and re-naming of Monsanto to Pharmacia or British Airways' and British Gas's dropping of the label "British" from their names represent corporate attempts to shape public opinion. We return to a discussion of reputation management as a theme for the future later in this chapter.

Social Capital

Social capital has been defined as an asset that inheres in social relations and networks (Leana and Van Buren, 1999). It is understood roughly as the good will that is engendered by the fabric of social relations and that can be mobilised to facilitate action (Adler and Kwon, 2000). From a BCM perspective, a concern with social capital emanates from the notion that networks of social relationships give rise to collective action that might not have been possible without those social relationships. Elliott and Johnson (2008b) assert that at least two patterns emerge from the various definitions of social capital. These relate to models of social capital based on "public" or "private" goods and mirror what Adler and Kwon (1999) recognise as internal "socio-centric" or external "egocentric" perspectives respectively. For Coleman (1990) and Nahapiet and Ghoshal (1998) social capital is a resource that is jointly owned, rather than controlled by any one individual or entity, or as Leana and Van Buren (1999: 541) suggest "an attribute of the collective, rather than the sum of individuals' social connections".

To illustrate this, Elliott and Johnson (2008b) describe the outbreak of a water-borne E. coli contamination in Walkerton, a small town in Ontario, causing seven people to die and 2,300 to become sick. Following restructuring, the local authority and affected communities were uncertain of their respective responsibilities. This acted as a catalyst for the mobilisation of local community social capital and an emergent self-organised response (Murphy, 2007). Structurally, almost three-quarters of Walkerton's residents were involved in some sort of community or group-based activity prior to the crisis, suggesting a potential for many and diverse group or network ties. During the crisis, about a third of voluntary activity was related to being involved in community activity prior to the event. A similar figure relied on the networks for assistance during the event. The community-based groups exhibited appropriable organisation as many of the groups collectively managed an unplanned emergency bottled water distribution system. This suggests the group or network ties established prior to the crisis played an important role in the community's capacity to adapt to changing conditions, providing a conduit for resource exchange – information as physical help.

As a small town located within a rural, farming landscape Walkerton was the functional centre for the region – the psychological, physical, and financial impacts of the crisis affected virtually every household. Cognitions, local knowledge and a shared understanding of the priorities and problems to overcome contributed to bridging the gaps in the local authority's response. The Walkerton case focuses upon social capital at the community level. Murphy (2007) suggests that formal vertical links between local authority and communities are likely to be complemented when combined with horizontal links at community level when planning for, and dealing with, anticipated or unanticipated events. In other words, "top-down" approaches to contingency planning and response could benefit from recognising and utilising the "untapped" resources that reside within community social capital networks.

Within a BCM context, a fuller understanding of social capital may provide the basis for both resilience and more effective recovery. Elliott and Johnson (2008b) identified a number of instances in which social capital played a vital response to interruptions. In one case relationships within the civil construction industry were critical to a quick recovery following a fatal rail accident and resulting damage to a main north–south route. Contractual arrangements meant far less than the reservoir of social capital which brought a multi-organisational team together. A second example concerned a group of small firms pooling resources on a day-to-day basis which proved vital when their region was severely affected by floods. It is our view that the study of social capital within this context is a neglected area and yet there is evidence that it is taken for granted in practice. This is one area, we suggest, worthy of future research and one that may feed into the development of BCM. However, where high-profile disasters are concerned, analysis, understanding and, thus, learning will be shaped and constrained by preconceptions, media coverage and deep-seated prejudices as may be seen with regard to the aftermath of Hurricane Katrina.

Box 8.3 Hurricane Katrina, Rita and the Prescience Borne of Pam

New Orleans experienced one of the worst natural disasters in the summer of 2005, repercussions of which are still being felt in the city and across the Gulf of Mexico. Recovery efforts continue as this text goes to press, and have been slow and problematic. However, the value of pre-planning and preparedness training emerged as having been critical in enabling the authorities to cope as well as they did during the unprecedented disaster.

Hurricane Katrina hit the area on 29 August 2005, setting off a mass exodus of 1.3 million people from the area. The Louisiana Recovery Authority estimates property losses exceeded $100 billion. More than 1,400 residents of New Orleans lost their lives and more than 60,000 residents across the southern part of Louisiana were evacuated. Many of these rescues were from rooftops (62,000) – 78,000 were rescued by bus and aircraft. Ninety per cent of the regional population in the state was evacuated, with 40,000 finding shelter at the Louisiana Superdome.

Hurricane season in the Gulf of Mexico is an annual event that is taken extremely seriously. Given the scale of the Katrina and Rita storms, as well as the structural vulnerabilities of the New Orleans parishes, it would appear that emergency agencies regarded the number of deaths as far fewer than would have been expected under the circumstances. In July 2004, a hurricane simulation entitled Pam was undertaken in the Louisiana area, envisaging the scenario of a slow moving category three hurricane hitting New Orleans and its environs and flooding the city – a scenario eerily similar to Katrina. Hurricane Pam was funded by FEMA and fifty state and local government organisations participated in the event, the purpose of which was to develop more targeted plans and provisions. Some of these were being worked on at the time that Katrina struck, but FEMA had apparently run out of funding to enable a second scenario to be run for the summer of 2005.

As this book goes to print the debate about the impact and effectiveness of the response to the disaster continues. A review of the response by emergency management agencies leading up to and during the disaster provides a picture of the complexity of the conditions which state and federal agencies had to contend with. One of the unforeseen events that made conditions so difficult was the breaching of levees, causing 80 per cent of the city to be overwhelmed. This caused flooding and made access in and out of the city difficult by leaving only one route safe to traffic. In addition, the key role of communications technology became evident. High winds and driving rain damaged communications infrastructure, while the sheer numbers of emergency personnel compromised the available channels for emergency communications. Interoperability of communications devices and channel redundancy became critical issues to be resolved by emergency agencies. Satellite communications and the use of Blackberry's were key in enabling communications to continue. Additional issues that challenged the response included regulations that hampered the use of emergency medical personnel from other states as they were not legally able to practise in Louisiana without the appropriate paperwork. State law did not allow for them to be deployed under emergency situations. Medical facilities were found to be the most challenging of group habitations to evacuate, something that could have been predicted and planned for. Finally, lack of ownership of vehicles by many of the poor and elderly also presented unusually difficult challenges.

Many critics of the response contend that this again should have been anticipated as New Orleans has historically had a poverty rate more than double the national average, with 28 per cent of the city's families living below the poverty line (Boettke et al., 2007). Notwithstanding the concerns about the areas where effectiveness was limited, it is universally acknowledged that the response to the storms were effective primarily because of learning done during hurricane Pam. In addition, the Herculean efforts of individuals who were involved in the rescue efforts eased the coordination efforts of the emergency authorities. Finally, the willingness of other states to support Louisiana and Mississippi contributed to limiting the loss of life. Informal social networks around particular groups of artists, especially musicians, ensured that those who were not immediately accounted for were searched for and found. Communities of individuals also came together to set up non-profit organisations to raise funds to support artists and musicians in the city (http:// www.nomrf.org/index.html). Such efforts continue today to ensure that healthcare and housing can be restored to those without a regular income or savings.

The rebuilding efforts in New Orleans have been marred by a lack of achievement. The US media regularly carry stories about problems with resettling families and rebuilding the city. Boettke and colleagues (2008: 363–364) highlight the fact that, both before and after the 2005 hurricanes, government-subsidised flood insurance made possible building in areas that were extremely vulnerable to flooding. These authors quote John Stuart Mill on the resilience that economies naturally appear to have in the face of natural disasters:

> Mill argued that the possibility of rapid recovery mainly depends on whether or not the country has suffered massive depopulation or not. But there are other issues involved as well as the human capital embodied in the population. The free flow of labor and capital seems to be an important aspect, as well. In addition, the ability to quickly reestablish clearly defined and enforced property rights seems to be a characteristic in common with rapid recoveries from disaster.

In addition to rebuilding in areas subject to flooding, there was also the social, economic and political issues peculiar to New Orleans that Boettke and colleagues (2008) believe cause the problems with rebuilding of the city. New Orleans is a very poor city, racked by political corruption with an under-educated population, who have to interpret signals and rules that are inconsistent and distorted. Signal distortions occur when government intervention in the form of emergency financial support subverts the efforts of individuals or communities because of the expectation of payoffs. This leads to rent-seeking behaviour and the problems that have come to light with sub-optimal uses of government funds. Organic recovery can best be supported by providing very clear and consistent messages about what government will provide and when and, in addition, trying to avoid any financial support that would lead to distortion of local economies. Boettke and collleagues (2006) suggest that the best means of ensuring this would be to have local citizens be in charge of making policy decisions.

Sources: Boettke et al. (2008); Louisiana Office of Homeland Security & Emergency Preparedness (2005); Hurricane Pam (2008)

Political

Global Web Crime – Efforts at Protection and Regulation

The year 2000 should not be noted for the lack of chaos caused by the millennium bug as much as for the jolt given to significant online companies such as Yahoo! and Amazon.com by denial of service attacks. The major developments in regulation witnessed during recent months have sought to control the "dark side of the internet!" The most significant of these may turn out to be those that are global in nature. During October 2000 the Organisation for Economic Cooperation and Development (OECD) led calls for a global effort to enforce internet security. The OECD appears to be setting itself up as a coordinating body, the aim of which would be to encourage information sharing worldwide (Grande, 2000).

Corporate Governance

A key driver of continuity services is regulatory intervention. Within the UK, companies are expected to demonstrate satisfactory risk management and internal control mechanisms. The Turnbull Report (1999) represented an important step in the evolution of the UK's self-regulatory regime, developed by the Higgs Code (2003). Where earlier reports were concerned with strengthening audit controls and the roles of non-executive directors following a number of scandals (for example, Maxwell, Polly Peck, Bank of Credit and Commerce International), Turnbull was concerned with board responsibilities for a wide range of risks from market and financial through to operational risks, a convenient catch-all. The failure of these efforts may be seen in Higgs (2003), which has been seen as a response to Enron and Worldcom.

At the risk of generalising, business and government in the US regard themselves as remarkably free of the kind of intervention that Turnbull and Cadbury represents. Culturally there is a preference for specific, tight industry regulation that has to be enforced, rather than the British model of "gentlemanly codes". Food and Drugs Administration (FDA) agencies will come down hard on businesses should they not comply. On Friday, 16 February 2001 the pharmaceutical company Schering-Plough announced that they had to shut down some factories in North America as their practices were found to be out of compliance with FDA production guidelines. The company issued a statement indicating that the FDA would be tying approval for a new allergy drug to successful resolution of their quality control problems (*Financial Times*, 2001). The size and complexity of US industries elevate federal regulations. This does not mean that all companies do comply with the letter and spirit of the law. For example, in February 2001 it was revealed that many manufacturers of seafood products did not comply with regulations, and that the FDA did not audit these companies as tightly as they might. The presence of many small companies in this fragmented industry presented a "logistical nightmare".

Economic

Partnership and Prevention

A growing feature of strategic management concerns partnership. Increasingly, the supply chain is recognised as the fundamental unit of competition. Frey and Schlosser (1993) indicate the limitations of traditional competitive bidding within the automotive supply chain, the antithesis of partnership. Put simply, the competitive bids system discourages research and development investment because there is a real risk that such costs will not be recovered. For Womack and colleagues (1990), the adversarial nature of supply chain relations within this industry was identified as a key factor in the decline of the Anglo-US car industry, while supplier partnerships were seen as key to the success of the Japanese car industry.

Increasingly, BC recognises that any one interruption will impact upon a number of organisations. Where organisations are tightly coupled, as in just-in-time manufacturing systems, cross-organisational impacts will be virtually immediate. Interruptions may arise where the activities of organisations meet. For example, control of the UK railways is divided between Network Rail, who maintain the tracks, and the operating companies who manage the trains. The immediate causes of the Paddington crash in 1999 (in which thirty people died) included the layout of the track and signals, Railtrack's (NetworkRail's predecessor) responsibilities, and staff reductions and extended working hours (the railway companies' responsibility). Following the Paddington crash and the subsequent Hatfield crash, the consequences were immense. Railtrack was forced to invest millions in an immediate track improvement scheme; the resulting disruptions forced train cancellations and delays to the cost of the railway companies; virtually every company dependent upon staff commuting by train (for example, every London-based corporate headquarters or institution) saw an increase in absenteeism or lateness as staff struggled to get to work.

The railways provide the most obvious example of how the repercussions of an interruption may be widespread. However, few interruptions are firmly bounded. In 2001 an outbreak of foot and mouth in the UK had a significant impact upon the farming industry. Livestock hauliers lost their livelihoods. Yet the economic costs to tourism were even greater as large tracts of British countryside were closed. The ripples of crisis spread wide with tourist attractions and hoteliers seeing dramatically reduced numbers of customers. Increasingly, the liability of, response towards, and prevention of, crises of this type will require attention in partnership-type arrangements. BCM plans will not only span organisations, but span across them. This is one of the key tasks facing the discipline and can only evolve from a value-based approach. Where a sharp focus upon technical systems and buildings exist, the potential for partnership is limited. As we argued in Chapter 1, building a BC capability is, in part, dependent upon nurturing of relationships with a view to increasing the resilience of the organisation.

At another extreme, the effect of a sudden jump in fuel prices during 2008 had consequences for companies across the globe. Keeley (2008) reported lorry drivers' blockades across Spain and Portugal cutting food supplies and leaving supermarket shelves empty. Nissan, Seat, Ford and Citroen were reported to have closed due to lack of automobile parts. In Chile a lorry drivers' strike saw supermarkets run out of meat and a threat to hospital oxygen supplies (Carroll, 2008). Protests against gas price increases and petrol station closures swept across South Asia, from Bangkok to Beijing (McKinnon and Watts, 2008). Such issues cannot be solved or even managed effectively at an organisation or local level. They reveal, starkly, global interdependencies. In Africa the most significant effects of rising oil prices have been sharply higher food prices. Machine-intensive farming methods rely upon expensive diesel. Also, a switch to bio-fuels made more attractive by the high price of oil and European environmental policies to encourage sustainable fuel sources have seen farmland switch from food to bio-fuel production. The basics of global supply and demand have contributed to the sharp increases in food prices. From a continuity perspective, understanding the influence of what some call "peak oil" may be key to securing long-term competitive advantage (Aleklett, 2007).

Continuity Service Providers

On the supply side, changes in the BCM industry structure itself are of great importance. Consolidation continues with large players acquiring scarce skills and offering a one-stop continuity shop, from the "man-in-a-van" situation during the 1980s and 1990s, to the provision of "e-continuity" services provided from anywhere in the world today. The market has matured greatly over the last two decades. Bolstered by regulations and new standards, a wide range of e-continuity services continue to be added to the more traditional recovery sites and training services, targeted not only at larger organisations but at small and medium-sized companies also.

The potential for the data storage industry to expand beyond storage for industry is potentially also huge, should the "democratization of data" continue (Lyman and Varian, 2001). Lyman and Varian predict how business in the future will be affected by the greater access to data by individuals made possible by the decreasing real cost of data storage and communications. They conducted research on data storage and found that, despite the growth of industry giants in data storage, such firms store only around 16 per cent of the total digital storage internationally; 56 per cent is stored on individually owned personal computers.

The outlook for the data storage and services industry is therefore attractive at present. In part this is due to the trends outlined above, but also to the commercial explosion of the web. The internet has boosted the earnings potential of data storage companies such as EMC, one of the most successful companies of the past decade (Hemp, 2001). The average rate of profit and revenue growth for the company over the last fourteen consecutive quarters has been 20 per cent. Box 8.4 demonstrates how the market has changed and will continue to move away from a highly fragmented industry dominated by smaller players, to one which is controlled by larger companies. Changes in how companies are using technology (web-hosting and the emergence of application service providers) mean that the higher overheads associated with having the correct infrastructure and knowledge competencies will increasingly erect higher barriers to entry to smaller companies.

Box 8.4 The Rise and Development of EMC

EMC began life as a manufacturer of computer motherboards. Based in Hopkinton, Maryland, US it was worth $120 million by 1988. In 1989, Michael Ruettgers was appointed CEO and, due to quality control problems with their existing manufacturing operation, he decided to redirect the company towards data storage instead of motherboard production. By 1992 he had accelerated the company's concentration on data storage, doing battle with the likes of IBM and many other, smaller competitors. The company has grown through its ability to anticipate and capitalise on changes in the data storage industry. This it has done by being customer-focused and using input from these stakeholders to make changes to EMC products and services. For instance, in the early 1990s, the company, through talking to large clients, realised that corporations wanted to move away from decentralised computing with data stored on local area networks back to centralised storage. This led them to move into open storage, where different servers are linked to a single storage system (Hemp, 2001). At present the company is set to capitalise on the growth of the networked information storage market which is undergoing rapid growth. IDC estimates that, in this market, EMC had a total market share of 30.5 per cent in 2000. This market grew from $2.8 billion in 1999 to $6.7 billion in 2000. EMC recently also reported that it was increasingly selling into international markets. A company spokesman reported in January 2001 that international markets represented about 64 per cent of future business opportunities, with non-US revenue accounting for 60 per cent of total revenue in 2000.

Source: Foremski (2001)

The BCM market still has a mix of smaller and corporate providers but consolidation will increase. Large consultancy and computer groups have also become very active in the area, notably Accenture, ICM, IBM and the like. Indeed, what is instructive is that the product offerings of such organisations appear to be mainly influenced by technological developments such as convergence between client and supplier systems, or internet-based trade. For instance, American International Underwriters has launched an internet liability insurance product covering losses incurred through computer attacks (*South China Morning Post*, 2000). A number of firms in the industry also appear to be working on setting up international security assessment standards for internet-based business. These standards should help to protect critical information and will be used to define insurance products to cover the product exposure of companies involved in such transactions. While corporate governance and the needs of individual businesses will continue to be the major drivers of BCM, it is clear that the internet and technology convergence will also have an increasing influence on BCM. It is to some extent inevitable that the negative aspects of using the internet will have a very big impact on the regulatory environment, reinforcing demands that some control be exercised over the cyber environment. Attacks on internet sites during early 2000, the increasing number of viruses that affect computer users, as well as concerns over the criminal use of the internet, have led in the US to demands for government surveillance of the medium. There are new rules to enable digital wire-tapping by the FBI. The measure is aimed at tracking the physical location of cellular phones but could potentially be used to monitor internet traffic (Waldmeir, 2000). The law that enables this practice is the 1994 Federal Communications Assistance for Law Enforcement Act, which mandates that telecommunications companies must design their networks to enable monitoring. Privacy activists, including the American Civil Liberties Union, were, during May 2000, engaged in challenging the provisions to engage in digital wire-tapping that would enable emails and other internet communications to be scrutinised. During November 2000 the US Justice Department released a report on the FBI's "Carnivore" surveillance system that gave the software a clean bill of health but the Illinois Institute of Technology Research Institute, the body that had reviewed the software, admitted their concerns at the lack of provisions that would ensure the FBI did not abuse the system and the power they possess.

Social

In recent years it has become evident how powerful and well-organised organisational stakeholders can affect companies. January 2001 saw the culmination of a concerted effort by animal rights activists to close down the Huntingdon Life Sciences (HLS) animal testing laboratories, based in Cambridge, UK. Whatever the rights and wrongs of animal testing, and despite evidence of past malpractice, the HLS laboratories provide a legal service to the pharmaceutical industry. The anti-HLS campaign demonstrates the vulnerability of organisations to seemingly powerless groups. The main effort has been to target key investment groups, including the company's bank, the Royal Bank of Scotland (formerly NatWest), which was due to consider an overdraft facility to the company during January 2001. By 2007, a new Pro-Test group campaigned in support of HLS and animal testing, on the grounds of the benefits accrued for science and medicine (Gaines, 2008). This represented the public face of what Walker

(2007) described as the shared objectives of government and key investors in research perceive to be "blinkered anti-science fanaticism". Other examples abound of how stakeholders, including the mass media, can have a powerful effect on how companies deal with issues of service or product quality.

Information and Ambiguity

The internet is commonly perceived as a fast way to communicate and gather information. For organisations, this represents as much of a threat as a benefit. Disinformation (cf. FUD), rumours and protests may quickly spread across nations and time zones, thereby requiring crisis communications to be ready to address incidents as they happen (in order not to exacerbate the situation or compound a crisis) and adopt internet crisis communications strategies in addition to their regular crisis communications strategies. Several issues spring to mind:

1   Regular internet scanning to ensure that organisations are quickly aware of false or malicious information.
2   Policies towards newsgroups, discussion forums and unofficial sites.
3   Strategies to respond effectively to this information in the electronic domain as well as regular media.
4   Knowledge of differences in legal systems where negative information may be sourced.
5   Dealing with incidents instigated by rival companies.

"Consumerism and Continuity" or "The Accidental Accused"

Consumer affairs programmes (for example, *Watchdog*) and magazines such as *Which?* highlight the enormous appetite that the UK public has for the "outing" of reckless (or worse) companies trading in the UK. However, recently, a number of companies have found that they have had to respond to (and been seen to be to blamed for) problems with products and service, when the problem may reside with the supplier. For example, when two children died as a result of carbon monoxide poisoning at a Corfu holiday site organised by Thomas Cook, the company was criticised for failing to ensure that its suppliers followed appropriate practice, although it should be noted that charges for negligence were levelled at the suppliers and not the travel agent. Although companies may have continuity plans that deal with supplier crises, the downstream, more visible, organisation frequently takes the public "rap" for an incident. In the media, the culpable party is not always the one that is chastised, and with the increased integration between products, this is likely to continue. For instance:

* Digital operators have faced extensive media criticism when "Tivo"

failed to integrate fully with EPG (electronic programme guides) for Sky digital and OnDigital satellite television services.

• Hardware manufacturers face media criticism due to DVD software (that is, films) which does not follow the DVD forum code, and thereby fails to operate on budget DVD players.

• Internet service providers offer erratic or slow service – telephone companies, such as BT (ironically), receive blame for opening exchanges.

• Organic farmers in the Third World are found to be less than organic – in the UK, the retailer Iceland has faced public or media criticism.

Reputation Management

Two hundred years ago the vast majority of the world's population was virtually self-sufficient in essentials; risk and safety from food contamination was a personal responsibility. A feature of commerce in the twenty-first century is the growing separation between producer and consumer; the scale, complexity and remoteness of food production all contribute to the potential for contamination. Consumers are forced to place their trust in producers and regulators to ensure the safety of the produce they consume. Trust has been eroded because of fears arising from the threat to health posed by BSE, the extravagant use of antibiotics, and the uncertainty surrounding the growing use of genetically modified foodstuffs. At a macro level, popular and media concern about food production methods in agriculture, processing plants and additives is growing. At a micro level, there appears to have been an increase in product contamination incidents. Some involve malicious product tampering such as the lacing with cyanide of Johnson & Johnson's Tylenol painkiller drug. Other incidents may arise from errors in production or from the use of contaminated raw materials as happened with the contaminations experienced by Perrier (in 1990) and Coca-Cola (1999).

The proliferation of channels of communication has changed the context in which communications occur – managers are deluged with information, problems are widely disseminated. Some commentators describe this as the "age of information" although, more cynically, Pilger (1998) refers to a media age in which information is distorted or sanitised by the media and organisations. The social reports published by companies including Merrill Lynch, Barclays and Shell indicate the importance corporations place on publicising a "socially responsible face". The management of reputation has gained increasing relevance to organisations in the "media age" (see, for a full discussion, Riel, 1995; Fombrun, 1997; Gray and Balmer, 1998; Balmer and Soenen, 1999; Fombrun et al., 2000).

Elliott and colleagues (2001) in an analysis of Perrier (1990) and Coca-Cola's (1999) response to product contamination crises offers some insight into the process of reputation management. First, organisations need to communicate in an open and consistent manner. A disjointed approach to communication can create serious problems for a company as witnessed by Perrier. Communications should be unambiguous and free from attempts at the projection of blame elsewhere. The media and consumers often view with considerable suspicion any attempt to blame others.

Second, contingency plans must be tested. Developing such plans without testing them or providing training for staff will severely inhibit their effectiveness. A core element of such a planning process should involve media training for key staff and the creation of media-friendly background information which can be given out in the early stages of the crisis. There was little evidence of such plans in the responses of either Perrier or Coca-Cola. It seems inconceivable that Coca-Cola did not possess such plans, suggesting that it was a failure in their implementation that lay behind the poor crisis response.

A third issue concerns the role of trust in stakeholder management. Organisations that appear to prioritise profit over safety will find that their attempts to manage their image will be plagued by a persistent lack of trust among stakeholders. This process is not something that can be established during a crisis but should be an integral part of a company's strategy. Organisations must be aware of the variety of stakeholder groups, their interests and power in planning for and when managing crisis events. Some utility companies maintain databases of vulnerable groups who might require special attention should there be an interruption in supply (for example, hospitals, residential care homes, etc.). Politicians or vociferous pressure groups may also be listed in order that potentially embarrassing media coverage can be anticipated. Since the Brent Spar difficulties, Shell has employed environmental activists as consultants to provide input at board level.

Closely linked to stakeholder management is historical context which combines the record of media relations, perceptions of openness and ongoing marketing communication activity. Certain product attributes may be more vulnerable to threat, such as "natural purity". Alternatively, there is the context in which an incident occurs. For Perrier, the disillusionment of key investors and weak links with the media isolated the company from potential allies during the crisis. Media support for Johnson & Johnson was vital in their recovery from the Tylenol incidents. For Coca-Cola, the coincidence of the contamination with the high-profile dioxin problems in Belgium created an ultra-sensitive environment for their own difficulties. Continuity plans, including crisis communication blueprints, can only assist an organisation's crisis response. Effective crisis response requires ongoing environmental scanning in order that such plans can be used in a flexible manner and adapted to the particular circumstances of each incident. For the global company there are likely to be many local difficulties that have the potential to trip them up.

Finally, the recognition of a company's intangible assets is an important, but neglected, aspect of the strategic management process. All too often, organisations fail to take account of their intangible asset base when developing contingency plans for crisis events. As the cases discussed here illustrate, the reputational costs of a crisis can be considerable (see Box 8.5).

A number of practical lessons may be learned from the experiences of Perrier and Coca-Cola:

- Product contaminations do not necessarily result in a full-blown crises. Poor media relations, and disillusioned investors were key factors in allowing the escalation to develop into a full-blown crisis for Perrier. The coincidence of a scare with the Belgian dioxin contamination was unfortunate for Coca-Cola, yet the frequency of such scares is increasing rapidly. Coca-Cola's response, in public perception, was that of a distant corporation with little real interest in Western European consumers. Globalisation requires that companies manage information flows to ensure that they remain abreast of "local key issues".
- Second, where national or product divisions exist, an overall coordinating structure within a crisis management team is necessary to distinguish between strategic, tactical and operational matters (as discussed in Chapter 6).
- Third, effective communication is based on a thorough understanding of all stakeholders and their needs during a crisis. This understanding will be evident in the messages communicated. Perrier and Coca-Cola's initial responses created an impression of self-interest to the detriment of customer care.
- Fourth, communicating the message requires a good understanding of context. For Perrier, an unsympathetic media, coupled with a fickle customer base concerned with health and purity, provided an unfavourable context. Coca-Cola's scare was inextricably linked to the dioxin contamination and the associated political furore. Effective communications and public relations require significant intelligence and environmental scanning (see Stone, 1995; Regester and Larkin, 1997; Elliott et al., 2001).

Box 8.5 Reputational Crisis – Coca-Cola Emulates Perrier?

In early 1990 Perrier experienced a major business interruption from a crisis triggered by suspected contamination. On 2 February the Food and Drugs Adminstration in the US notified Perrier that minute traces of benzene had been found in its product. However, it was not until 12 February that Perrier recalled its American stocks. Perrier perceived the problem as affecting the US only, despite rumours that the French source had been polluted. British supermarkets began to remove Perrier water from their shelves in the absence of clear communications from the company. On 14 February, Perrier announced a worldwide recall of Perrier water.

Perrier's management of the crisis was widely criticised for a number of reasons. First, the length of time taken by the company between identifying a problem and acting was too long. This indicated that there was no crisis plan. The crisis was pushed through public and media pressure and was allowed to pass beyond the control of the Perrier Group. There was an apparent lack of a coordinated response, with action in the UK and US targeted at reassuring consumers and media. The response of Source Perrier was focused upon poorly thought-through attempts to reassure investors. Perrier's handling of the disaster was described as: "uneven at best, ranging from head in the sand refusal to talk, to announcements in arch corporatese, to bursts of pique". Another commentator called it "the caveman approach to public relations".

Perrier had ignored warnings of contamination that had circulated for some six months preceding the crisis. There was no clear view of who the key stakeholders were at each stage of the crisis or the message that should be targeted towards each group. There was evidence of significant differences in opinion regarding the strategic direction of the Perrier Group, between key shareholders and the management team, personified in its chairman, Leven. Such division may cause problems for an organisation at the best of times. During a crisis it may of course create a common sense of purpose or, alternatively, one party may exploit the troubles to meet their own objectives. Perrier had developed a strong brand image, founded on natural purity. Its crisis communications did not appear to have considered this. Its post-crisis communications included messages emphasising the technical nature of the production process, which might be perceived to be at odds with the natural purity of the water. As Raymond Perrier (no relation) pointed out, "The images of peasants filling empty bottles from gushing springs was destroyed." There is much evidence that the behaviour of the different divisions of the Perrier Group was uncoordinated. This added to the potential for contradiction and reinforced, in the minds of the media and financial institutions, the view that Perrier was poorly managed. The lack of a proper BC plan was clear.

Sources: Crumley (1990); Sipika et al. (1993); *Economist* (1999)

Coca-Cola

In June 1999 the suspected contamination of Coca-Cola prompted the largest product recall in the company's history. Although the "contamination" affected much of Western Europe, the events were centred on Belgium. Fears of contamination occurred in the midst of a major health scare in which the Belgian government's handling of the dioxin contamination of chicken and eggs had been widely criticised and had led to the resignations of the ministers for Agriculture and Public Health.

Almost 200 people reported feeling ill after drinking Coca-Cola. Although the symptoms were limited to consumers in France and Belgium, the suspect plants supplied the Netherlands, Germany, Luxembourg, Spain and Switzerland. Government bans against consumption of the beverage across north-western Europe created the impression that Coca-Cola was reluctant to act. Control of the crisis passed to government agencies creating an impression that Coca-Cola was uncaring.

Defective carbon dioxide and a fungicide were identified, initially, as the immediate causes of the contamination, although the evidence for this was mixed. Most important was that the identification of these "causes" was interpreted as an attempt by Coca-Cola to deflect blame for the contamination onto two suppliers. Coca-Cola's crisis response was perceived as lackluster and was extensively criticised. The *Economist* (1999) described this response:

> Coca-Cola's public-relations error is to have seemed keener to protect its own back than to allay the understandable fears of consumers . . . the firm's legal-sounding insistence that there were no "health or safety issues" and that the drinks "might make you feel sick, but are not harmful" were hardly going to reassure people. . . . A statement on June 16 from Douglas Ivester, the firm's chairman, expressing his regret, arrived hopelessly late.

It is likely that analysts at Coca-Cola's Atlanta headquarters were not fully aware of this recent history and thus of the likely strength of concerns. The quick introduction of government bans may have been excessive in the light of the real hazard to health, as identified later. However, given resignations less than two weeks earlier, it would be a brave politician who failed to act quickly and assertively. It seems that, as with Perrier ten years previously, Coca-Cola did not fully appreciate the implications of the potential for damage associated with an alleged contamination. Ivester later admitted that he did not capture the depth of the problem early enough and that he had relied on subordinates to manage the incident, rather than seizing the opportunity to reassure government ministers early enough.

Sources: Kielmas (1999); *Economist* (1999); Elliott et al. (2001)

Internet and Reputation

The internet provides great opportunity for companies to communicate directly with consumers, facilitating a "militant tendency" to organise against companies, whether warranted or not. Indeed, the ability to communicate with customers is one of the most important facets of truly building a loyal customer base through establishing a sense of community. Unfortunately this positive aspect of the internet has an associated weakness in that electronic billboards or chat sites also provide disaffected consumers with the power to communicate negative news about organisations to vast numbers of consumers, often sparking copy-cat actions. Moss-Kanter (2001b) reports how a Toshiba customer created an internet site for the express purpose of publicising how poor was the company's after sales service. The customer had allegedly bought two VCRs which were discovered to be defective and Toshiba representatives did not repair the machines properly. The company representative had also apparently refused to apologise and the website contained an audio recording of this. The company responded to this public "outing" with an apology and compensation but by then the damage was done – the website had received 7 million visits and sparked off copy-cat sites.

Summary

Chapter 8 has outlined some of the potential developments for business and continuity management. It is our view that the future of BC rests in the imaginations of the BC managers of today and tomorrow. Globalisation, growing interdependencies, growing regulations, social demands, the influence of new standards and expectations and the internet all form part of the context in which BC will evolve. The role of the continuity manager is here to stay. We have argued that effective continuity requires commitment, access to the senior echelons within an organisation but, perhaps most importantly, a mindset that regards organisational assets as a means to an end. Within such a mindset, creative solutions to continuity problems will always be possible.

In this last chapter our intention has been to be thought-provoking rather than to provide a comprehensive list of issues for the future. In the first edition of this text we admitted that we possessed no crystal ball and our expectations around the replacement of an auditing mindset with a value based one have proved optimistic. A key task for BC professionals remains to ensure that, as a process, BCM becomes normalised within organisations. Our fear is that the auditing mindset will shape and constrain practice as organisations seek the comfort blanket of conforming to an external agenda rather than consider the needs of their business. As many respondents have asserted, your business should be driving your BC.

Indeed, we suggest that while there is much to be gained from the study of BC tools and techniques, nothing can replace a rich understanding of the business and how it creates value. This is the foundation of effective BC and requires that it be seen as a strategic issue.

Study Questions

1 How will BC evolve during the next five years? You may choose to use the headings, political, economic, social and technological to help structure your answer. Apply these to your organisation and consider what recommendations you would make to your company's board of directors about its BCM plans and practices at the present time and how these should evolve.

2 How will e-business affect your organisation?

3 What do you perceive to be the opportunities and threats to your organisation in the event social media such as Facebook, Twitter or some similar application were to be used for marketing purposes? What policies currently exist that guide employees and managers in the use of these technologies? Evaluate whether these are adequate or not to guide organisational use of social media.

4 Prepare a 1,250-word report identifying and highlighting the likely concerns of key stakeholders, affected by an interruption in the following:

   a an international oil company
   b a general hospital
   c a large grocery retailer
   d a manufacturer of computer memory chips.

5 Find examples of two organisations – one which you consider to have effectively managed its reputation in the aftermath of a crisis, and another which has been less effective. What are the key differences in their response? What advice would you give to the less effective organisation?

Further Reading

Clair, J.A. (1998) "Reframing crisis management", *Academy of Management Review*, 23 (1): 59–76.
Financial Times (2000) "Mastering RISK, part eight", *Financial Times*, pp. 1–4.
Gray, E. and Balmer, J.T. (1998) "Managing corporate image and reputation", *Long-Range Planning*, 31 (5): 695–702.
Pearson, C.M. and Rondinelli, D.A. (1998) "Crisis management in central European firms", *Business Horizons*, May–June: 50–60.
Smith, D. and Elliott, D. (eds) (2006) *Issues and Concepts: A Crisis Management Reader*, Routledge: London.

Sutcliffe, K.M. and Vogus, T. (2003). "Organizing for resilience", in K.S. Cameron, J.E. Dutton, and R.E. Quinn (eds), *Positive Organisational Scholarship: Foundations of a New Discipline*, San Francisco: Berrett-Koehler, pp. 94–110.

Walker, P. (2007) "Animal rights militants losing the war", *The Guardian*, Tuesday 1 May, p. 11.

Wiersema, M. and Bowen, Harry P. (2008) "Corporate diversification: the impact of foreign competition, industry globalization, and product diversification", *Strategic Management Journal*, February, 29 (2): 118–132.

Notes

1 The content of this chapter should not be construed as legal advice and readers should not act upon this information without professional counsel.
2 Although the Act does not explicitly refer to Business Continuity Planning (BCP) or plans, section 19 of The Civil Contingencies Act 2004 (Contingency Planning) Regulations 2005 refers to the duty under section 2(1)(c) of the act as a "duty to maintain business continuity plans or emergency plans".
3 An internet-based distributed denial-of-service (DDoS) attack is when many "compromised systems" focus an attack upon a single target. This results in a denial of service for its users. The target system is overwhelmed by the number of incoming messages.
4 Requires a standard to be set to ensure the security and confidentiality of customer information; protect against any anticipated threats or hazards to the security or integrity of such information; and protect against unauthorised access to or use of customer information that could result in substantial harm or inconvenience to any customer (FDIC, 2001).
5 CERT is a federally funded internet security research centre based at Carnegie Mellon Software Engineering Institute.
6 Wilson (1992) identifies three approaches. However, two of these fall within the "cultural/behavioural" category.
7 Thirty people died when a train crashed leaving Paddington station in October 1999. Four people died in a train accident near Hatfield in October 2000.
8 The US-based stock exchange that lists primarily technology stocks. In 2006, the companies listed on the exchange had a combined market capitalisation approaching $4 trillion. The exchange has become more international in recent years, is available as a screen-based and internet-based service, and provides access to liquidity for small, emerging company and large company stocks (Greifeld, 2006).
9 To some extent the debate on whether BCM should have board representation echoes that of whether risk management should have board representation. In some companies risk management takes care of much the same issues that BCM does – particularly in insurance-related businesses.
10 The "love bug" virus that affected both domestic and corporate computer systems during May 2000 is a good example of this.

Bibliography

Abbott, H. (1992) *Product Risk Management*, London: Pitman Publishing.

Adler, P.S., and Kwon, S. (1999) "Social capital: the good, the bad, and the ugly", modified version of a paper presented at the 1999 Academy of Management Meeting, Chicago, IL.

Adler, P.S. and Kwon, S. (2000) "Social capital: The good, the bad and the ugly", in E. Lesser (ed.), *Knowledge and Social Capital: Foundations and Applications.* Boston: Butterworth-Heinemann.

Adler, P.S. and Kwon, S. (2002) "Social capital: Prospects for a new concept", *Academy of Management Review*, 27: 17–40.

Afuah, A. (2002) "Mapping technological capabilities into product markets and competitive advantage: The case of cholesterol drugs", *Strategic Management Journal*, 23: 171–179.

Aglionby, J. (2005) "Indonesia starts installing tsunami early-warning system", *The Guardian*, 8 October, p. 14.

Ahuja, G. and Katila, R. (2004) "Where do resources come from? The role of idiosyncratic situations", *Strategic Management Journal*, 25: 887–907.

Aleklett, K. (2007) *Reserve Driven Forecasts for Oil, Gas and Coal*, discussion paper 2007–18. Online: http://internationaltransportforum.org/jtrc/Discussion Papers/DiscussionPaper18.pdf (accessed 16 June 2008).

Alexander, D. (2000) *Confronting Catastrophe*, Harpenden: Terra.

American Red Cross (2007) "Business and industry guide". Online: http://www.redcross.org/services/disaster/0,1082,0_606_,00.html (accessed 23 March 2007).

Anderson, L. (2007) "Beyond competence: identifying and understanding non-technical competencies for crisis management team members", *Business Continuity Journal*, 2 (1): 6–31.

Anderson, R.E. (1992) *Bank Security*, Woburn, MA: Butterworth.

Argyris, C. (1994) "Good communication that blocks learning", *Harvard Business Review*, July–August, 72 (4): 77–85.

ARPA (2005a) *Prudential Standard GPS 222 Business Continuity Management*, Sydney: The Australian Prudential Regulation Authority.

ARPA (2005b) *Prudential Standard APS 222 Business Continuity Management*, Sydney: The Australian Prudential Regulation Authority.

Ashmos, D.P, Ducho, D. and Bodensteiner, W.D. (1997) "Linking issue labels and managerial actions: A study of participation in crisis vs. opportunity issues", *Journal of Applied Business Research*, 13 (4): 31–45.

Awazu, Y., Baloh, P., Desouza, K.C., Wecht, C., Kim, J. and Jha, S. (2009) "Information-communication technologies open up innovation", *Research Technology Management*, 52 (1): 51–58. Online: http://www.proquest.com/ (accessed 5 April 2009).

Balmer, J.T. and Soenen, G.B. (1999) "The acid test of corporate identity management", *Journal of Marketing Management*, 15: 69–92.

Bangemann, M. (1994) "Europe and the global information society", recommendations to the European Council, Brussels: European Commission.

Bank of Thailand (2003) *Strategic Risk Manual: Risk Assessment and Information and Technology System Department (Financial Institutions Supervision)*, Bangkok: Bank of Thailand.

Barney, J.B. (1989) "Asset stocks and sustained competitive advantage: a comment", *Management Science*, 35 (12): 1511–1513.

Barney, J.B. (1995) "Looking inside for competitive advantage", *Academy of Management Executive*, 9 (4): 49–61.

Barney, J.B. (2001) "Resource-based theories of competitive advantage: a ten-year retrospective on the resource-based view", *Journal of Management*, 27: 643–650.

Barney, J.B. (2007) *Gaining and Sustaining Competitive Advantage*, Upper Saddle River, NJ: Pearson Prentice Hall.

Basel Committee on Banking Supervision (1999) "A new capital adequacy framework", consultative paper, Basel: Bank for International Settlements.

BBC (2001) "London shares chaos". Online: http://news.bbc.co.uk/hi/english/business/newsid_702000/702573.stm (accessed 7 February 2001).

BBC (2002) "Six ways the UK has changed". Online: http://news.bbc.co.uk/1/hi/uk/2248658.stm (accessed 8 September 2009).

BBC (2005) "Bridgestone ends Ford recall row". Online: http://news.bbc.co.uk/1/hi/business/4335324.stm (accessed 10 January 2007).

BBC (2008) "Eyewitnesses on Heathrow incident". Online: http://news.bbc.co.uk/1/hi/uk/7194268.stm (accessed 18 January 2008).

BCI (2001) "10 standards". Online: www.thebci.org.

BCI (2002) *Good Practice Guidelines*, London: Business Continuity Institute.

BCI (2003) "The Business Continuity Institute 10 standards of professional competence". Online: http://www.thebci.org/certificationstandards.htm (accessed 25 July 2006).

BCI (2007a) "Good practice guidelines 2007". Online: http://www.thebci.org/CHAPTER1BCIGPG071.pdf (accessed 2 October 2007).

BCI (2007b) "Good practice guidelines 2008". Online: http://www.thebci.org/gpgdownloadpage.htm (accessed 29 September 2007).

Beazley, H., Boenisch, J. and Harden, D. (2002) *Continuity Management: Preserving Corporate Knowledge and Productivity when Employees Leave*, Hoboeken, NJ: John Wiley and Sons.

Belbin, R.M. (1981) *Management Teams: Why They Succeed or Fail*, Oxford: Butterworth-Heinemann.

Bell, E. (2006) "The media have yet to harness the power of citizen journalism", *The Guardian*, Saturday 8 July, p. 24.

Bellovin, S.M. (2001) "Computer security – an end state?", *Communications of the ACM*, March, 44 (3): 131–132.

Bird, L. (2002) "Business continuity for SMEs", *International Journal of Business Continuity*, 2 (1): 8–11.

BIS (2006) *International Convergence of Capital Measurement and Capital Standards: A Revised Framework Basel Committee on Banking Supervision*, Bank for International Settlements, June. CH-4002 Basel, Switzerland.

Blaney, J., Benoit, J. and Brazeal, L.M. (2002) "Blowout! Firestone's image restoration campaign", *Public Relations Review*, 28: 79–92.

Bloor, I. (2004) "The lawyers are coming". Online: http://www.itanalysis.com/technology/security/content.php?cid=6845> (accessed 12 February 2004).

Body Shop International (2000) *Annual Results*, London: Body Shop International Plc.

Boettke, P., Chamlee-Wright, E., Gordon, P., Ikeda, S., Leeson, P. and Sobel, R. (2007) "The political, economic and social aspects of Katrina", *Southern Economic Journal*, October, 74 (2): 363–377.

Bowe, C. (2001) "Ford and Firestone settle high-profile lawsuit", *Financial Times*, 8 January.

Bowman and Brooke LLP (1999) "International product liability laws". Online: http://library.findlaw.com/1999/Aug/1/129312.html (accessed 25 July 2006).

Bozarth, J. and Menkus, B. (2003) "Changes that could affect the IS business Continuity Plan", in K. Doughty (ed.) *Business Continuity Planning*, Boca Raton: Auerbach.

Braithwaite, J. and Fisse, B. (1987) "Self-regulation and the control of corporate crime", in C.D. Shearing and P.C. Stenning (eds) *Private Policing*, London: Sage.

Broadbent, D. (1979) *Contingency Planning*, Manchester: NCC.

Broder, J.F. (2000) *Risk Analysis and the Security Survey*, 2nd edn, Oxford: Butterworth-Heinemann.

Brown, J.M. and Campbell, E.A. (1994) *Stress and Policing: Sources and Strategies*, Chichester: John Wiley.

BSI (2005) "BS ISO/IEC 20000–1: 2005 Information technology – Service management – Specification". Online: http://www.bsi-global.com/ICT/Service/bs15000–1.xalter (accessed 25 July 2006).

BSI (2006) *BS25999–1 Code of Practice for Business Continuity Management and BS25999–2 Specification for Business Continuity Management*, London: British Standards Institute.

BSI (2007) *Draft BS25999–2 Business Continuity Management Part 2: Specification*, London: BSI

Burkhill, P. (2008) Video comments of pilot to news conference. Online: http://news.bbc.co.uk/1/hi/uk/7195921.stm (accessed 19 January 2008).

Burnes, B. (2004) *Managing Change: A Strategic Approach to Organisational Dynamics*, London: Pitman.

Bursa, M., Hunston, H., Lewis, A. and Wright, C. (1997) *The Automotive Supply Chain – New Strategies for a New World Order*, London: Informa Publishing Group.

Business Week (2006) "Web 2.0: the new guy at work", *Business Week*, 19 June, p. 59.

Cabinet Office (2005) *Emergency Preparedness – Guidance on part 1 of the Civil Contingencies Act 2004, its Associated Regulations and Non-statutory Arrangements*, London: The Stationary Office.

Cameron, K.H. (1994) "An international company's approach to managing major incidents", *Disaster Management*, 3(2).

Camp, J.L. and Tsang, R.P. (2001) "Universal service in a ubiquitous digital network", *Ethics and Information Technology*, 2 (4): 211–221.

Campbell, K., Gordon, L.A., Loeb, M.P. and Zhou, L. (2003) "The economic cost of publicly announced information breaches: empirical evidence from the stock market", *Journal of Computer Security*, 11: 431–448.

Canadian Underwriter (2005) "Electrifying business impact analysis", *Canadian Underwriter*, August, pp. 22–23.

Cappelli, D. (2005) "CERT preventing insider sabotage: lessons learned from actual attacks", CERT. Online: http://www.cert.org/search_pubs/search.php?sort=author&keyword=&topic=&step=search.

Cardline (2005) "Cybersource hopes deal will change visa's mind about card-systems", *Cardline*, 30 Sept, 5 (39): 1. Online: http://find.galegroup.com. libaccess.fdu.edu/gps/start.do?prodId=IPS (accessed 7 September 2009).

Carley, K. (1991) "Designing organisational structures to cope with communication breakdowns: a simulation model", *Industrial Crisis Quarterly*, 5 (1): 19–57.

Carrington, D. (2000) "Virgin on a disaster". Online: http://www.news.bbc.co.uk/hi/english/sci/tech/ (accessed 18 January 2000).

Carroll, R. (2008) "Protests spread as prices soar – Caracas". Online: http://www.guardian.co.uk/business/2008/jun/14/oil (accessed 16 June 2008).

Castillo, C. (2004) "Disaster preparedness and business continuity planning at Boeing: An integrated model", *Journal of Facilities Management*, 3 (1): 8–26.

CCTA (1995a) *An Introduction to Business Continuity Management*. London: HMSO.

CCTA (1995b) *A Guide to Business Continuity Management*. London: HMSO.

Chadwick, T. and Rajagopal, S. (1995) *Strategic Supply Management*, London, Butterworth-Heinemann.

Chandler, A.D. (1962) *Strategy and Structure: Chapters in the History of the Industrial Enterprise*, Cambridge, MA: MIT Press.

Chattopadhyay, P., Glick, W.H., Chet Miller, C. and Huber, G.P. (1999) "Determinants of executive beliefs: comparing functional conditioning and social influence", *Strategic Management Journal*, 20: 763–789.

Chemical and Industry (1998) "UK warned over risk assessment", *Chemical and Industry*, 3: 587.

Chesbrough, H. (2003) *Open Innovation: The New Imperative for Creating and Profiting from Technology*, Boston: Harvard Business School Press.

Civil Contingencies Act 2004. c.36, London: The Stationery Office.

Clark, J. and Harman, M. (2004) "On crisis management and rehearsing a plan", *Risk Management*, 51, May. Online: http://www.rmmag.com/MGTemplate. cfm?Section=MagArchive&NavMenuID=304&template=/Magazine/Display Magazines.cfm&Archive=1&IssueID=215&AID=2348&Volume=51& ShowArticle=1.

Clegg, S. (1992) *Modern Organisations: Organisation Studies in the Postmodern World*, London: Sage.

Clemons, E. (2000) " 'Gauging the power play in the new economy', mastering RISK, Part eight", *Financial Times*, 23 March, pp. 1–4.

CNN (1997) "Computer maker says $194 million purchase allows it to grow server line", *CNNfn*, 19 June.

Coleman, J.S. (1990) *Foundations of Social Theory*, Cambridge, MA: Harvard University Press.

Collins, D. (1998) *Organisational Change: Sociological Perspectives*, London: Routledge.

Commercial Union (1995) "Don't make a drama out of a crisis" video, Commercial Union.

Cooper, S. (2006) "A preview of disaster", *Harvard Business Review*, May, 84 (5): 36.

Cornell (2006) "Products liability", Legal Information Institute, Cornell Law School. Online: http://www.law.cornell.edu/wex/index.php/Products_liability (accessed 25 July 2006).

Cox, T. (1978) *Stress*, London: Macmillan Education.

Cranwell-Ward, J. (1990) *Thriving on Stress*, London: Routledge.

Croft, J. and Eaglesham, J. (2007) "Banks want Treasury to pay if lost data lead to ID theft", *Financial Times* (London), 24 November, p. 2.

Crowe, M.K. (1996) "Information and business process", *Systems Practice*, 9 (3): 263–272.

Crumley, B. (1990) "Fizzzzz went the crisis", *International Management*, 45 (3): 5.

Datamonitor (2007) *Eastman Kodak Company*, May 2008.

Davis, B. (2008) "Global ties under stress as nations grab power: trade, environment face new threats: balkanized Internet", *Wall Street Journal*, 28 April: A1–A16.

Day, D.V. and Lord, R.G. (1992) "Expertise and problem categorization – The role of expert processing in organisational sense making", *Journal of Management Studies*, 29: 35–47.

Day, R. (1997) "Planning for disaster", *Business Consultancy*, 1 (2): 62.

Deal, T.E. and Kennedy, A.A. (1982) *Corporate Cultures: The Rites and Rituals of Corporate Life*, Reading, MA: Addison Wesley.

DeWoskin, K. (2007) "The 'Made in China' stigma shock", *Far Eastern Economic Review*, 170 (7): 9–14.

Dhamija, R., Tygar, J.D. and Hearst, M. (2006) *Why Phishing Works*, CHI, April 22–27. Online: http://people.deas.harvard.edu/~rachna/papers/why_phishing_works.pdf (accessed 25 June 2006).

Dietrich, S., Dittrich, D., Mirkovic, J. and Reiher, P. (2004) *Internet Denial of Service: Attack and Defense Mechanisms*, New York: Prentice Hall.

Dill, W. (1958) "Environment as an influence on managerial autonomy", *Administrative Science Quarterly*, 2 (4): 409–443.

Doemland, T. (1999) "Awareness through auditing, testing and training", in A. Hiles, and P. Barnes (eds) *The Definitive Handbook of Business Continuity Management*, Chichester: John Wiley.

Dolan, A. (2003), "New Bug Ship Storm", *The Daily Mail*, p. 4.

Doswell, B. (2000) *Guide to Business Continuity Management*, Leicester: Perpetuity Press.

Doughty, K. (2001), *Business Continuity Planning – Protecting Your Organisation's Life*, Boca Raton: Auerbach.

Doyle, P. (1994) *Marketing Management and Strategy*, London: Prentice Hall.

Dunphy, D.C. and Stace, D.A. (1987) "Transformational and coercive strategies for planned organisational change", *Organisational Studies*, 9 (3): 317–334.

Dutton, J.E. and Dukerich, J.K. (1991) "Keeping an eye on the mirror: the role of image and identity in organisation adaptation", *Academy of Management Journal*, 34: 517–554.

Earl, M.J. (1989) *Management Strategies for Information Technology*, Hemel-Hempstead: Prentice-Hall.

Earl, M.J. (1996) "Information systems strategy . . . Why planning techniques are not the answer", *Business Strategy Review*, 7 (1): 54 (retrieved 4 September 4 2009 from ABI/INFORM Global, Document ID: 9389169).

Easterby-Smith, M., Thorpe, R. and Lowe, A. (1991) *Management Research: An Introduction*, London: Sage.

Economist (1999) "Coca-Cola: bad for you?", *Economist* (USA), 19: 62.

Egan, C. (1995a) *Competitive Advantage*, London: Butterworth-Heinemann.

Egan, C. (1995b) *Creating Organisational Advantage*, Oxford: Butterworth-Heinemann.

Eisenhardt, K.M. and Zbaracki, M.J. (1992) "Strategic decision making", *Strategic Management Journal*, 13: 17–37.

Elliott, D. (2005) "Risk and crisis management", in M. Gill (ed.) *International Security Handbook*, Leicester: Perpetuity Press.

Elliott, D. (2006) "Crisis management into practice", in D. Smith and D. Elliott (eds) *Issues and Concepts: A Crisis Management Reader*, Routledge: London.

Elliott, D. (2008) *Business Continuity Interim Report*, University of Liverpool.

Elliott, D. and Johnson, N. (2008a) *Interim Report on Benchmarking Business Continuity Project*, University of Liverpool.

Elliott, D. and Johnson, N. (2008b) *Business Continuity Project: Interim Report*, University of Liverpool, unpublished report.

Elliott, D. and MacPherson, A. (2009) *Policy and Practice: Recursive Learning from Crisis*, OLKC Conference Amsterdam.

Elliott, D. and Smith, D. (1993) "Coping with the sharp end: recruitment and selection in the Fire Service", *Disaster Management*, 5 (1): 35–41.

Elliott, D. and Smith, D. (2000) "Opening Pandora's box", in E. Cole, D. Smith and S. Tombs (eds) *Managing in the Risk Society*, Cambridge: Kluwer.

Elliott, D. and Smith, D. (2001) *Learning from Crisis*, Leicester: Perpetuity Press.

Elliott, D. and Smith, D. (2006) "Patterns of regulatory behaviour in the UK football industry", *Journal of Management Studies*, 43 (2): 291–318.

Elliott, D., Frosdick, S. and Smith, D. (1997) "The failure of legislation by crisis", in S. Frosdick and L. Walley (eds) *Sport and Safety Management*, Oxford: Butterworth-Heinemann.

Elliott, D., Harris, K. and Baron, S. (2005) "Crisis management and services marketing", *Journal of Services Marketing*, 19 (5): 336–345.

Elliott, D., Smith, D. and Sipika, C. (2001) "Message in a bottle: learning the lessons from crisis, from Perrier to Coca-Cola", University of Sheffield mimeo.

Elliott, D., Swartz, E. and Herbane, B. (1999a) *Business Continuity Management – Preparing for the Worst*, London: Incomes Data Services.

Elliott, D., Swartz, E. and Herbane, B. (1999b) "Just waiting for the next big bang: business continuity management in the UK finance sector", *Journal of Applied Management Studies*, 8 (1): 43–60.

Ellison, R.J., Fisher, D.A., Linger, R.C., Lipson, H.F., Longstaff, R. and Mead, N.R. (1999a) *Survivable Network Systems: An Emerging Discipline*, Carnegie-Mellon Software Engineering Institute, CERT. Online: http://cert.org/research/97tr013.pdf (accessed 26 July 2005).

Ellison, R.J., Fisher, D.A., Linger, R.C., Lipson, H.F., Longstaff, T. and Mead, N.R. (1999b) *Survivability: Protecting Your Critical Systems*, Carnegie-Mellon Software Engineering Institute, CERT. Online: http://www.cert.org/archive/html/protect-critical-systems.html (accessed 15 June 2006).

Engwall, M. and Svensson, C. (2001) "Cheetah teams", *Harvard Business Review*, 79 (2): 20–21.

Ernst and Young (2004) *Global Information Security Survey 2004*, London: EYGM Limited.

Ernst and Young (2005) *Global Information Security Survey 2005*, London: EYGM Limited.

Evers, J. (2006) "Computer crime costs $67 billion, FBI says", CNET News.com, 19 January 2006 Online. Available <http: //news.com.com/Computer+crime+ costs+67+billion,+FBI+says/2100–7349_3–6028946.html> (accessed 29 June 2006).

Evers, J. (2005) "Credit card suit now seeks damages", *ZDNet News*, 7 July. Online: http://news.zdnet.com/2100–1009_22–5777818.html (accessed 29 June 2006).

Eysenck, H.J. (1952) *The Scientific Study of Personality*, London: Routledge & Kegan Paul.

Fallows, Deborah (2003) *Spam: How It Is Hurting Email and Degrading Life on the Internet*, Washington DC: Pew Internet and American Life Project. Online: http://www.pewinternet.org/pdfs/PIP_Spam_Report.pdf (accessed 7 August 2005).

Federal Deposit Insurance Corporation (FDIC) (2001) *Examination Guidance*. Online: http://www.fdic.gov/news/news/financial/2001/fil0168.html (accessed 25 January 2008).

Federal Trade Commission (2006) *Card Systems Solutions Settles FTC Charges*, February. Online: http://www.ftc.gov/opa/2006/02/cardsystems_r.htm.

Feldman, P. (1998) "Surviving internet disasters", *Risk Management*, 45 (2): 56.

Felstead, A. (2007) "Executives are finding that they live in interesting times. Directors' insurance: new fears are boosting the market", *Financial Times Surveys Edition*, 1 May. Online: http://www.proquest.com/ (accessed 7 April 2009).

Ferre, R. (2000) *Building Confidence in Business Continuity*, London: Institute of Directors.

FFIEC (2003) Business *Continuity Planning Booklet – March 2003*, Federal Financial Institutions Examination Council.

Financial Times (1996) "Financial Times focus: IT in financial services", 4 September.

Financial Times (2000a) 7 April, p. 8.

Financial Times (2000b) "Mastering risk, part eight", 23 March, pp. 1–4.

Financial Times (2001) 16 February, p. 15.

Finkelstein, S. (2007) "Is Google just the tip of the iceberg of concerns about online privacy?" *The Guardian*, 21 June, p. 14.

Finkelstein, S. and Hambrick, D. (1988) "Chief executive compensation: a synthesis and reconciliation", *Strategic Management Journal*, 9: 543–558.

Fisher, S. (1986) *Stress and Strategy*, London: Lawrence Erlbaum.

Fitzgerald, K.J. (1995) "Establishing an effective continuity strategy", *Information Management and Computer Security*, 3 (3): 20–24.

Flin, R. (1996) *Sitting in the Hot Seat*, London: John Wiley.

Florida, R. (2008) "Megaregions: the importance of place", *Harvard Business Review*, March: 18–19.

Folke, C., Colding, J., Berkes, F. (2003) "Synthesis: building resilience and adaptive capacity in social–ecological systems", in F. Berkes, J. Colding and C. Folke (eds) *Navigating Social–Ecological Systems: Building Resilience for Complexity and Change*, Cambridge: Cambridge University Press, pp. 352–387.

Fombrun, C. (1997) *Reputation: Realising Value from the Corporate Image*, Boston, MA: Harvard Business School Press.

Fombrun, C., Gardberg, N. and Sever, J. (2000) "The reputation quotient: a multi-stakeholder measure of corporate reputation", *Journal of Brand Management*, 7 (4): 241–255.

Foremski, T. (2001) "Siebel beats estimates in fourth quarter", *Financial Times*, 24 January, p. 26.

Foster, S.P. (2005) "Building continuity into strategy", *Journal of Corporate Real Estate*, 7 (2): 105–119.

Fowler, D. (2006) "Power struggles", *Networker*, December, 10 (4): 5.

Fox, S. (2005) *Spyware: The Threat of Unwanted Software Programs Is Changing the Way People Use the Internet*, Washington DC: Pew Internet and American Life Project, July. Online: http://www.pewinternet.org/pdfs/PIP_Spyware_Report_July_05.pdf (accessed 7 August 2005).

Freeman S.F., Maltz, M. and Hirschhorn, L. (2003) "Moral purpose and organisational resilience: Sandler O'Neill & Partners, L.P. in the aftermath of September 11, 2001", in D. Nagao (ed.), *Academy of Management Best Papers 2003*.

Frey Jr, S.C. and Schlosser, M.M. (1993) "ABB and Ford: creating value through cooperation", *Sloan Management Review*, Autumn: 65–72.

Friedman, T. and Kaplan, R. (2002) "States of discord", *Foreign Policy*, 129: 64–70 (retrieved 14 September 2009, from ABI/INFORM Global, document ID: 110197680).

Frost, C. (1994) "Effective responses for proactive enterprise: business continuity planning", *Disaster Prevention and Management*, 3 (1): 7–15.

FSA (2005) *Resilience Benchmarking Project*, discussion paper December. Online: http://www.fsc.gov.uk/upload/public/Files/9/Web%20%20Res%20Bench%20 Report%2020051214.pdf.

FSA (2006) *Feedback Statement on the Resilience Benchmarking Project Discussion Paper*, July, London: The Financial Services Authority.

Gaines, S. (2008) "Campaigners to march in support of animal testing", *Society, The Guardian*, 4 February, p. 5.

Galliers, R.D. and Sutherland, A.R. (1991) "Information systems management and strategy formulation: the 'stages of growth' model revisited", *Information Systems Journal*, 1 (2): 89–114.

Galliers, R.D. and Sutherland, A. R. (1994) "Information systems management and strategy formulation: applying and extending the stages of growth concept", in R.D. Galliers and B.S.H. Baker (eds) *Strategic Information Management: Challenges and Strategies in Managing Information Systems*, Oxford: Butterworth-Heinemann.

Garnham, R. (2007) *Scrutiny Inquiry into the Summer Emergency 2007*, Gloucester: Gloucestershire County Council.

Gartner (2001) *Business Continuity and Disaster Recovery Planning and Management: Perspective*, Gartner Research, 8 October, DPRO-100862.

Gaudin, S. (2007) "Two universities hit by security breaches", *Information Week*, 11 June 11. Online: http://www.informationweek.com/news/internet/show Article.jhtml?articleID=199903218 (accessed 6 April 2009).

Gavetti, G., Henderson, R. and Giorgi, S. (2005) "Kodak and the digital revolution (A)", Harvard University Business School Case Study, Ref 9–705–448.

Gerlach, K.P. (2002) "The role of states and of international and national organisations as super risk managers", in M. Wieczorek, U. Naujoks and B. Bartlett (eds) *Business Continuity: IT Risk Management for International Corporations*, Berlin: Springer.

Ghemawat, P. (2008) "Globalization is an option not an imperative. Or, why the world is not flat", *Ivey Business Journal Online*, Jan/Feb, 72 (1).

Gibson, C. and Nolan, R.L. (1974) "Managing the four stages of EDP growth", *Harvard Business Review*, 52 (1): 76–88.

Giles, A. (2005) *SOX: What Does it Mean for UK Companies?* Online: http://www.continuitycentral.com/feature0203.htm (accessed 1 February 2009).

Ginn, R.D. (1989) *Continuity Planning: Preventing, Surviving and Recovering from Disaster*, Oxford: Elsevier Advanced Technology.

Gluckman, D. (2000) "Continuity . . . Recovery", *Risk Management*, 47 (3): 45.

Goetsch, S.D. (1996) "Products liability", *Defence Counsel Journal*, 63 (3): 399–401.

Goodden, R.L. (1995) *Preventing and Handling Product Liability*, New York: Marcel Dekker.

Goodden, R.L. (1996) "Lawyers can provide unique product-liability perspective", *Hydraulics and Pneumatics*, 49 (2): 10–12.

Goodhart, C. (1998) "Regulation from the inside – the politics of managerial control", *Chartered Banker*, January, pp. 20–23.

Google Watch (2007) "And then there were four". Online: http://www.google-watch.org/bigbro.html (accessed on 1 October 2007).

Gould, S.J. (1996) *Mismeasure of Man*, London: Penguin Books.

Government Centre for Information Systems (CCTA) (1995a) *An Introduction to Business Continuity Management*, London: HMSO.

Government Centre for Information Systems (CCTA) (1995b) *A Guide to Business Continuity Management*, London: HMSO.

Grande, C. (2000) "Innovators are back to net a second e-fortune", *Financial Times*, 17 October, p. 8.

Grant, R.M. (1991) "The resource-based theory of competitive advantage", *California Management Review*, 33 (3): 114–135.

Gray, E. and Balmer, J.T. (1998) "Managing corporate image and reputation", *Long Range Planning*, 31 (5): 695–702.

Green, C. (2006) "You can't manage what you can't measure", *The Business Continuity Journal*, 1 (1): 9–20.

Greifeld, B. (2006). "The business of being a stock market", *Vital Speeches of the Day*, 72 (13): 408–411. (Retrieved 23 April 2008, from ABI/INFORM Global database).

Greiner, L.E. (1972) "Evolution and revolution as organisations grow", *Harvard Business Review*, July–August: 37–46.

Greve, H.R. (1998) "Managerial cognition and the mimetic adoption of market positions: What you see is what you do", *Strategic Management Journal*, 19: 967–988.

Grimshaw, A.S. and Wulf, W.A. (1997) "The legion vision of a worldwide virtual computer", *Association for Computing Machinery, Communications of the ACM*, 40 (1): 39–46.

Guardian (2008) "Series of sensitive data losses call into question safety of National Biometric Database", *The Guardian*, 21 January. Online: http://www.guardian.co.uk/military/story/0,,2244578,00.html.

Hall, R. (1992) "The strategic analysis of intangible resources", *Strategic Management Journal*, 13: 135–144.

Hamilton, A. (2003), "Full steam ahead", *The Times*, 4 November, p. 1.

Hammer, M. (1990), "Re-engineering work: don't automate, obliterate", *Harvard Business Review*, July–August, pp. 104–112.

Handy, C. (1990) *The Age of Unreason*, Boston, MA: Harvard Business School Press.

Hanson, N. (1969) "There is more to seeing than meets the eye", in M.J. Smith (ed.) *Social Science in Question*, London: Sage.

Hansson, S.O. (2005) "Seven myths of risk", *Risk Management – An International Journal*, 7 (2): 7–17.

Hardin, G. (1971) "Nobody ever dies of overpopulation", *Science*, 171: 524–532.

Harrison, A. (2006) "Can airlines recover after terror ordeal?", *The Observer*, 20 August, p. 14.

Hearnden, K. (1993) "Up the creek – the perils of computer failure", Loughborough University Report in association with Computing Services Association and The Kingswell Partnership for IBM.

Hemp, T. (2001) "Managing for the next big thing: EMC's Michael Ruettgers", *Harvard Business Review*, January: 130–141.

Hemphill, T.A. (1996) "The new era of business regulation", *Business Horizons*, 39 (4): 26–31.

Heng, G.M. (1996) "Developing a suitable business continuity planning methodology", *Information Management and Computer Security*, 4 (2): 11–13.

Henry T. (2006) "Review", *Business Continuity Journal*, 1 (1).

Herbane, B. (1997) "Business Continuity: Facts and Effects", in B. Herbane (ed.) (1997) *Centre for Business Continuity Planning; Proceedings of the Launch Symposium*, London, Institute of Directors, 16th April, pp. 79–88.

Herbane, B. (2004) "Basel Committee on Banking Supervision", *Risk Management – An International Journal*, 6 (1): 65–66.

Herbane, B. and Rouse, M.J. (2000) *Strategic Management: An Active Learning Approach*, Oxford: Blackwell.

Herbane, B., Elliott, D. and Swartz, E. (1997) "Contingency and continua: achieving excellence through business continuity planning", *Business Horizons*, 40 (6): 19–25.

Herbane, B., Elliott, D. and Swartz, E. (2004) "Business continuity management – time for a strategic role?" *Long Range Planning*, 37 (5): 435–457.

Higgs, D. (2003) *The Combined Code On Corporate Governance*. Online: http://www.fsa.gov.uk/pubs/ukla/lr_comcode2003.pdf (accessed 7 June 2008).

Hiles, A. and Barnes, P. (eds) (1999) *The Definitive Handbook of Business Continuity Management*, Chichester: John Wiley.

Hirokawa, R. (1988) "Understanding the sources of faulty decision making", *Small Group Behaviour* 19: 411–433.

Hirschheim, R., Earl, M., Feeny, D. and Lockett, M. (1988) "An exploration into the management of the information systems function: key issues and an evolutionary model", *Proceedings Information Technology Management for Productivity and Strategic Advantage, IFIP TC-8 Open Conference Singapore*.

Hirschheim, R.A. and Verrijn-Stuart, A.A. (1996) *Office Systems*, London: Elsevier Science.

HKMA (2002) *Supervisory Policy Manual TM-G-2 Business Continuity Planning*, Hong Kong: The Hong Kong Monetary Authority.

HMSO (2004) Civil Contingencies Act 2004. Online: http://www.opsi.gov.uk/acts/acts2004/20040036.htm (accessed 25 July 2006).

Hofstede, E. (1990) "Measuring organisational cultures: a qualitative and quantitative study across twenty cases", *Administrative Science Quarterly*, June: 286–316.

Hogge, B. (2008) "The sky's the limit", *New Statesman*, 5 May, 137 (4895): 48.

Home Office (1997a) *Business as Usual: Maximising Business Resilience to Terrorist Bombings*, London: Home Office.

Home Office (1997b) *Bombs, Protecting People and Property*, 3rd edn, London: Home Office.

Honour, D. (2002) "Lessons from 11 September", *International Journal of Business Continuity*, 2 (1): 13–17.

Honour, D. (2006) "The BIA under the microscope, II", *The Business Continuity Journal*, 1 (1): 36–45.

HSE (2001) "Health and Safety Executive guidance notes on stress". Online: http://www.hse.gov.co.uk/pubns/stress2.htm (accessed 4 June 2001).

Huber, P. (1997) "The health scare industry", *Forbes*, 160 (7): 114.

Hughes, J. Eaglesham, J., Cox, A. and Croft, J. (2009) "FSA had HBOS risk fears in 2002", *The Financial Times*, 12 February. Online: http://www.ft.com/cms/s/0/98f6f584-f8a5–11dd-aae8–000077b07658.html (accessed 12 February 2009).

Hurley-Hanson, A.E. (2006) "Organisational responses and adaptations after 9–11", *Management Research News*, 29 (8): 480–494.

Hurricane Pam: a failure of initiative. Online: http://a257.g.akamaitech.net/7/257/2422/15feb20061230/www.gpoaccess.gov/katrinareport/hurricanepam.pdf (accessed 13 June 2008).

Huws, U. and O'Regan, S. (2001) *eWork in Europe: Results from the EMERGENCE 18-country Employer Survey*, London: Institute for Employment Studies.

Huy, Q.N. and Mintzberg, H.(2003) "The rhythm of change", *MIT Sloan Management Review*, Summer, 44 (4).

Imerson, M. (1997) "Helen Liddell: taking a tough approach to regulation", *Chartered Banker*, December, pp. 10–15.

International Organization for Standardization (2005) *ISO/IEC 17799: 2005 Information Technology – Security Techniques – Code of Practice for Information Security Management*. Online: http://www.iso.org/iso/en/prods-services/popstds/informationsecurity.html (accessed 25 July 2006).

Intertek (2004) *Product Safety in Europe: A Guide to Corrective Action Including Recalls*, London: Intertek Research and Testing Centre on behalf of the UK Consumers Association.

Irwin, R. (2001) *What is Fud?* Online: www.geocities.com/siliconvalley/hills/9267/ (accessed 20 January 2001).

ISA (2004) *Business Continuity and Disaster Recovery*. Online: http://www.ida.gov.sg/idaweb/marketing/infopage.jsp?infopagecategory=factsheet:marketing&infopageid=I2259> (accessed 25 July 2006).

ISF (2005) "The ISFs standard of good practice – the standard for information security (Version 4.1)", *Information Security Forum*.

ISO (2008a) *ISO/DIS 22399 Societal Security – Guidelines for Incident Preparedness and Operational Continuity Management*, Geneva: International Organization for Standardization.

ISO (2008b) *ISO 24762 Security Techniques – Guidelines for Information and Communications Technology Disaster Recovery Services*, Geneva: International Organization for Standardization.

IT 2000 (1997) *A Legal Guide for Users and Suppliers*, London: Monitor Press.

Jablonowski, M. (2006) *Precautionary Risk Management – Dealing with Catastrophic Loss Potentials in Business, the Community and Society*, Basingstoke: Palgrave Macmillan.

Jackson, C.B. (2001) "The business impact analysis process", in K. Doughty (ed.) *Business Continuity Planning: Protecting Your Organization's Life*, Boca Raton, FL: CRC Press.

Jacobs, J.A. and Portman, R.M. (1998) "Beware the threat of product liability litigation", *Association Management*, June, pp. 81–82.

Janis, I. (1982) *Groupthink*, Boston: Houghton Mifflin.

Janis, I. (1983) *Victims of Groupthink*, 2nd edn, Boston: Houghton Mifflin.

Johnson, G. and Scholes, K. (2008) *Exploring Corporate Strategy: Text and Cases*, 8th edn, London: Prentice Hall.

Johnson, G., Scholes, K. and Whittington, R. (1997) *Exploring Corporate Strategy: Text and Cases*, 7th edn, London: Prentice Hall.

Jones, M., Rahman, B. and Newman, C. (2000) "Dismay as BNFL agrees to take back Japanese fuel", *Financial Times*, 12 July, p. 2.

Jones, M.E. and Sutherland, G. (1999) *Implementing Turnbull: A Boardroom Briefing*, London: Institute of Chartered Accountants in England and Wales.

Karakasidis, R. (1997) "A project planning process for business continuity", *Information Management and Computer Security*, 5 (2): 72–78.

Kasperson, R.E., Renn, O. and Slovic, P. (1988) "The social amplification of risk: a conceptual framework", *Risk Analysis*, 6: 177–187.

Kassler, P. (1995), "Scenarios for world energy: barricades or new frontiers?" *Long Range Planning*, 28(6): 38–47.

Keeley, G. (2008) "Protests spread as prices soar". Online: http://www.guardian.co.uk/business/2008/jun/14/oil (accessed 16 June 2008).

Keeney, M., Kowalski, E., Cappelli, D., Moore, A., Shimeall, T. and Rogers, S. (2005) *Insider Threat Study: Computer Systems Sabotage in Critical Infrastructure Sectors*, May 2005, National Threat Assessment Center, U.S. Secret Service and CERT/SEI. Online: http://www.cert.org/archive/pdf/insidercross011105.pdf (accessed 7 July 2006).

Kelleher, E. (2005) "MasterCard sales boost", *Financial Times* (London), 3 August, p. 21.

Kharbanda, O. and Stallworthy, E. (1991) "Industrial disasters – will self-regulation work?", *Long-Range Planning*, 24 (3): 84–89.

Kielmas, M. (1999) "Interest in recall covers rises: Coca-Cola scare fuels awareness of risks", *Business Insurance*, 33 (28): 18–22.

King, J. (1997) "Business continuity is focus of disaster recovery", *Computerworld*, 1 September, 31 (35): 17.

Kirshenbaum, A. (2004) *Chaos, Organisation and Disaster*, New York: Marcel Dekker.

Klay Management Ltd. (2003) *Mitigating Operational Risk – Not Just for the Field Anymore*. Online: www.kimc.com/KLAY/pdfs/Mitigating_Op_Risk.pdf.

Kochan, A. (1999) "Rover's e-build process assembles cars in the virtual world", *Assembly Automation*, 19 (2): 118–120.

Kotter, J.P. and Schlesinger L.A. (1979) "Choosing strategies for change", *Harvard Business Review*, March/April: 123–136.

Krcmar, H., Bjorn-Andersen, N. and O'Callaghan, R. (1995) *EDI in Europe*, Chichester: John Wiley.

Krell, E. (2006) "The case for business continuity management", *Business Finance*, 12 (4): 20–26.

Kumar, N., Scheer, L. and Kotler, P. (2000) "From market driven to market driving", *European Management Journal*, 18 (2): 129–142.

Kuong, J. and Isaacson, J. (1986) *How to Prepare an EDP Plan for Business Contingency*, Wellesley Hills, MA: Management Advisory Publications.

Kurzweil, R. (2007) "Frontiers", *The Atlantic Monthly*, 300 (4): 14–15 (accessed 15 April 2009 from ABI-Inform).

L'Engle, M. (1995) *A Wrinkle in Time*, New York: Bantam Doubleday Books.

La Porte, T. and Consolini, P. (1991) "Working in practice but not in theory: theoretical challenges of 'high-reliability organisations' ", *Journal of Public Administration Research and Theory*, 1 (1): 19–47.

Lagadec, P. (1993) *Preventing Chaos in a Crisis*, Maidenhead: McGraw-Hill.

Lawrence, F. (2004) "Things get worse with Coke", *The Guardian*, 20 March, p. 21.

Lazarus, R.S. (1966) *Psychological Stress and the Coping Process*, New York: McGraw-Hill.

Lazarus, R.S. (1999) *Stress and Emotion: A New Synthesis*, London: Free Association Books.

Lazarus, R.S. and Folhman, S. (1984) *Stress, Appraisal, and Coping*, New York: Springer.

Lazarus, R.S. and Launier, R. (1978) "Stress-related transactions between person and environment", in L.A. Pervin and M. Lewis (eds) *Internal and External Determinants of Behavior*, New York: Plenum.

Leana, C. and Van Buren, H. (1999) "Organisational social capital and employment relations", *Academy of Management Review*, 24 (3): 538–555.

Lederer, A.L. and Sethi, V. (1992) "Meeting the challenges of information systems planning", *Long Range Planning*, 25 (2): 69–80.

Lee, R.G. and Russo, R.J. (1996) "Dealing with disasters takes careful planning ahead of time", *Building Design and Construction*, 37 (9): 37–38.

Lee, Y.J. and Harrald, J.R. (1999) "Critical issue for business area impact analysis in business crisis management: analytical capability", *Disaster Prevention and Management*, 8 (3): 184–189.

Leemhuis, J.P. (1985) "Using scenarios to develop strategies", *Long Range Planning*, 18 (2): 30–37.

Lemos, R. (2006) "U.S.B. drives pose insider threat", *SecurityFocus*. Online: http://www.securityfocus.com/brief/239 (accessed 29 June 2006).

Lengnick-Hall, C.A and Beck, T.E. (2003) "Beyond bouncing back: the concept of organisational resilience", paper presented at the *National Academy of Management Meetings*, Seattle, WA.

Lengnick-Hall, C.A. and Beck, T.E. (2005) "Adaptive fit versus robust transformation: how organisations respond to environmental change", *Journal of Management*, 31 (5): 738–757.

Lettice, J. (2002) *Chopped Cable Knocks dabs.com off the Web*. Online: http://www.theregister.co.uk/2002/10/25/chopped_cable_knocks_dabs_com/> (accessed 25 October 2002).

Levitt, B. and March, J.G. (1988) "Organisational learning", *Annual Review Of Sociology*, 14: 319–340.

Levitt, T. (1965) "Exploit the product life cycle", *Harvard Business Review*, Nov–Dec, 43: 81–94.

Lewin, K. (1951) *Field Theory in Social Science*, New York: Harper & Row.

Lewis, S. (2005) "Business continuity and disaster recovery plans – things overlooked", *EDPACS*, 33 (1): 19–20.

Locke, E.A. (1968) "Toward a theory of task motivation and incentives", *Organisational Behaviour and Performance*, 3: 157–189.

Löfstedt, R. and Frewer, L. (1998) *The Earthscan Reader in Risk and Modern Society*, London: Earthscan Publications Ltd.

Louisiana Office of Homeland Security & Emergency Preparedness (2005) *Lessons Learned, Event Name Hurricane Katrina/Rita 26 Aug–29 Nov 2005*. Online: http://www.katrina.lsu.edu/downloads/LOHSEP%20LESSONS%20LEARNED.pdf (accessed 13 June 2008).

Lower Manhattan Development Corporation (2007) Online: http://www.renewnyc.com/plan_des_dev/130Liberty/overview.asp (accessed 23 March 2007).

Lyman, P. and Varian, H (2001) "The democratization of data", *Harvard Business Review*, January: 137.

Macalister, T. (2006) "Shell accused over oil rig safety", *The Guardian*, 23 June, p. 17.

Mandela, N. (1994) *The Long Walk to Freedom*, London: Abacus Books.

Marlin, S. (2005) "Visa system targets credit-fraud rings", *InformationWeek*, 20 June, 1044: 32.

Martin, K. (2006) "U.S. gov't mandates laptop security", *SecurityFocus*. Online: http://www.securityfocus.com/news/11397 (accessed 25 June 2006).

Martinson, J. and Elliott, L. (1999) "Ministers seek to still stock market panic G7 meeting: financial leaders forced to address dollar's fall and crash predictions", *The Guardian*, 25 September, p. 23.

MAS (2003) *Business Continuity Management Guidelines*, Singapore: Monetary Authority of Singapore.

Maurer, H. (2007) "O.K. we bid too high", *Business Week*, 15 October, p. 30.

McCubbins, T.F. and Mosier, G.C. (1998) "Effects of product liability laws on small business: an introduction to international exposure through a comparison of US and Canadian law", *Journal of Small Business Management*, 36 (3): 72–79.

McFadden, T. (1993) "World Trade Center", *New York Times*, 6 February, p. 5.

McGregor, R. and Russell, A. (2008) "African protests repel arms ship", *Financial Times*, 23 April, p. 10. (retrieved 23 April 2008, from ABI/INFORM Global database).

McKenna, E. (1994) *Business Psychology and Organisational Behaviour*, Hove: Lawrence Erlbaum Associates.

McKinnon, I. and Watts, J. (2008) "Protests spread as prices soar – Asia and Beijing". Online: http://www.guardian.co.uk/business/2008/jun/14/oil (accessed on 16 June 2008).

McManus, D.J. and Carr, H.H. (2001) "Risk and the need for business continuity planning", in K. Doughty (ed.) *Business Continuity Planning: Protecting your Organization's Life*, Auerbach Best Practices Series, Boca Raton: CRC Press LLC.

Mellish, S. (2000) "J Sainsbury and the fuel crisis", *Continuity*, 4 (4): 3–6.

Mellish, S. (2000) "When a BCP really comes into its own", *Continuity*, 4 (4): 4–6.

Menkus, B. (1994) "The new importance of business continuity in data processing disaster recovery planning", *Computers and Security*, 13 (2): 115–118.

Meredith, W. (1999) "Business impact analysis", in A. Hiles and P. Barnes (eds) *The Definitive Handbook of Business Continuity Management*, Chichester: John Wiley.

Meyer, A.D. (1982) "Adapting to environmental jolts", *Administrative Science Quarterly*, 27: 515–537.

Meyer, J.W. and Rowan, B. (1977) "Institutional organizations: formal structure as myth and ceremony", *American Journal of Sociology*, 83: 340–363.

Microsoft (2006) *Enabling an Adaptable, Aligned, and Agile Supply Chain with BizTalk Server and RosettaNet Accelerator*. Online: http://www.microsoft.com/technet/itsolutions/msit/ecomm/scmbiztalktcs.mspx (accessed 17 July 2006).

Mintzberg, H. (1983a) *Power In and Around Organisations*, Englewood Cliffs, NJ: Prentice Hall.

Mintzberg, H. (1983b) *The Structuring of Organisations*, Englewood Cliffs, NJ: Prentice Hall.

Mintzberg, H. (1994) *The Rise and Fall of Strategic Planning*, London: Prentice Hall.

Mintzberg, H. and Waters J. (1985) "Of strategies, deliberate and emergent", *Strategic Management Journal*, 6: 257–72.

Mintzberg, H., Quinn, J.B. and Ghoshal, S. (1998). *The Strategy Process*, rev. European edn, London: Prentice Hall.

Mitchell, R.K, Agle, B.R. and Wood, D.J. (1997) "Toward a theory of stakeholder identification and salience: defining the principle of who and what really counts", *Academy of Management Review*, 22 (4): 853–886.

Mitroff, I., Pauchant, T. and Shrivastava, P. (1988) "The structure of man made organisational crisis", *Technological Forecasting and Social Change*, 33: 83–107.

Mitroff, I., Pauchant, T., Finney, M. and Pearson, C. (1989) "Do (some) organisations cause their own crises? Culture profiles of crisis-prone versus crisis-prepared organisations", *Industrial Crisis Quarterly*, 3 (4): 269–283.

Mitts, J.S. (2005) "Business continuity and disaster recovery plans: how and when to test them", *EDPACS*, November, 33 (5): 8–24.

MOD (2006) *Joint Service Publication 503 Business Continuity Management*, 3rd edn, London: Ministry of Defence.

Moore, T. and Lakha, R. (2006) *Tolley's Handbook of Disaster and Emergency Management*, London: Butterworth-Heinemann.

Morgan, O. (2003) "Besieged BA left with strike baggage", *The Observer*, 27 July, p. 16.

Moss-Kanter, R. (2001a) *E-volve!: Succeeding in the Digital Culture of Tomorrow*, Cambridge, MA: Harvard University Press.

Moss-Kanter, R. (2001b) "The ten deadly mistakes of wanna-dots", *Harvard Business Review*, January: 91–100.

Moyer, K. (1996) "Scenario Planning at British Airways – a case study", *Long Range Planning*, 29 (2): 172–181.

Mumford, E. and Hendricks, R. (1996) "Business process re-engineering RIP", *People Management*, 2 May, pp. 22–29.

Murphy, B.L. (2007) "Locating social capital in resilient community-level emergency management", *Natural Hazards*, 41 (2): 297–315.

Mwende, J. (2002) "Kenyans add too much realism to their crash exercise", World News, *The Times* (London), 22 August.

Nahapiet, J. and Ghoshal, S. (1998) "Social capital, intellectual capital and organisational advantage", *Academy of Management Review*, 23 (2): 242–266.

National Bureau of Standards (1979) *Guideline for Automatic Data Processing Risk Analysis*, FIPS PUB 65, Washington, DC: U.S. General Printing Office.

National Fire Protection Association (2004) *NFPA 1600 Standard on Disaster/Emergency Management and Business Continuity Programs 2004 Edition*. Online: http://www.nfpa.org/assets/files/PDF/NFPA1600.pdf> (accessed 25 July 2006).

National Fire Protection Association (2007) *NFPA 1600 Standard on Disaster/Emergency Management and Business Continuity Programs 2007 Edition*, NFPA, 1 Batterymarch Park, Quincy, MA.

National Hi-Tech Crime Unit (2004) *Hi-Tech Crime: The Impact on U.K. Businesses*, London: NHTCU/NOP.

Nash, W.A. (1998) *Schaum's Outline of Theory and Problems of Strength of Materials*, New York: McGraw-Hill.

NECSI (2008) *About Complex Systems: New England Complex Systems Institute*. Online: http://www.necsi.org/guide/study.html (accessed 20 January 2008).

Negroponte, N. (1996) *Being Digital*, New York: Vintage Books.

NERC (2002) *Security Guidelines for the Electricity Sector*, Version 1.0, 14 June, Princeton, NJ: North American Electric Reliability Council.

NFA (2003) *RULE 2–38. Business Continuity and Disaster Recovery Plan*, New York: National Futures Association.

Nielsen, J. (2006) "BCM & corporate governance – the chicken or the egg?" *ContinuitySA*. Online: http://www.continuitysa.co.za/Article1.asp (accessed 25 July 2006).

NIST (2002) *Contingency Planning Guide for Information Technology Systems – Recommendations of the National Institute of Standards and Technology*, NIST Special Publications (SP) 800–34, Washington: US Department of Commerce.

Nocera, J. (1995) "Fatal litigation", *Fortune*, 132 (8): 60–74.

Nolan, R. (1979) "Managing the crises in data processing", *Harvard Business Review*, 57 (2): 115–126.

Norton-Taylor, R (2008) "Recruits' banks alerted after theft of laptop", *The Guardian*, 21 January, p. 321.

O'Leary, M. (2006) "Can airlines recover after terror ordeal?" *The Observer*, 20 August, p. 14.

OCC (2006) Online: http://www.occ.treas.gov/pubs1.htm.

Olins, R. and Lynn, M. (1997) "A class disaster", *The Sunday Times* (London), 16 November, p. 14.

Pabrai, U.O.A. (2005) "Contingency planning: business impact analysis", *Certification Magazine*, May, pp. 30–31.

Panko, R.R. (1988) *End User Computing*, New York: Wiley.

Paraskevas, A. (2006) "Crisis management or crisis response system? A complexity science approach to organisational crises", *Management Decision*, October, 44 (7): 892–907.

Parris, D. (1999) "Image conscious", *Survive*, August, pp. 11–15.

Parthasarathi, P. (2005) *Operational Risk Management – Business Continuity Planning, DBS.CO.IS Audit. No. 19/31.02.03/2004–05*, Department of Banking Supervision, Mumbai: Reserve Bank of India.

Pascale, R.T. and Athos, A.G. (1982) *The Art of Japanese Management*, London: Penguin Books.

Paton, D. (2003) "Stress in disaster response: a risk management approach", *Disaster Prevention and Management*, 12 (3): 203–209.

Pauchant, T. and Douville, R. (1993) "Recent research in crisis management: a study of 24 authors' publications from 1986 to 1991", *Industrial and Environmental Crisis Quarterly*, 7 (1): 43–66.

Pauchant, T. and Mitroff, I. (1988) "Crisis-prone versus crisis avoiding organisations: is your company's culture its own worst enemy in creating crises?", *Industrial Crisis Quarterly*, 2: 53–63.

Pauchant, T. and Mitroff, I. (1992) *The Crisis-Prone Organisation*, San Francisco: Jossey-Bass.

Perrow, C. (1997) *Normal Accidents*, New York: Basic Books.

Perry, K. (2000) "Cruise down the Swanee: *Aurora*'s maiden voyage halted", *The Guardian*, 3 May, p. 5.

Peters, T.J. and Waterman, R.H. (1982) *In Search of Excellence*, New York: Harper & Row.

Petroni, A. (1999) "Managing information systems' contingencies in banks: a case study", *Disaster Prevention and Management*, 8 (2): 101–110.

Pettigrew, A.M. and Whipp, R. (1991) *Managing Change for Competitive Success*, Oxford: Basil Blackwell.

Pettigrew, A.M., Whipp, R. and Rosenfeld, R.H. (1989) "Competitiveness and the management of strategic change processes", in A. Francis and P. Tharakan (eds) *The Competitiveness of European Industry*, London: Routledge.

Pew Internet and American Life Project (2007) *Teens and Online Stranger Contact*, 14 October. Online: http://www.pewinternet.org/pdfs/PIP_Stranger_Contact_Data_Memo.pdf (accessed 14 June 2008).

Pilger, J. (1998) *Hidden Agendas*, London: Vintage.

Pitt, M. (2008) *The Pitt Review: Lessons Learned from the 2007 Floods*, London: HMSO.

Pitt, M. and Goyal, S. (2004) "Business continuity planning as a facilities management tool", *Facilities*, 22 (3/4): 87–99.

Plant, R. (1987) *Managing Change and Making it Stick*, London: Fontana.

Plunkett Research Ltd. (2006) *Telecommunications Industry Center*. Online: http://www.plunkettresearchonline.com.libaccess.fdu.edu/Profiles/Default.aspx?Industry=3 (accessed 12 July 2006).

Porter, M.E. (1980) *Competitive Strategy*, New York: The Free Press

Porter, M.E. (1985) *Competitive Advantage*, New York: The Free Press.

Powell, T.C. (2001) "Competitive advantage: logical and philosophical considerations", *Strategic Management Journal*, 22: 875–888.

Power, M. (1997) *The Audit Society: Rituals of Verification*, Oxford: Oxford University Press.

Power, P. (1999) *Business Continuity Management – Preventing Chaos in a Crisis*, Management Action Notes, London: Department of Trade and Industry.

Pritchard, J.A.T. (1976) *Contingency Planning*, Manchester: NCC.

Prowse, R. (1998) "A legal moose on the loose?", *Motor Industry Management*, October, p. 17.

Punch, M. (1997) *Dirty Business*, London: Sage.

Putnam, R. (1993) *Making Democracy Work*, Princeton: Princeton University Press.

Quinn, J.B. (1980) *Strategies for Change*, New York: Irwin.

Rahman, B. (2000) "Nuclear hopes dashed by furore", *Financial Times*, 12 July, p. 2.

Raiffa, H. (1968) *Decision Analysis*, Reading, MA: Addison Wesley, cited in C. Smart and I. Vertinsky (1977) "Designs for crisis decision units", *Administrative Science Quarterly*, 22: 640–657.

Ramprasad, A., Ambrose, P. and Komarov, M. (1998) "The power of stakeholders in continuity", *Disaster Recovery Journal*, Fall, 11 (4): 11–13.

Ramsay, C.G. (1999) "Protecting your business: from emergency planning to crisis management", *Journal of Hazardous Materials*, 65: 131–149.

Raphael, B., Meldrum, L. and McFarlane, A.C. (1995) "Does debriefing after psychological trauma work?", *British Medical Journal*, 310: 1479–1480.

Rayport, J. and Sviokla, J. (1995) "Exploiting the virtual value chain", *Harvard Business Review*, November–December: 75–85.

Reason, J. (1997) *Managing the Risks of Organisational Accidents*, Aldershot: Ashgate.

Reason, J. (2008) *The Human Contribution – Unsafe Acts, Accidents and Heroic Recoveries*, Ashgate: Farnham.

Red Cross (2008) "Leading CEOs launch alliance with American Red Cross to strengthen nation's preparedness for disasters", press release. Online: http://www.redcross.org/portal/site/en/menuitem.94aae335470e233f6cf911d-f43181aa0/?vgnextoid=96fc0f3cba57b110VgnVCM10000089f0870aRCRD &vgnextfmt=default.

Reed, R. and DeFillippi, R.J. (1990) "Causal ambiguity, barriers to imitation and sustainable competitive advantage", *Academy of Management Review*, 15 (1): 88–102.

Regester, M. and Larkin, J. (1997) *Risk Issues and Crisis Management*, London: Kogan Page.

Reiman, K.M. (2002) "Position of the internal audit department in a BCP project", in M. Wieczorek, U. Naujoks, and B. Bartlett (eds) *Business Continuity: IT Risk Management for International Corporations*, Berlin: Springer.

Rick, J. and Briner, R. (2000) *Trauma Management vs. Stress Debriefing: What Should Responsible Organisations Do?* London: HSE Books.

Rider, B. (2003) "RPO and RTO redefined for the decision maker", *Continuity Insights*, Jan–Feb, 1 (1): 40.

Riel, V.C. (1995) *Principles of Corporate Communications*, London: Prentice Hall.

Risk Management (2002) "Dealing with disaster", *Risk Management*, December, 49 (12): 12–17.

Robinson, J. (2006) "Measuring continuity", *Business Continuity Journal*, 1 (1): 25–33.

Rohrer, Carly (2003) "Move retailers from dial-up to high-speed payment transactions", *Business Solutions*. Online: http://www.bU.S.inesssolutionsmag.com/Articles/2003_11/031114.htm (accessed 7 August 2005).

Rothschild, M. (2006) "The threat from within: the evolution of cyber attacks", *Computer Technology Review*, March/April, XXVI (2). Online: http://www.w-wpi.com (accessed 7 July 2006).

Royal Sun Alliance (1996) "The Manchester bombing incident" video.

Ryan, R. (2005) "BA staff begin returning to Heathrow", *The Guardian*, 12 August.

Sarbanes-Oxley (2002) *An Act to Protect Investors by Improving the Accuracy and Reliability of Corporate Disclosures made Pursuant to the Securities Laws, and for Other Purposes*, 23 January.

Schein, E. (1992) *Organisational Culture and Leadership*, 2nd edn, San Francisco: Jossey-Bass.

Schneider, R.O. (2000) "Knowledge and ethical responsibility in industrial disasters", *Disaster Prevention and Management*, 9 (2): 98–104.

Schwartz, H. (1987) "On the psychodynamics of organisational disaster", *Columbia Journal of World Disaster*, 22, Part 1.

Searcy, D. (2005) "Consumer alert, technology: the journal report", *The Wall Street Journal*, 18 July, p. R6.

Searle, D., Charter, D. and Bird, S. (2003), "Straw protests at spanish closure of Rock border", *The Times*, 4 November, p. 11.

SEC (2002a) *Interagency Paper on Sound Practices to Strengthen the Resilience of the U.S. Financial System*. Online: http://www.sec.gov/news/studies/34–47638.htm (accessed 25 July 2006).

SEC (2002b) *NYSE Rulemaking Self-Regulatory Organisations; Notice of Filing of Proposed Rule Change by the New York Stock Exchange, Inc. Relating to Business Continuity and Contingency Planning*. Online: http://www.sec.gov/rules/sro/34–46443.htm (accessed 25 July 2006).

SEC (2003) *NASD Rulemaking re: Business Continuity Plans and Emergency Contact Information*. Online: http://www.sec.gov/rules/sro/34–48503.htm (accessed 25 July 2006).

Semelka, S. (2007) "Hackers hit university's staff records", *Knight Ridder Tribune Business News*, May, 8 (1). Online: http://www.proquest.com/ (accessed 7 April 2009).

Sheffi, Y. and Rice, J. (2005) "A supply chain view of the resilient enterprise", *MIT Sloan Management Review*, Fall, 47 (1): 41–48.

Shipley, D. (1998) "Marketing strategies for growth, maturity and decline", in C. Egan and M.T. Thomas (eds) *The CIM handbook of Strategic Marketing*, London: Butterworth-Heinemann.

Shrivastava, P. (1987a) *Bhopal*, London: Ballinger.

Shrivastava, P. (1987b) "Are we ready for another Three Mile Island, Bhopal, Tylenol?", *Industrial Crisis Quarterly*, 1 (1): 2–4.

Shrivastava, P. and Mitroff, I. (1987) "Strategic management of corporate crises", *Columbia Journal of World Business*, 22 (1): 5–11.

Shrivastava, P., Miller, D. and Miglani, A. (1991) "Understanding industrial crises", *Journal of Management Studies*, 25, Part 4.

SHRM (2001) "Poll predicts change in the workplace as a result of terrorist attacks". Online: www.shrm.org.

SHRM (2002) "HR implications of the attack on America". Online: www.shrm.org.

Siegfried, W.A. (1998) "Guard against suits", *Design News*, 53 (11): 230.

Simon, H.A. (1957) *Administrative Behaviour*, 2nd edn, New York: Macmillan.

Sinha, I. (2000) "Cost transparency: the net's real threat to prices and brands", *Harvard Business Review*, March–April: 43–50.

Siomkos, G.J. and Kurzbard, G. (1994) "The hidden crisis in product-harm crisis management", *European Journal of Marketing*, 28 (2): 30–41.

Sipika, C., Smith, D. and Elliott, D. (1993) "Message in a bottle: Perrier", *Proceedings of the World Academy of Marketing*, University of Istanbul, pp. 559–563.

Sirignano, M.A. (1997) "Unsafe hamburgers and unreasonably hot coffee", *LI Business News*, 14: 7.

Skapinker, M. (2000) "FT survey", *FT Director*, 31 March.

Slovic, P. (1998) "Perception of risk", in R. Löfstedt and L. Frewer (eds) *The Earthscan Reader in Risk and Modern Society*, London: Earthscan Publications Ltd, pp. 31–43.

Smart, C. and Vertinsky, I. (1977) "Designs for crisis decision units", *Administrative Science Quarterly*, 22: 640–657.

Smith, D. (1990) "Beyond contingency planning: towards a model of crisis management", *Industrial Crisis Quarterly*, 4 (4): 263–275.

Smith, D. (2000) "Crisis management teams: issues in the management of operational crises", *Risk Management: An International Journal*, 2 (3): 61–78.

Smith, D. and Elliott, D. (2007) "Exploring the barriers to learning from crisis organisational learning and crisis", *Management Learning*, 38 (5): 519–538.

Smith, D. and Tombs, S. (1995) "Beyond self-regulation: towards a critique of self-regulation as a control strategy for hazardous activities", *Journal of Management Studies*, 32 (5): 19–37.

Smith, J. and Frisby, J. (2004) "A five-step plan for comprehensive information security and privacy", *Bank Accounting and Finance*, June, pp. 31–37.

Smith, M. and Sherwood, J. (1995) "Business continuity planning", *Computers and Security*, 14: 14–23.

Smith, R. (1996) "Planning for contingencies", *Industrial Management and Data Systems*, 96 (6): 27–28.

Smith-Spark, I. (2005) "New Orleans violence 'overstated' ". Online: http://news.bbc.co.uk/1/hi/world/americas/4292114.stm (accessed 27 January).

Snellen, M. (2003) "How to build a 'dark site' for crisis management – using internet technology to limit damage to reputation", *Strategic Communication Management*, April/May, 7 (3): 18–21.

Snyder, A.V. and Ebeling Jr, H.W. (1992) "Targeting a company's real core competencies", *Journal of Business Strategy*, 13 (6): 26–32.

Soo Hoo, K.J. (2000) "How much is enough? A risk management approach to computer security", working paper, The School of Information Management and Systems (SIMS), The University of California, Berkeley. Online: www2.sims.berkeley.edu/resources/affiliates/workshops/econsecurity/econws/06.doc.

South China Morning Post (2000) 15 March. Online: http://www.globalarchive.ft.com/search-components/index.jsp (accessed 15 March 2000).

Spillan, J. and Hough, M. (2003) "Crisis planning in small businesses: importance, impetus and indifference", *European Management Journal*, 21 (3): 398–407.

SPRING (2005) *Technical Reference (TR19: 2005) on BCM*. Online: http://www.spring.gov.sg/Content/WebPage.aspx?id=3179f0f0–0a7a-4142–905d-6f24bd7ddaa4> (accessed 25 July 2006).

Standards Australia (2004) *BH 221: Business Continuity Management*, 2nd edn, Sydney: Standards Australia.

Starbuck, W.H. (1996) "Unlearning ineffective or obsolete technologies", *IJTM* (Special Publication on Unlearning and Learning) 11 (7/8): 725–737.

Starbuck, W.H. and Milliken, F.J. (1988) "Challenger: fine-tuning the odds until something breaks", *The Journal of Management Studies*, 25 (4): 319–340 (retrieved 4 September 2009, from ABI/INFORM Global, Document ID: 1177177).

Starbuck, W., Greve, A. and Hedberg, B. (1978) "Responding to crisis", *Journal of Business Administration*, spring. Reprinted in J. Quinn and H. Mintzberg (eds) (1992) *The Strategy Process*, Englewood Cliffs, NJ: Prentice Hall.

State Bank of Pakistan (2003) *Risk Management Guidelines for Commercial Banks & DFIs*, Karachi: State Bank of Pakistan, Central Directorate.

Stefanik, M. (2007) "Fear, uncertainty and doubt". Online: http://mstefanik.spaces.live.com/blog/cns!E265B99124714E68!145.entry (accessed 2 October 2007).

Steves, B. (2006) "Ready, set . . . recall", *Insurance Journal*, 8 May. Online: http://www.insurancejournal.com/magazines/west/2006/05/08/features/69887.htm (accessed 25 July 2006).

Stewart, T.A. and Champion, D. (2006) "Leading change from the top line", *Harvard Business Review*, Jul/Aug, 84 (7/8): 90–97.

Stirpe, A. (1999) "Apple will focus on distribution in new year", *Channel Webnetwork*. Online: http://www.crn.com/it-channel/18833092 (accessed 29 September 2007).

Stone, N. (1995) *The Management and Practice of Public Relations*, London: Macmillan.

Strohl Systems (1995) *The Business Continuity Planning Guide*, King of Prussia, PA: Strohl Systems.

Stucke, C. and Straub, D. (2005) "Business continuity and the protection of informational assets", in D. Straub, S. Goodman and R. Baskerville (eds) *Information Security and Management*, New York: M E Sharpe.

Sun Microsystems (2001). *Official Fudwatch Index*. Online: java.sun.com/features/fudwatch/ (accessed 29 January 2001).

Sun Microsystems (2007) "Think thin: thin client and server based computing group blog", Online: http://blogs.sun.com/ThinkThin/entry/protocol_fud (accessed 2 October 2007).

Survive (1996) "A risk too far", *The Business Continuity Magazine*, August, pp. 20–22.

Sutcliffe, K.M. and Vogus, T. (2003) "Organizing for resilience", in K.S. Cameron, J.E. Dutton and R.E. Quinn (eds) *Positive Organisational Scholarship: Foundations of a New Discipline*, San Francisco: Berrett-Koehler, pp. 94–110.

Swartz, E., Elliott, D. and Herbane, B. (1995) "Out of sight, out of mind: the limitations of traditional information systems planning", *Facilities*, 13 (9/10): 15–21.

Swartz, E., Elliott, D. and Herbane, B. (2003) "Greater than the sum of its parts: Business Continuity Management in the UK Finance Sector", *Risk Management – An International Journal*, 5 (1): 65–80.

Tait, N. (2001) "Firestone in wider tyre recall", *Financial Times*, 2 January.

Taleb, N.N. (2007) *The Impact of the Highly Improbable*, London: Penguin Books.

Tamburro, M. (2008) "Passenger criticises BA treatment", *BBC News online*. Online: http://news.bbc.co.uk/1/hi/uk/7196128.stm (accessed 19 January 2008).

Tangen, S. and Seigel, M (2008) "ISO/PAS 22399 provides international best practice for preparedness and continuity management", *ISO Management Systems*, January–February, pp. 5–9.

Taylor, A. (2000) "Jac Nasser's biggest test", *Fortune*, 18 September, 142 (6): 71–74.

ten Berge, D. (1990) *The First 24 Hours*, Oxford: Basil Blackwell.

Thomas, J.B., Clark, S.M. and Gioia, D.A. (1993) "Strategic sense-making and organisational performance – linkages among scanning, interpretation, action and outcomes", *Academy of Management Journal*, 36: 239–270.

Tilley, K. (1998) "Fire shows disaster plans wanting", *Business Insurance*, 5 October, 32 (40): 57.

Toft, B. and Reynolds, S. (1997) *Learning from Disasters*, 2nd edn, Leicester: Perpetuity Press.

Toigo, J.W. (2003) *Disaster Recovery Planning, Preparing for the Unthinkable*, 3rd edn, Englewood Cliffs, NJ: Prentice Hall.

Traynor, I. (2007) "Russia accused of unleashing cyberwar to disable Estonia", *The Guardian*, 17 May, p. 9.

Tripsas, M. (2009) "Technology, identity, and inertia through the lens of 'the digital photography company' ", *Organization Science*, 20 (2): 441–460, 479–480 (retrieved 14 September 2009, from ABI/INFORM Global, document ID: 1687270151).

Trompenaars, F. (1993) *Riding the Waves of Culture*, London: Nicholas Brearley Publishing.

Trosa, S. and Williams, S. (1996) cited in M. Bowerman, G. Francis, A. Ball and J. Fry (2002) "The evolution of benchmarking in UK local authorities", *Benchmarking: An International Journal*, 9 (5): 429–449.

Tucker, E. (2006) "Business continuity planning", in J.F. Broder (ed.) *Risk Analysis and the Security Survey*, 3rd edn, London: Butterworth-Heinemann.

Turchin, V. and Joslyn, C. (1999) "The metasystem in transition", in F. Heylighen, C. Joslyn, and V. Turchin (eds) *Principia Cybernetica Web* (*Principia Cybernetica*, Brussels). Online: http://pespmc1.vub.ac.be/MST.html (accessed 27 June 2005).

Turnbull, N. (1999) *Internal Control: Guidance for Directors on the Combined Code*, London: Institute of Chartered Accountants in England and Wales.

Turner, B. (1976) "The organisational and interorganisational development of disasters", *Administrative Science Quarterly*, 21: 378–397.

Turner, B. (1978) *Man-Made Disasters*, London: Wykeham.

Turner, B. and Pidgeon, N. (1997) *Man-Made Disasters*, 2nd edn, London: Butterworth-Heinemann.

UK Online for Business (2000) *Business in the Information Age*, London: Department of Trade and Industry.

UKresilience (2006) *Civil Contingencies Act*. Online: http://www.ukresilience.info/ ccact/index.shtm (accessed 25 July 2006).

Vancoppenolle, G. (1999) "What are we planning for?" in A. Hiles and P. Barnes (eds) *Business Continuity Management*, London: Wiley.

Vasagar, J. and Tremlett, G. (2003) "Anglo-Spanish relations on the sick list as cruise liner sails out, *The Guardian*, 4 November, p. 3.

Vaughan, D. (1996) *The Challenger Launch Decision: Risky Technology, Culture, and Deviance at NASA*, Chicago: University of Chicago Press.

Vaughan, D. (1997) "The trickle-down effect: policy decisions, risky work, and the challenger tragedy", *California Management Review*, 39 (2): 80–102.

Vodafone (2007) "Flooding at Vodafone UK headquarters fails to dampen employee spirits", Vodaphone.

Wagner, C.G. (2006) Information security's biggest enemy, *The Futurist*, July–August, p. 11.

Waldmeir, P. (2000) "Monitoring poses threat to cyber-anonymity", *Financial Times* 11 May, p. 4.

Walker, B. and Meyers, J.A. (2004) "Thresholds in ecological and social–ecological systems: a developing database", *Ecology and Society*, 9 (2): 3. Online: http://www.ecologyandsociety.org/vol9/iss2/art3/.

Walker, P. (2007) "Animal rights militants losing the war", *The Guardian*, 1 May, p. 11.

The Wall Street Journal Report Online (2005) "The journal report", *The Wall Street Journal*, 18 July, p. R2.

Walsh, C. (2001) "Leadership on 9/11: Morgan Stanley's challenge", *HBS Working Knowledge: Leadership*. Online: http://hbswk.hbs.edu/item.jhtml?id=2690&t= leadership> (accessed 7 July 2005).

Warr, P. (1990) "The measurement of wellbeing and other aspects of mental health", *Journal of Occupational Psychology*, 63: 193–210.

Waterman, R.H., Peters, T. and Phillips, J.R. (1980) "Structure is not organisation", *Business Horizons*, 23 (3): 14–26.

Weick, K.E. (1993) "The collapse of sensemaking in organizations: the Mann Gulch disaster", *Administrative Science Quarterly*, December, 38: 4.

Weiner, S. (1995) "Business risk, internal control and audit implications of EDI", *The CPA Journal*, November, pp. 56–58.

Wieczorek, M., Naujoks, U. and Bartlett, B. (eds) (2002) *Business Continuity: IT Risk Management for International Corporations*, Berlin: Springer.

Wiersema, M. and Bowen, H.P. (2008) "Corporate diversification: the impact of foreign competition, industry globalization, and product diversification", *Strategic Management Journal*, February, 29 (2): 118–132.

Wildavsky, A. (1988) *Searching for Safety*, New Brunswick, NJ: Transaction Press.

Wilkinson, S. (2004) "Focus group research", in D. Silverman (ed.) *Qualitative Research, Theory, Method and Practice*, London: Sage.

Williams, A., Dobson, P. and Walters, M. (1989) *Changing Culture*, 2nd edn, London: Institute of Personnel Management.

Williams, D.M. (2001) Private communication with the authors.

Williams, R. (2007) "Global hackers threaten net security in cyber warfare aimed at top targets", *The Guardian Online*. Online: http://www.guardian.co.uk/ technology/2007/nov/29/hacking.news (accessed 25 January 2008).

Wilson, D.C. (1992) *A Strategy of Change*, London: Routledge.

Womack, J.P., Jones, D.T. and Roos, D. (1990) *The Machine That Changed the World*, New York: Rawson Associates.

Woodman, P. (2006) *Business Continuity Management, Chartered Management Institute*. Online: http://www.ukresilience.info/publications/bcm2006.pdf (accessed 28 August 2006).

Worren, N., Ruddle, K. and Moore, K. (1999) "From organisational development to change management: emergence of a new profession", *The Journal of Applied Behavioural Science*, 35 (3): 273–286.

Wu, T. and Yoo, C.S. (2007) "Keeping the internet neutral?: Tim Wu and Christopher Yoo Debate", *Federal Communications Law Journal*, 59 (3): 575–592, 456 (retrieved 30 April 2008 from ABI/INFORM Global database).

Yeoh, P. and Roth, K. (1999) "An empirical analysis of sustained advantage in the U.S. pharmaceutical industry: impact of firm resources and capabilitites", *Strategic Management Journal*, 20: 637–653.

Zsidisin, G.A., Melnyk, S.A. and Ragatz, G.L. (2005) "An institutional theory perspective of business continuity planning for purchasing and supply chain management", *International Journal of Production Research*, 43 (15/16): 3401–3420.

Index